Wine Marketing

Wine Marketing: A practical guide

C. Michael Hall
and
Richard Mitchell

ELSEVIER

AMSTERDAM • BOSTON • HEIDELBERG • LONDON • NEW YORK • OXFORD •
PARIS • SAN DIEGO • SAN FRANCISCO • SINGAPORE • SYDNEY • TOKYO

Butterworth-Heinemann is an imprint of Elsevier

Butterworth-Heinemann is an imprint of Elsevier
Linacre House, Jordan Hill, Oxford OX2 8DP, UK
30 Corporate Drive, Suite 400, Burlington, MA 01803, USA

First edition 2008

Notice
No responsibility is assumed by the publisher for any injury and/or damage to persons
or property as a matter of products liability, negligence or otherwise, or from any use or
operation of any methods, products, instructions or ideas contained in the material herein.

British Library Cataloguing in Publication Data
A catalogue record for this book is available from the British Library

Library of Congress Cataloging-in-Publication Data
A catalog record for this book is available from the Library of Congress

ISBN: 978-0-7506-5420-3

For information on all Butterworth-Heinemann publications
visit our web site at books.elsevier.com

Typeset by Charon Tec Ltd (A Macmillan Company), Chennai, India
www.charontec.com

Printed and bound in Hungary
07 08 09 10   10 9 8 7 6 5 4 3 2 1

Working together to grow
libraries in developing countries

www.elsevier.com | www.bookaid.org | www.sabre.org

ELSEVIER   BOOK AID
             International   Sabre Foundation

Contents

List of Boxes

List of Figures

List of Tables

List of Plates

Acknowledgements

This book takes a contemporary look at the marketing of one of the world's oldest products. The book is designed to provide practical insights into the marketing of wine. However, this does not mean that the book is without theory. Applying the old adage from Kurt Lewin that 'there is nothing so practical as a good theory' (Lewin, 1951, p. 169) the book has utilised some of the recent developments in marketing theory and application with respect to ideas of co-creation, service, value and value chains, experiences and relationships. The book is also shaped differently from many other marketing texts in that while the various 'Ps' of marketing are noted we emphasise how they – and other marketing concepts – apply differentially along the wine distribution and value chains. Not all wine businesses and wine growers are the same so why should we write a book that acknowledge the facts that those in the industry already know?! Importantly, we also stress how the value of wine to the consumer, and therefore the return to wine businesses, can be added to over all points of the distribution and value chain. Therefore, the importance of cooperative behaviour and positive B2B relationships in wine marketing is also stressed in the book.

The contemporary wine marketing concepts that the book provides have been combined with numerous examples and cases as well as a list of practical wine marketing insights at the end of each chapter. The wine world is so diverse that we do not provide a check list of 'what to do', such an approach is simplistic and provides no basis for giving winegrowers and wine businesses a source of competitive advantage, getting a better return on investment and in growing the wine market. Instead, we have provided a set of tools and a series of conceptual tools along with an outline of critical issues in the contemporary wine business environment that will enable students of wine and wine marketing to better understand the complex nature of the industry and how wine actually gets from the winegrower to the consumer and enable wine businesses to make better informed decisions.

This book has been a while in coming, not least because Richard managed to, literally, get run over by a truck. We would therefore like to thank not only Sally North and the team at Butterworth-Heinemann for persevering with the project but all the medical staff that helped put Richard back together again. We would also like to thank our various students and colleagues who have helped contribute to some of the ideas in the book as well as the various members of the wine industry from the vineyard all the way through to the retail store – and the tasting. We would also especially like to thank Louisa Aitken, David Christensen, Nicollete Le Cren, Clare and Hamish Nicholls, Carleigh Randall, Tsasha Russek, Egil Thorsen, Nicola van Tiel, the New Zealand Food and Wine Tourism Network and Hillebrand Wine Estates for being willing to share some of their insights with us in the book. Finally, we would like to thank our families and significant others especially Jody, Carleen, James and Emma to whom the book is most sincerely dedicated.

C. Michael Hall   Richmond
Richard Mitchell   Pine Hill

Reference

Lewin, K. (1951) *Field Theory in Social Science: Selected Theoretical Papers*. D. Cartwright (ed.), Harper & Row.

Introduction: A practical approach to wine marketing

Chapter Objectives

After reading this chapter you will

- Appreciate the dynamic nature of the wine industry
- Understand the importance a market-driven approach to the business of wine
- Appreciate the complex nature of the supply chain for wine
- Identify the 8 Ps of wine marketing
- Understand how this book is used

The context for wine marketing

Wine is one of the most civilized things in the world and one of the natural things of the world that has been brought to the greatest perfection, and it offers a greater range for enjoyment and appreciation than, possibly, any other purely sensory thing which may be purchased. One can learn about wines and pursue the education of one's palate with great enjoyment all of a lifetime, the palate becoming more educated and capable of appreciation and you having constantly increasing enjoyment and appreciation of wine even though the kidneys may weaken, the big toe become painful, the finger joints stiffen, until finally, just when you love it the most you are finally forbidden wine entirely.

Ernest Hemingway (*Death in the Afternoon*, 1932, p. 14)

Wine is a complex, almost enigmatic, product. At once it is:

- a provider of sustenance and a luxury item;
- associated with healthy living, while in excess it can lead to death;
- a symbol of status and a 'peasant' drink;
- of immense religious and cultural significance and can be associated with hedonistic and debauched behaviour;
- a fashion item, experience and commodity all in one.

Wine comes in many varieties, vintages, styles and from many parts of the world. It can range from 'two buck chuck,' retailing for US$1.99, to a bottle of 1787 Chateau Lafitte (a red Bordeaux wine), which sold at auction in 1986 for US$160,000 or a bottle of Chateau d'Yquem (a sweet white Bordeaux wine) from the same vintage purchased for US$100,000 in 2006.

Charters (2006) provides a very detailed account of just how complicated wine is, but he also suggests that at a very basic level wine can be divided into two broad categories: bulk wines and premium wines. This binary is important to any discussion of wine marketing as the two are historically very different products but, despite the fact that bulk wines account for a significant proportion of production, 'almost invariably those who discuss, sell or write about wine refer to it as if it were a single, homogeneous product, albeit in various styles' (Charters, 2006, p. 51). Of bulk wine Charters (2006, p. 51) says, that it:

> may or may not be mass produced, but [it] is nevertheless generally purchased in large volumes (either direct from a vat, or in containers larger than the traditional 750 mL bottle).... Consumption of this product takes place substantially in countries which produce wine – but not exclusively in Europe. Bulk wine consumption is widespread, for instance, in Australia and New Zealand. This kind of wine – consumed merely as a beverage – receives little focus from the wine industry which naturally tends to promote its premium product, and almost no attention from wine critics and writers. Nonetheless, it is economically important.

Premium wines, on the other hand, are:

> designated explicitly as such in Australia (Geene et al., 1999), when [sic.] it is based on price, or as 'quality wine produced from a specified region' (QWPSR). Premium wine is not sold in bulk form. Its distinguishing feature in Europe is likely to be its region of origin and in most of the new producing countries that it carries a vintage date. It is almost invariably sold in 750 mL bottles.
>
> (Charters, 2006, p. 52)

Charters continues that this distinction is fundamentally about the nature of the wine being consumed and not about market segmentation. He suggests that they can also be distinguished from each other on the basis of the aesthetics and social purpose of wine consumption and, often, by the place from which they originate. Premium wines provide greater aesthetic outcomes (rather than sustenance or lubrication), they are a marker of social status and social capital and they tend to come from cooler climate regions (while bulk wines come almost is exclusive from hot regions where growing conditions allow for higher yields) (Charters, 2006). The dimensions of aesthetic consumption, social status and the cultural capital necessary to understand premium wines (and to distinguish between premium and bulk wine) are complex. However, it is important to note that bulk wines are also not bereft of cultural meaning. Indeed, the experiential dimension of all wine is a cornerstone of the approach of this book. For example, in the Old World bulk produced wines are typically markers of tradition, family, the rural idyll, place and/or the authentic. One of the reasons why reform of the wine sector in the EU, for example, has been so difficult (see Chapter 2) is because of the cultural and experiential overlay that people from wine producing areas have with respect to all the wine that is made and the cultural landscape that produces it. As Barthes (1957/2000) observed, wine of all kinds is a 'totem-drink' for all French; imbued with meaning and significance. The wine market is therefore as complex as the product itself.

In the 'Old World' of wine (primarily mainland Europe), wine is a part of everyday life for millions of people. They grew up with wine, drinking it at every meal, and learning of its provenance, production and quality through this experience and exposure. For these people wine is sustenance, culture and spirituality melded into one. Here, the consumption of wine (albeit in differing levels of 'quality') knows no class distinction. In the 'New World' (primarily the grape growing regions of South and North America, Asia, South Africa, Australia and New Zealand), on the other hand, wine has become a symbol of status, knowledge and power. It is associated with special occasions and has typically been the preserve of a relatively small portion of the middle classes. For many of these people (and for the upper echelons of Old World society), wine has become a fashion item unashamedly consumed to show who they are and what they have achieved. Indeed, accord to Brook (2000b, p. 21) fashion, 'has come to influence not merely the style of wine production, but the very colour of wine'. Wine is therefore consumed as an experience, an event, an emblem (Unwin, 1996; Brook, 2000a; Charters, 2006). However, these historical distinctions between Old World and New World consumers are just the tip of the iceberg when it comes to the complexity of the increasingly changing marketplace of wine:

- While wine consumption is on increase in many New World wine markets, it has been in decline in most Old World markets for at least the last three decades (see Chapter 2).
- Wine growing has become identified as an important tool of regional development. However, at the global level wine production is increasing faster than wine consumption making for an increasingly competitive wine business environment.
- The growing body of wine marketing literature has identified differences in the wine consumer behaviour of men and women, between different generations, amongst different ethnic groups (especially in the USA) and in different countries. It is also possible to identify different markets depending on how they purchase and consume wine and the meanings it has for consumers.

● Other research has explored the way in which different markets use wine on different occasions and in different situations.

What is clear from all of this research is that there is no such thing as the wine market nor is there a typical wine consumer. Instead the wine market is made up of several, sometimes very niche, segments that are influenced by demographics, psychographics and the situation in which it is being consumed.

Research into wine consumers and their behaviour is becoming increasingly sophisticated so that it now includes explorations of personality, levels of involvement (see Chapter 9) and the milieu of motivations for purchasing wine. Unfortunately, however, much of this research is still not filtering down to those that need it the most – the wineries themselves and those that control its sale and distribution – while many other parts of the wine supply and distribution chains are also unaware about how their business success is interrelated with the success of the chain as a whole in meeting consumer demands. Furthermore, it has been suggested that around half of all published wine marketing research comes from New Zealand and Australia (Lockshin and Spawton, 2001) and therefore some parts of the global wine market still remain relatively poorly understood.

Lockshin (2003, p. 5) asks 'What do we know empirically about wine marketing?' In response he suggests that

Wine marketing includes many sub-areas of research. Traditionally, we would speak of the 4 Ps of marketing, product, pricing, promotion, and placement and their concomitant areas in wine marketing, such as branding, new product development, pricing, public relations, managing the sales force, and distribution. Beyond this, the area of wine marketing should include specialty topics, such as consumer behaviour for wine, wine tourism and cellar door (direct sales), supply chain management from the vineyard and supplier to the end user, labelling and packaging, wine events, medals and show awards, promotional activities, exporting including market choice and channel within market choice, selecting and managing agents, protecting intellectual property (names and logos), and world regulation of wine and alcohol.

(Lockshin, 2003, p. 5)

Given the complex nature of the product itself and of the market for wine, plus the fact that research has only relatively recently begun to understand wine consumer behaviour, it is no surprise that wine is one of the most difficult consumer products to market. This book attempts to unravel some of this complexity and provides some insights into the way in which an understanding of the product and its market can be used to more effectively market and sell wine. This chapter highlights the value of a market-driven approach to the business of wine, demonstrates the complexity of the wine distribution chain and introduces 8 Ps of wine marketing that differ quite substantially from the 4 Ps of marketing. The value of understanding the wine distribution chain is that this book emphasises that value should be added over all the elements of the chain to the long-term benefit of all the individual firms and stakeholders in the chain. The chapter concludes with a précis of the structure of the book and some hints on its use. Firstly, however, we will discuss the highly dynamic nature of the wine industry and what this means for wine marketing.

Wine: an industry in flux

In many wine regions around the world, wineries are riding the crest of a wave that has seen record export volumes and prices for wine. At the turn of the 21st century, for example, New Zealand could boast that its wine industry was winning awards for its wine in France, the UK, North America and Australia, beating all comers in show categories normally dominated by domestic and/or European wines. The value of New Zealand's wine exports also grew, skyrocketing from around NZ$29.2 million in 1994 (New Zealand Winegrowers, 2004) to NZ$512.4 million in 2006 (New Zealand Winegrowers, 2007). Winegrowers of New Zealand, in their *Scenario 2010* for the New Zealand wine industry, promoted New Zealand wine, '... as a high added value, innovative product New Zealand wine is marketed and sold to appeal to fashion leaders, opinion leaders, consumers with high disposable income, new age wine connoisseurs, the new generation, 18–30 year old women, and the health conscious' (New Zealand Wine Grower, 1999, p. 8).

If some commentators are to be believed New Zealand's success can only be bettered by that of Australia. In fact Anderson (2000) suggested that the fifth and latest boom in Australian wine production (beginning in 1987) differs substantially from previous booms, none of which lasted much more than a decade. Anderson suggests that the current boom is different as it is: overwhelmingly export oriented; mainly market driven; quality driven allowing the industry to build brand, regional and varietal images; riding on the back of heavy promotion of the health benefits of moderate (red) wine consumption that has seen consumers seek quality rather than quantity and still exceptionally good value for money in Northern Hemisphere markets. As such the Winemakers Federation of Australia's

Strategy 2025 suggests that wine is 'the late 20th century lifestyle beverage of moderation. It is more than just a beverage, it has become a lifestyle product with a high degree of complementarity with food, hospitality, entertainment, the arts and tourism' (Winemakers Federation of Australia, 1996, p. 196). Anderson (2000, n.p.) suggests that

These are all reasons to be optimistic about Australia's long-term future as a successful exporter of premium wines. Within the next five years export sales could well account for the majority of Australian wine sold. How long the current boom lasts therefore depends heavily on export demand for Australian wine. That in turn depends both on the export marketing skills and efforts of the industry and on developments elsewhere in the world wine market.

These national figures, however, are hiding the real story for the vast majority of wineries, as 86% of Australia's branded bottle wine sales (both domestic and export) come from just 22 companies (Winetitles, 2006). That's only 1.1% of Australia's 2008 wine companies! As a result 1986 wineries (98.9%) vie for just 14% of sales and it is here that the benefits of Australia's boom have not been evenly distributed. It is these small-scale wine producers that have not necessarily gained from the Australian boom. Smaller wineries have less capacity to compete in the export market than their larger counterparts, both in terms of the costs involved and their ability to supply larger retail buyers. In Australia this has lead to some dire figures in terms of profitability. In fact, Peter Barnes (President, Winemakers Federation of Australia) reported in February 2004 that:

Since 1997–98 winery profits have declined by 45% as a comparative return on assets, the greatest drop among established industry groupings. This impact is felt across the wine industry, especially among small wineries where the decline in profitability has been acute. In fact, wineries with annual turnover of less than $5 million suffer from average profitability of just one per cent or less.

(Kilikanoon Wines News, 2004, n.p.)

Meanwhile, in New Zealand, *Doubtless Strategic* director Hugh Ammundsen has suggested that a predicted large increase in the supply of New Zealand wine, combined with the rise of the New Zealand dollar, make a shakeout in the wine industry inevitable (Carpinter, 2004). Ammundsen (cited in Carpinter, 2004, n.p.) also observes that 'wine producers face greater pressures than at any time in the last 18 years – since the fallout from oversupply and price wars that led to the government-financed vine pull of 1986'. These comments were made less than five years after Peter

Simic (Editor/Publisher, Winestate Magazine) said, lauding the growth and success of the Australasian wine industry, 'if you're not excited by what is happening in the Australasian wine industry at the moment then you're probably dead!' (Simic, 1999).

It is widely recognised that the wine industry in New Zealand and Australia is prone to high levels of boom-bust development (Hall et al., 2000; Treloar, 2004), with government-sponsored vine-pull schemes in the 1980s being the last evidence of a significant bust period. Evidence that perhaps this massive growth is about to slow comes from all over the world, with French wine exports continuing to decline in both volume and value (Styles, 2004a), including the traditionally strong region of Bordeaux, restructuring of one of Australia's largest wine companies (Australian Associated Press, 2004) and, despite massive growth in the overall value and volume of wine exports, the price per litre for American (Wine Institute, 2004), New Zealand (New Zealand Winegrowers, 2004) and Australian (Wine Business Monthly, 2004) wine has continued to decline for most of the last five years.

In Australia, this situation is predicted to worsen, with a grape surplus in Australia that began in 2003 (Gettler, 2004) and this has several implications for New Zealand wineries. The first is that Australian producers will be forced to discount their wines in a number of export markets in order to stay competitive, which New Zealand will struggle not to have to follow. Secondly, Australia will look to New Zealand as a market to 'dump' stock unwanted elsewhere and this will compete with New Zealand wines domestically (New Zealand Winegrowers, 2003). Finally, New Zealand too has a predicted grape production surplus and this will further force New Zealand wineries to discount in export markets. As such, Philip Gregan (CEO, New Zealand Winegrowers) states that, to keep pace with predicted grape production increases, New Zealand needs to increase exports to '... around 9 to 10 million cases per annum by 2007 ... a three-fold increase from the current level!' (Gregan, 2004, n.p.). Meanwhile, the New Zealand Winegrowers (2003, n.p.) suggest that in the domestic market

Whether or not New Zealand producers can recover a substantial market share from imported bottled wines ... will largely depend on their competitiveness in the under $12 per bottle market segment. Currently the vast majority of New Zealand producers, given their costs of production, do not compete in this market segment.

Joseph (2005) goes further suggesting that there is already a crisis for the wine industry as production far outstrips production (see also Chapter 2). He suggests that there has been an explosion of new wine producers all vying for an ever-decreasing slice of the wine market.

Cast your eyes anywhere in the world and you will find similar statistics. The skills of these newcomers at both making and selling wine vary widely. In Australia, many of the labels that have recently begun to appear on the market belong to people who never intended to make wine. Encouraged by tax breaks to plant vineyards, these lawyers, doctors and bankers expected to sell their grapes to bigger wineries. It was only when those companies either failed to buy or offered less per tonne than had been allowed for in the business plans that they had to go looking for winemakers, and names, labels and, most crucially, customers.

(Joseph, 2005, n.p.)

So, with a honeymoon period of the current boom for some New World wine producers seemingly nearing an end, continuing declines in domestic consumption in most European markets and declining returns on exports (despite increasing volumes of sales) for all but a few countries, there is a need for an increasingly market-driven focus for wineries around the world. Turrentine (2001, n.p.) suggests that this requires '... industry self-knowledge, self-control and efforts to expand markets. But it takes wisdom to see the need for self-control when business is booming, guts to be bold when business slows and – most difficult of all – cooperation to expand the market'.

Despite unabated growth in the number of new entrants into the wine industry, there is evidence, in New Zealand and Australia at least, that existing wineries are heeding this advice and they are exercising self-control and seeking evermore sophisticated knowledge of winemaking and wine marketing. Wineries are now more eager than ever for information and tools to aid in the sales of their wine. Some have a market-driven approach, but many still have a primary focus on the product. So what, then, are the differences between a market-driven approach and a product-driven approach to the business of wine?

A market-driven approach

Variously known as a 'market orientation', 'market led' or 'market driven' (amongst others), a market-driven approach is critical for wineries to survive in today's competitive environment (Barclay, 2001). Such an approach is common in most other sectors, but has not always been the case for the wine industry.

In France, for example, wine producers have long been focused on the production of their wine rather than the market that they sell to. This has been enshrined in appellation laws (see Chapters 2 and 10) which have severely limited French winemakers' ability to adapt to changing market conditions. In the New World, on the other hand, a product focus has resulted from the complex interaction of the romantic notions associated with all things rural, wine and winemaking that has blinded many winemakers to the reality of selling wine. In both France and the New World of wine, the result is often a winemaker or winery owner that is completely impassioned by his/her wine but who makes little deference to the wine market. For these winemakers the wine is their *raison d'être*, knowing who is going to buy it from them and why is someone else's problem.

Arguably, the basic distinction between a market-driven approach and a production-driven approach to the business of wine is in realising who ultimately determines the quality of the wine produced in commercial terms. In a market-driven approach producers realise that it is the consumers who decide on the quality of their wine by virtue of their decision to purchase it, not just once, but as part of an ongoing purchasing relationship. In contrast, a production-driven approach may result in the making of a quality wine as defined by the producer or by certain empirical standards, but there is no particular consumer or market in mind. There is instead an inherent belief that the product is there and because it is 'good' it will sell. Firms which follow a market-driven approach 'concentrate on developing distinctive wines, build long-term customer relationships, and understand what's happening in their various chosen markets. They know their products create a niche that their competitors cannot penetrate and develop marketing plans with measurable objectives and specific goals' (Barclay, 2001, n.p.).

An experiential (experience-driven) approach

This book builds on the idea of a market-driven approach. But perhaps more than that, it emphasises that ultimately wine is an experience that includes everything from the intangible elements of wine and its brand image (e.g. symbolism, emotional value and meaning) to the more tangible service elements of economic exchange surrounding wine (e.g. the services provided by intermediaries, winery staff and retailers). Indeed, we agree with the insights of a number of marketing scholars that the 'strategy of differentiating services from goods should be abandoned and replaced with a strategy of understanding how they are related. Service is the common denominator in exchange, not some special form of exchange' (Vargo and Lusch, 2004a, 334; see also Vargo and Lusch, 2004b). The physical good, or the physical aspect of wine becomes only 'one element among others in a total service offering' (Gronroos, 2000, p. 88) and the intangible, and perhaps more powerful, emotional and symbolic content is the true provider of value (Charters, 2006). The application of an approach that accounts for these experiential elements of wine calls for a much wider approach than Barclay's market-driven approach. According to Mitchell et al. (2000, p. 129), Holbrook and Hirschman's (1982) 'experiential view' of consumer behaviour '...recognized the special nature of products and services that have a hedonic component such as wine, leisure activities and pleasure travel'. This approach suggests that many products and services are consumed for non-utilitarian reasons such as 'fun, amusement, fantasy, arousal, sensory stimulation and enjoyment' (Holbrook and Hirschman, 1982, p. 135). As such the experiential view of consumer behaviour allows for the '...stream of consciousness or sensory, imaginal and affective complex that accompanies an experience' (Lofman, 1991, p. 729). The application of this approach to consumer behaviour to wine has recently been discussed in terms of wine tourism (e.g. Mitchell et al., 2000; Mitchell, 2004) and wine consumption more broadly (Charters, 2006).

In line with both Vargo and Lusch's (2004a, b) service-dominant approach and Holbrook and Hirschman's (1982) 'experiential view' of consumer behaviour, this book takes a more humanistic view of a market-driven approach. Therefore, we term the approach taken by this book as an experiential (experience-driven) approach in order to emphasise how wineries and all the actors in the wine production and supply chains need to focus on the values that consumers derive from wine and other competing products as a whole and from the wines that they are providing in particular. This means that we pay specific attention to the needs and experiences of consumers and customers and how we create and add value for customers in all elements of the chain.

Charters' (2006) triadic approach to wine consumption acknowledges that wine may be consumed for various reasons that fall loosely into three categories: utilitarian, symbolic and experiential. Charters suggests that the symbolic and experiential motivations for wine consumption are more important than the utilitarian (see Plates 1.1 and 1.2). The implication, then, is that traditional marketing models do not easily apply to wine and that a different approach is required and this is what we are advocating here too. To make his point, Charters (2006) provides evidence from several qualitative interviews, finishing with a discussion of how complex wine consumption was for one particular consumer:

Wendy is a winemaker who has also been a show judge, having finely tuned organoleptic [(sensory)] skills to supplement a technical analysis. Yet ultimately the combination of flavours and the structure of the wine do something for her – with all her knowledge and skill – she cannot explain. Clos de Mesnil [(the experience of which she is describing)] is a very expensive single-vineyard Champagne produced by Krug; she can dissect it, and see how it has been produced, she can correct it in the winery, yet the way it 'transports' her remains a mystery. The fact that she chooses an exclusive and expensive wine suggests that such a quasi-spiritual response may not be appropriate for all wines, but at least for some that she drinks it is the case, and it is clearly an experience to be aspired to....

At this level wine consumption can combine almost all of the various factors which prompt consumption. Wendy clearly sees the consumption of Clos de Mesnil as fitting into her lifestyle, and it is probable that she sees it as helping to shape her image. There is also no doubt that it gave her immense pleasure, both organoleptically and in the sense of the challenge offered by the exploration of its complex taste. It also provided a socially cohesive experience (she talks of 'we...') and there may also be a sense of ritual to it; it was drunk at the end of the last day of the working week, the classic time for marking out private time. Yet all of these complex factors together make something that to Wendy is greater than the sum of their parts.

(Charters, 2006, p. 155)

As part of this approach we discuss the significance of providing hospitality, which goes beyond the traditional view of service as a rationalised commercial process. This can create a true comparative advantage where service can only ever create a competitive advantage which can ultimately be copied. In fact a purely market-driven approach or a largely service-driven approach has a tendency to reduce consumption to a commercial (transactional) act, doing little to add value beyond that which is purely economic. For example, in Chapter 4 we highlight how hospitality can go beyond a purely economic transaction, creating an emotional and meaningful connection that results in a lasting bond with the consumer. These principles are also discussed at various points in the value chain throughout the book.

Table 1.1 compares the differences between a production-driven, market-driven and an experiential approach to the business of wine and to wine marketing. In reality a winery will typically have a mixed approach to wine business. However, firms that

Table 1.1 Production-driven and market-driven approach versus an experiential approach in wineries

Topic	Production driven	Market driven	Experiential
Products	Winery sells whatever it makes	Winery makes what it can sell	Winery develops experiences that complement their wine
Role of sales force	Sell to the customer – don't worry about the rest of the winery	Help the customer buy if the wines fit their needs, coordinate planning with other winery departments (production, accounting, etc.)	Provision of experiences that highlight values of the wine, intimately involved throughout the supply/value chain
Attitudes toward customers	They should be glad we're here	Customer needs determine our winery plans	Customers seek meaning from our wine, our brand values need to facilitate meanings
Advertising focus	Product features and quality	Need satisfying benefits	Emotional benefits, meanings and occasion based
Innovation	Focus on technology	Focus on finding new opportunities	Focus on tailoring to individual customer meaning
Packaging	Cost and product protection	Designed as a selling tool	Designed as a marker of meaning
Transportation	Viewed as an extension of storage	Viewed as a customer service	Viewed as not adding value and meaning, therefore viewed as cost
Profitability	A residual – what's left over after costs are covered	A primary objective before production begins	A primary objective achieved by adding value rather than reducing costs

Adapted from Barclay (2001, n.p.).

adopt a strong experiential focus are the ones that are most likely to succeed.

An experiential approach means that, from the grape to the glass, a winery goes beyond understanding its primary target market and their markets' needs to develop approaches to know their market and the meanings that they place on their wine/brand. It also means that they keep abreast of political, economic, environmental, socio-demographic and technological trends in all of their major markets through constant environmental scanning and by measuring themselves against benchmarks that they have set for themselves. These benchmarks are qualitative as well as quantitative, as wineries identify wines and other products with brand values that most closely resemble those of their target market. They are not only able to identify their strengths, weaknesses, opportunities and threats but they are able to identify who their main competitors are and what they are doing (Barclay, 2001). Experience-driven wineries recognise that all staff must engender their brand values and not just the physical dimensions of the product that they sell because they realise they are selling an experience and a service that must satisfy customer needs in order to be successful. In addition, all staff realise that each point of contact that a consumer has with their product, whether it be advertising, ordering their wine in a restaurant, purchasing their wine at an outlet, or looking at the website will influence the consumer's equity in their brand(s) and is an opportunity to develop a relationship with that customer. The creation of long-term positive customer relationships will in turn lead to long-term loyalty in customer purchasing as well as positive word-of-mouth.

Brand is vital to an experience-driven winery as this allows them to further differentiate their wine from others. The brand is developed with the target market in mind and there is a high degree of consistency in the communication of brand values through all channels (e.g. labels, marketing collateral, press releases, websites, newsletters, cellar door/tasting room design and signage). The value of the brand is ultimately derived from consumers. Therefore, wineries that seek to develop their brands and maximise their value have a strong customer focus.

For an experience-driven wine company relationships are core to the way they do business. Developing and maintaining relationships directly with their customers is especially important and this requires a coordinated communication strategy that engages them and develops their loyalty. The most effective tool in this strategy is the cellar door/tasting room, where the winery has complete control over the way in which the wine and its brand values are presented to consumers (see Chapter 4). Where it is not possible to invite the consumer directly into the tasting room other ways must be found to give the customer the experience of being invited into the cellar door. Relationships with a range of individuals and companies within the wine supply chain are also critical to the success of a winery as these are the people that are ultimately responsible for the effective communication of their brand values. Importantly, an experiential approach emphasises that relationships are developed over time and therefore a long-term perspective on relationship building is integral to the marketing strategy.

The supply chain for wine is very complex. In fact a single-supply chain that is exactly the same from country to country, and arguably even from winery to winery, does not exist and there are an almost unlimited number of routes that a wine can take from winery to consumer.

The complexity of the wine supply chain

It is difficult to describe the sheer number of permutations there are for a winery to get their wine to the consumer. The wine supply chain is a minefield of choices each with the potential to make or break a winery. Unfortunately, too few new entrants into the wine business are aware of this complexity and of how to navigate their way successfully through to the consumer. Even for experienced wine industry campaigners it can be difficult as there are constant shifts in the nature of the supply chain as the chain becomes increasingly globalised (see Chapter 2). For example, in several large markets supermarkets have now become extremely powerful and are now playing roles in every part of the supply chain, including winemaking itself. The large number of different players means that it can be difficult for wineries to juggle loyalties and meet their many and varied demands. Each player also interprets and uses each wine brand in a unique way and this can influence everything from the ultimate target market for the wine to the final retail price and the way the wine is presented in the marketplace and perceived by the consumer.

The choices that wineries make regarding how their wine is distributed are therefore a critical component of the marketing strategy for a market-driven wine company. This means that wineries must understand the wine supply chain in order to evaluate which route, and which players, provide the best opportunities to reach their target market and effectively communicate their brand values.

In order to demonstrate the complexity of the wine supply chain, a series of models are presented here that gradually build a picture of the potential number of permutations presented to wineries. Figure 1.1 shows how the supply chain can be simply divided into three broad areas: the wine industry, which is

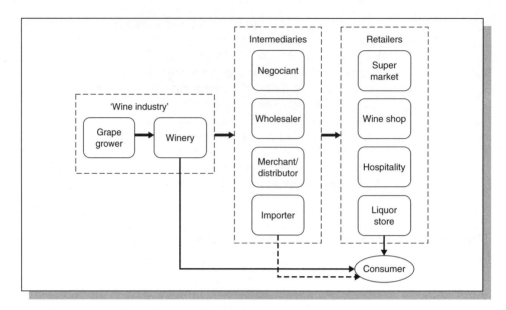

Figure 1.1
The basic wine supply chain

responsible for producing wine and developing brand values; a range of intermediaries, with varying roles and levels of power, depending on the market within which they operate and; a range of different retailers. A winery can choose to use intermediaries and retailers, (or in fact may be forced to use them by legislation: see Box 1.1 for the USA's three-tier system), or can use various direct sales avenues to by-pass one or other of these elements of the chain (see Chapter 4 for discussion of cellar door/tasting room sales and Chapters 6 and 9 for discussion of the internet).

There are also a number of elements that lie outside these basic components of the wine supply chain. These include such things as wine and food festivals, wine shows and wine clubs (Figure 1.2). While wine shows and festivals have been in existence for many years, it is only relatively recently that they have become a conduit for wine sales and/or a tool for communicating brand values to consumers (see Chapter 7 for discussion of wine and food festivals and Chapters 7 and 9 for a discussion of wine shows). It is often important that wineries choose to take part in these events for reasons that will reinforce their brand values and reach their target markets. In doing so they need to research the target markets for the wine and food festivals and know which, if any, wine shows are most influential to their target market.

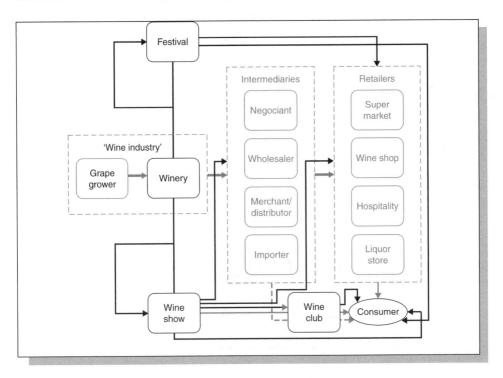

Figure 1.2
The role of festivals, wine shows and wine clubs

Wine clubs are an interesting case, as they may be run by intermediaries, wine retailers, independent wine societies, wine and food media, unrelated organisations with large direct mailing databases (e.g. credit card companies) or the winery themselves. Obviously the most beneficial to the winery is the club that they operate themselves as they control the content of all communication and set prices and methods of distribution. These are also likely to have the most loyal consumers as members and, while they may not necessarily purchase through the club, the communications that they receive may prompt sales at other outlets and/or visits to the winery. At the other extreme are those wine clubs run by credit card companies, who are most likely to operate the club as a service to their members that reinforces their own brand values and therefore they are likely to have little interest in maintaining your brand values. The sheer buying power of these clubs also makes it nigh on impossible for small producers to break into this arena, let alone control the price. (See Chapter 9 for further discussion of wine clubs.)

Figures 1.1 and 1.2 do not however reveal anything of the true complexity of the wine supply chain. In realty there are multiple

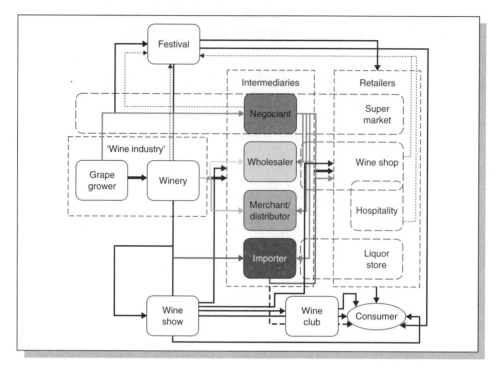

Figure 1.3
Complexity of the wine supply chain

pathways between and within each of the three basic components of the industry, intermediaries and retailers. It is not possible to explain all of these pathways in detail here, but Figure 1.3 should help to highlight at least some of the potential pathways. Some of the relationships between different elements of the supply chain are discussed throughout this book. For example the role of negociants is discussed in Chapter 5.

Figure 1.3 also demonstrates the blurring of the boundaries between the different elements of the supply chain. This has, at least in part, resulted from the transnationalisation and corporatisation of the wine industry. Large multinational drinks corporations such as *Pernod Ricard* not only control production but control distribution of their own brands and others. *LVMH* (Louis Vuitton Moët Hennesey) has an even greater level of control as they are a conglomerate of luxury brands (not just wines and spirits) and they have their own distribution networks and major international retail outlets like *DFS Galleria* (with more than 150 stores in Asia-Pacific) and *Sephora* (with more than 500 stores in Europe and North America). There is also consolidation of many of these larger companies (e.g. *Pernod*

Ricard's, 2005 acquisition of *Allied Domecq* and the *South Corp – Fosters* merger in Australia). This can sometimes result in changes in distribution for individual brands within these port-folios and/or the selling off of unwanted brands to other com-panies and therefore lead to further changes in distribution.

Companies that have not traditionally been involved in wine production and distribution have also recently begun to assert more control over all elements of the supply chain. Supermarkets, in particular, have moved to have a wider involvement in the wine industry. For example, a number of UK supermarkets, such as Tesco and Sainsbury, have contracts with wine produc-ers around the world to make their 'own brand' wines and/or for exclusive distribution of all of a winery's production, while Wal-Mart is also increasingly active in the wine market. The distinction between supermarkets and other wine retailers is also becoming increasingly blurred, with the *Woolworths* group in Australia purchasing *Dan Murphy's* (which was one of Australia's largest independent wine retailers) and *First Estate Wine Merchants* (now re-branded as *BWS: Beer Wine Spirits*). The result is a degree of both vertical (e.g. supermarkets owning other retailers) and horizontal integration (e.g. supermarkets effectively controlling production or branding) within the wine supply chain. This can be the source of much confusion for wineries and can make it difficult for smaller wine producers to gain shelf space in retail outlets.

The internet has also begun to change the way the supply chain works, but it has not been explicitly included in our sup-ply chain model. This is because it is primarily used as a tool at all levels in the chain, rather than a distribution network in its own right. It can be used by wineries for direct sales, where reg-ulatory systems allow, as well as by intermediaries to facilitate business-to-business transactions and retail outlets for sales to consumers. The internet provides opportunities for sales and as a promotional and communication tool and can add value to all businesses in the supply chain (see Chapters 6 and 9). However it is also adding to the multiplicity of distribution pathways already available to wineries and therefore increases the chances of poor choices being made.

Figure 1.3 demonstrates the complexity of the wine supply chain but it is not the full story. There are also a series of overlays that modify the supply chain in different markets around the world (Figure 1.4). Each market operates in a different cultural system which influences everything from: the relative importance of different types of intermediaries (e.g. negotiants being more important in parts of France than in other parts of the world); to the role and status of wine producers in society (e.g. peasant or

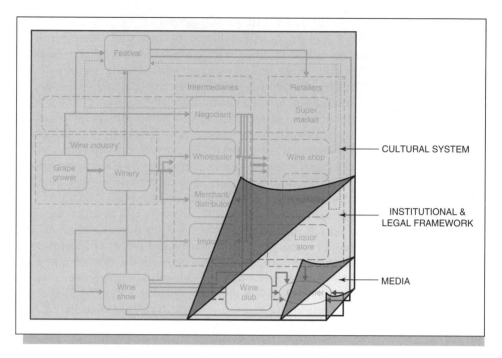

Figure 1.4
Media, legal and cultural overlays

farmer in some Old World wine regions versus entrepreneur or business operator in many New World wine regions); to attitudes towards different types of retailers (e.g. the relatively high significance of supermarkets in the UK and New Zealand).

Each national system also has a series of cultural influences and institutional and legal frameworks that determine how wine is sold and distributed. In Finland, Norway, Sweden and most of Canada, for example, wine is sold to the public through state monopolies, while the US mandates intermediaries (see Box 1.1). Similarly, in Australia wine sales in supermarkets are prohibited while in New Zealand 65% of all wine (53 million litres/70.7 million bottles) is sold via supermarkets (Corbans Viticulture, 2007).

Also within these cultural systems there is a range of media that can influence both the production and consumption of wine. In the USA, Robert Parker (a wine critic and journalist) is the single most influential individual in the wine media. His recommendations can be the difference between success and failure in the USA for a winery, a region or even an entire country (see Chapter 9 for further discussion of Robert Parker and other wine media). In other countries, individuals are less powerful

Box 1.1 The USA's three-tiered wine distribution system

One example of the complexity of the wine supply chain and the institutional frameworks that have been set up to reinforce this is the three-tiered system of distribution in the USA. US legislation makes it mandatory for foreign wine to be distributed via an importer, then a distributor and then a retailer. Until recently this also applied to all interstate wine shipments and it still applies in some states. This box shows how this system arose and discusses its implications for wineries.

Prohibition of Alcohol: the root of the three-tiered system

This situation is the result of the repealing of prohibition laws that were in place between 1920 and 1933 that saw the '… manufacture, sale or transportation of intoxicating liquors' and its importing and exporting prohibited throughout the USA. Prohibition formed part of the American Constitution (United States Constitution Amendment 18, ratified 16 January 1919) and it reflected strong temperance movements that had begun in the 1840s. The movement then waned for several decades especially around the time of the Civil War before being rekindled in the 1880s by the Woman's Christian Temperance Union and the Prohibition Party (Hanson, 2007). These movements were followed by powerful political groups in the 1900s, including the Women's suffrage movement, who felt that alcohol was the root of much of the poverty, crime and disorder of the time (Hanson, 2007). As such prohibition, not only reflected a movement against alcoholism, but also an affirmation of women's rights and an outcry against perceived declining moral standards.

Amendment 21: Repeal of Prohibition of Alcohol

Although not wholly attributable to prohibition itself, the period of Prohibition was in fact characterised by greater levels of disorder. In particular organised crime took off as gangs rallied to produce and supply illegal alcohol. As a result nationwide prohibition was repealed in 1933 (although it still remained in several States right up to 1966) by the 21st Amendment which simply states:

Section 1: The eighteenth article of amendment to the Constitution of the USA is hereby repealed.

Section 2: The transportation or importation into any State, Territory, or Possession of the USA for delivery or use therein of intoxicating liquors, in violation of the laws thereof, is hereby prohibited.

(United States Constitution Amendment 21, ratified 5 December 1933)

For the wine industry Section 2 was important as it gave the states power over the regulation of wine (and other alcohol), which lead to the three-tiered system of distribution. This resulted in all states having some form of control over wholesale and retail operators. Around one-third of the states operate a state monopoly where the government owns and operates all wholesale and retail alcohol sales. The remainder have a strict set of regulations that require alcohol to be handled by State-licensed wholesalers and retailers.

According to Royce (1981, p. 42), because of varying levels of ongoing sympathy with temperance movements, State control of alcohol has also led to 'The fifty states [having] varied and even conflicting laws; for example, in one state food must be served in the same place as liquor, while in an adjoining state not one but two walls must separate food from liquor'. This further complicates the three-tiered system for those wishing to import wine into the USA.

Challenging the Three-Tiered System

A number of States have seen legal challenges to their three-tiered systems from within the USA as wineries seek to directly ship wines to interstate consumers. These include North Carolina, South Carolina, New York, Michigan and Virginia (Wehring, 2005). A case of particular significance was the case taken against Michigan and New York in the US Supreme Court. This case, depending on which side is reporting the ruling, found that: these '… state laws banning direct shipments from wineries to consumers are discriminatory and, therefore, unconstitutional' (Wehring, 2005); or that the three-tiered-system was 'perfectly legal' and 'unequivocally legitimate' provided that it did not discriminate between in-state and out-of-state wineries (Virginia Wine Wholesalers Association, 2005).

These varying views of the same Supreme Court decision suggest that there are still many deep-seated divisions in the US surrounding alcohol, not to mention wine wholesalers wishing to preserve their monopolies. Despite this, changes are occurring that suggests that this system of distribution is on the decline, for US wineries at least (these changes do not apply to wines from outside of the US). In the 1980s there were just four states allowing direct-to-consumer wine shipments (Free the Grapes, 2007). By August 2006, 33 states allow wineries to ship wine directly from out-of-state via licensed shippers, but just 12 states allow wine retailers to do the same (Free the Grapes, 2007).

See the following for further discussion of the ongoing developments surrounding the three-tiered distribution system in the USA:

For both sides of the ongoing debate:
www.freethegrapes.com
The website of *Free the* Grapes, proponents of continued freeing up of US distribution laws.
www.wswa.org/public/index.html
The website of the *Wine and Spirits Wholesalers Association*, the opponents of change.

For notes on each states regulations on wine distribution see the following documents:
Houchins, R.C. (2006) *Notes on Wine Distribution*. http://shipcompliant.com/blog/document_library/dist_notes_12_0.pdf
Barber, N. and Dodd, T. (2006) *An Analysis of State Direct Wine Shipment Laws*. Technical Report No. 06-03, October 2006, Texas Wine Marketing Research Institute, Texas Tech University, Lubbock. http://www.hs.ttu.edu/texaswine/2006/technical_report_0603.pdf

but wine (and food and lifestyle) magazines can be very influential. Australia has *Australian Gourmet Traveller (AGT) Wine Magazine*, New Zealand has *Cuisine* magazine, the USA has *Wine Spectator* and *The Wine Advocate* (for which Robert Parker writes) and the UK *Decanter*. Beyond wine-dedicated media, movies and television programmes can have a huge influence on consumer preferences. Perhaps the most notable example of this is the cult movie *Sideways*, which changed consumption patterns in the US overnight. Known as the 'Sideways Effect', consumers began drinking Pinot Noir in preference to Merlot because of one line in the movie (see Chapter 9 for more discussion of the Sideways Effect). Movies such as the *Lord of the Rings* Trilogy have also increased the desirability of all things New Zealand and wine has been no exception.

From supply chain to value chain

The supply chain described in the previous section is one that has traditionally seen little value added between when the wine leaves the winery and when it reaches the consumer. This is especially the case where legislative frameworks and cultural systems have legitimised unnecessarily complicated pathways between winery and consumer (e.g. the US three-tiered system or the system of negotiants and merchants in Bordeaux). One of the desirable things for wineries and consumers is for the system of distribution to add value, not just cost, to the wine. A market-driven/experience-driven approach can facilitate this, turning a cost-driven supply chain into a value-driven value chain. A value chain is therefore a sequence of productive, value adding, activities leading to end use.

A production-driven approach does not necessarily allow, or even require, the addition of value by actors in the chain. A production-driven winery will see distribution as a necessary evil and treat it is a cost of production, while an experience-driven winery will see it as an opportunity to add value for its consumers. For example, in an ideal world an experience-driven winery might carefully select a distributor that is going to concentrate on placing its wines into retailers that provide a level of service and type of experience that meets their target market's needs. They would also treat the distributor as any other customer, developing a relationship with them, communicating consistent brand values and providing added value through education and experiences that support these brand values. This should in turn allow them to communicate the winery's brand values to the retailer and so on. Value can also be added by exploring what other brands are associated with a particular distributor or retailer so that they closely match those of the wine in question. Alternatively, it might be an association with a particular restaurant that specialises in a cuisine that matches both the wine's characteristics and brand values (e.g. a local restaurant using only local ingredients or one that only uses organic ingredients matched with a biodynamic wine).

The distinction might also be made here between bulk wine producers and premium wine producers. Bulk wine producers, being primarily production driven, have traditionally focussed on distribution as a supply chain mechanism. However, they too can benefit from a strategy which results in a value chain rather than a supply chain distribution system. For example, Chapter 6 indicates how large, transnational retailers have sought to add value even with respect to their bulk wine sales via various sub brands of their own label wines. In short, anything that adds value to their wine must have a positive impact on their bottom line. In practice the strategies of bulk producers will be different to those of premium producers because of the nature of the product itself, but the principles espoused in this book can apply equally to both bulk and premium producers. This is especially true for discussions relating to several areas of the value chain, including: the marketing value of production (Chapter 3); the cellar door and direct sales (Chapter 4); intermediaries (Chapter 5) and; wine retail (Chapter 6); as well as the wider business context for wine (Chapter 2). Other parts of this book are likely to have more value for premium producers than bulk producers but there is clear value in bulk producers having an understanding of all parts of the value chain, especially as many bulk producers are moving into premium production in many parts of the world (Charters, 2006) while a number of existing wine businesses combine premium and bulk wine production.

There are many factors that can conspire to make this task difficult or, in some circumstances, impossible. These might include the availability of choice of distributor or retailer in any given market, the power held by different players in the value chain or legislative frameworks that remove choice. However, this should not detract from what is in essence an attitude: add value not just cost!

This kind of approach requires a wine producer to have a thorough understanding of the supply chain and the tools necessary to add value and therefore convert it into a value chain. It also requires an investment of time and effort in the development of relationships and communication to support these relationships. In short, it requires a focus not on the wine, but on the people that are responsible for adding value to it and giving it its true brand value: everyone from intermediaries to retailers, media and, most importantly, the consumer themselves (see Box 1.2).

Box 1.2 Australia's Marketing Strategy and Wine Australia market programmes (2007)

In 2007, the Australian Wine and Brandy Corporation (AWBC) released a new industry strategy and set of market programmes as part of 'a roadmap for wine sector sustainability'. The new strategy was regarded as important because the Australian wine industry has undergone a dramatic transformation since the publication in 1996 of the Strategy 2025 document that set a target of A\$4.5 billion in annual sales by 2025 – a figure already surpassed in 2005. According to Winemakers' Federation of Australia Chief Executive Stephen Strachan 'In the decade since the release of the Strategy 2025 document, the global operating environment has changed markedly with increased global competition, wine producer and retail sector consolidation, as well as a wine oversupply' (AWBC, 2006).

The new Wine Australia market programmes had been developed so as to move Wine Australia (the banner under which the AWBC promotes Australian wine internationally) from a 'one-size-fits-all' national generic brand to one that developed sub-brands that fitted in better with the various elements of the wine supply chain, such as those indicated in the various chapters of this book, but particularly different retail outlets. Thereby adding value through more of a value chain emphasis. According to the AWBC, Australia seeks to represent itself:

… as a broad and inclusive producer that seeks to champion quality and excitement whatever the price point. As we extend our brand footprint, so our market activities develop and fall into the following four sub-brands or 'personalities' that reflect new market and channel opportunities. The benefit to all is to clearly differentiate our product offering and direct it toward intended target markets. These are two skills usually conspicuous by their absence in generic marketing and will ensure improved collective benefit and individual brand profile.

(AWBC, 2007a).

The four sub-brands and their characteristics are

1. *Brand Champions*: The 'standard bearers' of Australian wine. 'Category champions, popular premium brands, audacious commercial newcomers and wineries that aspire to a mainstream presence in either the Retail or Restaurant channels' (AWBC, 2007a)
2. *Regional Heroes*: focussed towards the development of regional identities under the Australian wine brand umbrella that illustrate varietal choice and/or styles linked to place
3. *Generation Next*: focussed towards innovation in winemaking (new blends), viticulture (new varieties) and marketing (packaging and communication)
4. *Landmark Australia*: focus on Australian 'ultra-premium collectables and image makers' (AWBC, 2007a).

See AWBC: http://www.wineaustralia.com/

One way that this can be done is to consider the various elements of wine marketing at each of stage of the wine value chain. In this text we introduce 8 Ps of the wine marketing mix that will help readers identify and understand the different elements that are important to wine marketing and we will apply a number of these Ps at each stage of the value chain.

The 8 Ps of the wine marketing mix

Traditionally marketing texts have used McCarthy's (1960) 4 Ps to describe the marketing mix: product, pricing, place and promotion. Others have extended these Ps to also include: public relations and political power (Kotler, 1984); people, physical evidence and process (Magrath, 1986) and packaging (Sin, 2006). There are also many different ways that each of these elements are interpreted and in some cases their meaning is widely debated. These Ps are also applied across a wide range of marketing situations but are not necessarily all applicable to wine marketing and/or can have a number of different connotations when used in the context of wine.

Table 1.2 shows the focus of the 8 Ps of wine marketing and how they might be applied. These elements are sometimes quite similar to the traditional marketing definitions, but in each case they have been altered to be more directly applicable to wine marketing. *Place*, for example, is an important element of wine production, consumption and marketing that has too many strong connotations to be used in its traditional marketing sense. One of the core concepts associated with wine is *terroir*, which is a French term with no literal English translation that describes how all elements of a place (natural and cultural) combine in a way that cannot be replicated in any other place. It is what gives wines their complexity and it breathes life into it, giving wine its soul (see Chapter 10 for a more detailed discussion of terroir). The traditional use of place in marketing also tends to be more suggestive of a supply chain (i.e. it is about process and cost) rather than the value chain concept espoused here.

Planning is often a given in traditional marketing and it could be suggested that this is in fact what marketing is all about. However, it is our experience that for many wine producers and some others in the value chain (especially wine retailers and restaurateurs) marketing planning is not given the level of attention that it should (Box 1.3).

Table 1.2 8 Ps of the wine marketing mix.

	Traditional focus	Wine marketing focus	Wine marketing application

Product	• Actual, core and augmented
	• Quality
	• Attributes
	• Brand
		• As for traditional
		  – greater emphasis on the augmented product
		  – increasing emphasis on understanding the product from the perspective of consumer needs
		  – co-creation
			• More than just the wine, especially at the winery:
			  – wine service
			  – food matching
			  – consumer experience

Place	• Distribution
	• Retail outlets
	• Warehousing
	• Sales territories
		• Applications of sense of place
		  – traditional definition is considered to be more production driven
		• Location of business
			• Application of *terroir* and geographically designated origins
			  – Country/region of origin
			  – regional characteristics/appellation
			  – winery sense of place
			  – connection of consumer to the intangibles of place
			  – environmental dimensions of place

Pricing	• Costs
	• Distribution and retailer mark ups
	• Discounts
		• Adding value to consumers rather than based on costs
		• Traditional understandings augmented with greater knowledge of what provides value for customers
			• Pricing based on
			  – rarity and novelty
			  – quality (as determined by the consumer)
			  – place (appellation or origin)
			  – service (restaurants)

(Continued)

Table 1.2 (Continued)

	Traditional focus	Wine marketing focus	Wine marketing application
Promotion	• Advertising • Sales promotion • Personal selling • Publicity	• As for traditional – but account for different actors in the value chain	• Different for: – Winery – Intermediary – Retailer – Post retail – Region – Integrated wine businesses
Packaging	• Design • Labelling	• As for traditional – PLUS bundling with other products	• Traditional: – labels, bottles, etc. • Bundling: – Tourism products – Food and wine matching – Event programming
People	• Service creators/ providers	• As for traditional – including all actors in value chain, but also recognising role of champions	• Cellar door staff • Restaurateurs and waiters • Sommelier and bar staff • Key actors
Planning	• None	• Marketing planning • Value chain planning/strategy • Understanding business environment	• Marketing plans and strategies • Value chain strategy • Research
Positioning	• Attempting to control perceptions of the product	• As for traditional – complicated by number of intermediaries	• Value chain strategy

Box 1.3 How *not* to plan for a new winery

This fictitious example is not intended to reflect any single winery's approach to marketing and selling their wine when establishing a new winery. However it is drawn from a combination of real world examples observed by us over the past 10 to 12 years of researching wineries. In fact many of the aspects of this example are far too often repeated in wine regions around the world, but especially in the New World, where becoming a wine producer is a middle-class romantic dream.

The Dream: Nigel Poyndexter purchases some land in the Yarra Valley wine region near Melbourne Australia with the intention of 'planting a few grapes' so that he can make some wine to show off to his friends with a little left over that he will sell to cover the production costs. He pays a premium for the land because it is right next door to a famous vineyard and he does not get any advice from viticultural or winemaking consultants [mistake #1].

Living the Dream: Nigel plants a few hectares of grapes, manages them himself on weekends and holidays for the first 12 months [mistake #2]. However he soon realises that his busy professional career does not allow him the time that he needs to tend the vines, so employs a consultant viticulturalist to manage the grapes for him. The consultant says that there are some issues with the soils on the site and recommends that some of the grapes be moved and Nigel pays him to move them.

Honeymoon Period: After around three years Nigel has some grapes. He thinks that it might be a good idea to try and make some of his own wine at this stage [mistake #3], but he has too few grapes for any contract winemaker to deal with as a stand-alone wine. He is forced to sell his grapes to a larger, well-established winery at less than market rates [mistake #4].

Fruits of Your Labour: After five years Nigel is nearly in full grape production, and over the last two years he has planted an additional 20 hectares of grapes [mistake #5]. He now has enough wine to make his own label. He contracts the winery that he has been selling his grapes to and they make one barrel (300 bottles or 12 cases) into Nigel's own label. Nigel also spends several thousand dollars paying a design company to design a name and a label for his bottles: *Mount Misery* being the result [mistake #5]. Nigel keeps five cases of *Mount Misery* for himself and sells the rest to friends at cost [mistake #6]. Nigel's friends love it so he decides to increase production of *Mount Misery*.

Into a 'Lifestyle Career': In year seven Nigel is still selling most of his grapes to another winery, but he now has around 300 cases of *Mount Misery*. Last year he had 100 cases (1200 bottles) and managed to sell all of these to friends and a couple of local restaurants. With 300 cases, he now realises that he has to make a more directed effort to market *Mount Misery* so he quits his job and concentrates on selling his wine [mistake #7].

Early Success (a.k.a false sense of security): It's now year eight and last year *Mount Misery* managed to sell all 300 cases as they won a gold medal at the Yarra Valley Wine Show and a distributor decided to put *Mount Misery* on her portfolio and she duly sells 250 cases. Despite the fact that *Mount Misery* is far from making a profit (as they are servicing a very high level of debt) Nigel is buoyed by the enthusiasm from the distributor and the fact that he has managed to sell everything and he decides to go it alone [mistake #8]. He starts building a winery [mistake #9] with a cellar door/tasting room and café [mistake #10]. He also increases production to 1000 cases, while still selling grapes to other wineries [mistake #11].

Reality Bites: Year 10 and *Mount Misery* has just completed its first solo vintage and they have 3000 cases of wine to sell. Last year was a poor vintage and the distributor struggled to sell 700 cases of the 1000 they produced. Nigel sacks his distributor and tries to go it alone again [mistake #12]. He spends three months and tens of thousands of dollars travelling to major export markets [mistake #13] but he has little luck as they have too many wines on their portfolio from Australia and are now finding it hard to sell the varieties and styles of wine that *Mount Misery* is producing. In desperation Nigel slashes his trade price [mistake #14] to below cost just to have some turn over. A major domestic supermarket chain buys 1500 cases [mistake #15], but he discovers that they further discount his wine as a 'loss leader'. This in turn has a negative impact on cellar door/tasting room sales, as visitors are reluctant to buy because they know that they can buy it from the supermarket for 35% less than Nigel sells direct to the public. The only saving grace is that Nigel manages to sell 1000 cases for his original asking price via an importer in Brazil [mistake #16]. At the end of the year, however, the importer discovers that he could have bought it from a supermarket chain for much less and he unceremoniously dumps Mt Misery from his portfolio.

End of the Dream: It is now year 13 and Nigel has struggled through the last two vintages by discounting [mistake #17] and picking up the odd distribution deal in the export market. He has not been able to recover his price following the major discounting of year ten and he is now faced with the inevitable and he is forced to sell up. His initial investment of a few hundred thousand dollars 13 years prior has now ballooned to around $2 million, while the value of the vineyard and grapes is far less than it should be because of poor decisions made ten years prior. The brand itself is also worthless and the best the Nigel can hope for is to minimise his losses.

All of the mistakes above could have been avoided by using a market-driven approach and saved Nigel a lot of money and perhaps even turned growing debts into profits. Some mistakes are not in themselves mistakes, but rather the lack of market analysis and planning makes them a mistake. For example, Mistake #10 (the development of a cellar door and café) could have been a major positive for *Mount Misery* if Nigel had undertaken research into the wine tourism market in the Yarra Valley, their needs, how to reach them and how to distribute the wine tourism product.

How this book works

In this chapter we have highlighted the complexity and significance of the wine supply/value chain. This book is therefore organised to address a cross-section of issues throughout the chain. As such the chapters are organised with both the value chain and 8 Ps in mind (see Table 1.3). This application across the value chain is also designed to demonstrate how the principles of an experience-driven approach can be used by different players in the value chain and not just wineries.

As is evident in this chapter, this book also has a series of boxes with real world examples of 'how to' apply some of the principles discussed in the chapter. There will also be 'how not to' examples that will be based on observations of the real world, but which may be exaggerated and/or slightly altered in order to make the lessons very clear. Each chapter will also conclude with a series of short practical wine marketing insights.

Table 1.3 The 8 Ps in each chapter

	Chapter 1 Introduction	Chapter 2 International business environment	Chapter 3 Production processes	Chapter 4 Cellar door	Chapter 5 Intermediaries
Product	X	X	X	X	
Place	X		X	X	X
Pricing	X				
Promotion	X		X	X	X
Packaging				X	
People	X			X	X
Positioning	X	X	X	X	X
Planning	X	X	X		X

	Chapter 6 Retailing	Chapter 7 Licensed premises	Chapter 8 Events	Chapter 9 Wine brand image agents	Chapter 10 Marketing cooperation	Chapter 11 Conclusion
Product	X	X	X		X	X
Place					X	X
Pricing	X	X	X			X
Promotion	X	X	X	X	X	X
Packaging	X		X		X	X
People	X	X	X	X	X	X
Positioning	X	X	X	X	X	X
Planning	X		X	X		X

As understanding the wine consumer and their behaviour is critical to effective wine marketing, there are several wine consumer behaviour insights throughout the book. These will relate directly to the topics being discussed in the chapter and will be drawn from research undertaken by a wide range of researchers from around the world. Given Lockshin and Spawton's (2001) assertion that around half of all research into wine marketing comes from Australia, however, many of the examples will come from these two countries.

Before entering into discussions of the various elements of the value chain, Chapter 2 provides more detail on the international context for the wine trade. This includes more discussion of a range of institutional and legal frameworks from around the world and figures on the production and consumption of wine around the globe. Chapter 3 highlights the significance of the production process as an element of wine marketing, which has hitherto been largely ignored in wine marketing literature. In Chapter 4, we explore several layers of marketing opportunity at the cellar door including direct sales, relationship marketing, brand building and using it as a place to gather market intelligence. A range of different intermediaries make up the next part of the value chain and these are discussed in Chapter 5, relationship marketing also being a key element of the discussion in this chapter. Various retail outlets are most likely to be the point of sale to the end consumer of the wine and these can include small specialised retailers right through to vertically integrated multinationals such as supermarket chains. At all retail outlets the 'servicescape' is an important element of wine marketing and this is one of the core themes of Chapter 6. Licensed premises have the potential to add the most value for wine consumers as they are often the site of special occasions, almost always involve experiential consumption and may involve a dining experience and these are discussed in Chapter 7. There are a range of events that can add real value to the wine value chain. Chapter 8 explores a range of these events including those primarily targeted at the wine trade, as well as those with more of a consumer focus. Chapter 9 moves away from the value chain to explore how various external image formation agents (i.e. advertising, media, shows and critics) can influence perceptions of a wine brand. The penultimate chapter discusses the value of marketing cooperation amongst wineries and with other sectors such as tourism. In doing so Chapter 10 explores some of the differences between New World and Old World approaches to cooperation including some discussion of the concept of terroir and how it has driven Old World wine producers. Chapter 11 concludes the book with a discussion of some of the themes that emerge throughout this book, as well as discussion of the future of wine production and consumption through to 2015.

Chapter summary

This chapter has introduced the reader to several core concepts that are used as a framework for what follows. In particular it has highlighted the nature of the wine industry around the world and established the need for the adoption of a more market-driven approach. It has also described the complexity of the wine supply chain and suggested that, by taking an experiential approach to its management, this can be perceived and utilised as a value chain. Finally the chapter has introduced the 8 Ps of wine marketing: Product; Place; Pricing; Promotion; Packaging; People; Positioning, and; Planning.

Further reading

Barclay, V. (2001). Is Your Winery Production or Marketing Driven? *Wine Business Monthly*, 8(9), http://www.winebusiness.com/html/MonthlyArticle.cfm?dataId=11390.
An introduction to some of the key aspects of a market-driven approach for wineries.

Charters, S. (2006). *Wine and Society: The social and cultural context of a drink*, Elsevier Butterworth Heinemann.
An introduction to the context of modern wine consumption including its symbolic and experiential value and the social and cultural context of wine.

Holbrook, M.B. and Hirschman, E.C. (1982). The experiential aspects of consumption: consumer fantasies, feelings, and fun. *Journal of Consumer Research*, 9(2), 132–140.
As the original proponent of an experiential view of consumer behaviour, this article outlines the key aspects of this way of viewing consumption.

Lockshin, L. (2003). *Consumer purchasing behaviour for wine: what we know and where we are going*. Marchés et Marketing du Vin Cahier de Recherche (Markets and Marketing of Wine Research Paper) No. 57-03 August 2003, Centre de recherche de Bordeaux Ecole de Management, Bordeaux. Available at: http://www.bordeaux-bs.edu/download/recherche/larry_Lockshin.pdf.
A good summary of the 'state of play' in wine market research.

Vargo, S.L. and Lusch, R.F. (2004). The four service marketing myths: Remnants of a goods-based, manufacturing model. *Journal of Service Research*, 6(4), 324–335.

Provides a good overview of a service-dominant view of exchange.

Virginia Wine Wholesalers Association (2000). *Intervenor–defendant VWWA's memorandum of law in support of its motion for summary judgment.* Available: http://www.coalitionforfree-trade.org/litigation/virginia/VWWA.MSJ2.pdf
Legal arguments surrounding the abolition of three-tiered system of distribution in Virginia, USA.

The international business environment of wine

Chapter objectives

After reading this chapter you will

- Understand the international nature of the business of wine
- Understand some of the key factors influencing the competitiveness of the international wine market
- Appreciate some of the factors that are affecting the macro-environment for wine
- Identify specific competitive factors in the international business environment of wine

We are now totally export driven and at the whim of the international market-place (Croser, 1997).

It is also more *fun* than investing in pork bellies. And if the market does crash, you can at least take solace in drinking up your position (Stimpfig, 2007).

Introduction

Wine is an international business. On average, over the past two decades 25% of the wine produced in the world is traded internationally. However, the extent of international trade has been gradually increasing over time. At the beginning of the 1980s approximately 18% of wine consumed in the world market monitored by the OIV (Organisation Internationale de la Vigne et du Vin) had been imported. In 2005 this figure had reached almost 33.4% of wine consumption (OIV, 2006) (the OIV estimate that their figures account for approximately 94% of world trade in wine). The total figure for world exports, which is an indicator of the size of the market, has also been expanding with world wine exports being 44 million hectolitres on average in the years 1986–1990, and 67 million hectolitres for 2002 (European Commission, 2006a). For 2004 78.7 million hectolitres was traded internationally (OIV, 2006).

Even if a winery is not exporting and is concentrating on the local market it is still competing with imports, while the supply chain of wine production in many countries not only relies on the importation of yeasts and oak barrels, but also wine-making equipment and labour. The phenomena of flying wine-makers – a term used to describe wine-makers who move seasonally between the southern and northern hemispheres to make wine or advise on wine-making – for example, demonstrates the increased internationalisation of wine-making and the globalisation of some wine styles (Lagendijk, 2004). Indeed, increasingly it is not just the wine-makers who are part of a global wine labour market but also seasonal labour that may harvest grapes or prune vines.

An example of the internationalisation of the wine industry is the range of wines stocked by the Swedish wine retail monopoly Systembolaget. Apart from a few small vineyards in the south-east of the country, Sweden produces little grape wine. Therefore, the range of wines sold by Systembolaget provides a good indication of the potential sources of wine in the international market. Table 2.1 indicates the origin areas of wines planned for launch from October 2007 to March 2008 with some 27 countries being identified as sources of wines that the state monopoly would like to launch in addition to its existing selection. Therefore, because of the competitive environment within which wineries and all elements of the wine value chain find themselves in it is therefore increasingly important that businesses systematically evaluate their environment.

This chapter provides an overview of some of the major factors that are influencing the business environment in which wine businesses operate. This is undertaken through an analysis of the 'micro-environment' or 'task environment' of the firm which is the immediate industry environment in which it operates and the 'macro-environment' which is the environment in the form of wider influences that affect the industry as a whole (Figure 2.1). The majority of wine businesses probably analyse their industry environment, although typically on an informal non-systematic basis and often only in consideration of their immediate local environment. However, the internationalisation of the wine industry means that, for many wineries, the local business environment is now global. Only a limited number of wine businesses, such as some retailers and restaurants, can now afford to solely have a local focus with respect to their competitive environment. However, even those businesses that have traditionally sold to locals are increasingly looking to the implications of the global wine trade, if not for their own stock, then for their competitors.

The business environment surrounds the wine business and its products. It is important to distinguish between the two as different products, such as fortified wine versus a varietal chardonnay or even different brands, will often have different factors operating in their environments as compared to that of the business overall. The industry environment represents the core of the business environment that affects wine businesses

Table 2.1 Systembolaget wine launches October 2007–March 2008

Country of origin	Fixed range white (Oct. 7)	Fixed range red (Oct. 7)	Temporary range white (Nov. 7)	Temporary range red (Nov. 7)	Temporary range white (Dec. 7)
Argentina	2	3	–	1	–
Australia	3	3	4	2	1
Austria	–	–	3	1	–
Brazil, Bolivia, Peru	–	–	1	1	–
Bulgaria	–	1	–	–	–
Chile	1	1	1	2	–
Croatia/Slovenia	–	–	–	–	–
France	2	4	3	6	2
Germany	2	–	–	–	3
Greece	–	–	–	1	–
Hungary	–	–	–	–	1
Italy	2	5	1	1	1
Lebanon	–	–	–	–	–
Macedonia/Serbia/ Montenegro	–	–	–	1	–
Moldavia	–	–	–	–	–
New Zealand	–	–	1	2	–
Portugal	–	1	–	–	1
South Africa	1	3	–	2	2
Spain	1	4	–	3	2
Uruguay	–	1	1	1	–
USA	3	2	–	2	1

Country of origin	Temporary range red (Dec. 7)	Temporary range white (Feb. 8)	Temporary range red (Feb. 8)	Temporary range white (Mar. 8)	Temporary range red (Mar. 8)
Argentina	1	2	1	–	1
Australia	2	–	4	–	1
Austria	–	–	–	1	1
Brazil, Bolivia, Peru	–	–	–	–	–
Bulgaria	–	–	1	–	1
Chile	2	3	–	–	2
Croatia/Slovenia	–	1	–	–	–
France	5	3	5	3	–
Germany	–	–	–	1	2
Greece	–	–	–	–	1
Hungary	–	–	–	–	–
Italy	6	1	1	2	2
Lebanon	–	–	–	1	1
Macedonia/Serbia/ Montenegro	–	–	–	–	–
Moldavia	–	–	1	–	–

(Continued)

Table 2.1   (Continued)

Country of origin	Temporary range red (Dec. 7)	Temporary range white (Feb. 8)	Temporary range red (Feb. 8)	Temporary range white (Mar. 8)	Temporary range red (Mar. 8)
New Zealand	1	–	–	1	–
Portugal	2	–	–	1	1
South Africa	1	2	3	2	2
Spain	1	–	3	2	3
Uruguay	–	–	–	–	–
USA	1	–	1	2	2

Note: Excludes sparkling, fortified and mulled wines.
Source: Derived from Systembolaget (2007).

and includes its network of business relationships both current and desired. Therefore, it includes suppliers in the business' supply chain and customers referring to both end-customers and business to business customers, which for a winery may include wholesalers, retailers and restaurants depending on how they sell their wine. Customers are a subset of consumers with customers being all previous or current consumers who have purchased the business' products and consumers being the set of all possible purchasers, as well as those that may have consumed the wine without purchasing it (e.g. the wine was given to them as a gift).

Competitors, such as other wineries, are also an important part of the industry environment. However, it should be stressed that on many occasions wineries compete and cooperate simultaneously. Indeed, this is often a characteristic of smaller wineries. For example, while wineries compete to sell their own wines they may also cooperate in terms of joint and regional marketing exercises, particularly in export markets; sharing viticultural and wine-making expertise and even equipment; and, for small wineries, even sharing transport costs to export markets by sharing container space. Chapter 10 has a more detailed discussion and several examples of this type of cooperation.

The final element of the industry environment is stakeholders. This includes interest groups, organisations and individuals that influence the business environment though are not suppliers, competitors or customers. These include organisations such as national and regional wine associations, wine

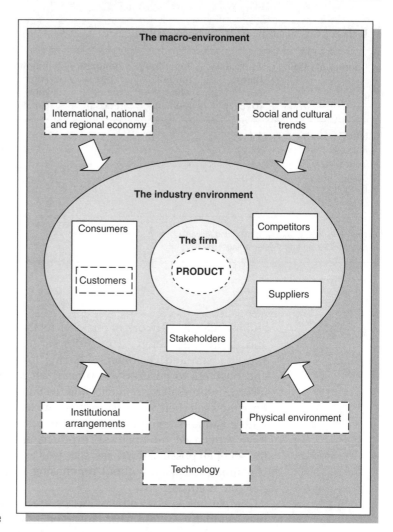

Figure 2.1
The international
business
environment of wine

tourism networks, environmental groups, licensing bodies and
consumer groups that may all influence a wine business and its
products. For example, because of concerns over food miles
from environmental and consumer groups there are increased
pressures on supermarkets and other retailers, as well as legis-
lators, to change labelling requirements to indicate how far
food, including wines has travelled, and what the impact is in
terms of greenhouse gas emissions (Box 2.1).

This chapter provides a discussion of major issues in the international business environment of wine. It does not provide a
specific analysis for a specific business as that needs to be done on

Box 2.1 From food miles to wine miles

The term 'food miles' was first used in a 1994 report by a British non-profit organisation (SAFE Alliance) now known as Sustain UK (DEFRA, 2005). Food miles are a term primarily used to describe the distances travelled by foodstuffs from producer to consumer. They are generally measured as tonne kilometres, that is, the distance travelled in kilometres multiplied by the weight in tonnes for each foodstuff. However, to measure the environmental impact of food miles it is necessary to convert them into vehicle kilometres, that is, the sum of the distances travelled by each vehicle carrying food. More recently, the term has been used as a generic description of the amount of energy and consequent greenhouse gas (GHG) emissions that food travels.

Between 1978 and 2005, the annual amount of food moved in the UK by heavy goods vehicles has increased by 23%, and the average distance for each trip has increased by over 50% (DEFRA, 2005). In North America, the most widely cited study on food miles is the Leopold Center for Sustainable Agriculture's report *Food, Fuel, and Freeways* (Pirog et al., 2001) which is based on arrival data for the Chicago Food Terminal which specified the origin of all food items passing through the terminal. They found that food items travelled on average 1518 miles (approximately 2429 kilometres) to get to Iowa destinations in 1998, a 22% increase over 1981. This average distance was 33 times greater than the 45-mile average distance travelled by food items in a local farm-to-institution programme in Iowa. The food items sourced from the terminal also used 4–17 times more fuel and produced 5–17 times more GHG emissions than the locally sourced ones (Xuereb, 2005).

In Canada a study by Foodshare, a Toronto non-profit organisation (Bentley and Barker, 2005), took the approach of purchasing the same dinner ingredients at a grocery store and a farmers' market, reading product labels to identify source locations, and contacting producers to identify the mode of transport. The study found that the local food items travelled an average of 101 kilometres versus 5364 kilometres for the imported items. The imported food items created 100 times more GHG emissions than the local ones (Xuereb, 2005). An alternative approach developed by the Lifestyles Project based in Victoria BC has been to create an on-line database of food items imported into British Columbia. The Lifecycles website is able to instantly call up the average food miles for imports of selected food items. Based on the average distances of all food imports, and then compare the GHG emissions created by the imports to locally sourced versions of the same food items (see http://www.lifecyclesproject.ca/).

Xuereb (2005) adopted the above approach to determine the average distances travelled by imports of selected food items to the Waterloo Region in Ontario, Canada (just north of the Niagara wine region), and the GHG emissions associated with their transport. Xuereb's (2005) study demonstrated that imports to the Waterloo Region of 58 commonly eaten food items travelled 4497 kilometres on average, and account for 51,709 tonnes of GHG emissions annually. Significantly, all of the food items included in the study could have been grown or raised in the Waterloo Region, leading to a finding that replacing all the studied food items with products of Southwestern Ontario origin would produce an annual reduction in GHG emissions of 49,485 tonnes, equivalent to taking 16,191 cars off the road.

Concern over GHG may have an affect on the behaviour of wine consumers. For example, Carbon Footprint (http://www.carbonfootprint.com/) advises 'Think twice about buying a bottle of wine from the other side of the world – you may be able to find much more local wine, which will have traveled far fewer miles' as part of its tips to reduce an individual's emissions. Sedlescombe Organic Vineyard in the UK has also used the fact that its wine has fewer 'wine miles' than imported wine as a selling feature noting 'Wine flown in from New Zealand/Australia creates 3302 kg CO_2. Wine from Kent/Sussex creates 5 kg CO_2. The Sunday Times, Nov 19th 2006' (http://www.englishorganicwine.co.uk/). Concern over wine miles may therefore become a means for local wineries to reinforce reasons to purchase local wines. However, such concerns may still be addressed by exporters. For example, the Grove Mill brand (see Chapter 3) was recommended for its 'greenie' points value in *The Times* newspaper in the UK:

… here is a way to ease your conscience. Drink the world's first carbon-neutral wine. New Zealand winery Grove Mill offset over 300 tonnes of carbon dioxide last year by investing in carbon-balancing schemes that plant trees and finance renewable energy projects. It accounts for the eco-impact of production as well as transport. Drinking European wine still wins when you consider the wine miles, but this is a decent second best.

(Sheppard, 2007)

However, while food miles or wine miles are an important concept for thinking about sustainable consumption they do not account for the full amount of GHG emissions that come from wine. In order to do this it is important that the energy costs of production at the winery and in the vineyard are also calculated and included in the figure and these are rarely calculated by those promoting local consumption, which may overstate the difference in impact between imported and locally produced wines.

Lifecycles Food Miles Project: http://www.lifecyclesproject.ca/

a product-by-product, business-by-business, country-by-country and market-by-market basis. Nevertheless, many of the issues discussed will be relevant to how you consider the marketing of wine in the present and future marketing environment. The key reason for discussing these issues is they affect the profitability of wine businesses and while wine is, for many small producers, part of a lifestyle decision, the reality is that a lifestyle is easier to maintain if the accounts are in the black.

Fundamentally, wine business profits will be determined by three factors:

1. The value of the product to customers.
2. The extent of competition between producers.
3. The relative bargaining power of firms at different stages of the wine production and distribution chain.

All of these factors provide challenges to wine businesses in the contemporary business environment for wine.

The first section of the chapter will discuss the industry environment particularly with respect to issues of competitiveness and changing wine consumption. The second section will discuss the macro-environment under the headings provided in Figure 2.1.

The competitive industry environment for wine

'What started out as a hobby ... became an economic liability. Now we have to make a profit ... or break even' Dean Bender, Lawton Ridge Vineyard in Van Buren County, Michigan speaking at the 31st Wineries Unlimited Conference and Trade Show.

(Silfven, 2007)

Return on investment (ROI) is the ratio of capital gained or lost, relative to the amount of capital invested. It is the fundamental driver for establishing a business and in business competition. The ROI is determined by five sources of competitive pressure (Porter, 1980):

1. *Competition from suppliers of substitute products*: In wine this includes not only other wines but also, for many wine markets, other types of alcoholic beverages (in fact in France bottled water is seen as one of wine's biggest competitors).
2. *The threat of competition from new entrants*: This can include new wineries being established in the same region as producers as well as new entrants in the form of wine from other regions in markets where it had never previously been available before.
3. *Competition from existing producers*: This can include existing competitors changing their price structures, new branding strategies and/or the introduction of new brands.
   These three types of competition may be referred to as 'horizontal competition'. Two other types of competition referred to as vertical competition are:
4. *The bargaining power of suppliers*: In the case of a winery this will include such suppliers as wine-making and viticultural

equipment suppliers, bottle suppliers. In the case of a whole-saler the primary suppliers are the wineries.

5. *The bargaining power of purchasers (buyers)*: In the case of a winery this may include both the end consumer and other businesses in the supply chain to the end consumer.

These factors are indicated in Figure 2.2.

As a result of increasing internationalisation of the wine industry, which has gone hand in hand with a lessening of trade barriers, the growth of new entrants, and high levels of production, most wine markets are at their most competitive level ever. Australia, for example, is perhaps the one of the most aggressive markets for new entrants into the wine industry. As a result of

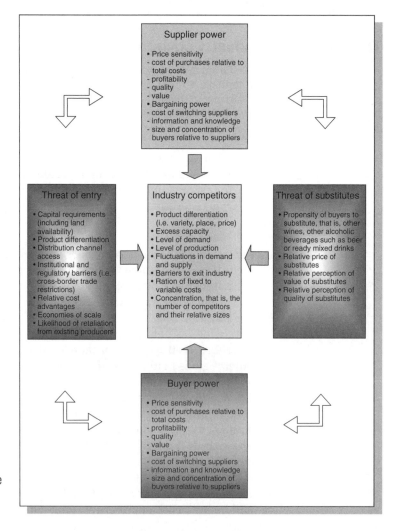

Figure 2.2

The competitive framework for wine (based on Porter, 1980; Hall, 2008)

this recent explosion in development, Michael De Palma, the director of the Australian Wine and Brandy Corporation (a statutory authority of the Australian government), said in March 2007 that the large number of vineyards with fewer than 50 hectares (as many as 75%) were struggling compared to those of more than 150 hectares. According to De Palma (in Akerman, 2007):

The majority of our growers really can't hang in there to ride out these tough times ... There has to be another way, shape or form for them to exit the industry or to adapt. The drought has given us the opportunity to refocus our future direction as an industry ... A lot of focus has now been on trying to lift the consumer to try to look at the higher prices – a bigger buffer when it comes to profitability.

Although Australian wine exports remained strong, with records set for volume and value in the year ending to January 2007 (volume grew 9% to 768 million litres and value grew 2% to A$2.85 billion) the average price declined 7% to A$3.71 a litre. However, because of the drought in Australia it was expected that the 2007 harvest would be the smallest since 2000 and about a third less than the previous year's production. In fact, the market situation and the drought had arguably reached a situation where some growers could potentially make more money by selling water than grapes. De Palma argued that increased competition from Spain and Italy in the premium-range market was threatening the profitability of the Australian wine industry, arguing 'We've gone now from being the leader of the pack to be amongst the pack ... The great love affair with Australian wine has tarnished a little bit. We've certainly punched above our weight, there's no doubt about it, but I think those good times have gone and the world market is now starting to say, "OK, what else have you got to offer?" ' (Akerman, 2007).

Unfortunately, concern over the viability of the wine industry is not isolated to Australia. For example, in 2006 US wine exports, 95% of which were from California, totalled US$876 million and 404.5 million litres, an increase of 30% in value and 4.0% in volume compared to 2005. In Europe, which receive more than half of US sales abroad, exports surged 48% by value, while wine exports to Canada grew 29% by value (Wine Institute, 2007). Even though the 2006 number represented a 106% increase in exports by value in the last decade a study of the contribution of wine and grape products on the US economy by MKF Research (2007) reported a number of significant challenges in terms of long-term competitiveness including:

- scarcity of skilled labour,
- market risk for grapes,

- shortage of quality wine grapes in emerging wine regions,
- scarcity of financing,
- access to market,
- consolidation in wine distribution and retailing,
- a crowded market,
- a highly competitive market for wine.

With respect to the latter MKF Research (2007, p. 14) reported:

The continued growth of the US wine industry faces increasing challenges as wine's retail and wholesale channels continue to consolidate
and as foreign wine producers target the US market with growing
inventories, government support and saturated home markets. ... the
US and Canada are the only markets in which demand is growing for
wine priced above $5 per 750 ml bottle. In fact, the US is among the few
markets in which demand for wine is growing at all.

The scale of the competition can be judged by the fact that by the
end of 2006 there have been some 219,000 wine labels registered
by United States Alcohol and Tobacco Tax and Trade Bureau
since 2003, from all producing regions (MKF Research, 2007).

Enormous competitive pressures are also being felt in the
European Union (EU), which is responsible for well over half of
world trade in wine, as EU member states' share of the world
wine export market has fallen in recent years. As the European
Commission (2006a, p. 22) has reported:

France, Italy and Spain form the leading trio of exporting countries,
accounting for almost 60% of world exports (average quantities from
2001 to 2003 – including intra-Community trade). In a decade, their
exports increased significantly, i.e. from France by 34%, Spain 31%
and Italy 21%. By contrast, they fell in Greece (−30%), Hungary
(−19%) and Germany (−10%).

But it is the 'New World' countries which have seen a spectacular
growth in their exports: South Africa (+770%), Australia (+500%),
Chile (+270%) and the United States (+160%).

Between 1995 and 2005 imports into the EU were increasing at
around 10% per annum, as a result the European Commission
concluded that European producers are 'facing competition from
two sides' (2006a, p. 24) because of increased competition in the
world market and within Europe itself as a result of substantial
importation of New World wines. European wine production in
2004 represented 5.4% of EU agricultural output, and more than
10% in France, Italy, Austria, Portugal, Luxembourg and Slovenia.
The EU has more than 1.5 million holdings producing wine,
covering 3.4 million hectares, or 2% of EU agricultural area.
On current trends, and without major restructuring, excess wine

production in Europe will reach 15% of annual production by 2010/2011 (European Commission, 2006b). Such is the European wine crisis that the European Commission has called for a comprehensive reform of the Common Market Organisation (CMO) for wine (Box 2.2). According to Mariann Fischer Boel, Commissioner for Agriculture and Rural Development:

European wines are the best in the world ... Our wine sector has huge potential for further growth, but we need to use this potential actively.

Box 2.2 The EU wine sector

Europe is the:

- leading global producer with over 45% of vines and 60% of production;
- leading consumer accounting for almost 60% of global consumption;
- leading exporter and largest import market.

EU production

From 2000 to 2005, average production in the EU-25 amounted to 178 million hectolitres (between 166 and 196 million hectolitres) worth around $$16.1 billion. With the accession of Romania and Bulgaria, production will increase by roughly 7 million hectolitres.

- France is the largest producer, with an average of 55 million hectolitres, representing 30.6% of the EU total. It accounts for half the production of the EU-25 in terms of value – with €7.7 billion.
- Italy follows France with roughly 51 million hectolitres (28.5% of the EU) with a value of €4.2 billion (25.8% of the European total).
- Spain, the third largest European producer, has an annual production of 43 million hectolitres (23.2%), worth €1.2 billion (7.6%).
- Germany's production in terms of value nearly equals that of Spain (€1.1 billion) despite a considerably lower production volume (roughly 10 million hectolitres).
- Portugal produces roughly 7.2 million hectolitres of wine for a value close to €1 billion.
- Next come Hungary (4.5 million hectolitres for €181 million), Greece (€3.6 million hectolitres for €46 million) and Austria (2.5 million hectolitres for €437 million).
- Finally come other small producers such as Slovenia (1 million hectolitres), the Czech Republic (520,000 hectolitres), Slovakia (440,000 hectolitres), Cyprus (425,000 hectolitres), Luxembourg (140,000 hectolitres) and Malta (67,000 hectolitres).

The mid-term outlook for the EU wine sector until 2010/2011, without reform and on the basis of the expected trends in production, consumption and trade dynamics, is that excess wine production will increase to 27 million hectolitres (15% of production), or to 15 million hectolitres (8.4% of production), if the quantities distilled with aid to the potable alcohol sector are not considered surplus.

Trade

- The EU exports more than €15 billion worth of wine. In terms of volume (excluding intra-EU commerce), exports are roughly 13 million hectolitres.
- The EU is beginning to be caught by the New World exporters. The four main producers have seen their exports develop in spectacular fashion: South Africa (+770%), Australia (+500%), Chile (+270%) and the USA (+160%) between 1991/1993 and 2001/2003.
- European wine imports in 2005 reached almost 12 million hectolitres, compared to 13 million hectolitres of exports.
- The global decline is accounted for by two distinct and contradictory situations: the EU's gradual drop, and its main competitors' staggering development of production capacity: USA: +26%; Chile: +48%; Australia: +169%; New Zealand: +240%.

'Quality wines' and 'table wines'

- The wines of the EU can be divided into two principal categories. Roughly 40% of the land is dedicated to 'table wines' and 60% to 'quality wines produced in specific regions' (QWpsr). This distribution varies enormously between the member states, notably based on the wine classification system adopted at national level. Certain Member States consider almost all their production as quality wines.
- The rigidity of procedures for adopting and adapting wine-making practices hinders competitiveness. EU regulations are too complex, notably on definitions, wine-making practices and classification, that is, QWpsr, table wine with a GI and table wine.
- On QWpsr, there is no 'quality' concept at an international level and no reference in EU legislation to the concept of 'geographical indication' as defined by the WTO's Trade-Related Aspects of Intellectual Property Rights (TRIPS) Agreement.
- In recent decades, there has been an increase in the number of QWpsr and table wines with GIs, which leads to customer confusion, weakens EU GI policy, and contributes to the decline of the market situation.
- Consumers are confused by wine labels resulting from a complex legal system. Inflexible labelling rules hamper the marketing of European wines. A major drawback is the prohibition of the indication of the vintage and the wine variety on table wine without a GI.

Source: Adapted from European Commission (2006) *EU Wine Reform: Background Information on the Wine Sector, Memo/06/245*, Brussels, June 22.

Despite our history and the quality of so many EU wines, the sector faces severe problems. Consumption is down, and exports from the New World are making huge inroads into the market. We in Europe are producing too much wine for which there is no market. We spend far too much money disposing of surpluses instead of building our quality and competitiveness. Over-complex rules hold back our producers and confuse our consumers. I am not advocating cutting the budget, of about €1.2 billion a year, but we must use this money more intelligently. This is a great opportunity to put the EU wine sector back at the top where it belongs – we must not waste it.

(European Commission, 2006b)

The objectives for a new EU wine policy are (European Commission, 2006c, p. 1):

- Increase the competitiveness of the EU's wine producers; strengthen the reputation of EU quality wine as the best in the world; recover old markets and win new ones in the EU and worldwide.
- Create a wine regime that operates through clear, simple rules – effective rules that balance supply and demand.
- Create a wine regime that preserves the best traditions of EU wine production and reinforces the social and environmental fabric of many rural areas.

The European Commission (2006b, c) has recommended that there needs to be a profound reform of the Wine CMO via:

- Abolition of distillation programmes and other aid measures.
- Introduction of national envelopes.
- Promotion of the use of rural development measures.
- The prohibition of chaptalisation (the addition of sugar to grape juice before fermentation) using sucrose and a stricter regulation of the use of concentrated must (grape juice concentrate) for enrichment.
- A clearer, simpler and more effective wine quality policy, including production and labelling. For example, facilitating the production of 'vins de cépage', wines composed of a single variety or of a blend of two or more varieties in order to counterbalance such wines developed by third countries.
- Greater versatility in wine-making practice.

Because of the size of the EU in export and marketing terms the proposed changes to EU wine policy will have profound affects on the competitiveness of wine businesses throughout the world. As noted in the above discussion a key element in the competitiveness of wine businesses are changing wine consumption patterns.

Although it may come as a surprise to some readers, total global wine consumption and production has changed little in the past 40 years (Table 2.2) despite the fact that there has been enormous population growth over the same period. This means that in real terms at a global scale wine consumption has fallen per capita. Summaries of global wine production and consumption in key markets are provided in Tables 2.3 and 2.4.

At the same time as there has been a decline in wine consumption in some European countries, but particularly in the traditional wine countries of France, Italy, Portugal and Spain, there has been a corresponding increase in northern European countries such as Denmark, Sweden, Finland and the UK as well as in New World wine countries such as the USA, Canada, New Zealand and Australia. Wine consumption has also started to increase in emerging markets in Asia where European style grape wine is not a traditional beverage but in which wine consumption is growing as a result of increased western influence on lifestyles. Arguably, the development of new markets for wine has allowed not only for opportunities for the growth on wine industries in the New World (the Americas, South Africa, Australia and New Zealand) but has also helped sustain the wine industries in Europe which have been substantially affected by declines in domestic consumption. Nevertheless, there is a substantial gap in production and consumption which has led to the creation of what is often termed a 'wine lake'.

Europe, which is the major contributor to the world wine lake has sought to manage the problem by a number of measures including subsidies to distil lower-quality wine into industrial alcohol and vine-pull schemes. The extent of wine distillation in Europe is enormous. In 2005 Bordeaux alone distilled the equivalent of around 23 million bottles of wine into ethanol or biofuel (Wyatt, 2006). The EU pays a subsidy for each litre, plus a small extra tranche of money from the local wine growers' cooperative, making it more profitable for some growers to distil their wine into undrinkable pure alcohol than to sell it. In 2005 France, Italy and Spain received more than €180 million from the EU to distil some of their excess wine, both table and quality, into industrial alcohol or biofuel. According to Bernard Farges of Chateau de l'Enclos in Bordeaux:

The crisis distillation is by its very nature a proof of failure ... But this failure is the result of bad decisions taken over a long period by our

Table 2.2 World production and consumption of wine ('000 hectolitres)

	1961–1964	1965–1969	1970–1974	1975–1979	1980–1984	1985–1989	1990–1994	1995–1999	2000–2004*	2005*
Global production	261	278	312	319	341	303	269	263	272	278.3
Global consumption	231	250	278	286	284	249	232	236	229	235.6
Consumption per capita (l)	0.075	0.075	0.075	0.070	0.064	0.056	0.044	0.042	0.038	0.037
Consumption of adults (20+ years) (l)								0.069	0.062	0.058
Balance (consumption − production)	−31	−28	−34	−33	−57	−54	−37	−27	−43	−42.7

Note: Consumption per capita calculated from estimated world population of first year of time period.
*Estimates only.
Source: Anderson and Norman (2003); OIV (2006); US Census Bureau, International Programs Center, International Data Base.

Table 2.3 World production of wine

Country	Rank	1961–1964	1965–1969	1970–1974	1975–1979	1980–1984	1985–1989	1990–1994	1995–1999	2000–2004
France	1	61,347	62,724	70,567	66,614	67,453	66,088	56,309	55,614	57,892
Italy	2	62,089	68,964	69,369	71,276	76,787	67,470	61,058	55,202	51,460
Spain	3	26,124	25,975	31,406	32,622	35,824	32,545	30,276	29,998	36,409
USA	4	7320	7993	11,353	15,574	17,630	17,362	16,186	19,820	23,550
Argentina	5	18,894	20,924	22,146	24,357	21,975	19,178	15,106	14,237	14,167
South Africa	6	3649	4557	5112	5812	8651	8152	8418	8709	10,983
Germany	7	5157	5582	8193	8708	9646	9542	10,648	9721	9757
Australia	8	1483	1709	2813	3535	3992	4391	4693	6772	8817
Portugal	9	12,921	10,805	10,861	9218	9162	8130	7987	6940	6854
Chile	10	4647	4531	5053	5399	7085	4007	3488	4364	6210
China	11						825	2860	3790	5475
Romania	12	5772	6305	7529	8183	8260	8062	5324	6425	5456
Hungary	13	3737	4215	4933	5139	5386	4086	4259	3924	4200
Greece	14	3592	4208	5181	5283	5170	4545	3602	3889	4079
Brazil	15	1479	1345	2157	2503	2810	3098	3091	2994	3352
Russia*	16	13,874	19,563	27,510	30,323	34,034	24,903	9402	2403	2952
Austria	17	1643	2035	2315	2868	3259	2461	2672	2329	2338
Bulgaria	18	3258	3694	3263	3404	4524	3356	2231	2740	2050
Croatia	19							2011	2075	1992

Moldova 20							1648	2796	1991
Uzbekistan 21							967	1314	1491
Japan 22	316	340	173	203	506	529	538	1051	1241
Switzerland 23	833	846	1030	1041	1246	1260	1228	1203	1225
Georgia 24							1033	804	1175
Uruguay 25	793	822	907	694	687	766	864	989	1080
Ukraine 26							1699	1014	710
New Zealand 27	60	103	253	343	429	475	439	561	566
Canada 28	341	438	595	503	490	389	342	347	512
Azerbaijan 29							1050	475	315
Turkey 30	361	447	429	399	394	321	251	323	310
Benelux 31	140	126	170	119	151	159	173	141	157
Mexico 32	75	76	119	109	204	186	45	71	51
UK 33	5	10	7	10	10	10	18	15	15
The Netherlands 34				10	10	10	2		
Others or non-specified	21,226	19,471	18,279	15,096	14,860	10,276	9369	9659	8402
All nations	261,136	277,808	311,723	319,335	340,625	302,582	269,287	262,709	277,234

*Includes figures for former Soviet Union.
Source: After Anderson and Norman (2003); OIV (2006).

Table 2.4 World consumption of wine

Country	Rank	1961–1964	1965–1969	1970–1974	1975–1979	1980–1984	1985–1989	1990–1994	1995–1999	2000–2004
France	1	58,339	57,200	55,121	52,731	47,354	42,234	38,019	35,622	34,858
Italy	2	55,189	59,404	59,422	51,827	48,009	39,127	34,315	32,323	30,498
USA	3	6763	7872	12,204	15,360	19,509	21,321	17,881	19,874	21,800
Germany	4	11,395	12,052	14,948	18,518	19,894	18,399	18,965	18,893	19,695
Spain	5	19,266	20,628	23,508	25,202	21,637	17,615	15,884	14,618	14,521
Argentina	6	18,127	19,486	20,000	22,086	20,951	17,899	16,256	14,036	12,833
Russia*	7	11,835	19,469	31,626	29,297	30,194	16,631	11,087	10,076	11,326
UK	8	1104	1411	2346	3374	4596	6208	7353	9313	9321
China	9						330	2822	4075	7855
Romania	10	5197	5280	5527	7001	6364	5909	4942	6764	7476
Portugal	11	9097	9113	7630	7527	7765	6575	5700	5364	5076
South Africa	12	1483	1858	2432	2397	2683	3058	3388	3891	4700
Australia	13	586	814	1238	1968	2871	3358	3174	3481	3940
The Netherlands	14	327	510	1027	1594	1975	2243	2422	3238	3721
Japan	15	176	319	376	554	771	1028	1278	2445	3393
Brazil	16	1577	1657	1938	2777	3253	2712	2747	3110	3343
Hungary	17	3071	3492	3904	3640	3353	2385	3035	2962	3032
Switzerland	18	2099	2366	2812	2832	3119	3190	3058	2922	2950
Greece	19	3187	3320	3436	3720	4168	3079	3219	2863	2749
Chile	20	4585	4366	4939	4903	5146	4128	3133	2545	2662

#	Nation									
21	Benelux	1223	1246	1634	1785	2102	2309	2295	2476	2555
22	Canada	435	583	1030	1591	2235	2498	2180	2211	2551
23	Austria	1740	2349	2674	2694	2721	2583	2597	2509	2372
24	Croatia							2072	2059	2015
25	Bulgaria	1620	2068	2073	2147	2099	1965	1895	1805	1743
26	Denmark	169	216	404	629	872	1095	1301	1563	1559
27	Uzbekistan								1323	1460
28	Sweden	301	392	588	738	867	1040	1122	1176	1199
29	Uruguay	759	749	719	716	826	743	844	1000	1080
30	Georgia								775	779
31	New Zealand	60	101	221	314	430	497	551	614	647
32	Moldova								1052	532
33	Ireland	40	49	66	98	86	144	185	323	423
34	Azerbaijan								288	403
35	Finland	81	124	195	224	242	257	275	330	391
36	Ukraine								543	370
37	Turkey	210	281	291	205	232	274	265	250	253
38	Mexico	68	83	123	129	202	213	180	179	183
	Others	10,446	11,369	13,410	17,267	17,171	17,468	17,693	16,759	16,361
	All nations consumption	230,555	250,227	277,862	285,845	283,697	248,515	232,133	235,650	242,625

*USSR to 1991, Russia thereafter.
Source: After Anderson and Norman (2003); OIV (2006).

collective masters. Somehow, they thought wine wasn't a product like any other. But alas, it is – and however nice it is to drink, we can't carry on producing more than we can sell.

(Wyatt, 2006)

In March 2007 the EU opened a tender to sell unwanted wine from France, Greece, Italy and Spain. The tender would offer roughly 653,381 hectolitres of wine alcohol for exclusive use as bioethanol in the fuel sector with a view to reducing community stocks of wine alcohol and ensuring the continuity of supplies (Reuters, 2007). In 2006 when EU Agriculture Commissioner Mariann Fischer Boel presented four broad policy options for overhauling the EU wine sector she stated that she favoured abolishing the existing system of 'crisis distillation', as an emergency market tool used as a short-term measure to correct supply imbalances. Ironically, such suggestions are being made at the same time that the EU has set a target that at least 10% of their transport fuel must be biofuel thereby potentially creating a significant new market for the European wine lake. Nevertheless, according to the Commissioner:

We must put the wine sector on a more competitive footing. We must restore balance. Any reform which did not do this would not be worthy of the name.

Among other things, this means that the whole sector must learn to walk on its own two feet without crutches for uncompetitive production, such as distillation. And it means that a 'grubbing-up' scheme, which would give less competitive producers capital to leave wine-making with pride and invest in a more profitable activity, has much to recommend it. When we abolish distillation there will be producers who cannot survive, I want them to leave the sector with dignity and use the single farm payment to help them get into other areas of production.

(Fischer Boel, 2007, p. 3)

Importantly, with respect to marketing Fischer Boel noted her disappointment that the EU 'have been spending half a billion euros every year on distillation and only €14 million on promotion. This is wrong. Something has to be done to help the EU wine sector both internally and on external markets'. Nevertheless, she went on to add 'promotion cannot be done without a strong initiative from the wine sector itself and I hope to see many new innovative ideas from you!' (Fischer Boel, 2007, p. 3).

Changes in European policy (see above) may have a considerable impact on grape production, particularly by small growers. Nevertheless, the core problem is that Europe is producing too much wine for which there is no market. Vine-pull schemes have been utilised before to try and create a better balance between wine production in the EU and consumption. For example, in 1988 the EU financially encouraged growers, mainly in southern France and southern Italy, to pull out 320,000 hectares (790,400 acres) of vineyard. This was the equivalent to the then entire vineyard area of the world's fourth largest grower of grapes, the USA (Robinson, 1999). However, the global imbalance in the 1980s and 1990s was arguably eased by a number of other vine-pull schemes. For example, in the Soviet Union the total area under vine dropped from more than 1.3 hectares million (3.2 million acres) to 880,000 hectares (2.2 million acres) between 1985 and 1990 as a result of President Gorbachev's attempts to curb alcohol consumption (Robinson, 1999). The mid-1980s also saw government sponsored vine-pull schemes in Argentina, Australia, Chile and New Zealand.

The present highly competitive position with respect to wine production has not only lead to calls for vine-pull schemes in Europe but also in Australia. For example, in 2006 Barossa Valley vigneron Leo Pech who has grown grapes in the region for 54 years, and is a past president of both state and federal grape grower associations argued that a government-subsidised vine-pull scheme was the only option to ensure the industry's future. 'I think government intervention is the only way to save the industry. A vine-pull scam [sic.] will cost the government a lot of money, but at the end of the day this may be the minor implication over all the total downfall of the industry' (Haxton, 2006). Nevertheless, as Croser (1997) commented, 'The Australian wine industry has traditionally been a victim of over and undersupply of its raw materials, in similar manner to the hog cycle. We are currently in the grips of a premium grape shortage, which is escalating grape prices and driving planting response to unprecedented levels.' Indeed, immediately following the vine-pull scheme the unplanned for and unprecedented growth of exports plunged some varieties of grapes into serious shortage in 1988 and 1989, driving up grape prices which in turn encouraged large grape plantings, resulting in oversupply again by 1991–1992 (Croser, 1997).

Although the goals of vine-pull schemes are well intended their application has to be carefully managed so as to ensure that they do not have unanticipated consequences. For example, in reviewing the impacts of the 1986 Australian vine-pull scheme in the Southern Vales region of South Australia Barrett (1989, p. 189) observed, 'In some respects the scheme may lead to an improvement in the industry because a high proportion of over-supplied varieties were removed. But, on the other hand, so too were large quantities of varieties in strong demand'. Indeed, Barrett concluded that a vine-pull scheme was 'not an appropriate means of restructuring the wine grape industry as the focus is far too broad' (1989, p. 189). However, such a conclusion had actually been reached by the South Australian Department of Agriculture prior to the implementation of the scheme. In its submission to the Australian Royal Commission of Inquiry into the Grape and Vine Industries the Department expressed a number of reservations with respect to a vine-pull scheme that remain relevant to the present day (McKay, 1985):

- There are problems in ensuring that a vine-pull scheme stimulates removal of the varieties in oversupply rather than removal of all varieties.
- There is substantial unpredictability in forecasting long-term demand trends.
- With respect to agricultural restructuring there may be a lack of alternative crops and there is also a possibility that oversupply problems may be shifted from the wine industry to another agricultural sector.
- The least efficient producers will not necessarily be removed.
- Growers in most need were not likely to participate as they would be better off selling a vineyard as a going concern.

Indeed, it should also be noted that one of the conclusions of the Australian Royal Commission was that there also needed to be an improved marketing effort in order to promote the consumption of Australian wine. Nor should such schemes be regarded as necessarily preventing new wine business introductions. For example, Cloudy Bay, the New Zealand winery that is arguably the benchmark for Sauvignon producers around the world, was established at the same time as the New Zealand government vine-pull scheme of 1986/1987 and when interest rates were 25% (Boothman, 2006). From the beginning the business focussed on quality and even after being taken over by LVMH (Louis Vuitton Moët Hennessy) that focus remained, with no reserve labels or second-tier brands. As wine-maker Kevin Judd commented, 'They're only interested in top quality, not in any mass-market wine' (in Boothman, 2006, p. 282).

The marketing response to the problems of imbalance between wine production and consumption is to stimulate consumption and ensure that there is a market for the wine product. As noted above the global per capita consumption of wine is tiny. Even allowing for the exclusion of approximately 25% of the potential world market on religious grounds, the potential to increase the attractiveness of wine to the market and therefore increase consumption remains sound. To put this into perspective if the world's adult population (20+, and excluding religious reasons for not consuming alcoholic wine) were to drink one glass of wine a year the problem of over production would be solved! (Box 2.3)

Box 2.3 Stimulating a new market: the case of China

One significant way of overcoming overproduction is to stimulate consumption in a new market. For example, Australian wine exports to China soared in 2005 leading Kakaviatos (2006a) to comment, 'the Australian wine lake has found a new outlet: the Chinese middle class'. In 2005–2006 Australian wine exports to China grew by 482% to 11.75 million litres with the main sales growth occurring in the discount or bulk end of the market. With the average price per litre declining by 63% to A$1.75. However, Australian Wine and Brandy Corporation corporate affairs manager Eric Wisgard said wine-makers were encouraged by a recent reduction on tariffs on wine sold in China as a result of the WTO accession agreement, from 65% to 14%, and by rising Chinese affluence: 'There's a growing middle class, and there is quite a move to adopt Western symbols of success' (Kakaviatos, 2006a).

In 2005 China imported approximately US$75 million in wine with the market dominated by France and Spain (combining for a market share of 46%) and Australia and Chile with approximately 16% market share each. In 2005 in terms of highest average value New Zealand earned 4 times above average value, followed by Germany (2.9 times) and Australia (2.5 times) (Trade Law Centre of South Africa, 2006).

Since 2000 wine consumption per capita in China has doubled but in global terms remains low at 0.3 litres per head, although it is higher for urban residents at over a litre per head. China's consumers are very price conscious with domestic wines positioned at below US$4 a bottle and imported usually more than $15 a bottle (Rozelle and Sumner, 2006). Imported wines make up only 5% of the total Chinese wine market. However, the growth in consumption of western food, particularly in the large urban centres of Beijing and Shanghai along with the development of westernised places of consumption such as supermarkets, nightclubs, restaurants and hotels has helped lead the demand for wine, domestic and imported. Unfortunately, at times the potential of the Chinese market for wine sales may have been harmed by western exporters seeking to make quick sales. According to Sam Featherston, Manager of Montrose Food and Wines in Shanghai 'Some exporters, unable to offload low-standard wines onto Western markets, tend to sell these wines to the East at a cheaper price' with some markets at times affected by concern over quality (Sutherland, 2002). Nevertheless, in urban centres wine knowledge is increasing as wine education courses become available and more outlets stock international and domestic wines, thereby further encouraging the growth of wine consumption in China. It is also becoming more fashionable and a status symbol as wine is associated with what is perceived as a socially and culturally sophisticated lifestyle (Sutherland, 2002; Lixin, 2006).

Positive relationships between domestic and international wine brands are regarded as an important element of wine business strategies in China as growth in wine consumption is usually initially driven by local wine with local consumers tending to become interested in more international wine the greater the wine knowledge they develop. According to Lixin (2006) imported wines are particularly strong in the highly lucrative high-end wine market, where profit margins can be as high as 30–50%, compared to 11% margins for lower-grade brands. Wine education is therefore essential to the long-term development of the Chinese market. In addition, as Lixin (2006) comments:

While many imported wines enjoy strong brand recognition in their home countries, they all start from the same point in China, where hundreds of brands are now competing to establish their market positions and build brand loyalty. Most premium wineries are of generally small scale, and with marketing costs in China so high, many have had a difficult time establishing distinct brand perceptions – especially challenging in a market that lacks a strong wine culture.

Obviously, the authors of this book advocate marketing, including consumer and stakeholder education with respect to wine, as being integral to the management of the relationship between consumption and production at an international level as well as in domestic and emerging markets. However, just as importantly for the growth of wine businesses in the internationally competitive wine environment, marketing needs to be placed within an understanding of trends that impact the wine market.

International, national and regional economy

In order to be able to purchase wine people need to have an income. Because wine is usually regarded as a non-essential item, sufficient income needs to be earned by potential consumers so that they have a disposable income that may be used to make purchases of commodities such as wine. Therefore, the state of national and regional economies can be an important determinant in the potential value of a market. A good example of this situation is the rapidly developing economies of East Asia, such as China, Singapore and Japan. According to Rozelle et al. (2006, p. 56) it is demand in urban areas that is encouraging the development of the wine industry in China (see Box 2.3; also compare with Box 2.5 on India) with the income elasticity of wine being estimated at more than two, that is 'as income doubles, consumption increases fourfold.' The relationship between the amount spent on wine and income is also illustrated in the UK where the most affluent 10% of households devoted 60% of alcohol spending to wine in 2004, compared to 33% in the poorest 10% of households (Mintel, 2005). In addition, economic conditions will also influence investment in wine businesses as well as the extent to which wine itself becomes an investment.

Investments in fine wine have become a significant factor in increasing its price relative to other wine in the last 20 years. Nevertheless, it is the case that for a small number of wines their market value is based as much on speculation as it is on the consumer's desire to drink them. The wine firm Berry Brothers & Rudd provide a useful guide to the potential advantages of wine investment:

- *Finite product*: A chateau or domaine produces a finite quantity each vintage which then diminishes over time as the wine is consumed. This in turn leads to limitations on availability and prices can subsequently rise.
- *Tangible asset*: Wine is a physical product rather than just a certificate. If the worst happens the wine can always be drunk.
- *Wasting chattel*: In theory wines benefit from an exemption from Capital Gains Tax. However certain rules apply. We strongly advise speaking to and Independent Financial Advisor.
- *Potential returns*: If the correct wines are bought at the right time and at a good price then decent returns can be made. As a rule we estimate 8–12% compound interest per annum on your investment. Of course some wines do not perform as well and some far outperform these figures. Hence we advise seeking advice before investing in wine.

The value of wines, as with the stock market, can go down as well as up. Nevertheless, 2006 was the best year for the fine wine market in a decade. The Liv-ex 100 Index was up 47.5% to the end of November and the Liv-ex 500 up 27.5% although between 1996 and 2006 price had generally been quite flat having done only marginally better than inflation (Liv-ex, 2006). Stimpfig (2007) argues that a wine requires most or all of the following to be regarded as a good investment:

- be an instantly recognised label or brand with a long track record of quality and high to very high prices;

- come from a good or great vintage and be highly rated by leading wine critics on both sides of the Atlantic;
- have strong, consistent global demand for previous vintages of similar quality show consistent upward price movement beyond a minimum set return;
- have the ability to age and improve over a long period of time.

Social and cultural trends

Understanding belief systems and attitudes with respect to wine is extremely important in terms of determining not only the size actual of the wine market but also the extent to which attitudes can be changed or belief systems affect policy. Therefore, social and cultural values underlie consumer behaviours in relation to wine.

Wine is subject to a number of social and cultural trends which range from short-term changes in fashion to longer-term changes in culture. Changes in fashion can affect the style and varieties of wine that are being drunk and are primarily due to the influence of the media (see Chapter 9). Medium-term changes are often associated with demographic and lifestyle change, for example perspectives as to the health effects of wine, while more fundamental cultural change is often associated with changes in religious beliefs and/or attitudes, such as the sinfulness of drinking wine or the rise of consumerism (Brook, 2000a; Charters, 2006).

Cultural constraints play an important part in influencing production, the size of the potential market and trading regulations. A substantial proportion of the world's population does not drink wine because of religious reasons. For example, grape wine as well as other alcoholic beverages has generally been recognised as *haram* (prohibited) under Islamic law although the interpretation of this is not universal. Indeed, even within the Christian tradition attitudes towards wine are often mixed even though the first miracle of Christ was to turn water into wine.

Prohibition, the term usually applied to describe a prohibition in the consumption of alcohol, is typically applied to the USA to describe the period 17 January 1919 to 5 December 1933 in which under the 18th amendment to the Constitution of the USA the 'manufacture, sale or transportation of intoxicating liquors' was prohibited. Although it is worth noting that 33 of the then 48 states already had state mandated prohibition. However, the temperance movement had an impact far wider than the USA in western countries and particularly in those areas dominated by protestant religious groups such as Scandinavia, Australia and New Zealand. The influence of the prohibition movement on the business of wine is substantial because the social movement of temperance has a lasting legacy in the institutional arrangements that were established to satisfy the demands of the movement (see, e.g. discussion of the three-tier distribution system in the USA in Chapter 1) and therefore on viticultural and winery production, regulation of sales and shipping, taxation and international trade in wine (Geraci, 2004).

For example, in early 2007 politicians in the state of Georgia in the USA were debating as to whether to allow wine (and other alcohol) to be sold on Sundays. Georgia, along with Connecticut and Indiana, were the only states at the time which banned Sunday sales. In testimony before the state senate the Rev. Aaron McCullough stated that Georgia lawmakers who voted for a bill which would allow the sale of alcohol on Sunday would have 'blood on their hands' if a fatal accident resulted from alcohol purchased on the Sabbath. The bill's sponsor, Republican Senator Seth Harp, said the measure was about local control and fairness. Restaurants in Georgia can already sell alcohol on Sundays as can stores in neighbouring states. According to Senator Harp 'I do not believe this bill in any way defames or demeans the Sabbath ... It simply brings Georgia in line with the 21st century' (in McCaffrey, 2007). A January 2007 poll by Mason-Dixon Polling and Research commissioned by the *Atlanta Journal-Constitution* found that 68% of Georgians supported the legislation. Support was even stronger in metropolitan Atlanta, where 80% of respondents supported the bill (McCaffrey, 2007). Nevertheless, in March 2007 the sales measure was effectively dead for another year as the relevant Senate committee decided that there were insufficient votes for the bill to pass either the House or the Senate (Fain, 2007).

Changes in lifestyle and demographic change are having a significant affect on the wine market. For example, awareness of the health benefits of drinking wine in moderation (Ford, 2003), what is sometimes referred to as the 'French paradox' (Renaud and de Lorgeril, 1992), has had considerable influence on wine drinking habits in New World as well as the place of wine within a healthy lifestyle, particularly what is described as a 'Mediterranean' diet or lifestyle (Kromhout, 1999; Singh et al., 2002; Charters, 2006). Indeed, the impact of greater consumer knowledge of the relationship between moderate wine drinking and health is evidenced by the impact of the broadcast of the now-famous French paradox segment on 60 minutes in 1991. The programme indicated that despite eating food with high saturated fat and getting little exercise, the French had a lower mortality rate from heart disease and fewer heart attacks than Americans. The broadcast raised immediate awareness of the connection between wine and health, and red wine sales increased by 40% (Heeger, 2007). Just as importantly, as Curtis Ellison Professor of Medicine at Boston University School of Medicine, one of the principal speakers at an International Wine and Heart Health Summit, said 'It became politically correct for scientists to describe the beneficial as well as harmful effects of alcohol consumption' (Heeger, 2007).

Another potentially significant social dimension affecting wine consumption is demographic change, the most significant aspect of which is the aging of the world's population. This substantial demographic change has occurred because of dramatic improvements in health care and a decline in the birth rate in the developed world and is predicted to continue well into the coming centuries so long as the world's resources are able to support the increases in population. At the end of the 20th century 11% of the world's population was aged 60 years and above. By 2050, it is estimated that 20% will be 60 years or older; and by 2150, approximately one-third will be 60 years or older (Hall, 2005).

Just as significantly the older population itself is aging. The increase in the number of very old people (aged 80+ years) between 1950 and 2050 is projected to grow by a factor of from 8 to 10 times on the global scale. As well a general aging of the world's population there are also substantial regional differences in the aged population. For example, currently 20% of Europeans are 60 years or older, but 5% of Africans, are 60 years or older. The potential effects of aging on the wine market can be demonstrated by reference to the US market (Hall, 2005).

In 2000 the core wine-consuming population of the USA (defined as individuals who drink wine at least once a week aged 21 years and over), was estimated at 15.7 million, just 11% of the then total adult population of 142.6 million (ages 21–59 years). In 2000 core wine consumers drank the greatest amount of wine (88%), yet approximately 63% of this market was aged 40 years and over (Koerber, 2000). By 2006 core wine drinkers represented 17.4% of the US adult market and were responsible for 92% of wine consumption. According to the US Wine Market Council (2006):

Generation X adults, now mostly in their 30s, are finally taking to wine in significant numbers. Moreover, the Millennial generation, now entering young adulthood, is exhibiting the same receptivity to wine that leading edge Baby Boomers did more than 30 years ago. Like the Baby Boom generation, their numbers are so great as to make their dominance in the market inevitable, and they offer the wine industry the kind of growth potential not seen in more than thirty years.

There are 77 million Baby Boomers (ages 42 to 60 in 2006), compared to a 44 million Generation X population (ages 30 to 41 in 2006). But the Millennial generation is a group of some 70 million. The eldest among this group turned 29 in 2006. They add, on average, 5 percent more new adults to the U.S. population per year than did Generation X, and their taste and lifestyle choices will drive the beverage alcohol market for many years to come.

Therefore, as the population ages it clearly becomes extremely important to develop the next generation of wine drinkers (Box 2.4).

Box 2.4 Wine X: wine, food and an intelligent sense of vice

On 15 February 2007, Wine X a magazine specifically aimed at younger adults ceased publication after almost 10 years. At its height it sold 330,000 a month, and claimed 2 million readers per issue (Lechmere, 2007a). Since 1997 20 somethings have added 40% to per capita consumption in the USA and 25% to the core wine consumer group (Penn, 2007a). According to founder and publisher Darryl Roberts although the magazine had supporters among consumers and trade members, it failed to attract and retain enough wine industry advertisers to keep it going. 'There's a lot of talk within the wine industry about marketing to young adults … New wines have been created, new wine divisions have been formed by large wine companies, all with the idea of targeting young adults. Yet they give us absolutely no support' (in Penn, 2007a). In an interview with *Decanter* Roberts stated:

The wine industry says it's interested in young adults but spends all of its ad and promo money targeting the same people it's been targeting for the past 30 years – rich, old white people … I forgot I was dealing with the wine industry, an industry still stuck in the 80s. They don't want to market wine to young adults. Young adults don't drink wine. … It will be interesting to see what happens now that there are no national/international groups or organisations reaching out to young adults. It takes a peer-to-peer relationship to influence young adults … With Wine X gone, that … support is gone too.

In an interview with *Wines & Vines* Roberts cited lack of understanding and industry support for the magazine's demise. 'The decision-makers in the wine industry don't "get" the magazine … nor should they. It's not for them. It's not written for them and it's not designed for them. So they look at it and, since they don't like it, they dismiss it. They put their personal preferences in front of their company's best interests' (Caputo, 2007). According to Roberts the wine industry was not willing to make a real commitment to the younger demographic:

When's the last time that you saw a wine ad in a young adult publication, or heard one on a young adult radio station? If the wine industry is so interested in young adults, where are they spending their money to attract them? We had tasting clubs in 10 key markets for exclusive tastings and WineRaves. We had a network of college/university wine clubs available to advertisers and sponsors, too. You'd think that the industry, if it were serious about reaching young adults, would start there.

(Caputo, 2007).

A further influential factor with respect to demographic change and wine consumption in both relative and absolute terms is that it is estimated that among the major industrialised countries only the USA is estimated to have significant population growth by 2050 (Population Reference Bureau, 2004). The USA is expected to have reached a population of 420 million by 2050, an increase of 43%. But Europe is expected to have 60 million fewer people than today and some countries could lose more than a third of their populations. Japan, which currently has only 14% of its current population under 15, may have shrunk in size to approximately 100 million people by 2050. Over the same period Eastern Europe is also predicted to experience major population loss. Bulgaria is expected to return to pre-1914 population levels, losing 38% of its people, while Romania could have 27% fewer and Russia 25 million fewer people. Germany and Italy are expected to shrink by approximately 10% (Population Reference Bureau, 2004). The changes in population in traditional wine markets are therefore likely to have a substantial affect on future consumption overall as well as in market share.

In contrast developing countries are predicted to expand dramatically in population. Although the world's developed countries are expected to grow in total population by about 4% to over 1.2 billion, population in developing countries is predicted to grow by up to 55% to more than 8 billion. Under this scenario Western Asian nations are expected to gain about 186 million people by 2050 and sub-Saharan African countries more than one billion people. By 2050, India will be the largest country in the world, having long passed China (Population Reference Bureau, 2004). Therefore, in order to grow the world wine market it becomes extremely important to encourage the development of an appreciation of wine in countries, such as China and India, which traditionally have not had a wine culture (Box 2.5).

Box 2.5 Growth of wine culture in India

India has one of the fastest growing economies in the world. Going hand-in-hand with economic growth and the development of a large middle class is growth in wine consumption and production. Wine has become increasingly popular with the urban middle classes which are adopting a number of aspects of western consumer lifestyles. In addition, the health benefits of wine are also regarded as attractive in the Indian market. Nevertheless, 'It is also a style statement, as French wine, being so expensive in India, is consumed mainly by English speaking, Western-educated men and women' (Ahmed, 2004) – a market of course which is one of the fastest growing in Asia.

Wine's consumption is also about to enter a period of further change as western style supermarkets and retail outlets come to be established in the cities, which will compliment the already established restaurant and wine bar scene. Approximately 20% of wines sold in India are imported from France, Italy, South Africa and Australia with foreign wines being dominant at the upper end of the market. However, domestic wine production is expected to grow at an annual rate of 30% between 2004 and 2009 with growth being driven by the three largest wineries of Grover, Indage and Sula (Ahmed, 2004). Although some of this wine is exported, for example Sula Wines export to the USA and the UK and are comparable in price points to similar wines from Australia, Chile and France. The primary market for Indian producers is domestic, with wineries such as Sula acting as distributors for international wine brands while at the same time growing their own.

A significant barrier for entry into the Indian market has been that exporters face duties of up to 550% for spirits and 264% for wines as a result of 'additional duties' and 'extra additional duties' levied on top of the federal basic customs duty of 150% for spirits and 100% for wine. EU spirits exports to India in 2004 amounted to just €23 million (£16 million), while wine sales were just over €4 million. As a result of the Indian duties the EU requested the intervention of the World Trade Organisation to adjudicate on the dispute in November 2006 (BBC, 2006).

Institutional arrangements

The term 'institution' has many meanings, though there is some consensus about the importance of rules and the regulation of individual and group behaviour. Institutional arrangements provide a set of rules and procedures that regulates how and where demands on public policy can be made, who has the authority to take certain decisions and actions, and how decisions and policies are implemented. The main institutions of national governments include the elected legislatures, government departments and authorities, the judiciary, enforcement agencies, other levels of government, government business enterprises, regulatory authorities and a range of para-state organisations, such as trade unions or wine organisations that receive state funding or are state regulated. Such frameworks vary significantly between countries and between policy sectors within an individual country. 'These differences affect how political conflict is expressed, what strategies individuals and groups will employ in attempting to influence policy, and the weight that policy-makers ascribe to particular social and economic interests' (Brooks, 1993, p. 79).

With respect to prohibition for example, noted above, the National Prohibition Act of October 1919 (The Volstead Act) was a means of codifying the demands of the temperance movement. Ironically, the 21st amendment that repealed the 18th amendment provided for the states to regulate alcohol with the result that US laws with respect to wine sales and shipment remain chaotic by international standards as there is a 'patchwork quilt' of state and local regulations (Wiseman and Ellig, 2004; Riekhof and Sykuta, 2005) that make it difficult for both domestic US companies as well as firms seeing to export into the USA (see related discussion in Chapter 1).

A major regulatory focal point of wine businesses around the world is the tax that wine receives. Tax is often justified in being placed on wine because of health reasons. Saffer (1989) indicated that the greatest decrease in alcohol consumption results from an increase in spirits taxes, followed by beer taxes and then wine taxes. This suggests that a taxation policy of placing the highest tax on spirits, a lower tax on beer and the lowest tax on wine, would result in the greatest reduction in total alcohol consumption. However, the taxation regimes and overall policy settings of many jurisdictions would suggest that revenue-raising from what is seen as a luxury item, is often the main reason for levels of wine taxation.

The type of tax on wine, within the context of the overall taxation on wine businesses, may also affect different production segments. For example, a study of the introduction of the Goods and Services Tax (GST) introduced in Australia on July 2000, and the associated wine tax reform, concluded that the switch from to the previous ad valorem (by value) tax to a revenue-neutral volumetric tax on wine under the GST was shown to favour the premium segment of the industry, but at the expense of the non-premium segment (Wittwer and Anderson, 2002).

As well as the level of tax that wine receives, wine businesses are also concerned with consistency of taxation so as to reduce levels of uncertainty. In March 2007 tax on sparkling wine was increased by 7p per bottle, a move that surprised the UK wine and spirits lobby. At the same time duty on wine was increased by 5p, on a pint of beer and a litre of cider by 1p while there was no increase in duty on spirits. The chief of the Wine and Spirit Trade Association (WSTA), Jeremy Beadles, welcomed the freeze on spirits but strongly criticised the increase in sparkling duty. 'We are shocked and disappointed by the Chancellor's decision … Sparkling wine already suffers from a higher tax rate than still wine, but in previous years the Chancellor has seemed determined to get rid of this anomaly' (in Lechmere, 2007b). Significantly, he added that the 'U turn' would have a 'serious impact' on the English and Welsh wine market, of which 15% is sparkling and stated that the 'duty hike will deal a real blow to this domestic industry' which had already been experiencing a slowing in wine sales (Lechmere, 2007b).

Another important aspect of the institutional arrangements for wine are the laws with respect to labelling, geographical designation, alcohol levels, health and consumer information. Each country, and in some cases states and provinces, sets its own requirements. However, such a system has created a number of difficulties for exporters because of the costs of meeting different labelling requirements in different markets.

Because of the internationalisation of the wine trade the institutional arrangements for wine therefore need to be seen as occurring over a range of scales, from the local to the international, particularly as wine is increasingly subject to international trade agreements and negotiations (Table 2.5). For example, wineries in Argentina, Australia, Canada, Mexico, New Zealand, South Africa and the USA will be affected in terms of business practice by the decisions reached by national representative bodies at the World Wine Trading Group (WWTG). Established in 1998, the group plays an important role in developing access to international markets as well as growing the overall wine market. The WWTG currently accounts for almost a quarter of all wine exports. Examples of initiatives include the Agreement on the Requirements for Wine Labelling reached in January 2007 which enables wine exporters to sell wine into WWTG markets without having to redesign their labels for each individual market. The agreement allows the placement of four items of mandatory information (country of origin, product name, net contents and alcohol content) anywhere on a wine bottle label provided they are presented in a single field of vision. An earlier agreement on oenological practices signed in 2001 allows for wine made in a signatory country to be sold in the others markets despite differences in oenological practices, conditional on compliance with the World Trade Organisation (WTO) obligations to protect the health and safety of consumers and to prevent

Table 2.5 Examples of institutional arrangements for wine

Scale	Wine specific	Influences on wine
International	International Organization for Vines and Wines	World Trade Organisation; General Agreement on Trades in Services; UN Food and Agricultural Organisation
Supranational (regional, multilateral and/ or bilateral relations)	Assembly of Wine-Producing European Regions; World Wine Trade Group	North American Free Trade Agreement; European Union; European Commission, Directorate-General for Agriculture and Rural Development
National	Australian Wine and Brandy Corporation; Union of Champagne Houses	National legislation with respect to alcohol, taxation, agricultural support schemes
State/provincial	State legislation with respect to wine sales and shipping in the USA; Texas Wines Institute	State legislation on alcohol, taxation, trading hours, agriculture
Local/regional	Marketing and regulatory bodies	Planning law

consumer deception. Such agreements are extremely significant and have influenced the activities of the OIV. For example, the WWTG international standard on wine labelling is in line with the principles adopted by the OIV in its international wine labelling standard and amendments made in 2005 and 2006 on the presentation of mandatory information with respect to such issues as language, legibility, use of the word 'wine', alcoholic strength, additives, nominal volume, country or countries of origin, and labelling.

A key element of the institutional arrangements for wine has been the set of conventions, regulations and agreements with respect to the geographical designation of origin (Maher, 2001). Such designations represent a form of intellectual property of place and can have considerable brand value (i.e. champagne, port, burgundy). The EU in particular has therefore been extremely active in protecting such property rights and have made them an important part of world trade organisation negotiations as well as agreements with respect to exporting wine to the EU.

Countries that are party to the WTO (1994) *Agreement on Trade-Related Aspects of Intellectual Property Rights* (TRIPS) must comply with terms for the protection of geographical indications of wines and spirits which are stronger than that of other goods. Article 23.1 of TRIPS obliges Members to:

provide the legal means for interested parties to prevent use of a geographical indication identifying wines for wines not originating in the place indicated by the geographical indication in question or identifying spirits for spirits no originating in the place indicated by the geographical indication in question, even where the true origin of the goods is indicated or the geographical indication is used in translation or accompanied by expressions such as 'kind', 'type', 'style', 'imitation or the like'.

It means, in effect, that producers from different regions or countries cannot use a wine or spirit geographical indication, even in conjunction with a word such as 'like' or 'style'. For this reason the term 'champagne' can therefore now only be identified with sparkling wine from Champagne in France. As a result of the TRIPS agreement a multilateral system of notification and registration of geographical indications for wines eligible for protection in those members participating in the system is being developed, with many countries having already completed their registry (Box 2.6).

Box 2.6 The OIV

The OIV was established in 2001 as an intergovernmental organisation that by April 2006 had 42 member states including the following (as well as 4 observer states and 10 observer organisations):

South Africa	Georgia	New Zealand
Algeria	Greece	Norway
Germany	Hungary	Peru
Australia	Ireland	Portugal
Austria	Israel	Czech Republic
Belgium	Italy	Romania
Brazil	Lebanon	Russia
Bulgaria	Luxemburg	Serbia
Chile	FYR Macedonia	Slovakia
Cyprus	Malta	Slovenia
Croatia	Morrocco	Sweden
Spain	Mexico	Switzerland
Finland	Moldavia	Turkey
France	The Netherlands	Uruguay

The objectives of the OIV are:

(a) To inform its members of measures whereby the concerns of producers, consumers and other players in the vine and wine products sector may be taken into consideration.
(b) To assist other international organisations, both intergovernmental and non-governmental, especially those which carry out standardisation activities.
(c) To contribute to international harmonisation of existing practices and standards and, as necessary, to the preparation of new international standards in order to improve the conditions for producing and marketing vine and wine products, and to help ensure that the interests of consumers are taken into account.

To attain these objectives, the OIV's activities shall be:

- To promote and guide scientific and technical research and experimentation to draw up and frame recommendations and monitor implementation of such recommendations in liaison with its members, especially in the following areas: the conditions for grape production, oenological practices, definition and/or description of products, labelling and marketing conditions, methods for analysing and assessing wine products.
- To submit to its members all proposals relating to guaranteeing the authenticity of wine products, especially with regard to consumers, in particular in connection with the information provided on labels, protecting geographical indications, especially vine- and wine-growing areas and the related appellations of origin, whether designated by geographical names or not, insofar as they do not call into question international agreements relating to trade and intellectual property, improving scientific and technical criteria for recognising and protecting new vitivinicultural plant varieties.
- To contribute to the harmonisation and adaptation of regulations by its members or, where relevant, to facilitate mutual recognition of practices within its field of activities.
- To help protect the health of consumers and to contribute to food safety: by specialist scientific monitoring, making it possible to assess the specific characteristics of vine products, by promoting and guiding research into appropriate nutritional and health aspects, by extending the dissemination of information resulting from such research to the medical and healthcare profession.

Source: OIV, http://www.oiv.int/.

Technology

Technology has an enormous impact of wine and wine quality through the use of technology in the vineyard and the winery.

For example, the adoption of stainless steel fermentation tanks and the development of new temperature controlling systems in the New World wine industries arguably assisted them in developing a fresher more fruit driven style than many of their European competitors. The adoption or rejection of potential technologies can therefore have a substantial affect on wine styles. Just as significantly, changes in technology can help producers get wine to consumers in better condition. For example, adoption of screw-top caps can be seen in terms of technological innovation while the use of coolers designed specially for wine can help ensure that glasses of wine can reach the customer at an appropriate temperature.

Development of the internet has also provided impetus to wine businesses by providing not only another distribution and relationship marketing mechanism (Gebauer and Ginsburg, 2003) but also an opportunity for wineries, in jurisdictions which allow, to gain better returns on sales as well as lower costs for customers. Billingsley (2004) reported that online retail sales in the USA were growing at 10 times the rate of their 'brick-and-mortar' counterparts, however, wineries have suffered restrictions in their capacity to sell over the internet as a result of a combination of prohibitionism and protectionism. Nevertheless, the number of online wine purchases in the USA has continued to grow. In 2000, 5% of core wine drinker market and 1% of the marginal wine drinker market purchased wine online in the last 12 months, by 2006 that had grown to 20% and 8%, respectively. In the case of ever having purchased from an online winery site in 2003 6% of core and 1% of marginal said they had. By 2006 that had increased to 17% and 7% (Wine Market Council, 2006).

Physical environment

The environment has an enormous impact on the wine industry through both its direct effect on the health and growth of grapes and an indirect effect in terms of perception of the environment as part of the attributes of wine quality. Apart from the given element of the effect of geomorphological and climatic features on vine quality, changes in the environment can also have a substantial impact on the wine industry. For example, few students of wine are unaware of the damage wrought by phylloxera on vineyards throughout the world during the second-half of the 19th century (Ordish, 1987). Such was the effect of the aphid, native to the east coast of the USA, that French wine production fell from a peak of 84.5 million hectolitres in 1875 to 23.4 million hectolitres in 1889. With phylloxera consequently also affecting the wine industries of almost every country in the world and leading to the use of grafted vines as a response to the new environmental conditions of grape growing. However, the great wine blight was arguably not without some benefits in terms of the way that vineyards and businesses responded to this threat. Phylloxera had long-term positive impacts on the wine industry with several innovations occurring in viticultural practices as a result of the management of the pest, for example, cessation of mixed vineyards, consolidation of unviable vineyards and a greater emphasis on research and openness to experimentation, that otherwise might not have occurred without such a change in the business environment (Charters, 2006) (see Plates 2.1 and 2.2).

Importantly, the conditions that allowed the spread of phylloxera – international trade and transport – persist to the present day. In fact, they are obviously far more significant because the amount of international trade has increased so rapidly. Yet despite this many vineyards and wineries have only rudimentary precautions to the environmental threats posed by the introduction of new pests and diseases.

For example, since 1998 the State of California has provided funding for a statewide management programme and research to combat the glassy-winged sharpshooter (GWSS) and the deadly Pierce's disease (a bacterium, *Xylella fastidiosa*) that it carries. Accidentally introduced in 1989 through imported US nursery stock the GWSS has had a substantially impact on vine health in the counties it has infested. On 22 February 2007, an Agricultural Commissioner's Office inspector, found a live adult GWSS on a plant shipped from a large Orange County wholesale nursery to a large plant retailer in the Napa Valley, arguably California's premier wine region. This was the first live adult GWSS ever found in Napa County, and the first GWSS life stage found on a nursery plant shipment to Napa County in 2007 (Box 2.7).

Another potential environmental threat to wine businesses is the affects of climate change which may bring not only greater warmth to some wine regions but also greater variability with respect to floods, storms and droughts. Just as significantly, in some of the lower latitudes wine producing areas in the USA, Australia and Europe climate change will likely lead to greater competition with other users for scarce water resources for irrigation purposes (Gössling and Hall, 2006).

The impacts of climate change may be substantial. White et al. (2006) estimate that potential premium wine grape production area in the conterminous USA could decline by up to 81% by

---

Box 2.7 Biosecurity and wine tourism

Biosecurity refers to the protection of a country, region or location's economic, environmental and/or human health from harmful organisms. A survey of New Zealand wineries conducted in 2003 found that only 17% of the 121 respondents had a biosecurity strategy of any form in place (Christensen et al., 2004). However, the possibilities of the spread of disease or pests through winery visitation are substantial given the growth of wine tourism. A survey of 324 winery visitors undertaken in New Zealand in early 2002 (Hall, 2003) found that:

- Over 90% of respondents had visited a vineyard in the previous 12 months.
- Almost half of the domestic visitors also having visited a vineyard overseas in the previous 12 months.
- In response to a question derived from agricultural and custom's surveys over 60% of respondents stated that they did not recognise a vineyard as a farm and therefore did not acknowledge such a visit on their customs form.
- 45% of respondents believing that they had worn the same footwear on their last visit to a vineyard as they had on the current visit (a possible vector for many soil-borne diseases, including Phylloxera).
- 10% believed they were wearing another piece of clothing they had worn or carried with them on their previous vineyard visit (another possible disease vector).

---

the late 21st century. While increases in heat accumulation will shift wine production to warmer climate varieties and/or lower-quality wines, and frost constraints will be reduced, increases in the frequency of extreme hot days (>35°C) in the growing season are projected to eliminate wine grape production in many areas of the USA. In such a scenario, grape and wine production will likely be restricted to a narrow West Coast region and the Northwest and Northeast. These climatic changes may also open up new areas to viticulture in places around the world where it is currently too cold. However, impacts will not only affect where wine is grown but also the varieties and styles of wine that are produced as a result of a longer growing season, increases in photosynthetic rate, changes in the range of certain floral and faunal pest species, and increased water stress.

Concern over climate change has already led to new investment strategies by wine companies in an effort to minimise the environmental threat to their wine portfolio. For example, French champagne houses have been investigating the potential of sparkling wine in southern England, an area with similar chalk deposits to that of the Champagne region, while Spanish producers have also sought to diversify their vineyard holdings as a result of increasing environmental pressure on their existing holdings. For example, the chief of one of Spain's largest wine producers, the Torres wine company, wrote in a 2005 company memo that heat and drought and the process of climate change required a 'move towards the north, closer to the Pyrenees, to acquire new land' (Kakaviatos, 2006b). According to Spanish wine-makers, such as Anna Martin Onzain who owns vines all over Spain, climate change 'is going to have a very important influence on wine-making in Spain ... Every year, we see higher alcohol levels because of hotter weather, so in the future, we may have to make red wine in the north.' With excess heat and sunlight not only leading to higher levels of alcohol, but also 'dangerously low acidity' (Kakaviatos, 2006b).

In response to climate change issues, as well as broader concerns over the state of the environment, many wineries and vineyards are seeking to expand the sustainable credentials of a product which is often promoted as part of the rural idyll. The drivers for embracing more environmentally friendly practices are complex but include both institutional (government and regulatory requirements) and individual (from within the business as well as from consumers) influences (Marshall et al., 2005). In addition to concerns over wine miles (see Box 2.1) there are many national and regional schemes to reduce the use of biocides, increase biodiversity and grow wine sustainably (see Chapter 3). The outcomes of many such schemes are, not only are they good for the environment, and therefore the long-term health of the vineyard, but they also make good business sense in an increasingly environmentally conscious market. For example, in 2006 Cullen Wines in Western Australia, became the first winery in Australia to adopt a carbon-neutral policy (Port, 2007) in addition to their organic and biodynamic 'A' Grade status with the Biological Farmers Association of Australia. Such an approach therefore helps provide support for their positioning statement of 'quality, integrity and sustainability' (see http://www.cullenwines.com.au/wines.htm).

In Marlborough Grove Mill has also used a strong environmental philosophy to gain environmental accreditation for their cellar door in the hope of reinforcing their brand image through visitation to the winery. As part of their commitment to the environment they have developed wetlands and environmental interpretation for visitors (see also Box 3.3). In 2006 they applied for and were awarded Green Globe 21 accreditation – an international environmental accreditation scheme for businesses involved in tourism. This is a clear recognition that the cellar door plays an important role in educating consumers on their environmental practices and promoting the business as well as the brand values that they perceive from sustainable practices (see http://www.grovemill.co.nz).

A significant issue for firms that are seeking to utilise their environmental values as part of their marketing, will be the investment in time and money for accreditation schemes as well as the extent to which it becomes a competitive advantage. For example, with respect to the growth of biodynamic vineyards consultant Alan York, who works with winery clients in California, Oregon, Chile and Italy stated, 'Right now, a lot of producers are looky-loos … Some are fascinated and embrace the time commitment and discipline; others are really looking for the halo effect,' referring to the public relations value in the green-conscious marketplace (McCoy, 2007). Nevertheless, improvements in vineyard health will likely help the production of better grapes, while the market (including retailers), particularly in developed countries, is becoming increasingly aware of sustainably produced wine (Box 2.8).

Box 2.8 Gathering market intelligence

The key to the marketing of any product is market research and market intelligence – gaining information to help in understanding products, business trends, markets and competitors – wine is no exception. Importantly, marketing intelligence not only provides information about the current business situation but also gives you insights into where it might be heading. This box provides some tips on how to gather market intelligence:

1. *Do not reinvent the wheel*: There is already a range of material 'out there' that can suit your needs for the cost of searching the web, going to the library and reading it yourself.
2. *Gathering market intelligence should be done systematically and regularly*: Allow a small amount of time each week to read through material you have gathered. It is strategically important as it allows you to consider your marketing strategy and your overall business strategy.
3. *Use resources such as search engines (i.e. google and google scholar for more academically oriented material), newspapers and magazines, business journals, trade press and online newsletters, subscriber news services and RSS feeds for relevant websites*: Some suggestions regarding source material are made in the further reading section at the end of the chapter.

Search engines also make it easy to find PowerPoint presentations, speeches and white papers. Use search terms such as .ppt, .doc and .pdf.

4. *Use the resources on 'meta-sites'*: These are sites that centralise a range of information from various sources as well as often containing statistical material. Much of this information is available for free or via membership of trade associations.

5. *Examine the websites of competitors*: When visiting competitor's websites look beyond immediate product and service information although this is obviously significant in marketing terms. You can also learn a great deal by viewing a competitor's financial reports (through their annual report if a publicly listed company), employment opportunities, organisation chart, distributor and vendor lists if available, and press releases. Some competitor sites will have a news/press area, here you can often download their press kit or even become a subscriber to their newsletter.

6. *Be systematic (again!)*: There is a lot of material out there. We usually suggest people to have a general 'browse' first to become familiar with what might be available before launching on particular tasks. Remember general information is readily available via some excellent wine news feeds (see below) or there are even free sites on the web that allow you to customise your own daily news page, such as NewsPage by NewsEdge Corp (www.newspage.com). Often you may focus on a particular aspect of what competitors do with aspects of their business and marketing (e.g. labelling, distribution method, pricing, image, positioning and communication strategy). In this situation it can be good to undertake your analysis by seeking to answer certain questions that help your search, for example, How are your competitors' products similar to yours? How are they different? Do they have websites, and how deep are they? Do they sell online or just offer information? What key benefits do their marketing materials communicate? Can you offer additional benefits that are valuable to prospects?

7. *Look at relevant government and research agency sites*: Often government departments or university extension services have programmes available by which they will undertake market research for you as part of a broader programme of initiatives. Many country's government departments for example, have free or low-cost services to help wine exporters and will often be an important first point of contact, along with wine business associations, for gaining information on access issues, legislative and regulatory requirements, distribution and the market.

8. *Look for potential marketing partners*: If exporting or even promoting into domestic markets it is often possible to not only participate in joint and cooperative marketing schemes with other businesses but also to agree to share costs of undertaking research.

The Internet is an extremely useful source for macro analyses of the wine marketing environment. This should not, however, be used as a substitute for market research at the micro-level that is specific to the brand and/or target markets for the company. If you are not confident of undertaking specific marketing research then qualified and professional market researchers (including university extension programmes) should either be employed or contracted to undertake this research.

Conclusions

This chapter has provided an overview of some of the key issues associated with the international business environment for wine. One of the key lessons lies in realising just how internationalised the wine business is and how globalisation has meant that the wine trade is becoming more international, and hence more competitive, not less. In addition, the factors affecting the macro-environment for wine businesses also create significant new issues with respect to understanding the consumption, production and supply of wine to the consumer.

As a result of no significant increase in consumption over the past 40 years on a global basis and the development of new production capacities, the wine trade is also extremely turbulent. For example, the old world producers of Germany, Spain, France, Italy and Portugal accounted for 75.6% of world wine exports in the first half of the 1980s but only 62.1% forecast for 2005. In contrast the New World producers of China, Argentina, South Africa, Australia, New Zealand and the USA have grown from 1.6% to 25.5% over the same period (OIV, 2006). As a result of such changes the EU is looking to dramatically revise its support structure for the wine industry which may lead to substantial economic restructuring in rural areas of Europe. However, Europe is not alone in its concerns over production and many producers in New World countries are also worried by the world wine lake.

One response to the present state of the industry is to remove some vines. In some cases this may be appropriate. However, in many others it may not be, as valuable stock can be lost and rural lifestyles changed. Such a comment is not to romanticise the vineyard and the winery but to reinforce the fact that wine is a part of culture. Nevertheless, one of the clear paths to take is with respect to increasing the level of wine consumption via education of consumers, and of those who seek to restrict others enjoying their wine, of the benefits and culture of wine. Such an approach is fundamental to the marketing of wine and in recognising the importance of marketing in wine businesses as much as the vineyard and the winery.

Practical wine marketing insights

- Understanding the local, regional, national and global business environment of wine is fundamental to the strategy of a wine business.
- You are competing in an international market even if you only sell your product domestically. This market is highly turbulent and competitive.
- Globally there has been little change in consumption or production for the past 40 years with per capita consumption actually falling.
- Some markets are increasing their consumption but because of globalisation processes producers from many countries are seeking to access these same markets.
- There are a range of macro-environmental factors that affect a firm's consumers, stakeholders and competitors as well as the firm itself, these include economic, socio-cultural, technological, institutional and environmental influences.
- In a global business environment local wine businesses are affected by decisions and agreements entered into at a national and international level. Knowledge and understanding of trends and issues allows for the development of sound strategies and proactive decision-making. Market intelligence is therefore fundamental to the business of wine.

Further reading

http://www.winebusiness.com/news/
Provides a daily news guide for the wine industry although the site primarily has an American focus it also provides good international coverage.

http://www.decanter.com
This is the website of Decanter wine magazine, one of the world's leading wine magazines. Their website has a valuable news service that keeps readers abreast of wine trends. In conjunction with Berry Bros. & Rudd Decanter also provide an excellent wine investment guide (http://www.decanter.com/specials/104729.html).

http://www.winespectator.com/
The Wine Spectator magazine is the North American equivalent of Decanter. There is a useful news service and well as tasting reports and information on collecting and auctions.

http://www.winebiz.com.au/dwn/
Wine@biz Daily Wine News provides information and news articles with an Australian focus. They also have a free subscriber news service that provides daily updates of relevance to the Australian and New Zealand wine industries.

http://www.winesandvines.com/
Website of Wines and Vines magazines. Has primarily a North American focus, and is particularly good in discussing issues directly affecting smaller wineries.

http://www.liv-ex.com
The London International Vintners Exchange (Liv-ex) is one of the leading marketplaces for fine wine.

http://www.wineinstitute.org/
The wine institute provides excellent information on a number of contemporary wine business issues including sustainable wine production, the campaign to allow direct wine shipments in the USA, policy issues and statistics.

http://www.freethegrapes.org/index.html
Campaign to allow direct shipments of wine in the USA

http://www.oiv.int/
The OIV is the International Organization for Vines and Wines. It is an intergovernmental organisation of a scientific and technical nature that is concerned with all vine-based products and which has considerable importance with respect to the international wine trade in terms of standards and activities.

http://www.tizwine.com
A predominantly New Zealand wine focussed website, but with both consumer and industry relevant news on the site and via a weekly news service. WineBiz News is for industry news and Tipple News is primarily for consumers. The latter, however, is useful for identifying trends in the global and domestic market place.

World Trade Organisation, TRIPS agreement: http://www.wto.org/english/docs_e/legal_e/27-trips_01_e.htm

Brook, S. (ed.) (2000). *A Century of Wine: The Story of a Wine Revolution*, Mitchell Beazley, London.
Provides a good overview of some of the trends and influences affecting the business of wine in the 20th century.

Ford, G.A. (2003). *The Science of Healthy Drinking*, Wine Appreciation Guild, South San Francisco.
Provides a good introduction to the health benefits of wine.

Gebauer, J. and Ginsburg, M. (2003). The US wine industry and the Internet: an analysis of success factors for online business models. *Electronic Markets*, 13(1), 59–66.
Details the advantages and disadvantages of online wine business models in the US.

Hall, C.M. (2003). Biosecurity and wine tourism: is a vineyard a farm? *Journal of Wine Research*, 14(2–3), 121–126.
Discusses some of the biosecurity implications of wine tourism for wineries including potential management strategies and impacts.

Marshall, R.S., Cardano, M. and Silverman, M. (2005). Exploring individual and institutional drivers of proactive environmentalism in the US wine industry. *Business Strategy and the Environment*, 14(2), 92–109.
Provides an analysis of the factors leading to increased environmental stewardship in the US wine industry.

The marketing dimensions of production processes: adding value to the vine

---

Chapter objectives

After reading this chapter you will

- Understand the importance of the intangible dimensions of wine production for consumers and marketing
- Appreciate difficulties of flexibility in responding to market change from the perspective of vineyard production
- Identify the marketing significance of sustainable wine production
- Further appreciate that value is added to wine brands at all stages of wine production, distribution and consumption where the consumer makes contact

Introduction

In the same way that the vineyard is the starting point for great wine so it is also the starting point for thinking about wine marketing. Although vineyards and wine production processes are usually not thought of in marketing terms, the market has an enormous influence on what happens in the vineyard and the winery, including not only what variety of grapes are planted but also how they will be managed and processed. Historically, wine businesses have been product as opposed to market oriented. Therefore, the vast majority of wine literature and focus of people in the wine industry is on the production process rather than the values derived from the product by the consumer. However, in marketing terms we are interested in the consumer's response to production rather than the production itself.

There are many good books on how to make wine and how to manage a vineyard. These processes will not be repeated here except to note that each management decision in the vineyard and the winery that leads to the wine product that is eventually available on the market will have marketing implications:

- *Price*: What are the costs of production and distribution? What earnings per bottle are required for reinvestment and distribution to shareholders? How will the price be received in the market in comparison with out competitors?
- *Place*: Where do we source our grapes from? Are they local so we can provide a geographic indication of origin or are they widely sourced?

- *Production*: How sustainable are our production methods? What are our environment impacts? How do our methods underlie our market position in terms of brand and image?

Figure 3.1 provides an indication of the interrelationships between price, geographical indicator and sustainability of viticultural and winery practices. It is important to bear in mind that while grape and wine production are tangible operations and processes they also have an intangible dimension to them in that the consumer places values on those operations. Issues such as the manner of pruning and trellising grapes, whether barrels or stainless steel are used, the yeasts that are used, the length of time spent in barrels can all have an influence on perception of the wine and purchasing behaviour as they influence the equity or sense of value that a consumer associates with specific wines (Figure 3.2).

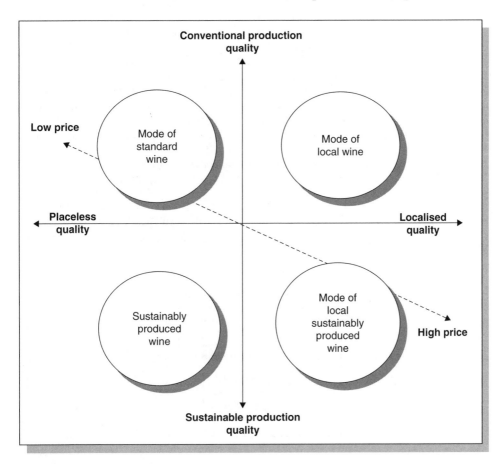

Figure 3.1
A model for modes of designed qualities in wine products

An example of the values associated with wine production is the consumer concerns over the application of biotechnology to grapes and wine. While genetic modification is an integral element of grape and wine production with respect to such things as grapevine varieties, wine yeasts and malolactic bacteria there is enormous public concern in some markets with respect to the dangers of such technology to the extent that it is not only influencing regulatory behaviours of government but also the purchasing behaviour of consumers. While wine producers may be able to argue that empirically the use of biotechnology can enhance the physical characteristics of the wine product the values associated with such technology by some consumers may lead to the product not being purchased. Such concerns are increasingly important for the wine industry. As Hoj and Pretorius (2005, p. 84) noted:

Wine is arguably one of the most natural of all the long-life food substances; compared with most packaged foods, the number of added substances not naturally present in wines is tiny. Moreover, the laws of most wine-producing countries are extraordinarily restrictive; a list of permitted additives exists and anything not on that 'positive' list is banned, however harmless (or indeed beneficial) it may be. In addition to these restrictions, much of the wine industry is also bound by tradition and regional culture. This segment of the industry is particularly unreceptive to any changes that might conflict with their image of wine as a natural beverage produced by time-honoured procedures and cloaked in a mantle of romanticism. Furthermore, the marketing of wine relies to a great extent on label integrity and product identity.

For many people the vineyard almost seems like a constant in the world of wine. However, this is not the case. New varieties of grapes and clones of existing varieties are utilised in order to

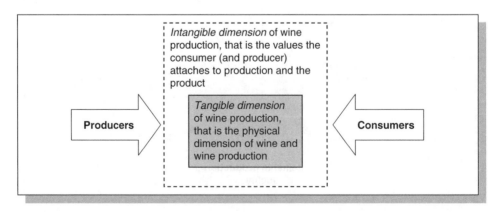

Figure 3.2
Tangible and intangible dimensions of wine production

develop a more product acceptable to the market. New wine regions and vineyards are also developed for a variety of different business reasons and even the grape stock in existing vineyards is replaced over time. For people who are interested in making wine for themselves the selection of grape varieties can be a matter of personal choice but for those who are in the business of wine it reflects a market oriented decision as they are seeking to antici- pate what the market will be demanding over the life of the vine. Indeed a key business issue for wineries and vineyards is the capacity to be flexible in the face of changing consumer demands and production requirements (see Chapter 2).

Flexibility of production

Given that a vine usually takes up to seven years to reach full production and the flavour characteristics of its grapes will change over the life-span of the grape the planting of a vineyard represents a substantial fixed asset the value of which can change depending on level of demand for the grapes planted and the overall level of supply. Wineries can adopt a number of strategies to respond to changing demands and cost of production in terms of what is grown in a wineries own vineyard, what is grown on contract and what is purchased on the market at spot prices. Growing grapes under winery control whether it be in its own vineyards or with contract growers can allow for greater cer- tainty in terms of level the quality of production. However, this may be considerably more expensive than purchasing grapes at spot prices. Figure 3.3 illustrates some of these issues.

Decisions regarding the flexibility of grape production are made with respect to the spread of risk and the desired quality of production for different wine brands. Therefore, a common strategy of mid- to large-sized wineries is to combine produc- tion in its own vineyards and that of contract growers with any shortfall in required juice being made up with purchases on the spot market. However, at times of low-price and/or low-income wineries may not renew contracts in order to take advantage of low market price for grapes and grape juice. Where there are major changes in market conditions entire vineyards may be ripped up and even replanted with other crops. The vineyard, like the market, is subject to rapid change.

The grape and the vineyard

The selection of grape varieties and the location of vineyards is a result of the interplay between three major sets of factors: the

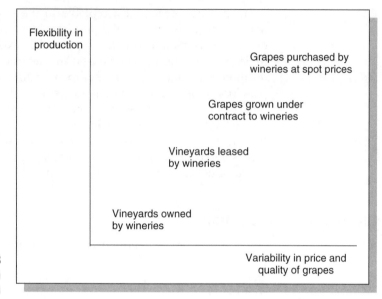

Figure 3.3
Flexibility in
production

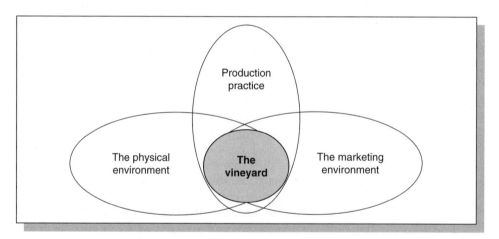

Figure 3.4
Business influences on the vineyard

physical environment, production practices and the marketing environment (Figure 3.4).

The physical environment of wine refers to the physical factors that affect the choice of a vineyard location and the selection of grape varieties. These include:

- climatic factors such as temperature, wind, rain, hail and heat units in a growing season;
- soil;

- water supplies and availability;
- pests and diseases;
- topography.

The production practices refers to:

- the management factors that occur in the development of a new vineyard or the redevelopment of an existing one;
- the cultural practices that are employed over the growth cycle and life-span of the vine, and of the vineyard;
- the wine production practices that will be utilised in the winery;
- financial considerations in the selection and management of vineyards and the conduct of cultural practices.

The marketing environment in the case of the vineyard refers to the behaviour of consumers with respect to their preferences in relation to:

- the intrinsic characteristics of the wine, that is, red versus white, variety, flavours and fruit characteristics;
- the extrinsic characteristics of the wine, that is, the location at which it is grown, the practices by which it is grown, the price at which it is available, its acceptance in the market which, in turn, are influenced by media, consumer preferences and fashion.

The three sets of factors do not occur in isolation of one another. For example, the availability of funds will influence where and the type of land that can be purchased for a new vineyard. In addition, funds will also influence the cultural practices that are employed and even the selection of grape varieties to be planted depending on the financial capacity to invest in vineyard development without there being any return from grape production for several years until the vines mature. Ultimately, market forces also come into play here and may influence the selection of varieties for which a market is already established versus new or unusual varieties that may only be known by a relatively small number of the buying public. Furthermore, in order to reduce the cost of fixed plant many new small wine businesses will often have their wine made under contract at another winery so that they do not have to fund winery equipment at an early stage of business development.

An example of a trade-off in development terms of a new vineyard is the decision to plant grafted or ungrafted rootstock. Rootstock is the plant that forms the root system of a vine on which a scion (fruiting variety) is grafted. The grafting of rootstock is undertaken because the variety of rootstock may be well adapted to the local physical environment but may only produce grapes of poor quality. Therefore, by grafting a better fruiting stock onto the rootstock a vine with both good environmental and fruiting qualities can be grown. In many parts of the world the grafting of European 'classic' or *Vitis vinifera* varieties onto North American species of grapevine or hybrids of European and North American varieties is undertaken because the North American vines are less susceptible to the affects of the root louse phylloxera, which devastated many of the world's vineyards in the Nineteenth Century (see Chapter Two), as well as nematodes. The difference in production of grapes and wine quality on grafted versus ungrafted varieties may be substantial. Australian research in the 1980s with Shiraz indicated that in the Murimbidgee area vines on the rootstocks Ramsey and Dog Ridge outyielded ungrafted vines by 46% and 48%, respectively. Vines on the rootstock Dog Ridge also produced wines with higher pH values than wines from ungrafted control vines (Hedberg et al., 1986a, b). Studies in the Barossa Valley, also with shiraz, also found that juice from the fruit of ungrafted vines had lower pH than that from rootstocks. However, wine made from this juice had higher colour density and the lowest wine colour hue (Cirami et al., 1984), a situation that also illustrates the trade-offs that exist between juice production and characteristics.

However, grafted rootstock is often twice, if not sometimes three times, more expensive than ungrafted vines. Therefore in developing a vineyard there is a trade-off in terms of cost, risk and the characteristics of the fruit that will develop on whatever is planted in the vineyard. As well as significant issues with how much juice can be produced and what its character will be there are also other marketing values associated with the type of rootstock that is used. The use of ungrafted vines may contribute to the appeal of a wine by being promoted as more original or authentic to the consumer, even if this is never stated explicitly. For example, Root:1 a partnership between Chilean producer Viña Ventisquero and US company the Click Wine Group bottles a cabernet sauvignon (with 15% Shiraz) for the American market designated 'The Original Ungrafted', with the partnership's website stressing the qualities that being ungrafted provide to the wine:

The ungrafted

Character comes from your Roots

Introducing a new Chilean wine from some of the oldest rootstock in the world.

Chile is a true rarity in the wine world. Unique geographic and climatic forces have allowed it to remain one of very few grape-growing regions in the world where the original European rootstocks survive.

> Root:1 Cabernet Sauvignon is crafted exclusively from grapes grown on the original, ungrafted root systems tended by our master Winemakers, giving the wine its pure, rich fruit flavours and aromas (http://www.root1wine.com/)

The use of ungrafted wines may also be promoted at a regional or national level. The Toro region of Spain promotes the fact that the majority of its vines, which are local varieties such as Tinta de Toro (Tempranillo), Garnacha, Malvasía and Verdejo are not grafted onto American rootstocks. Chile is also increasingly promoting the fact that, as a result of its sandy coastal soils, which were hostile to the phylloxera louse, it is phylloxera free and consequently has almost no grafted rootstocks (Box 3.1).

Box 3.1 Vieilles Vignes Françaises – An Ungrafted Champagne

In 2006, the *New York Times* ran a story on one of the rarest champagnes, Bollinger's Vieilles Vignes Françaises, which is a pinot noir grown on its own stocks (Azimov 2006). First commercially produced in 1970 only 3000–5000 bottles are made in vintage years and usually retail at around US$450 a bottle. The grapes for the wine come from two vineyards with a total area of about half a hectare, Clos Chaudes Terres and Clos Saint-Jacques near Epernay in Champagne. Unfortunately, the previous year a third vineyard of ungrafted pinot noir, Croix Rouge near Tauxières, had an infestation of phylloxera. Though only about 1300 square metres, or a third of an acre, it represented 22% of Bollinger's grape supply for Vieilles Vignes Françaises. According to Azimov (2006):

It is both easy and impossible to know what to make of a wine like this. To be literal-minded, consider the importance that most grape-growers place on selecting the right rootstocks, clones and soils for their wines. They have a buffet of choices, and they know that the roots on which they choose to graft their vines can play an enormous role in how vigorous the vine is, how it absorbs nutrients and sunlight, and how the grapes ripen. Why wouldn't a vine's own roots also affect the quality of the grapes?

But objectivity is often useless with wine. The same bottle will taste different at a candlelight dinner with your sweetheart than it will, say, in a fluorescent office. With the lore and romance of history and fantasy, of what might have been, bubbling up from the bottom of each glass, how can Vieilles Vignes Françaises ever be judged as merely a wine?

It is not a wine. It is the dream of a wine.

Nevertheless, while Vieilles Vignes Françaises is promoted in terms of its viticultural heritage. 'the old French way', Ghislain de Montgolfier, head of Bollinger, admits 'We have no scientific reason that I know for why we don't have phylloxera... We might not be able to produce a single bottle next year' (Azimov 2006).
See: http://www.champagne-bollinger.fr/vvf_en.pdf

Sustainable Wine growing as Sustainable Marketing

Arguably one of the best demonstrations of the connection between winegrowing practices and marketing is the development of sustainable vineyard and wine production management programmes. These programmes often make not only good environmental sense but become an important element in appealing to an increasingly environmentally and socially conscious market (Bisson et al., 2002; Miles and Munilla, 2004). For example, in a study of dimensions of wine equity in terms of the benefits sought by wine consumers, Orth et al. (2005) found that quality, price, social acceptance, emotional, environmental value and humane value were strong and significant predictors of consumer preferences for wine from three US states (California, Oregon, Washington) and six countries (Australia, Chile, France, Italy, New Zealand, Spain). The promotion of the quality of wine products is often understood to be in relation to price, brand advertising (more typical of New World wine) and geographical indicators (more typical of Europe) (Fluett and Garella, 2002; Barham, 2003). However, in both cases the understanding of quality is built up over time via a relationship of the subjective dimensions of quality to the actual objective production process. Consumer knowledge of the lowering of production standards in relation to their existing equity of a wine product can have devastating and even long-term impacts on the quality values associated with wines at a national, company or regional level (Levitan, 2001).

A sustainable agricultural system (Poincelot, 1990) is one in which:

- Resources are kept in balance with their use through conservation, recycling and/or renewal.
- Practices preserve agricultural resources and prevent environmental damage to the farm and off-site biophysical resources including land, water and air.
- Production, profits and incentives retain their importance, because not only agriculture needs to be sustained, but so do farmers and society.

Sustainable viticulture is generally regarded as having developed out of the sustainable agriculture and organic farming movements. However, sustainable viticulture and wine production is not necessarily organic. Indeed, organic production methods can be seen as one particular approach to producing grapes and wine that concentrates on the environmental dimensions of sustainability (see Crescimanno et al., 2002). The Walla Walla

Valley Vinea Winegrowers' Sustainable Trust (2004) defines sustainable wine growing as:

a holistic system of recognized cultural production methodologies that employ environmentally-friendly and socially responsible viticultural practices that respect the land, conserve natural resources, support biodiversity, exercise responsible relationships with workers, neighbors and the community and provide continuing economic and biological vineyard viability.

The goals of the Walla Walla Valley Winegrowers Vinea Sustainable Trust with respect to sustainable winegrowing are a mixture of sustainability and marketing considerations:

Membership: Attract Walla Walla Valley winegrowers dedicated to investing in sustainable viticulture and implementing these practices over the long term.
Stewardship: Implement proven holistic, environmentally friendly viticultural practices that respect the land, conserve natural resources, support biodiversity and provide for the long-term vineyard viability.
Obtain international recognition through certification with the International Organization of Biological Controls.
Quality: Produce world-class wines of distinction by further strengthening the partnership between growers, vintners and consumers.
Viability: Enhance the image and prestige of Walla Walla Valley winegrapes, specifically those grown by members of Vinea, the Winegrowers Sustainable Trust.
Establish Walla Walla as a leader in sustainable viticulture and generate awareness and regard for this position among Washington state vintners, growers, elected officials, the community at large, members of the trade, media and consumers.

Ohmart (2002, p. 3) regards sustainable winegrape viticulture as 'a systems view of winegrape growing that considers soil building as the foundation, minimizes off-farm inputs, emphasizes economic profitability, and concerns itself with environmental health and social equity'. However, he notes that it is difficult to adhere to such an approach to sustainable viticulture particularly when dealing with individual viticultural practices. Therefore, he addresses sustainable viticulture as a problem solving tool similar to how integrated pest management has addressed pest management and notes that 'integrated viticulture' may be a better term to use. Though he goes onto define sustainable viticulture as 'a long term approach to managing winegrapes which optimizes winegrape quality and productivity by using a combination of biological, cultural and chemical tools in ways that minimize economic, environmental, and health risks' (Ohmart and Matthaiasson, 2002, p. 3).

The adoption of improved environmental management practices is a combination of external regulatory and market pressures and internal drivers to improve the sustainability of winegrowing practices. The increasing internationalisation of environmental issues means that meeting international standards may be required for access to some markets, while it may also be perceived favourably by consumers. The International Standards Organisation (ISO) has established a range of standards that affect international trade including standards for safety and health and the environment. In the case of ISO 14001 Environmental Management System van Schoor and Visser (2000) argued that South African wine companies 'trading in foreign markets … have a choice either to play the international game according to the internationally acceptable rules or to capitulate and concentrate on the internal market'. The first winery to be awarded ISO 14001 certification in South Africa, the Rupert and Rothschild Winery in the Franschhoek Valley, led a multi-site certification initiative of nine wineries and a bottling plant in the Valley. Interestingly, Dominic Burke from La Couronne, one of the members of the Eco-Association suggested that the initiative was good for marketing as well as for the environment: 'On a collaborative note, this acknowledgment has allowed the Franschhoek Valley a unique advantage over other wine growing regions as being the first South African wine production region to be granted such an accolade, which can also benefit the region from a marketing point of view' (Walsdorff et al., 2005, p. 86).

The increased adoption of sustainable viticultural management practices in some regions is illustrated in the Lodi-Woodbridge area of California where grape growers demonstrated increased adoption of sustainable vineyard management practices between 1998 and 2003 (Table 3.1). The region is recognized as an inter-national leader in sustainable viticulture. In 2002 the California Wine Institute and the California Association of Winegrape Growers published the *Code of Sustainable Winegrowing Workbook* (Dlott et al., 2002) which was modelled after the *Lodi Winegrower's Workbook* (Ohmart, 2000). The Code defined sustainable winegrowing as using in terms of the three 'Es of sustainability':

1. *Environmentally Sound*: growing and winemaking practices that are sensitive to the environment.
2. *Socially Equitable*: responsible to the needs and interests of society-at-large.
3. *Economically Feasible*: to implement and maintain.

Table 3.1   Vineyard integrated pest management practices of winegrape growers in the Lodi-Woodbridge Commission 1998–2003

Practices	% used in 2003	% used In 1998	% change
Insect management			
Leaf pulling	79	68	11
Reduced insecticide rate	75	76	−1
Pheromones for OLR	25	16	9
Alternate row spraying	44	35	9
Cover crops for natural enemy refuge	53	46	7
Release Beneficial Insects	15	NA	
Mite management			
Irrigation management	76	71	5
Dust reduction	84	60	24
Cover crops for natural enemy refuge	50	34	16
Predatory mite release	15	13	2
Reduced miticide application rates	57	58	−1
Alternate row spraying	38	36	2
Disease management			
Using computer disease forecasting model	30	12	18
Irrigation management	81	79	2
Leaf pulling	75	65	10
Modified trellising	50	44	6
Remove mummies and clean berms	58	51	7
Weed management			
Monitoring and needs based spraying	87	82	5
Reduced herbicide application rates	78	66	12
Mechanical weed management	45	47	−2
Use only contact herbicides/No pre-emergents	53	33	20
Narrowing the treated strip	41	NA	
Other management practices			
Use of compost in vineyards	31	37	−6
Owl boxed for rodent control	54	39	15
Enviromist-type shielded sprayer	42	27	15
Electrostatic sprayer	16	6	10

Source: Lodi-Woodbridge Winegrape Commission (2005, p. 37).

In 2006, the Lodi-Woodbridge Winegrape Commission (LWWC), which was formed in 1991 and promotes the Lodi region as a producer of premium winegrapes and wine, won The Governor's Environmental and Economic Leadership Award, the State of California's highest and most prestigious environmental honour. The Commission, which represents almost 800 wine-growers farming more than 90,000 acres that produce 20% of California's winegrapes, promotes use of farming practices that are environmentally sound, economically viable, and socially equitable (LWWC, 2006). LWWC's programme includes (Box 3.2):

- grower education and outreach,
- field implementation with one-on-one assistance,
- the Lodi Winegrower's Workbook self-assessment, and since 2005,
- a third-party sustainable winegrowing certification programme, The Lodi Rules for Sustainable Winegrowing. The programme is being implemented on a region-wide basis; 1500 vineyard acres were certified in 2005, and 6000 acres were enrolled for 2006.

Box 3.2 The Lodi Rules

The Lodi-Woodbridge Winegrape Commission Rules for Sustainable Winegrowing Program (The Lodi Rules) has two components:

- Sustainable winegrowing standards;
- A pesticide environmental assessment system (PEAS) that measures the impact of all pesticides used in the vineyard

The Lodi Rules are third-party certified which means the standards have been reviewed and endorsed by an organisation not connected to the Commission. Vineyards in The Lodi Rules program are certified by an environmental non-profit organization, Protected Harvest, which is dedicated 'to advancing and certifying the use of environmentally and economically sustainable agriculture practices through the development of stringent, transparent and quantifiable standards, incentive-based eco-labelling and public education' (http://www.protectedharvest.org/aboutus/mission.htm).

The sustainable winegrowing standards consist of 75 farming practice standards divided into six areas:

- Ecosystem Management
- Education, Training and Team Building
- Soil Management
- Water Management
- Vineyard Establishment
- Pest Management.

A farming practice had to meet three criteria to be included as a standard:

1. It must be measurable, in other words there must be physical evidence indicating the practice was carried out.

2. The practice must maintain or enhance one or more of the three E's of sustainability.
3. The practice must be technically and economically feasible, and must not set an unachievable standard.

The PEAS model currently contains five component indices measuring:

- worker acute risks,
- dietary risks to people from acute and chronic exposure,
- acute risks to small aquatic invertebrates,
- acute risks to birds,
- acute risks to bees and pest natural enemies.

Each of the indices is used independently to assess relative risks to organisms on a treated area basis. PEAS is used to calculate multi-attribute risks spanning all of the five indices on an equal weighting.

The Lodi Rules of Sustainable Winegrowing: http://www.lodiwine.com/lodirules_home1.shtml

Protected Harvest: http://www.protectedharvest.org/

Numerous wine regions and vineyard associations have sustainable viticulture schemes. The Washington Wine Industry Foundation at the request of the Washington Association of Wine Grape Growers (WAWGG) have developed a 'Vinewise' programme that focuses on vineyard sustainability in environmental and economic terms. Paul Champoux, Chairman of WAWGG and owner of the Champoux Vineyards underlines the relationship between what happens in the vineyard and the positioning of the wine product when he states 'Sustainability supports Washington's signature to the world of premium quality grapes and wine' (Vinewise, 2006a) (see Plates 3.1 and 3.2).

In February 2005, WAWGG sent out a survey on sustainable viticulture to 418 growers to determine what growers knew about sustainability and the motivations they had with respect to the adoption of sustainable practices. Eighty-five growers responded (20.3% response rate) and included members and non-members from a range of different size vineyards and business. Highlights of the survey included (Vinewise, 2006b):

- 79.7% of respondents felt that practicing sustainable viticulture would make their crop more marketable and regarded sustainability as important to the industry as a whole.
- 75% of respondents practice at least some form of sustainability at the time of the survey with the top three areas of

practice being: (1) pest management, (2) soil and nutrient management and (3) vineyard management.

- Growers cited concern for the environment and the future as the reason to practice sustainable viticulture. Many noted overuse of pesticides and the effects of pesticides as a reason to move towards sustainable pest management.
- 53% of responding growers practicing sustainable viticulture at the time of the survey have faced challenges, with the most frequent being weed and pest management, water issues and initial costs. However, the same growers consistently cited better quality grapes and better soil as a result of adopting more sustainable practices as well as cost savings from less chemical use and less water use. Interestingly with respect to the social dimensions of sustainability many respondents also cited better relations with employees and wineries as a result.
- 79% agreed that sustainable practices would make their crop more marketable but were unsure how to market it.

The issue of the marketing benefits of sustainable viticulture is obviously important for the financial viability of wine businesses as there is often little short-term business incentive to introduce sustainable practices unless it helps in selling wine, although there is clear long-term incentives with respect to improving soil qualities and reducing pests and disease as well as with product positioning and the maintenance of industry standards. In the Waipara region of the South Island of New Zealand, the Waipara Valley Winegrowers have engaged in an active programme of revegetation and environmental conservation as part of a 'greening Waipara' programme that aims to build 'biodiversity back into the wine experience' (Greening Waipara, 2006). The programme is advertised in a number of vineyards as part of the cellar door experience and is also integrated into some wineries' marketing campaigns. For example, Muddy Water winery (see http://www.muddywater.co.nz/) has included information on the biodiversity project onto their wine labels.

In South Africa a Biodiversity and Wine Initiative (BWI) has been developed as a partnership between the South African wine industry and conservation groups in order to minimise the loss of natural habitat and contribute to sustainable wine production. The initiative aims to:

- Prevent further loss of habitat in critical sites.
- Increase the total area set aside as natural habitat in contractual protected areas.

- Promote changes in farming practices that enhance the suitability of vineyards as habitat for biodiversity, and reduce farming practices that have negative impacts on biodiversity, both in the vineyards and in surrounding natural habitat.
- Create marketing opportunities for the wine industry by positioning the biodiversity of the Cape Floral Kingdom, and the industry's proactive stance on biodiversity, as a unique selling point to differentiate Brand South Africa (World Wildlife Fund South Africa, 2004).

The initiative has a number of viticultural and marketing strategies to achieve its aims (Table 3.2) within the overall context of connecting biodiversity, terroir and wine (Figure 3.5). The initiative is part of a wider attempt to reposition South Africa in a premium wine niche and reduce its low-value/high-volume orientation. As of January 2007 there were 4 champions (Vergelegen, Graham Beck Wines, Cloof Wine Estate, Burgherspost Wine Estate), 4 cooperative cellar members and 70 members (BWI, 2007). The members and champions collectively conserve approximately 45,000 hectare. In marketing terms the biodiversity positioning was being used by Wines of South Africa as part of its 2006 'Variety in Our Nature' campaign in key markets including Germany, the UK and the USA. In the UK this included posters on the London underground, radio promotion and public relations, and promotion in magazines and at trade shows (Meropa Communications, 2006). However, the initiative is also regarded as a means of responding in marketing terms to both the development of environmentally conscious wine consumers as well as potential regulatory changes in key markets such as Europe. According to BWI project director Tony Hansen, 'the BWI is a useful tool to communicate how far ahead we are in SA as an industry, and as individual producers. The hope eventually is that sustainable wine production will be a motivation for overseas buyers to buy South African. We're trying to tighten that up, but the signal from the EU is that we're heading in the right direction' (Maxwell, 2005).

In Australia sustainable viticulture has been connected to wider attempts to restore native vegetation. Benefits of native vegetation in vineyards have been identified (Allan, 1999) as including:

- control of rising groundwater/salinity;
- reduction in run-off and siltation;
- improved soil structure and organic matter;
- provision of shelter and microclimate;

Table 3.2 Viticultural and marketing strategies of the South African Biodiversity and Wine Initiative

Strategy	Details
Incorporate biodiversity guidelines into Integrated Production of Wine (IPW) Guidelines	The BWI works closely with the wine industry to include relevant biodiversity guidelines in the IPW environmental guidelines. The biodiversity guidelines are designed to be practical and realistic for growers and producers to implement, with maximum conservation benefits.
Identify and enlist biodiversity and wine champions	Through marketing the BWI in wine industry publications, the BWI enlists interested producers and growers to champion the initiative. These champions are guided through the implementation of the biodiversity guidelines, and assist with building a biodiversity story into their winery identity. The role of champions is to test the implementation of the biodiversity guidelines, and to demonstrate the tangible benefits to the wine industry. The first champion was announced in 2005.
Extend conservation stewardship to the wine industry	Cape Nature's existing Conservation Stewardship Programme is extended to winegrape growers with endangered environments on their properties. Stewardship encourages landowners to enter into formal contracts with Cape Nature to conserve critical sites. Although this might only be a small portion of a landowner's farm, benefits to the land owner can include property rate rebates, securing the area for conservation, assistance with land management, alien plant clearing and positive media coverage.
Integrate biodiversity into Brand South Africa	The BWI aims to incorporate biodiversity into Brand South Africa, in order to give South Africa a competitive marketing advantage in the global wine market. The advantage is based on the unique attributes of the scenery and biodiversity of the Cape Floral Kingdom, which is also a World Heritage Site. The BWI aims to build on the idea that South Africa's complex terroir, unique in the world, results in complex biodiversity and complex wines.
Develop a biodiversity wine route	The BWI is establishing a biodiversity wine route where visitors are exposed to both the wine and the biodiversity experience of each participating producer. The biodiversity wine route is regarded as an opportunity to create employment and develop a new ecotourism dimension for South African wine tourism.

Source: World Wildlife Fund South Africa (2004) and Biodiversity and Wine Initiative (2004).

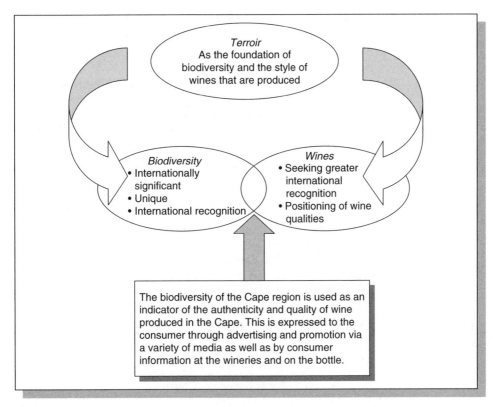

Figure 3.5
Connection between biodiversity, terroir and wine in the South African biodiversity and wine initiative

- provision of habitat for insects/bats/birds which can be useful natural predators;
- increase in biodiversity generally, including soil organisms (healthy ecosystems);
- aesthetics;
- commercial value of many native plants for seed, timber, flowers, etc.

One of the brands which has most sought to maximise the relationship between a conservation positioning for its product and its wine is Banrock Station. Banrock Station, a part of the Hardy Wine Company was established in 1994 on a 1750-hectare (4200 acres) property at the junction of Banrock Creek and the Murray River, about 200 kilometre north-east of Adelaide, South Australia. In 2002 its owner, BRL Hardy, formed a 50:50 joint venture partnership with US Constellation Brands to form Pacific Wine Partners in order to gain access to the three-tiered US market (importer, distributor and retailer). In 2003 Constellation

Brands bought out BRL Hardy, merged it with its own company and renamed the Australian subsidiary Hardy Wine Company. Approximately 65% of Banrock Station's earning comes from the export market.

Using the tagline of 'Good Earth Fine Wine' Banrock Station actively promotes wetland conservation values in the countries it exports to as well as with respect to restoration of wetlands on the Australian property where the grapes are grown. As of early 2007 Banrock Station had partnerships in Australia and nine other countries (Canada, Denmark, Kenya, Netherlands, New Zealand, Sweden, the UK, and the USA) with respect to wetland conservation programmes. The company's environmental conservation work is regarded as giving it a point of differentiation and a promotional advantage in environmentally conscious markets, such as Europe and North America (Pugh and Fletcher, 2002). Banrock Station Wines financially sponsor organizations that can develop projects that will lead to the conservation of wetlands or wetland species. Their first sponsorship was in 1996, and within 10 years Banrock Station wines had sponsored 60 projects in 11 countries, contributing more than A$3 million. According to a Banrock Station (2005) press release quoting Banrock Station manager, Tony Sharley:

This new international benchmark announced today [A$3 million of donations to environmental projects] is the culmination of a successful strategy that has played a key role in bringing the wine industry closer than ever to environmental projects throughout the world ... That makes perfect sense because wine is a product of nature ... If not for donations from sales of this wine brand, many of the wetlands we have helped restore – and the wildlife that depends so heavily upon them – would have continued to decline ... There is no reason why the achievements and successes of Banrock Station cannot be replicated many times throughout the world ... All it needs is more and more people to recognize the commitment they can make to this important environmental cause when next they buy wine.

In the USA the Banrock Station Wetlands Conservation program, a partnership project of Banrock Station Wines and The Conservation Fund (see http://www.conservationfund.org), provides seed grants to non-profit groups and/or public agencies in the USA that are planning and implementing wetlands and waterways conservation and/or restoration projects at the local level. In 2006, Banrock Station announced its largest single donation anywhere in the world by donating $1.25 million through the Banrock Station Wetlands Foundation Canada to Bring Back the Salmon, a five-year project to restore reproducing populations of native Atlantic Salmon to Lake Ontario. As part of the Bring Back the

Salmon announcement, Banrock Station also unveiled new, environmentally friendly one litre Tetra Pak wine packages. Available in three varietals – Unwooded Chardonnay, Shiraz, and Cabernet Sauvignon – these new wines were highlighted on feature displays from 27 April to 20 May 2006 in Liquor Control Board of Ontario (LCBO) stores across Ontario. The LCBO is also a partner in the Bring Back the Salmon project (Constellation Wines, 2006).

The discussion above has primarily highlighted viticultural practices and some of their marketing implications, especially with respect to the environment. However, winery practices are just as important with respect to consumer equity in the product. For example, with respect to sparkling wine value is not just accorded by consumers with respect to where the sparkling wine is from but also the method by which it is made, that is, bottle fermentation, tank fermentation or carbonation (Judica and Perkins, 1992; Lee et al., 2005). Similarly, the use of different oak by winemakers to provide different flavours in the wine will influence consumer choice not only in terms of the objective flavour but, where information is available, may also influence some consumers purchasing behaviour prior to consumption.

The reputation of wine is therefore based on a range of factors. In a study of consumers of Bordeaux wine Landon and Smith (1997) found that estimates of quality and reputation variables indicated a model of consumer decision making which incorporates information on reputation (past quality) and collective reputation (average group quality) ahead of alternative models that included current quality. The results also indicated that reputation has a large impact on the willingness to pay of consumers, that long-term reputation is considerably more important than short-term quality movements, and that consumers react slowly to changes in product quality. Reputational effects stem not only from the region or producer's reputation but also from the elements of the production processes that are used. When changes occur there is therefore potential to affect the reputational aspects of the wine product that are significant for consumers, particularly those consumers with a lower wine knowledge whose purchasing patterns may be more influenced by collective reputation variables when factors such as price are not a consideration. Nevertheless, it should also be noted that in a study of Bordeaux and Burgundy wines Lecocq and Visser (2006) observed that characteristics that are directly revealed to the consumer upon inspection of the bottle and its label (e.g. ranking, vintage and appellation) explained the major part of price differences. Sensory variables did not appear to play an important role, while prices were also hardly affected by the grades assigned by professional wine tasters. Although jury grades have a significant effect, their impact on prices was very small compared to the impact of ranking and vintage.

External Validation of Processes

One of the significant themes that emerge in examining the implications of production processes for wine marketing is that, in many of the cases discussed in this chapter, processes have been externally validated in some way. This can include generic labelling requirements (Marette and Zago, 2003; Zago and Pick, 2004), but more particularly can relate to appellation controls and geographic indicator requirements (Sanjuán and Albisu, 2004), as well as schemes with respect to the environmental and sustainable dimensions of viticulture and winemaking.

External validation of, for example, the contribution of a winery to environmental conservation or reducing greenhouse gas emissions, is extremely important as they help make business and product claims believable in an already cluttered and confusing market to the consumer. The identification of accreditation programmes in marketing and promotional activities such as advertising and labelling can therefore convey quality signals in wine marketing in the same way that exhibition awards can (Orth and Krška, 2002). New World wineries and emerging internal wine markets, in particular, have adopted the practice of signifying competition performance on bottle information as a way of signalling wine qualities (and often being able to get a higher return on the sale). In an increasingly production aware market environmental, social and other values can be appealed through creating consumer awareness of particular dimensions of production that can be a point of differentiation for the wine brand or company in an otherwise congested market (Loureiro, 2003) (Box 3.3).

Box 3.3 The New Zealand Wine Company Limited

The New Zealand Wine Company is an integrated wine company involved in growing grapes, winemaking and bottling, and in the marketing and sales of premium quality wines in New Zealand and to export markets with the brands Grove Mill, Sanctuary and Frog Haven. NZWC sources its grapes from a total land area of approximately 70 hectares of owned/leased vineyards and a further 76 hectares of Marlborough grapes under contract. The Company's 2006 vintage crush was 3017 tonnes and included 1489 tonnes of NZWC's own grapes. Formerly known as the Grove Mill Wine Company Limited the NZWC in listed on the New Zealand Alternative Market (NZAX) operated by the New Zealand Stock Exchange (NZX). For the financial year ended 30th June

2006 the company had a tax paid surplus of NZ$1.026 million on a total revenue of NZ$9.414 million, representing a 12% increase on 2005.

The New Zealand Wine Company's vision is to:

Build successful premium New Zealand wine brands globally through environmentally sustainable business practices.

The overall strategy is to develop the Grove Mill brand as the Company's flagship Ultra premium brand sold throughout the world whilst the Sanctuary and to a lesser extent Frog Haven brands will chiefly service the supermarket distribution as exclusive own label brands in export markets. The main export markets are the UK (where a supply arrangement exists with the UK supermarket chain Sainsbury), USA and Australia. Significant new markets include Belgium, Denmark, Germany, and Sweden in Europe; Barbados, Brazil and Canada in the Americas, and Hong Kong and Japan, and Thailand in Asia.

The company's principal business strategies are to:

- Build the Company's position through environmentally sustainable practices;
- Position the Grove Mill brand as a preferred provider of highest quality New Zealand wines to premium outlets globally;
- Use the Sanctuary, Frog Haven and other brands to support key customer needs for New Zealand wines;
- Expand the winery production infrastructure while maintaining and improving current quality, safety and environmental standards;
- Develop and maintain a diversified portfolio of cost effective, high quality owned and contracted vineyards producing grape varietals tailored to winery and market demands;
- Build on the performance culture that sets clear Board, management and individual targets, recognising and rewarding the maximising of Shareholder value;
- Expand the Company's existing business base and grow via acquisitions where these fit with existing strategy and add value for all Shareholders.

Brand development is regarded as critical in achieving a sustainable point of difference for the company so as to build volume while retaining value. This has been done from the company's approach with respect to sustainable environmental positioning. For example, the Grove Mill philosophy is to 'produce premium quality wine with minimal environmental impact' while the New Zealand Wine Company has an environmental policy with the philosophy: 'Sustainability meets our needs without compromising the ability of those who follow us to meet their own needs' where the environment is defined as including 'wherever our wines are made and enjoyed'. The goal of the company's environmental policy is continuous improvement in the areas of:

- Energy efficiency
- Waste management
- Greenhouse gas emissions

- Health and Safety
- Resource conservation
- Social responsibility
- Ecosystem enhancement.

These improvements have come through a variety of innovations (Table 3.3) in viticultural practice and wine production and management. As with a number of sustainable wine initiatives in the USA the Company has also utilised external accreditation as a means not only of quality control with respect to sustainable practice but also to ensure that the company's initiatives are regarded as being credible. These initiatives and their application are outlined in Table 3.4. The Grove Mill Pinot Noir 2005 was the first Marlborough wine to carry the Sustainable Winegrowing New Zealand logo while the aim is for all Grove Mill wines to be 100% accredited for the 2008 vintage.

Sources

New Zealand Wine Company (site contains access to the company profile and to the financial reports as well as other information): http://www.nzwineco.co.nz
Grove Mill (includes information on philosophy, the Grove Mill Frog, sustainable practices and environmental quality): www.grovemill.co.nz
Sanctuary Wines: www.sanctuarywine.co.nz
Sustainable Winegrowing New Zealand: http://www.nzwine.com/swnz/
carboNZero: http://www.carbonzero.co.nz
Enviro-mark: http://www.landcareresearch.co.nz/research/sustain_business/enviromark/

Conclusions

This chapter has focussed on some of the marketing dimensions of the production process. It has done this because historically the focus of wine producers on their product has been seen in manufacturing rather than service terms. That is primarily in terms of their perception of the quality of the end product rather than the value that a consumer derives from that product. Importantly in the case of wine that value is built over all aspects of the wine production process of which they have an awareness. This includes not only price and geographical location but the characteristics of production in terms of what is grown, how it is grown and the wine making process. The choice of oak and fermentation process, for example, not only contribute to the flavour of the wine but they also become part of the consumer's equity in the product. Similarly, as will be discussed later in the book, the selection of stopper for a bottle is not just an objective exercise in preventing oxidation or bottle

Table 3.3 The New Zealand Wine Company's/Grove Mill's innovations for sustainability

Innovation area	Activity
Heat recovery and waste heat system	Use of reclaimed energy lost through the refrigeration plant is used for heating purposes such as preparing wine prior to bottling and raising the temperature of tanks for fermentation as well as heating water that is used for cleaning purposes in the winery. The major benefit from these process enhancements is a reduction in electricity use.
Packaging	Use of lighter and thinner wine bottles that are able to use smaller cartons. This has resulted in up to 25% more wine being loaded into containers to the UK and USA. Overseas customers can now order more wine per container, which further reduces the company's carbon footprint.
Refrigeration and Temperature Control	Insulated refrigeration lines means lower energy use
Vineyard	The company is trailing a new organic product against Botrytis and uses organic fertiliser. In 2006 they used over 500 tonnes of waste grape marc on vineyards as a mulch.
CarboNZero project	Certification involves addressing climate change impacts with the aim of adding no net carbon dioxide (CO_2) emissions to the atmosphere in the production and distribution of wine. This is achieved by measuring and reducing emissions. All unavoidable emissions were then offset.
Habitat Restoration	Since 1996 a wetland beside the Grove Mill winery has been restored with the planting of over 4000 native plants. The Grove Mill symbol is the Southern Bell frog, which is found in the winery wetland and has become the icon for Grove Mill's philosophy.
Waste Water	The winery has a waste water system
Insulation	The winery and warehouse are both fully insulated. This has meant that no additional energy has been required to either heat or cool the warehouse as the insulation has ensured a constant internal temperature suitable for storing wine.
'Cold Cellar' Winery	Using passive cooling so as to minimise energy requirements for tank cooling
Distribution of products	The installation of a pallet wrapper has reduced the amount of plastic going out of the warehouse by one tonne per annum.
Recycling	Of plastic, paper, cardboard and aluminium

Source: After Grove Mill Sustainable Practices.
http://www.grovemill.co.nz/philosophy/SustainablePractices.aspx

Table 3.4 New Zealand Wine Company's/Grove Mill environmental accreditation programmes and their application

Programme	Energy efficiency	Waste management	Greenhouse gas emissions	Health and safety	Resource conservation	Ecosystem enhancement
Sustainable Winegrowing NZ The programme focuses on a range of environmental issues affecting the wine industry in New Zealand. It promotes a measured approach to use of sprays, water and energy. It also fosters staff awareness, safe chemical handling, plus waste reduction, reuse and recycling.	X	X		X	X	
Green Globe 21 Programme benchmarks environmental impacts	X	X	X	X	X	X
Enviro-Mark NZ Enviro-mark is an Environmental Management System is run by Landcare Research New Zealand. The Enviro-Mark certification process is a step-by-step approach to gaining objective evidence of accomplishments in health, safety and environmental management.	X	X	X	X	X	X
CarboNZero Is a carbon emissions reduction and offset scheme run by Landcare Research New Zealand.	X		X		X	

Source: After http://www.grovemill.co.nz/philosophy/EnvironmentalPolicy.asp

taint. This does not mean the wineries can attempt to differentiate themselves on the quality of their wine and winemaking practices alone – this is a claim that most wine producers can, and do, make about their wine. Rather it highlights the importance of considering the marketing value of all aspects of the winemaking process and utilising those aspects that add value for consumers and differentiate their wine from others in the market place.

Awareness of these issues help create a stronger consumer awareness by producers and also helps all members of the wine value and distribution chain understand how value is developed in wine brands from the vineyard on. The chapter has also focussed on issues of sustainable winegrowing as a way of drawing attention to how production elements are understood in terms of the market and how such initiatives may be used to differentiate product in an international wine market that is characterised by consumer confusion. However, the remainder of the book seeks to build on the concept of sustainable winegrowing in wider business and marketing terms as well as environmental values.

Practical Wine Marketing Insights

- Production processes and decisions in the vineyard and the winery all have marketing implications and wine brand managers should be knowledgeable of these processes and their associated brand value.
- Consumer values in relation to price, brand and geographical indicator are ultimately grounded in the reality of what occurs in the vineyard, winery and region.
- The consumers believability of claims with respect to the nature of the wine product and the processes that have led to its creation can take a long time to establish and can have a valuable reputational quality in influencing purchasing patterns but can be very quickly undermined.
- External accreditation and labelling can be a means of signalling quality with respect to production in the same way that exhibition awards can be an external validator of quality.
- The brand value of a wine is developed from the vineyard on.

Further reading

Banrock Station: http://www.banrockstation.com/
Brand of Constellation Wines that is a leader in using the environment as part of its marketing. The background music and sounds of Australian wildlife are also meant to reinforce the environmental positioning of the brand along with the virtual tour. There is also a wetland visitor centre available for visitation in the real world!

Biodiversity and Wine Initiative (South Africa): http://www.bwi.co.za/
Provides information on this South African project that connects the biodiversity of South Africa, arguably one of the country's most recognised features, with sustainable wine growing and wine promotion

Root:1 wine company: http://www.root1wine.com/
Promotion of ungrafted Chilean wine

Lodi-Woodbridge Winegrape Commission: http://www.lodiwine.com
The Commission has a very good website that provides details not only of sustainable viticulture and regional standards but also on regional wine tourism, festivals and wine club.

Walla Walla Valley Vinea Winegrowers' Sustainable Trust: http://www.vineatrust.com/
The sustainable trust has a very good website with respect to sustainable viticulture and technical guidelines.

Washington Association of Wine Grape Growers: http://www.vinewise.org/index.html
Vinewise – the Washington Guide to Sustainable Viticulture

Waipara Valley Winegrowers: http://www.waiparawine.co.nz/
New Zealand wine region just north of the city of Christchurch recognised for the quality of its riesling and pinot noir. The winegrowers are in active programme of promoting biodiversity including replanting of native vegetation.

Pugh, M. and Fletcher, R. (2002). Green international wine marketing. *Australasian Marketing Journal*, 10(3), 76–85.
A case study of the Banrock Station brand, which has achieved considerable success in its environmental positioning.

Orth, U.R., McGarry Wolf, M. and Dodd, T. (2005). Dimensions of wine region equity and their impact on consumer preferences. *Journal of Product and Brand Management*, 14(2), 88–97.
Findings suggest that wine region equity in terms of benefits sought by wine consumers originates in six motivational factors including environmental value and humane value.

Marshall, R.S., Cordano, M. and Silverman, M. (2005). Exploring individual and institutional drivers of proactive environmentalism in the US wine industry. *Business Strategy and the Environment*, 14(2), 92–109.
Examines the reasons behind the uptake of environmental stewardship in the US wine industry.

Crescimanno, M., Ficani, G.B. and Guccione, G. (2002). The production and marketing of organic wine in Sicily. *British Food Journal*, 104, 274–286.
A case study of the development of organic wine in Sicily and its marketing implications.

Walsdorff, A., van Kraayenburg, M. and Barnardt, C.A. (2005). A multi-site approach towards integrating environmental management in the wine production industry. *Water SA*, 30(5), 82–87.
Discusses the adoption of ISO4001 environmental management system by nine wineries and a bottling plant in the Franschhoek Valley, South Africa.

Tait, S.V., Hughey, K.F.D. and O'Connell, M.J. (2003). A comparison of the advantages and disadvantages of three voluntary environmental management systems used in the NZ wine industry. *The Australian and New Zealand Grapegrower and Winemaker* March, 70–72.
Discusses the advantages and disadvantages of different environmental management systems. Another evaluation arising from the same research can be found at Hughey et al. (2005).

Ardente, F., Beccali, G., Cellura, M. and Marvuglia, A. (2006). POEMS: A case study of an Italian wine-producing firm. *Environmental Management*, 38(3), 350–364.
An Italian case study of the environmental life cycle of a 750 millilitre bottle of red wine.

Cellar door: direct sales, brand building and relationships

Chapter objectives

After reading this chapter you will

- Appreciate the value of the cellar door as a marketing tool
- Understand some of the keys to maximising cellar door sales
- Understand how the cellar door can be used as a tool for building a winery's brand
- Understand how the cellar door is key to developing relationships with customers and the flow on effect of this for post-visit purchases and brand loyalty
- Appreciate the cellar door as a tool for gathering market intelligence

The marketing context of the cellar door

Variously known as cellar doors (especially in Australia, New Zealand and South Africa), tasting rooms (especially in North America), *caves* (France) or *cantine* (Italy) (we will use 'cellar door' from here on), a winery's shop front is one of the most important tools for sales, marketing and communication. Indeed the cellar door has become an important conduit for wine sales, for developing and maintaining relationships with clients and for reflecting and showcasing a winery's brand image.

Many wineries, especially those in the New World (e.g. Australia, New Zealand, South Africa and North America), are taking advantage of the relationship between wine and tourism and are now hosting visitors to their cellar door. European wine producers also host visitors and in some cases this has been happening for many years. Champagne Pommery in Reims, for example, have been hosting visitors to their caves since the 19th century and the large reliefs that were carved into the chalk *crayére* (underground wine cellars) to provide artistic decoration for the earliest visitors are still used to tell part of the Pommery story in tours of the caves.

Table 4.1 shows that there are several wine regions around the world that receive millions of visitors each year and therefore the winery visitor market cannot be ignored. The Napa Valley is undoubtedly the most highly visited wine region in the world. So much so that it has arguably become a victim of its own success and, with growing pressure on the wineries and infrastructure of the region, steps were take to demarket it so that the impacts of visitors could be reduced (Carlsen and Ali-Knight, 2004).

Table 4.1 Estimates of winery visitor numbers

Location	Year	Number of visits per annum	Source
USA			
California	1998	8 million	Skinner (2000)
Napa Valley	1998	5 million	Skinner (2000)
Sonoma and Napa	2001	10 million	Taylor et al. (2004)[1]
New York	2001	3 million	Taylor et al. (2004)[2]
Missouri	2001	1.8 million	Taylor et al. (2004)[2]
Ohio	2001	1.5 million	Taylor et al. (2004)[2]
Australia			
All visitors	1995	5.3 million	Macionis and Cambourne (2000)[3]
International only	1996	390,400	Foo (1999)
Domestic only	2003	4.3 million	Department of Industry, Tourism and Resources (2005)
International only	2003	524,000	Department of Industry, Tourism and Resources (2005)
Victoria	2002	2.2 million	Tourism Victoria (2003)
New Zealand			
Domestic	1997	2.5 million	Johnson (1998)
International	1997	554,000	Johnson (1998)
All visitors	2005	5.5 million	Mitchell (2004)
South Africa			
All visitors	2000	5.2 million	Bruwer (2003)
Stellenbosch	1999	1.7 million	Demhardt (2003)
Italy	1996	2.5 million	Cambourne et al. (2000)[4]

Location	Year	Number of trips including a winery	Source
All Australia	2003	4.8 million	Collins (2005)
Tasmania	1999	90,000	Patterson (2000)
South West (WA)	2000	1.4 million	Donaldson (2004)[5] (domestic trips only)
Adelaide (SA)	2000	629,000	Donaldson (2004)[5] (domestic trips only)
Hunter (NSW)	2000	565,000	Donaldson (2004)[5] (domestic trips only)
Perth (WA)	2000	626,000	Donaldson (2004)[5] (domestic trips only)

(*Continued*)

Table 4.1 (Continued)

Location	Year	Number of trips including a winery	Source
Barossa Valley (SA)	2000	143,000	Donaldson (2004)[5] (domestic trips only)
Peninsula (VIC)	2000	332,000	Donaldson (2004)[5] (domestic trips only)
NZ (domestic)	2001	259,000	Mitchell (2004)[6]
NZ (International)	2001	91,000	Mitchell (2004)[6]
Stellenbosch	1999	516,000	Demhardt (2003)

NSW: New South Wales; NZ: New Zealand; SA: South Australia; VIC: Victoria; WA: Western Australia.
[1]After *Wall Street Journal* (2001).
[2]After Shriver (2002) and includes visitors to wine festivals.
[3]After Australian Winemakers' Federation (1996).
[4]After Colombini, personal communication (1997).
[5]After BTR National Visitor Survey (2000).
[6]After Tourism Research Council New Zealand (TRCNZ) (2002, 2003).
Source: Adapted from Mitchell (2006, p. 31).

While wine sales are an important function of the cellar door, there are many other advantages to be gained from taking part in wine tourism (see Table 4.2). Table 4.2 also acknowledges that there are some disadvantages to operating a cellar door and, as Fraser and Alonso (2003) suggest, wineries need to weigh up the pros and cons of offering cellar door services and consider whether or not it will assist them to meet their overall business objectives and marketing strategy. Notwithstanding this, this chapter will highlight the advantages of operating a cellar door and discuss how these can be implemented so as to have their greatest marketing benefit. This chapter also highlights the importance of:

- *Promotion*: The role of personal selling skills at the cellar door.
- *People*: Cellar door staff as sales staff, brand ambassadors, relationship managers, educators and story tellers.
- *Place*: The role of cellar door in creating a sense of place and place-based brand identity.
- *Production*: The production process as a cellar door tourist attraction and marker of authenticity.

Table 4.2 Advantages and disadvantages of wine tourism for wineries

Advantages

- *Increased consumer exposure* to product and increased opportunities to sample product.
- *Brand awareness and loyalty* built through establishing links between producer and consumer, and purchase of Company-branded merchandise.
- *Increased margins* through direct sale to consumer, where the absence of distributor costs is not carried over entirely to the consumer.
- An *additional sales outlet* or, for smaller wine producers who cannot guarantee volume or constancy of supply, the only feasible sales outlet.
- *Marketing intelligence on products.* Wine producers can gain instant and valuable feedback on the consumer reaction to their existing products, and are able to trial new additions to their product range.
- *Marketing intelligence on customers.* Visitors to the winery can be added to a mailing list which can be developed as a customer database to both target and inform customers.
- *Educational opportunities.* Visits to wineries help create awareness and appreciation of wine and the wine industry, the knowledge and interest generated by this can be expected to result in increased consumption.

Disadvantages

- *Increased costs and management time.* The operation of a tasting room may be costly, particularly when it requires paid staff. While the profitability gap is higher on direct sales to the consumer, profit may be reduced if wineries do not charge for tastings.
- *Capital required.* Suitable facilities for hosting visitors may be prohibitively expensive, especially as wine-making is a capital intensive business.
- *Inability to substantially increase sales.* The number of visitors a winery can attract is limited and if a winery cannot sell all of its stock it will eventually need to use other distribution outlets.

Source: Hall et al. (2000, 11 after Dodd and Bigotte, 1995, Day, 1996).

Before discussing the different marketing functions of the cellar door it is useful to know something about the cellar door market and what motivates them to visit a winery. This is not intended to provide a full understanding of the winery visitor and it deliberately steers away from presenting large amounts of demographic data (see Further Reading at the end of this chapter for sources of more detailed wine tourism market information), but it does set the scene for discussion of the marketing functions of the cellar door.

Key motivations for the cellar door visit

Early stereotypical descriptions of winery visitors ranged from 'wine connoisseurs' (Edwards, 1989) to 'the passing tourist trade who thinks a "winery crawl" is just a good holiday' (McKinna, 1987, p. 85) and on to 'mobile drunks' (Spawton, 1986, p. 57). It is uncertain whether these descriptions are a reflection of the consumer of the time or just observations of the extremes. However, one thing is certain, recent research into cellar door visitors, who are referred too as wine tourists, is able to provide more accurate descriptions of visitors based on empirical data, perhaps dispelling the myths of the two extremes of the connoisseur and the drunkard.

Motivations for visiting wineries are important in understanding consumer behaviour and this understanding can be used by wineries to more effectively target winery visitors that are of the highest benefit to them. Table 4.3 summarises the motivations for visiting cellar doors that have been identified in four Australasian studies. The motivations that are most frequently

Table 4.3 Ranking of motivations for those visiting wineries

Motivation	Victoria (n = 1552)*	Canberra (n = 85)*	Canberra (n = 13)	New Zealand (n = 82)	Internal/ external
Tasting wine	1	1	1	1	External
Buying wine	2	2	1	2	External
A day out	–	3	7	3	–
Socialising	3	–	6	7	Internal
Learning about wine	4	6	5	4	Internal
Relaxation	–	–	3	5	Internal
Winery tour	6	–	9	6	External
Meeting wine-maker	7	5	4	8	Internal
Eating at winery	5	–	–	11	External
Picnic/BBQ	9	–	10	10	External
Entertaining	8	–	–	–	–
Rural setting	–	4	–	–	External

*Victoria and Canberra are based on visitors' self-reported motivations. Canberra and New Zealand based on wineries' perception of motivation.
Source: Mitchell (2004, p. 72) after: Victoria = Maddern and Golledge (1996); Canberra = Macionis (1994, 1996)* and New Zealand = Johnson (1998).

cited tend to be (external) 'pull factors' that draw the winery visitor to the winery and are in general characteristics or activities
of the winery. They are also the motives that people find easiest
to identify and articulate (i.e. they are usually more tangible)
and this can be one of the reasons that they are most often cited.
These include things like tasting and buying wine, tours and
dining services and the things that are income earners for wineries. However, according to Johnson (1998, p. 34), the study of:

... internal motivations [or 'push factors'] in addition to pull factors ...
allows operators to identify new products that can fulfill the same basic
needs. [A] level of abstraction also allows us to compare tourist motivation across a wide range of tourism types and to better understand
tourist demand. The study of internal motivations would reveal the simi-
larities in and differences between wine tourist demand and general
tourist demand, within different wine tourism market segments.

Hall (1996) also provides a typology of wine tourists based
on their motivations for visiting wineries and wine regions and
their behaviour. Based on Hall's work it is possible to identify
three segments:

1. The *'wine lover'*: Who is extremely wine interested (wine is a
   serious hobby and may be a career) and who is an experienced winery visitor, visiting the region solely for wine.
   They are likely to be mature with high income and education
   levels and are highly likely to purchase at the winery and
   add their name to any mailing list.
2. The *'wine interested'*: Who have a high interest in wine
   (include wine in wider lifestyle choices), who are likely to
   have visited other wine regions but wine is not the sole purpose of the visit to the destination. They will likely be in the
   moderate to high-income bracket and tend to be university
   educated. They are likely to purchase at the winery and add
   name to any mailing list and may become a repeat purchaser
   through having visited winery.
3. *'Curious tourist'*: Moderately interested in wine, who is
   motivated to visit the region by non-wine factors and wineries seen as 'just another attraction'. Their curiosity for the
   visit is likely to have been aroused by drinking or seeing winery product or general tourism promotion or pamphlets.
   They are likely to have a moderate income and education and
   they may purchase at the winery but will not join mailing list.
   Adapted from Hall (1996)

Following the publication of Hall's typology, which was based
on observations of winery visitors, Christensen et al. (2004)

attempted to measure the relative proportion of each of these segments by asking New Zealand wineries how they perceive the knowledge of their market (i.e. advanced knowledge for wine lovers, intermediate for wine interested and basic for curious tourists. Christensen et al. (2004) found that wineries felt that wine lovers accounted for around 27% of the perceived market, wine interested visitors accounted for around 65% and curious tourists the remainder. Similarly, Houghton (2002) identified the validity of the typology in a study of attendees at wine festivals (see also Chapter 7).

Mitchell (2004) used measures of wine knowledge in a nation-wide survey of New Zealand winery visitors conducted in 1999. He found that 52% had intermediate wine knowledge, 40% basic or no wine knowledge and 8% advanced wine knowledge. Of particular note in Mitchell's findings was the fact that many of the characteristics that had been ascribed to the wine lover from Hall's observations were also apparent in those with intermediate wine knowledge, suggesting that it is important to recognise these categories as part of a continuum rather than absolute distinctions. As a result of these characteristics and despite the small size of the advanced knowledge segment in Mitchell's study he concludes that they are an extremely important market as they exhibit behaviours that will be highly lucrative for wineries (see Table 4.4).

Charters and Ali-Knight (2002) also provided empirical support for Hall's typology in a survey of visitors to Margaret River (Western Australia) wineries. However they used interest in wine, rather than wine knowledge, to identify these segments and measure their behaviour. Their analysis found that not all wine lovers had an advanced level of wine knowledge and therefore they were able to identify a sub-segment of the wine lover that were all highly knowledgeable. This sub-segment was dubbed the 'Connoisseur' and, along with the newly identified 'Hanger-on', formed part of a new five-category segmentation (see Table 4.5). It is worth noting that there is some agreement between the Mitchell (2004) and Charters and Ali-Knight (2002) studies relating to the relative proportion of the moderately interested or intermediate knowledge wine interested segment (this is also supported by several other studies). However, Charters and Ali-Knights wine lover segment is significantly larger than that indicated by Mitchell's advanced knowledge segment.

Importantly, Charters and Ali-Knight's research provides an attempt to describe the lifestyle characteristics of these segments by analysing the wider wine behaviour and attributes of the winery visit that are considered to be important by each segment (see Table 4.4). For example, for wine lovers (including

Table 4.4 Potential of advanced wine knowledge segment

	Behaviour			
Wine purchasing and consumption	More than half are wine club participants	All consume wine at least once a week	Largest purchasers of wine	Shop for wine at a wide range of outlets
	Half of those participate >6 times per year	Half consume wine daily	Average 1.5 cases per month	Half have wine cellars of >250 bottles
			Most likely to buy at cellar door	
Winery visitation	Multiple visits to wineries each year	Least seasonal preferences	Most likely to spend more than NZ$60	
	Half visit more than 4 times			
	10% visit >12 times per year			
Pre-planning of visit	Almost 60% planned before leaving home	Use a range of sources to plan their visit	Almost a third use magazines as a source of information	
Regional travel behaviour	Most likely to be motivated by wine to visit a region	The longest average length of stay in the region	A range of commercial accommodation	
	Double all other segments	Average stay 5.4 nights	Stronger preference for hotels and B&Bs	

Source: Adapted from Mitchell (2004).

Table 4.5 Wine interest segments in a survey of winery visitors at Margaret River

Segment	%	Key Wine & Wine Tourism Behaviour
Wine lover	31	• Highly likely to attend wine courses, tastings and watch TV programmes on wine. • Winery visits are for buying, tasting and learning about wine. • Food and wine matching information important.
Connoisseur (sub-segment)	3	• As above but greater 'thirst for knowledge' (especially wine production and grape growing).
Wine interested	53	• Highly likely to have attended tastings. • Highly likely to have visited a winery before. • Food less important at wineries than others. • Learning is important (especially storing and ageing wine).
Wine novice (Hall's curious tourist)	15	• Likely to have attended tastings. • Winery motivation visit less clear. • Tours more important. • Tasting less important. • Eating at winery more important.
Hanger-on	2	• Goes to winery with no interest in wine. • Part of a group that decided to visit.

Source: Adapted from Charters and Ali-Knight (2002); Hall (1996).

connoisseurs), 'one could tentatively suggest that the entire "lifestyle package" is particularly important for the "wine lovers" – more so than the other segments. Food and gaining wine knowledge are key components of their motivation in making the visit' (Charters and Ali-Knight, 2002, p. 315).

Charters and Ali-Knight's wine interest research also identifies some of the internal and external motives of winery visitors. Internal motives (push factors) that they identified include various aspects of learning about wine (e.g. storing and aging, wine-making and grape growing, and wine and food matching). These internal motives were more appealing to wine lovers, while external motives such as tours of the winery or vineyard were more appealing to Wine Novices. Johnson (1998, p. 15) makes a similar distinction in the motivations of winery visitors when he makes the distinction between:

• a *wine tourist* 'who visits a vineyard, winery, wine festival or wine show for the purpose of recreation' and

- a *specialist wine tourist* 'who visits a vineyard, winery, wine festival or wine show for the purpose of recreation and whose primary motivation is a specific interest in grape wine or grape wine-related phenomena.'

Mitchell (2004) asked New Zealand winery visitors what their main motivation for visiting the wine region they were surveyed in was and found that 23% had wine-specific motivations, while the rest were motivated by general touring, visiting their friends and relatives, an event or other reason. Importantly however, Mitchell found few differences in the behaviour between the wine-motivated visitors and those motivated to visit for other reasons.

While the above research findings and the scores of research projects that describe the winery visitor are useful for wineries, Mitchell (2004) warns to be weary of the 'myth of the typical winery visitor' and to make sure that decisions are made on the basis of a picture of Mr and Mrs Average. These 'typical' winery visitors rarely exist and recognising the different needs, expectations and motivations of consumers is critical to a successful cellar door sales and marketing programme. This requires a commitment to market research and strategies that allow the winery to effectively identify and target the most lucrative visitor markets (see Box 4.1 for an example of how Hillebrand Winery implements such a strategy).

Gathering market intelligence at the cellar door

The cellar door provides an excellent opportunity to gather market intelligence about a winery's potential market. Aside from the descriptions of the potential of certain segments of winery visitors presented above, research has also found that there is a degree of planning prior to the visit. For example, studies in Victoria (Australia), South Australia and New Zealand have found that around three out of four visitors to wineries pre-planned their visit to a particular winery, compared with almost one in every two in Texas (Mitchell, 2004). Meanwhile Mitchell (2004) also found that around 40% of New Zealand winery visitors had planned their visit to a particular winery before leaving home to visit the wine region. This suggests that there has been a high degree of pre-selection and that the majority of visitors already have some degree of predisposition and, in some cases, commitment to the winery that they are visiting and its wines. As such they can be considered to be a market of high potential for on-going sales and therefore should be a target for marketing efforts. As they are also a 'captured audience' gathering information about them should prove to be very useful.

There are a number of wineries that already collect market intelligence at the cellar door and these can range from very simple systematic surveys to quite lengthy and detailed surveys and analyses of visitors. One example of winery that undertakes relatively simple, yet effective market research at the cellar door is Yering Station in the Yarra Valley just outside of Melbourne (Australia). Four times a year Yering Station implements a short survey at the cellar door that is based largely on three simple questions:

1. Where do you come from?
2. How did you hear about Yering Station?
3. What age group are you in?

As a result, Yering Station can reliably say that in 2004 57% of their visitors are from Melbourne and Suburbs, 23% are from interstate and 20% from overseas. They can also say that 25–35 year olds are the largest age group visiting Yering Station and, more importantly, they know that 70% of people heard about Yering Station by word of mouth, while the remainder used brochures, the Visit Victoria website (http://www.visitvictoria.com/) and advertising. This allows them to fine tune their advertising and promotional activities in terms of geographical location (i.e. which newspapers are of greatest value), the media to advertise in (if at all) and the content of advertising and promotional material (i.e. targeted at the appropriate age group). This is a simple, yet highly effective approach to market research that is relatively easy for staff to complete and for visitors to take part in. The survey occurs for a month each season and therefore gives them an idea of seasonal trends as well as an overall picture for the year. The secret to this research is that it is regular, systematic and easy to analyse. (See Further Reading on where to find more information about Yering Station's successful approach to cellar door management.)

Yering Station also regularly takes part in Tourism Victoria's extensive wine tourism research which allows them to get a sense of where they fit within the region and state as a whole and gives them more detail on visitors to their cellar door. Local, regional, state and national tourism offices often undertake research of visitors to wine regions and may enlist the help of wineries to distribute questionnaires. Provided that the winery receives reports on the findings, these present another excellent and cost effective way to gather market intelligence.

Undertaking research at the cellar door is as useful for wineries in remote parts of regions with a relatively few visitors as it is for those on main roads with large numbers of visitors. In the case of the former it will be important to find out about the visitors that have made the effort to visit a winery off the beaten track as they have clearly made a concerted effort to find the winery and are therefore already likely to be committed. The more a winery can find out about these visitors the better. For the latter it is important, as there is likely to be a cross-section of visitors with varying degrees of commitment and therefore ongoing market potential and it is useful to be able to identify what drives those with high degrees of commitment compared to those with lower levels of commitment.

In all cases, however, there are some very simple questions and techniques that can be used to gather information. Of course the opportunities for data collection are endless, but we feel that the following are a great starting point for a winery that is just starting to gather market intelligence at the cellar door.

Postcodes

The simplest question to ask is a visitor's postcode. This can help in terms of identifying geographical areas to target for advertising and promotion, but in many countries it is also possible to obtain some level of free information on socio-demographic characteristics of people living at these postcodes. There are also many consulting companies that specialise in providing data on postcode demographics and lifestyle statistics (see www.caci.co.uk/acorn/default.asp for UK example). This is only really useful however when the data is aggregated and patterns are identified (i.e. large concentrations in one area) as making assumptions from census data about individuals would be erroneous.

If the postcode is also able to be recorded on your POS (point of sale) management system or cash register with details such as the wine style purchased and how much was spent, then the picture that can be created is quite powerful: identifying preferences for particular wines with particular areas and/or the location of the biggest spenders.

Competitor/complementor analysis

Asking which wineries visitors have visited or intend to visit on their trip can reveal several things about your market, including who your competitors are, what type of winery they have a preference for (e.g. small family owned versus larger) and perhaps even the sorts of wines that they drink. It may also reveal the other wineries that would be most appropriate to undertake joint activities with when promoting the cellar door.

It is also useful to ask visitors which wines they preferred at the wineries that they visited. This can reveal wine style preferences that may not be revealed by asking the same questions about a winery's own wines, as people have a tendency to answer what they think that a winery wants to hear about their wines. This technique can be used also to determine which wines they might be more easily persuaded to purchased while at the cellar door.

This market intelligence also relies on knowledge of what other wineries in the region offer and keeping abreast of their wines. This is useful in terms of assessing what your local competition is doing (although in Chapter 10 we will suggest that local wineries should not always be considered as competitors), but also can help in determining how your own wine offerings stack up in terms of what your visitor market prefers.

Mailing list databases and surveys

Effectively managed mailing list databases are a very important tool for gathering information about your market. Databases, however, are only as good as the information that is entered into them. These should not simply be considered as mail merge lists for posting out information. Rather each list member should have data on their demographics (e.g. age, occupation and gender), their purchases at the cellar door (including merchandise) and their mail order purchases. Most, if not all, of this information can be gathered without even asking them a single question. However, mailing list sign up forms should include the following questions:

- Name
- Postal address (for mail order delivers and to gather postcode information)
- E-mail address (for newsletters and other correspondence)
- Key demographics (age, gender and occupation)
- Wine preferences (a simple tick box on the following red/ white, sweet/dry/off-dry, varieties)

Individuals that sign up to mailing lists are also indicating at least some degree of commitment to the company and therefore their opinions should also be of interest and regular surveys of their wine preferences, feelings about the company's offerings and purchasing behaviour would also be beneficial. This should be relatively easy to do, but where the company does not possess market research expertise, it is recommended that assistance is sought. In addition, it is also important to assure customers that such information will be kept confidential.

The cellar door as a sales outlet

Many wineries consider sales to be the most basic and fundamental function of a cellar door (although Table 4.1 suggests that sales are one of many functions of the cellar door). Box 4.1 shows that Hillebrand Winery (Canada) makes 30% of its revenue from cellar door activities, while cellar door sales account 65% of all sales from English wineries (Mitchell, 2004). Studies in New Zealand have found that cellar door sales account for on average around 15–20% of wine sales but that there are examples where more than 75% of revenue is gained through the cellar door (Mitchell, 2004). One winery in New Zealand also reported that just one bottle of their Reserve Pinot sold at the cellar door gave them the same return as seven bottles of their normal Pinot Noir sold via their New Zealand distributor even though the retail price for the reserve is only around 2.5 times that of the normal Pinot. As such direct sales can improve margins considerably as intermediaries and retailers take their cut, but it should be noted that cellar door operations are not without their own costs (i.e. the cost of cellar door operations must be factored in) and the margins may not always be as great as many wineries anticipate. Regardless cellar door sales can represent a significant proportion of a winery's sales and can and should be a very valuable contributor to profits.

The cellar door can also prompt those that have never purchased a winery's wine before to taste and then purchase the wine. For these new consumers of a wine and those with more experience, the tasting is the important factor in the cellar door purchasing experience as this allows the consumer to 'try before they buy'. Tasting is important because (premium) wine is an inherently risky purchase for people (Mitchell and Greatorex, 1989) as it is a discretionary spend (financial risk), has a high degree of symbolic meaning (social risk), it is used by many drinkers to indicate social status and/or cultural capital (social risk) and there is a high probability of error in its purchase (functional risk); much like haute-couture fashion (Charters, 2006). Mitchell and Greatorex (1989) also found in a study of UK consumers that the opportunity to taste wine was considered the most important way of reducing perceived risk (functional,

Box 4.1 Hillebrand: cellar door success

Hillebrand Estates in the Niagara-on-the-Lake region of Ontario, Canada, was established in 1982 following investment from a Swiss company. Now owned by Canada's Andrés Wines, Hillebrand Estates has one of the largest product lists of VQA wines in Canada and an enviable reputation for the quality of the wine experience provided to visitors. Below is an extract from a longer case study of Hillebrand Estates that outlines the five key contributors to their success.

Hillebrand and the wine experience business

Hillebrand Winery is proud to be in the 'wine experience business' and their philosophy is to provide the best 'experience' possible. Hillebrand is located near the township of Niagara-on-the-Lake (Ontario) which receives 3 million visitors per annum (less than 25% of its neighbour Niagara Falls). Hillebrand itself receives around 200,000 visitors a year and 30% of their revenue comes from sales at the winery.

A research focus

Overspending on research and planning has paid off – market segmentation has moved away from demographics to a focus on level of involvement with wine. Quarterly research focuses on 'wine lovers' – visitors who spend more than $100 on their visit. Research showed that 'wine lovers' purchased more wine than they expected not because of the quality of the wine but the quality of the staff/service.

The 'wine lover' rules

The '17:71 rule' is a key to why Hillebrand are so focussed on the wine lover. Analysis of their business resulted in the development of the 17:71 rule. In other words: 17% of Hillebrand's customers are responsible for 71% of revenue and around 90% of profit. Staff are trained to spot 'wine lovers' and, when identified, they are presented with an invitation to the 'Executive Tasting Lounge.' Sometimes this invitation is a written invitation from staff in the wine boutique (cellar door) or restaurant.

Passionate staff

They attract mature, semi-retired staff rather than younger students. They have a 'passion checker' that sits in on interviews to find the 'great people'. This allows them to develop a wine culture within the staff and this is reinforced by operating a monthly matching event using wines from around the world, matching with foods and comparing to their own wines.

The free independent traveller is king

Hillebrand do not allow weddings and want fewer corporate groups (e.g. conferences) so they can focus on providing the best experience to independent visitors.

A retail design focus

The retail design of the wine boutique (cellar door) has been upgraded to move the current conversion rate from 55% towards the 100% mark enjoyed by stores like Wal-Mart! Wine is king in the restaurant: they use lots of wine in the cooking and match wine with local produce and famed head chef Tony de Luca has even launched a cookbook with chapters that are based on wine varieties that include recipes for each of the four seasons.

http://www.hillebrand.com/
A copy of the full best practice case study can be found at:
http://www.nzte.govt.nz/common/files/tourism-hillebrand.pdf
More food and wine tourism best practice case studies are also available at:
http://www.nzte.govt.nz/section/14454/15090.aspx

financial and social risk) when it came to wine selection. Consumers always try on fashion clothing to see how it makes them look and feel in order to reduce any financial or social risks (i.e. not looking 'right'). Wine is no different. Further, as Charters and Pettigrew (2005) point out, wine can be seen as an aesthetic or quasi-aesthetic product and this has important implications for how it is sold.

Mitchell (1999, p. 174) suggests that '... perceived risk is a necessary antecedent for trust to be operative and an outcome of trust building is a reduction in the perceived risk of the transaction or relationship. As relationships develop and trust builds, risk will decrease.' Therefore trust is a key concept in wine sales at the cellar door and for building the relationships discussed later in this chapter. Developing a rapport and degree of trust with someone who may well be a stranger is a difficult skill and some would suggest not one that can easily be trained. In fact, some have suggested that trust is developed, at least in part, by a staff member who is empathetic (Beatty et al., 1996) which is considered by most to be a personality trait. Empathy has also been found to be an important factor for winery visitors, especially amongst females and those working in sales and clerical or management positions (O'Neill and Charters, 2000). Empathy is also seen as an important antecedent for 'true (non-commercial) hospitality' which can see a stranger socialised to become a friend (Scott, 2006) and therefore much more likely to be satisfied with their experience and committed to the company and its wines.

The above discussion makes one thing very clear: staff selection is critical. Arguably, empathy cannot be trained as it requires the staff member to have an innate ability to put themselves in the shoes of the customer, to put them at easy and understand their needs. An empathetic staff member can create an experience that is not a 'hard sell' but which is highly likely to result in trust and a sale (Beatty et al., 1996). Sadly, for whatever reason, cellar door recruitment processes very rarely use empathy as a criterion for selection.

While empathy is an inherent trait of an individual, sales skills can be taught. These skills are also sadly lacking at many wineries and investment in training would be beneficial for sales at the cellar door. Closing the sale requires skills that many hospitality trained staff that may be employed at cellar doors do not have and therefore it is important to assess the skill needs of staff and provide the necessary training. It can also be useful to train staff to provide alternatives to purchase for those that do not wish to buy (e.g. signing up to the mailing list or a list of distributors in their area).

Relationship marketing at the cellar door

O'Neill and Charters (2001, p. 120) suggest that:

> ... it may be surmised that the perceived level of service quality [at the cellar door] may in fact be a vital antecedent to any purchase being made.
>
> Connected with this is the critical factor of developing good 'relationship marketing' – an *efficient* cellar door should generate a number of one-off sales to visitors, using finely-honed sales techniques. An *effective* cellar door may generate lower immediate sales but, by placing emphasis on factors like empathy and responsiveness, generate very strong subsequent brand loyalty, at far greater profit to the winery in the long term. Winery operators need to understand this rather than focus on the short-term high profit margins generated by the distribution advantages of cellar door sales.
>
> (emphasis added)

An *effective* cellar door, then, is one that focuses on both the sales skills and the empathetic qualities of its staff outlined in the previous section while recognising that the use of metrics such as sales, turn-over and profit to measure cellar door benefits is hiding the real value of the cellar door. Put crudely, a visitor who buys a bottle at the cellar door and returns home as a loyal customer that purchases the winery's wine for life is infinitely more valuable than the visitor who walks out with a case of wine but never buys the brand again! Box 4.2 highlights the potential value of the winery visit and the on-going purchasing behaviour that it can generate.

Box 4.2   Wine consumer behaviour insight

Post-winery visit purchase of wine in New Zealand

Despite widespread recognition that the winery visit plays an integral part in on-going wine consumer behaviour, only three studies have attempted to track visitors' post-visit behaviour. King and Morris (n.d., 1999) studied visitors to wineries in the Augusta/Margaret River wine region tracking their behaviour between October 1996 and May 1998. Their study found that just 13% of visitors to Augusta/Margaret River wineries stated that they made a post-visit purchase of wine from the winery of survey. They concluded that 'these figures are disturbing' (King and Morris, n.d., 8) as the winery visit appears to be more about touring than serious wine tasting and purchasing.

O'Mahony et al. (2006) did not track brand-specific behaviour, but found that 20% of their respondents claimed some quantitative (i.e. consumed more or higher-value wine) and qualitative (i.e. higher quality of wine or type of wine) changes in their wine consumption in the five months post-visit. These findings have important implications for the relationship between the cellar door and wine consumption in general, but not brand-specific impacts.

Perhaps the most comprehensive study of brand-specific purchasing behaviour, however, is a nationwide study of visitors to New Zealand wineries undertaken in 1999 by Mitchell (2004), which found some positive longer-term outcomes of winery visits for wineries.

The study
Mitchell (2004) surveyed 1090 winery visitors at 33 New Zealand wineries in 1999 and 636 of the respondents to the survey were sent a second questionnaire six to eight months after their visit. A total of 358 second round questionnaires were returned. The second questionnaire was used to identify consumption and purchase behaviour and the reasons for purchase and non-purchase, as well as more experiential elements such as recollection of the visit, word-of-mouth behaviour and enduring levels of satisfaction.

Post-visit purchase behaviour
Mitchell's study provides evidence that the winery visitor present both an opportunity for sales at the cellar door and beyond. For example:

- Each respondent purchased an average of 3.5 bottles of wine at the winery:
  - around 10% to be consumed immediately;
  - around 40% to be consumed in under a year;

- – around 40% to be cellared for a year or more;
- – around 10% to be given away as gifts.
- At the time of the visit the vast majority of visitors reported at least some intention to visit again and purchase the winery's wine in the future:
  - – 95% at least some intention to visit in the future (52% strong intention);
  - – 89% at least some intention to purchase at a wineshop in the future (23% strong);
  - – 76% at least some intention to purchase at a restaurant in the future (20% strong);
  - – 34% at least some intention to purchase by mail order in the future (11% strong).
- 46% made a post-visit purchase of the winery's wine, especially:
  - – from restaurants (19%), supermarkets (17%) and specialist wine shops (16%);
  - – by visitors to medium and large wineries;
  - – by domestic visitors, but still more than one in four international visitors;
  - – by females;
  - – by those with intermediate or advanced wine knowledge;
  - – by repeat visitors to the winery (9 out of 10 of those visiting 2 or more times);
  - – by those with stronger intentions to make future purchases at the time of the visit.

One of the other important findings of the study was that post-visit purchases were made at a number of different wine outlet categories. In fact, while most respondents only listed one outlet category, the average was 1.6 categories and one in eight listed more than three categories. This suggests that post-visit purchasing was relatively widespread and, given the short time that had elapsed since the visit, there was a high degree of multiple purchases.

During the year of the study (1999), Mitchell (2004) estimates that there were as many as 10.5 million bottles of wine sold directly from New Zealand cellar doors. He also suggests that post-visit purchases were made by around 1.4 million winery visitors, including almost 160,000 that made purchases at three or more different categories of wine outlets.

It seems, then, that the New Zealand winery visitor presents excellent opportunities for sales that go far beyond the direct sales made at the cellar door, but what reasons did people give for purchasing (or not)?

Reasons for purchase

Not surprisingly 9 out of 10 respondents said that the taste of the wine had more than a moderate influence on there decision to purchase post-visit (67% said the influence was 'strong'). However, taste in itself does not provide the necessary motivation to purchase any given brand of wine. A winery visitor might have tasted anywhere between 5 and 25 wines while in the wine region and in the vast majority of cases they would have been of a high level of production and several were likely to have had a flavour profile that the visitor enjoyed. Mitchell (2006) suggests that, while wines must taste good (i.e. it is a 'hygiene factor' – whose absence leads to dissatisfaction, but whose presence does not guarantee any motivation to purchase a particular brand), other dimensions of the visit are likely to create a true point of different that results in the purchase of wine of a particular brand, variety and style. Availability of the wine and price were also considered to be hygiene factors, although they were less important in the decision to purchase.

Assuming that taste can be eliminated as a true satisfier/motivator, the most important motivator of post-visit purchase was *sharing the wine with others* (52% more than moderate influence). According to Mitchell (2006, p. 100) 'this is perhaps because of the generally social nature of wine consumption and ... this has important implications for the marketing of the wine.' *Service at the winery* (45%), *memory of the winery experience* (41%) and *sharing the winery experience with others* (36%) were also of some influence in the decision to make a post-visit purchase. A combination of these factors could be considered as the satisfiers of the winery experience and therefore influential in the decision to purchase 'Brand Y' over 'Brand X'. The cellar door experience, then, is an important element in motivating post-visit purchase.

The main reasons for non-purchase of wine related to *availability of the winery of survey's wine* (51%) and a *lack of knowledge of where to buy this wine* (42%). This has important implications for wineries as it implies that distribution and awareness of distribution channels are important factors in post-visit purchase and perhaps implies a latent demand for their wine.

Other post-visit behaviour
While purchasing behaviour is only one measure of brand loyalty, Mitchell's findings provide other indicators of brand loyalty (although these still remain as indicators, rather than true measures of loyalty). For example, recommendations to others:

- More than 9 out of 10 made a recommendation about their visit to someone else:
  - recommended the wine (59%), winery (65%) and wine region (56%, 15% only recommended the region);
  - for the recommended winery they recommended staff and service (25.4%), the setting (19.5%), value for money (12.3%) and the food (10.2%);
  - visitors to large winery's were less likely to recommend a visit;
  - post-visit purchasers were more likely to also recommend the wine and winery, but less likely to recommend the wine region.

Satisfaction levels with their experience and the wine from the winery also appeared to be relatively enduring. As such on-site and post-visit evaluations of satisfaction with the wine and the winery experience remained extremely consistent. Positive recollections of their visit related to the service/hospitality and wine (40% of respondents), the setting (33%) and the atmosphere

(25%). While negative recollections were far less frequently cited, they were most likely to relate facilities (39%), food (20%) and price (16%).

For more detail see:

Mitchell, R.D. (2006). Influences on post-visit wine purchase (and non-purchase) by New Zealand winery visitors. In Carlsen, J. and Charters, S. (eds.), *Global Wine Tourism: Research, Management and Marketing*, pp. 95–109, CABI.

Mitchell, R.D. and Hall, C.M. (2004). The post-visit consumer behaviour of New Zealand winery visitors. *Journal of Wine Research*, 15(1), 37–47.

For post-visit impacts on wine consumption more broadly, see also:

O'Mahony, B., Hall, J., Lockshin, L., Jago, L. and Brown, G. (2006). Understanding the impact of wine tourism on post-tour purchasing behaviour. In Carlsen, J. and Charters, S. (eds.), *Global Wine Tourism: Research, Management and Marketing*, pp. 123–127, CABI.

Many of the principles discussed in relation to cellar door sales above also apply to the development of longer-term relationships with consumers. In particular, trust is a key component of the development of on-going relationships. There are many other examples where trust is important and results in a consumer desire to develop a relationship. These might include businesses where there is a high degree of financial risk involved and trust in the information is important (e.g. financial services), where there is a high degree of perceived social/emotional risk and trust in skills and/or personal advice are important (e.g. hair dressers, clothing retailers, cosmetics, etc.) or where there is a combination of a high degree of both financial, functional and social risk and trust in skills and knowledge are important (e.g. real estate and car sales and service – which interestingly represent some of the least trusted professions in many countries). Most frequently, wine fits into the middle category where it is emotional and social risk that are most likely to be in play and therefore wineries need to reflect this at the cellar door.

It is not the wine that the consumer needs to trust (although product quality is of course an important hygiene factor) nor is it the wine that is the focus of the relationship. The brand is important as a source of trust, but only when the brand is imbued with personal experiences with staff, can a true relationship be developed. There is an argument to suggest that amongst some segments of wine consumer, brand is the complete focus of the relationship and these 'Beverage Drinkers' 'know what they like and like what they know' and have a very limited repertoire of brands that they regularly choose from (Spawton, 1991).

However, it is likely that they have developed this relationship following advice from an individual whom they trusted (most probably a close friend or relative). As such the long-term relationships with wine consumers may be perceived as being with the brand, but it is people that are important in either establishing and/or maintaining the trust associated with the wine.

The trick for cellar door operators, then, is to provide service that is a balance between espousing the quality of the wine, educating consumers on its qualities and brand values and a connection with a person or people that they can trust. Many wineries and cellar door training programmes focus on the first two aspects (i.e. the wine and the brand), with little reference to or understanding of the development of trust between winery staff and it may be useful to challenge a few of the principles that are currently espoused as being important at the cellar door. For example, the following, sometimes quite subtle, distinctions are important:

- Cellar doors should provide *hospitality* rather than just good service.
- Experiences should be *authentic* with 'real' stories and 'real' people in 'real' places rather than scripted, slick and shiny (or even contrived) – big and shiny is not always better.
- Learning experiences should be about *interpretation* rather than education – the distinction is very important.

Hospitality

The distinction between hospitality and service has become blurred by the commercialisation of hospitality (Scott, 2006). As Scott (2006, p. 128) suggests:

The (recent) ability to industrialise many components of commercial hospitality has led to increasing rationalisation. As a result, Korczynski's (2004) myth of consumer sovereignty is all pervasive in modern hospitality organisations and organisational efficiencies aimed at creating consumer satisfaction are privileged over culturally constructed concepts of hospitality. Perhaps the most disturbing symptom of this lauding of the consumer as king/queen is the ubiquitous satisfaction questionnaire that confuses service delivery for hospitality. Hospitality is thus commercialised as a consumer good within the economic system.

This means that when businesses talk of providing hospitality, they are generally referring to and training for the material and process-oriented elements of 'commercial hospitality' (Scott, 2006) (in this case the serving of wine and possibly food).

However, true hospitality (or 'performative hospitality' using Scott's terminology) is an 'act' that is, amongst other things: interactive, playful, mystical, temporal, doing, spiritual and authentic. As such it requires both an individual and organisational philosophy that allows for the '(re)enchantment of the hospitality experience' through a dynamic and honest ('inter-subjective') interplay between host and guest (Scott, 2006). This type of interplay is powerful, creating true and meaningful relationships between host (winery) and guest (visitor) that transcend the commercial imperative and which create true comparative (rather than competitive) advantage (Scott, 2006). Like empathy (which is perhaps a precondition for this type of hospitality) it is highly unlikely that this can be 'trained' but is dealt with by careful staff selection and an environment that allows for hospitableness.

A hospitality approach, rather than a service approach, also has implications for the design and management of the cellar door space. In particular, true hospitality is most often associated with the 'home', as the roots of true hospitality lie in welcoming the stranger into your home (Scott, 2006). As such design elements should replicate this sense of home. This can be as simple as the addition of personal photographs, fresh flowers or personal mementos or it could actually mean having the cellar door in the owners home. In the Gibbston Valley of New Zealand one winery, *The Wine House and Kitchen* (see *Plate 4.1)*, has even shifted an old house to their cellar door site and 'recreated every Kiwi's grandparents' home', right down to the 1950s wallpaper and electrical appliances (see www.winehouse.co.nz). Scale is also important and, where possible large spaces should be designed to ensure that they have a human scale and homely feel. Large winery buildings can also be very intimidating to some visitors from the outside and design elements can be used to once again give them a more intimate and welcoming feel from the outside. For example mature trees, meandering pathways and hedges can be used to screen and soften large geometric structures and create a more human scale or a sense mystery and mystique.

Authentic experience

The search for authenticity of experiences is part of the postmodern condition and is widely discussed and debated in the tourism and services marketing literature (Schmitt and Simonson, 1997; Lewis and Bridger, 2000; Boyle, 2003; Hall, 2007). In fact the term is very difficult to pin down and in reality has many meanings and is highly subjective. However, there is no escaping the fact that most consumers of premium wines will be seeking genuine experiences. Authenticity in this sense does not just relate to the wine and its production, rather it relates to the consumer's desire to experience a part of the symbolic value of the wine – the reality of its production, the real people behind the wine and the place that it comes from. As Hall (2007) commented, when considering authenticity it is important to consider the extent to which meaning is acquired through experience. 'The role of experience is particularly important because of its capacity to provide shared meanings through shared experiences. Yet replication is not intrinsically bad, what is important is the different experiential depth (i.e. historical depth, spatial depth, cultural depth, environmental depth, educational depth) between the original and the replication'.

Many visitors want to be enchanted (not entertained) by the stories that connect the land, the people and the wine, often wanting to become part of the story themselves. As Hall (2007) noted, authenticity is derived from the property of connectedness of the individual to the perceived, everyday world and environment, and the processes that created it and the consequences of one's engagement with it. This is played out through spontaneous acts, rather than contrived or scripted stories, that require all staff to be part of the story rather than employed to tell it. Most powerful are 'backstage' acts (MacCannell, 1973) that somehow seem more real, meaningful and memorable. Such acts might include a peek behind the scenes at the barrel hall; watching the winemaker 'doing his/her thing', however mundane he/she may think it is; a barrel tasting; tasting of grapes during harvest; observing or, better still, taking part in vintage; or tasting some museum stock that the wine-maker has been using as a baseline for the current vintage's blending. The list is endless, but it must not be (perceived as) contrived – today's consumers can spot fakery a mile away!

Interpretation

Closely linked with these discussions of hospitality and authenticity, is the critical distinction between interpretation and education. Unfortunately, the term education is often misused in such a way that it implies that the winery is in control of what the visitor learns. In contrast, interpretation is an educative process that allows for much more of a dialogue between host and guest that is much more of a process of discovery than what, if not careful, becomes a process of indoctrination. Interpretation therefore is imbued with the spirit of co-creation of experiences rather than an almost unidirectional relationship that is often implied in discussions of wine market or brand education. As Bill Nesto M.W. (in Calder, 1999, n.p.) commented, 'Brand specific knowledge doesn't free people or empower them … It breeds blind loyalty.'

According to Pitcher (2002) the work of Freeman Tilden, the 'father of interpretation', is useful here. Tilden (1957, p. 9) identifies six principles of interpretation that suggest that interpretation should somehow relate to a visitor's personality; is 'revelation based upon information', not information itself; is an art which can be taught; is about provocation, not instruction; should present 'a whole rather than a part' and, if addressed to children, should follow a fundamentally different, but undiluted, approach. These principles, except the last perhaps, have direct relevance to the cellar door and how the market can be engaged in the wine experience.

Wine interpretation at the cellar door is important for a number of reasons, including enhancing the overall tourism experience; self-development and learning for the individual; and appropriate advice on wine selection (Mitchell and Hall, 2001). However the real benefits of interpretation lie in its ability to be insightful, engaging and emotive, things which are not normally associated with education, but which are also highly conducive to relationship building. Once again empathy and understanding of the individual are critical; without this it is impossible to deliver effective interpretation. Interpretation is a dialogue, where the interpreter (cellar door staff) constantly assesses the level of understanding of the individual and how they can best adapt the information to the personality of the visitor. Table 4.6 provides some examples of how interpretation principles might be applied at the cellar door.

Other aspects of relationship marketing

Relationship marketing is about establishing, building and maintaining long-term loyal relationships with customers. Grönroos (1996, p. 5) suggests that there are '… three typical tactical elements of a relationship strategy: (1) seek direct contacts with customers and other stakeholders …; (2) build a database covering necessary information about customers and others; (3) develop a customer-oriented service system.' The cellar door allows the first of these to occur, while much of the discussion above has addressed the third point. We have also suggested above that mailing lists present an excellent opportunity to develop a database, but that it is only as good as the information that is entered into it.

Table 4.6 Examples of how interpretation and unidirectional education differ

Information	Education example	Interpretation example
Wine tasting	Describe how to taste	Insights into the cultural constructs that have driven the importance of wine tasting (why is wine tasting important to us?).
Flavour profiles	Describe the wine	Explain why particular flavours are present.
Vintage	Vintage information	Explain how vintage at the vineyard fits into the wider region.
Winemaking	Describe winemaking	Use stories of real events to bring the process to life.
The winery	History of the winery	Personal history of the winemaker alongside the history of the winery.
The region	Describe the wine region	Describe how wine fits into the local culture and economy or tell stories about local wine identities.

Using the mailing list as an effective relationship maintenance tool also requires the application of many of the principles discussed above. For example, newsletters should use interpretation, rather than simply provide information, to engage the reader: include stories about the people and the place and not just the wine; include candid photographs of what is happening on the vineyard and at the cellar door; and, where possible, personalise communication in some way. This latter point can be done by keeping detailed information about the client's preferences and using mail merges with e-mail software to customise content accordingly. In short, make them feel special and unique!

Events can be another way of maintaining the relationship. These might include events at the cellar door or at or near major market concentrations. Once again these should not just be about the wine, but should, where possible, include members of staff that have some association with either the winemaking or the cellar door. Remember clients have a relationship with the people not the wine.

Regardless of what approach is taken for ongoing communication, consistency is key. The message that is delivered at the cellar door must come through in both the content and delivery of the communication.

Relationship marketing is also more than just relationships between companies and their clients and also involves business-to-business (B2B) relationships with suppliers, inter-mediaries and retailers (Grönroos, 1996). In addition, relation-ship marketing is also integral to the development of cooperative marketing strategies undertaken by wine busi-nesses. As such relationship marketing will be returned to in Chapters 5, 6 and 10.

Brand building

The above discussion of aspects of relationship marketing and cellar door sales all contribute towards brand building for wineries and the cellar door represents the best opportunity to do this. The cellar door is particularly useful as wineries have full control over everything from how the wine itself is pre-sented, pricing and the brand image that they wish to associate with it. The approach introduced in this chapter allows wine brands to develop a 'personality' and to become associated with real people, places and events that have the added power of authenticity (see Plate 4.2). It is the combination of these ele-ments that create (and are created by) a winery's 'sense of place' and reinforcement of this along the wine value chain. This sense of place goes beyond just the physical attributes of place, in the same way that *terroir* is more than the soil and climate of a region (see also Chapter 10), requiring a human touch.

This approach removes the need for complicated and often expensive brand-building exercises constructed around scripted and contrived stories – the brand becomes built on philosophy, people and place. Communicating this at the cellar door is infin-itely easier than by other means, so this should start at the cellar door and other communications surrounding the brand (e.g. websites, newsletters, promotions, etc.) should be built on this experience.

The cellar door is also a location where influential media can be hosted to immerse them in the brand. This need not be limit-ed to wine media (who might not necessarily be that interested in brand values anyway), but should be extended to travel, food and lifestyle media who might be attracted by the wider experience and brand values surrounding the wine rather than the wine itself. One way to attract such media is to become involved with local and destination marketing organisations (DMOs) who have structured visiting media programmes that bring media on familiarisation tours of regions. Often the only cost involved in hosting these media representatives is some form of contra (e.g. a free tour, meal or tasting). These media should be treated with the same hospitality that is afforded to other guests as they can become powerful opinion leaders surrounding your brand, especially amongst those that do not normally read wine-specific publications which tend to have very narrow readerships.

The cellar door is where a true point of difference can be constructed/identified for a wine, as this is becoming increasingly difficult elsewhere in the wine value chain for a market that is saturated. People, their hospitality and their stories create this point of difference as they are derived from the unique attributes of the individual – these cannot be standardised and therefore cannot be replicated. The cellar door, then, can be the ultimate comparative, rather than competitive (competitive advantage can be copied) advantage.

Chapter summary

This chapter has suggested that the cellar door can be a valuable asset for a winery in terms of direct sales to the public, gathering market intelligence, relationship marketing and brand building. In particular we have emphasised the need for the cellar door to be considered as the place at which a winery can have complete control over the way its brand is portrayed and that experiences are critical in facilitating connections with the brand. This includes the provision of hospitality that goes beyond the often very transactional service provided at many wineries, as well as a focus on interpretation that opens the minds of visitors to new understandings of wine more broadly and not just the brand of the winery. This approach allows a winery to add real value without any substantial additional cost. It does, however, require wineries to think in different ways about their wine and brand(s), as this approach is about thinking, doing and being – a philosophy not just an approach to business.

This is not to deny the more traditional roles of sales skills, service and the wine itself. These three elements of the cellar door experience must be delivered to an increasingly high standard, as wineries, regions and entire countries lift their game in these endeavours, continually raising consumer expectations. These, however, can be considered to be 'hygiene factors' that do not necessarily create a comparative advantage and which are very transactional in nature. Comparative advantage is created by the more affective components of the visit (hospitality, authentic experience and interpretation). Figure 4.1 illustrates how these elements combine to lead to sales, relationships and brand building.

The key to implementing a successful cellar door marketing programme is therefore not the wine, but all that defines its meaning and value. This is best thought of in terms of the

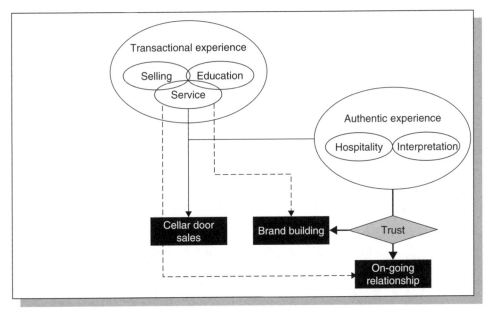

Figure 4.1
Cellar door experiential marketing approach

experiential approach advocated in this book. In the chapters that follow we will return to discussions of several of the aspects of cellar door marketing, as they can be equally valuable in other areas of wine marketing where the sales and marketing staff come into direct contact with the consumer.

Practical wine marketing insights

- The cellar door can be a significant contributor to overall sales for a winery, both at the cellar and post-visit.
- Trust is a core concept in the marketing of wine at the cellar door.
- As a captured market, the cellar door visitor provides an excellent opportunity to gather market intelligence.
- Selection of cellar door staff is critical to the brand image of a winery's wine.
- Hospitality, authentic experiences and interpretation are the key to effective relationship marketing and brand building at the cellar door.
- The cellar door can be used as a public relations and promotional venue for both wine-specific and wider lifestyle media.

Further reading

Carlsen, J. and Charters, S. (eds.) (2006). *Global Wine Tourism: Research, Management and Marketing*, CABI.
For research-based case studies of the cellar door and other aspects of wine tourism.

Hall, C.M., Sharples, E., Cambourne, B. and Macionis, N. (eds.) (2000). *Wine Tourism Around the World: Development, Management and Markets*, Butterworth Heinemann.
For a comprehensive discussion of the cellar door and other aspects of wine tourism, including some case study material.

Mitchell, R. and Hall, C.M. (2006). Wine tourism research: the state of play. *Tourism Review International* 9(4), 307–332 (available to Ingenta subscribers or for purchase at: http://www.ingentaconnect.com/content/cog/tri/2006/00000009/00000004/art00002).
A good summary of the 'state of play' in wine tourism research.

For best practice case studies of cellar door management from around the world (including Yering Station, Inniskillin and Hillebrand wineries) see: http://www.nzte.govt.nz/section/14454/15090.aspx

CHAPTER 5

The role of intermediaries

Chapter objectives

After reading this chapter you will

- Appreciate that there is a wide range of intermediaries that are present in the wine supply and value chains
- Understand the critical role that intermediaries play for wineries
- Understand the importance of relationships and relationship marketing in the producer–intermediary–retailer value chain
- Recognise that decisions relating to choice of intermediary are complex
- Recognise that choices relating to intermediaries are specific to each winery and situation

Introduction

Wine, perhaps more than any other industry, is an industry of intermediaries. Intermediaries (or 'middlemen') provide services of different forms that distribute wine from the producer to the retailer or consumer. There are many different forms of intermediary, each with a different role to play and each of whom has the potential to add cost and, hopefully, value to the wine. Because the types of intermediaries are many and varied, there are an overwhelming number of permutations for a winery when it comes to the selection of intermediaries (see Figure 1.3). This is especially the case for smaller wineries that, unlike their larger counterparts, do not usually have the selling power, volume of production or resources to by-pass intermediaries and sell directly to retailers or to negotiate contracts that benefit both winery and intermediary. The nature of the relationships between winery, intermediary and retailer is, therefore, critical to the ability of a supply chain involving intermediaries to add value to the wine.

In Chapter 4 we introduced the concept of relationship marketing at the cellar door, where wineries would develop relationships directly with consumers and we suggested that this concept was also useful in terms of B2B relationships (Grönroos, 1996). This chapter picks up these discussions and further explores the importance of trust in such relationships. It is, however, useful to begin the chapter with a discussion of

Plate 1.1
Old vintages of champagne stored in underground wine cellars. This sends strong symbolic messages about the history and heritage of champagne.

Plate 1.2
Gas station own-brand sekt
(German sparkling wine). A different
set of meanings and brand image to
champagne.

Plate 2.1
Phylloxera sign, South Australia. Although biosecurity is a major issue in many wine areas the impacts of wine tourism have often not been considered.

Plate 2.2
Vineyards in South-west Australia. Concerns over water availability, potentially worse under climate change, has necessitated the development of irrigation dams on many properties.

Plate 3.1
Sustainable winegrowing, Waipara, New Zealand

Plate 3.2
Greening Waipara project. The project
aims to enhance the biodiversity of
the region.

Plate 4.1
Wine House and Kitchen (Gibbston Valley, New Zealand) meeting room.
Design elements reflect a 1950s country home using the philosophy of the
warmth and welcome of 'Grandma's place' to engender a sense of home.

Plate 4.2
Olssen's of Bannockburn (Bannockburn, New Zealand) cellar door. Vernacular
and heritage architecture can be effective in creating a sense of authenticity by
providing a setting that has a strong sense of place.

Plate 6.1
Gourmet traveller shop. Located in Melbourne domestic airport the shop provides a retail outlet to a waiting audience.

Plate 6.2
Victoria Market, Melbourne. Direct selling provides an alternative distribution channel and close customer contact.

Plate 6.3
Retail choice. The customer is spoilt for choice at this specialist wine store illustrating the competitiveness of wine sales.

Plate 7.1
Restaurant and cafe. The wine focus of the restaurant is reinforced by the grape vine and signage.

Plate 7.2
Allan Scott Wines restaurant. Restaurants with a family focus can be an important way for wine consumers to have positive wine experiences and therefore they can be a useful marketing channel.

Plate 8.1
Appellation stand at Bordeaux Fête Le Vin. Visitors can taste a range of wines
from different producers in the same appellation.

Plate 8.2
Sign at the entrance to the Bordeaux Fête Le Vin. At this consumer event, exhibitors are grouped according to appellations.

Plate 9.1
Elements of a wine label – Clare Nicholls and Hamish Nicholls

Plate 10.1
French wine cooperative store. Wine cooperatives are common in many parts of France, where small growers collective own winemaking facilities, employ winemakers and market under one or a few brands.

Plate 10.2
Winemakers' and Fishermen's Route. Collaborations between wine and food producers can add real value to tourist trails.

Plate 11.1
Featherstone Vineyards, Ontario. Ontario grapes growers place a great emphasis on the quality of the wine in their branding. Vintners Quality Alliance Ontario (VQA) provides assurance to customers with respect to labelling, quality and origin. See http://www.vqaontario.com and http://www.featherstonewinery.ca

Plate 11.2
Experiencing wine. d'Arenberg in South Australia's McLaren Vale places great emphasis on providing a positive experience for visitors. See http://www.darenberg.com.au

the different types of intermediary that exist in the world of wine. In this chapter we will explore:

- *Place*: in the traditional marketing sense (i.e. distribution of wine).
- *Price*: how intermediaries can impact the price of wine.
- *People*: the importance of relationships between actors in the supply/value chain.

Intermediaries and their varied roles

According to Baritaux et al. (2006, after Yavas, 1992) there are two broad categories of wholesale intermediaries identified in several industries – 'marketmakers' and 'matchmakers' – although, they suggest, the terminology varies widely depending on author and research field. The distinction here is between those that take ownership of the product in the inter-mediation process (marketmakers), making their money from the 'bid–ask spread' (i.e. the difference between what they can buy it from the supplier – the bid – and what they can sell it to a retailer – the ask) and those that make economic gain through commissions on the transactions (matchmakers). In most wine markets around the world marketmakers dominate, but in France, matchmakers are more prominent, with wine brokers accounting for about 60% of bulk table and local (*vin de pays*) wine transactions and for about 80% of quality (*Appellation d'Origine Controlée*, AOC) wine exchanges (Baritaux et al., 2006). Baritaux et al. (2006) also distinguish between those that represent and therefore act on behalf of sellers and buyers of wine (agents) and those that remain independent (brokers). The following is a brief description of each of the categories of intermediaries outlined in Figure 5.1.

Négotiant

Négotiants are a special category of intermediary who may 'buy in grapes, must [grape juice], or wine, blend different lots of wine within an appellation, and bottle the result under their own name' (Robinson, 2006, p. 472). The key element that differentiates them from other intermediaries is their role requires them to transform the wine in some way, usually by blending and/or maturing it (Charters, 2006). While they are generally considered to be intermediaries, they may, to an extent, also act as a wine producers and/or retailer.

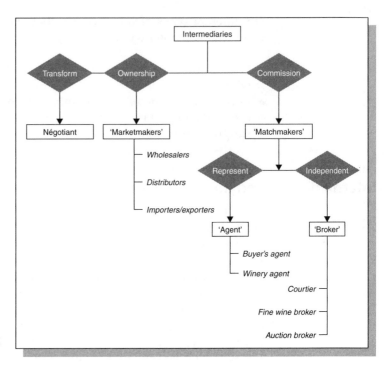

Figure 5.1
Taxonomy of wine
intermediaries
(derived from
Baritaux et al., 2006;
Robinson, 2006)

Négotiants have traditionally been most prevalent in Burgundy and Bordeaux (Robinson, 2006) and it can be argued that many Champagne Houses also fit into this category (Guy, 2003; Charters, 2006) as do Port Houses although they are not called this (Charters, 2006). According to Charters (2006, p. 71) 'Historically négociants have been very powerful' within the European wine market, as they had the capital necessary to make wine for small producers and to ship it to more lucrative markets in northern Europe and around the world. Charters (2006, p. 72) continues: 'In Burgundy, if not in Bordeaux, the influence of négociants has begun to rise again. This is in part due to a new wave of merchant, committed to making high-quality wine'. *Négotiants*, then, are primarily limited to France, but examples of a similar role do exist in the New World. In the New World these are sometimes known as 'virtual winemakers' who own no grapes or winemaking capacity and simply buy all of the services necessary to make wine that they bottle and label under their own brand.

Marketmakers: Wholesalers, Distributors and Importers/Exporters

As mentioned above, marketmakers are by far the most common form of intermediary around the world. These intermediaries buy wine as a commodity from the producer and on-sell it to others further along the supply chain. Also suggested above, they derive value and income from the wine by making a margin on the 'bid-ask spread' in the same way that someone does buying and selling shares or other commodities. It can also be argued that this is how many (large) wine retailers make their money (see Chapter 6).

In deriving value for themselves, most 'marketmakers' are simply adding cost to the wine and it is difficult to establish how they might add value in an effective value chain. However, it could be argued that in some situations they can provide a valuable service for a wine producer, including specialised or niche 'marketmakers' acting as a conduit to niche markets for a small producer (i.e. they also act as 'matchmaker'), or in new or emerging markets they can be the party to take the risk associated with establishing a market for wine as a category (i.e. the winery sells it to them and does not have to worry about how the market takes to wine as a product category). For example, in China, perhaps one of the most important emerging markets for wine, marketmakers can play a critical role, especially given the newly capitalising nature of its economy and the nuisances of cross-cultural trade. Box 5.1 provides a case study of China's largest wine marketmaker.

Box 5.1 ASC Fine Wines: China's largest wine marketmaker

Setting the scene: wine in China

A report on the Chinese wine market by Rozelle and Sumner (2006) highlights several things about this emerging market:

- Consumption is less than one-third litre per capita
  - but urban residents consume more than one litre per capita.
- Urban consumers present the greatest opportunity
  - to exceed the total population of the United States.
- Beijing and Shanghai the largest markets for on-licence consumption (e.g. hotels, lounges, night clubs, discos and upscale restaurants and banquets),
  - red wine is especially fashionable.
- Domestic wine satisfies most of the demand.
- Supermarkets are stocking more and more wine.
- Most wine consumers in China are price conscious:
  - domestic wines are typically below US$4 per bottle
  - imported wine is generally $15 per bottle or more.
- Few buy imported wine on their own.

According to Rozelle and Sumner (2006, p. 67), specialized wine-importing and distribution agents like ASC Fine Wines, '...are entirely responsible for getting foreign wine from the port to the consumer'. It is amongst this back-drop that ASC Fine Wines is operating.

ASC Fine Wines

ASC Fine Wines is China's largest importer/distributor of quality wines, with offices in Beijing, Shanghai, Guangzhou, Shenzhen and Xiamen. They have more than 800 wines and 87 winemakers from 13 countries. They have been operating in China since 1996, and import approximately 35% of all premium bottled branded wines.

They employ more than 220 staff and are suppliers to the top Hyatt Hotels and Resorts, Starwood Hotels and Resorts, the InterContinental Hotels Group, Marriott International and the Accor Group and several other hotels, plus supermarkets and hypermarkets including Carrefour, Metro, Wal-Mart and ParknShop.

A powerful position

ASC Fine Wines is hugely influential in the Chinese market. As China's largest importer/distributor of imported wines, selling one in every three bot-tles of imported wine it has considerable power to determine what sells and what does not. As Rozelle and Sumner (2006, p. 67) suggest:

These large firms typically have an established set of wineries that they represent. It is difficult to get onto the list of the most successful distributors.

For those smaller wineries that want to try to enter the Chinese market, they must turn to one of the hundreds of small (often fly-by-night) importers and distributors that are willing, but not necessarily able to import, distribute, sell, and promote the new wines.

Adding value through education

ASC Fine Wines not only supplies wine to the Chinese market, they also play an important role in educating the Chinese public on wine. In 2006 they became the first accredited provider in China of Wine & Spirit Education Trust (WSET) wine education programmes which are delivered in 35 countries around the world. Don St-Pierre Snr (founder/owner of ASC Fine Wines) also says: 'We organize a lot of wine events that include educational aspects, and we encourage newer wine drinkers to join in and learn more about wine. And we do an average of 30 training sessions each week for our trade customers' (http://www.asc-wines.com/). This function adds clear value to wine distribu-tion in China and is likely to pay dividends for those wishing to import wine into China, whether with ASC Fine Wines or another distributor.

For more information on ASC Fine Wines see:
http://www.asc-wines.com/

For more information on wine in China see:

Rozelle, S. and Summer, D. (2006) *Wine in China: Final Report to the California Association of Wine Growers*. University of California Agricultural Issues Center and UC Davis, California. Available at: http://aic.ucdavis.edu/research1/Wine_in_China.pdf

In the United States the wine and spirits wholesale business was worth US$31 billion in 2003 and the 20 largest wine and spirits wholesalers control 68% of US distribution, up from 49% in 1995 (National Wine and Spirits, 2004). Castaldi et al. (2006, p. 9) suggest that the large size of these companies and on-going consolidation of wholesalers 'has made it increasingly difficult for smaller producers to get their product onto the retailers' shelves. Wholesalers prefer to distribute only the top selling brands, in lieu of small or new labels, since their profits come from mark-ups on products they are able to replenish quickly'.

The following provide an illustration of the scale of one of these producers, National Wine and Spirits, the tenth largest wine and spirit distributor in the US in 2004:

- Sales of 12.2 million cases of wines and spirits
- Net sales of US$328.6 million, $140.9 million in wine sales (26.1%) accounting for approximately 10% of the value of all US wine and spirit sales
- 12,000 individual products
- 36,000 retail customers in three states
- 1388 employees
- 320 delivery vehicles
- 22 buildings (leased and owned)

(National Wine and Spirits, 2004)

Like other parts of the wine value chain (e.g. wine production and retailing), large companies clearly dominate in terms of the volume of wine sold, but there are also large numbers of small, often niche, marketmaker intermediaries. It is these intermediaries that are most likely to be matched with small producers and smaller specialist wine retailers and on-licence premises. In essence, while the distribution channel might look similar on the face of it, there are in effect two major systems (albeit with many variants within the systems): one based on volume and logistics and the other based on specialised niches and relationships (see Figure 5.2). Figure 5.2 highlights that there are some occurrences where there is a mixing of these two systems, but these are much less common than transactions within each

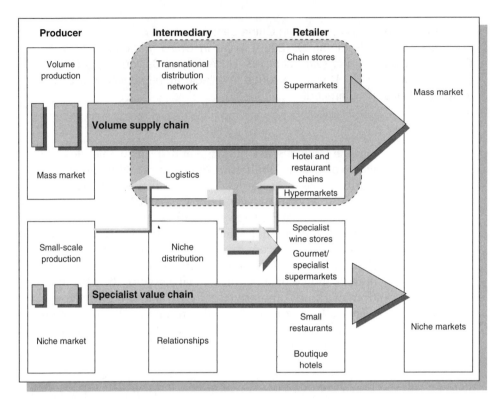

Figure 5.2
Volume versus specialist wine distribution

system. It also highlights the fact that there is an increasing level of consolidation and vertical integration between volume intermediaries and retailers (see also Chapter 6) and that this continues to reinforce the volume-driven ethos of this chain.

Matchmakers: Brokers and Agents

As mentioned already in this chapter matchmakers play an important role in the French context, accounting for well over half of all wine transactions in France. Brokers, in particular, play a vital role in getting the wine from the producer to the consumer in any wine market (Robinson, 2006). Baritaux et al. (2006, p. 376) distinguish between agents and brokers by suggesting that matchmakers '...can be representatives of one party or they can remain independent': agents representing producers or buyers and brokers remaining independent (see Figure 5.1). They also suggest that 'Wine brokerage is really poorly known. Moreover, these intermediaries often lack legitimacy vis-à-vis the other actors in the wine industry' (Baritaux et al., 2006, p. 376). Agents are less common than brokers in most wine markets but they still perform an important function for sellers and buyers of wine.

Robinson (2006) distinguishes between four different types of broker. The first, known as *courtier* in France, act as a middleman between vinegrowers and merchants or *négotiants*. They collect and exhibit hundreds of samples to merchants and *négotiants* and are paid a commission on the transaction between the parties. The second are fine wine brokers, who '…sell from a list of glamorous properties and vintages which may, but often do not, belong to them' (Robinson, 2006, p. 106). The third, she suggests, is one of the few parts of the wine industry that is highly profitable: brokers associated with wine auctions. These tend to be clustered mainly around London's two major auction houses (Christie's and Sotheby's), acting like stock brokers do for their clients and often brokering transactions for collectors and investors on wine that never leaves a bonded warehouse (Robinson, 2006).

Robinson's fourth category of broker would, under the taxonomy presented in Figure 5.1, be considered to be an agent. She suggests that they are further along the distribution chain than *courtier* and guide a 'stable' of wine producers to buyers '… in the manner of a literary agent representing a rollcall of authors' (Robinson, 2006, p. 106). These are winery agents and differ from buyer's agents in that they represent those selling the wine and as such are paid by the winery to act on their behalf. These winery agents are frequently used by small producers to assist them in export markets, especially when they are entering a new market. Winery agents may sell to further intermediaries or directly to retail outlets, but are highly unlikely to sell directly to the end consumer of the wine.

If a winery agent represents a winery then logically a buyer's agent represents a wine buyer further along the distribution chain (i.e. another intermediary, a retailer or an on-licence operator). In most cases these agents would be employed by the buyer (e.g. a supermarket or hotel wine buyer), but they may also be contracted by buyers to provide wines. Most commonly buyer's agents would represent restaurants, hotel, cruise line or airline, developing wine lists to match food styles and markets and acting as an agent between a winery, other intermediary or retailer and the restaurant, hotels, cruise lines or airlines. They provide expertise in wine and food matching, as well as knowledge of where to source the wine. In this case they may also be known as a wine consultant and they may have other roles in the wine industry (e.g. wine competition judge, wine critic or wine writer or may have been a sommelier in the past). In the case of a wine consultant that is also a critic or wine writer their 'celebrity status' may also be used by a restaurant or a specialist retailer in promotional material to attract consumers.

In some cases buyer's agents may also operate in a wine producing country and act on behalf of an importer, distributor or retailer (especially large supermarket chains) in another market (e.g. an agent who operates in France on behalf of an American importer). In this case they provide expertise on the market conditions of the producing country, including legal and regulatory issues, transaction and procurement procedures and local wine knowledge (e.g. vintage quality). They will also likely have relationships with producers that will assist in the procurement of the wine. They add value to the value chain through both their local knowledge and the relationships they have with producers.

Wine intermediaries and trust

Wine intermediaries hold considerable power in the distribution of wine as they are a necessary link between the winery and the consumer, especially in the export context. Their role can be seen as somewhat of a 'gatekeeping' role and '...gatekeepers are ultimately responsible for making or facilitating purchasing decisions related to imported foods [including wine] on behalf of millions of consumers' (Knight et al., 2003, p. 13). In this case power can be defined as '...the ability of one channel member to induce change in its behaviour in favour of the objectives of the channel member exerting the influence' (Ailawadi et al., 1995, p. 214, after Wilemon, 1972) and this power is legitimised by the position between the winery and the end consumer or retailer (also see Chapter 6 for a discussion of the power of supermarkets). In the US, for example, this is particularly true as the Three-Tier System of distribution legislates that wine must be distributed via these intermediaries (see Chapter 1).

As a result of this power relationship it is important that there is a degree of trust between the buyer and seller of the wine so that one party does not take advantage of the other. Svensson (2001) suggests that trust is a 'multi-dimensional concept' that has been found to include: confidence, predictability, ability, competence, expertness, intentions or motives, benevolence, motivation to lie, business sense and judgement, altruism, loyalty, integrity, congruence, consistency, fairness, character, openness of management, liking, respect, faith, acceptance and security. Following Svensson's (2001) categorisation of different forms of trust in a dyadic business to business relationship,

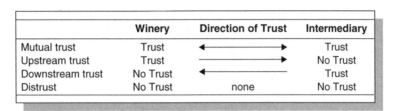

Figure 5.3
Classification of winery–intermediary trust

	Winery	Direction of Trust	Intermediary
Mutual trust	Trust	←——————→	Trust
Upstream trust	Trust	——————→	No Trust
Downstream trust	No Trust	←——————	Trust
Distrust	No Trust	none	No Trust

Figure 5.3 demonstrates the various ways that trust acts in the relationship between wineries and intermediaries.

This is further complicated by other actors in the wine supply/value chain as there are also dyadic relationships between other members of the chain. Svensson (2001) suggests that this results in what he terms 'trust chains' and posits a model which demonstrates how each of the actors is connected by trust. To be fully effective and increase the value of a wine brand these trust chains must be synchronised so that each actor in the chain trusts each of the others (Figure 5.4). According to Svensson (2001), these synchronised chains might be 'interrupted' by an event that sees the trust broken in a dyadic relationship, which may weaken other relationships in the chain and, we suggest, reduces any potential added value for a brand. In Figure 5.4, for example, a retailer's trust in an intermediary may be weakened because the wine that the intermediary supplied was not of the style the retailer ordered (e.g. an off-dry Riesling rather than a dry Riesling). This in turn weakens the trust between the winery and the retailer, as the winery has disappointed the retailer through no fault of the winery. Svensson (2001, p. 433) suggests, however, that 'these critical events of distrust, managed properly, may strengthen the trust in a dyadic business relationship, where the buyer's or the seller's corrective actions demonstrate the ability to handle unexpected situations adequately'. Alternatively, the situation may worsen and a 'distrust chain' develops. In Figure 5.4 if the intermediary does not rectify the situation with the retailer (e.g. supplying a dry Riesling from the same winery) and mistakes continue, then the retailer will loose all trust in the intermediary. It is also possible that this may lead to a lack of trust between the retailer and the winery and a weakening of trust between the consumer and the winery. In this case there are likely to be no opportunities for adding value to the wine brand and the value chain will be broken. Interestingly, the intermediary may be immune to any adverse impact of trust with the consumer. Trust between end consumer and intermediary is often implicit as the consumer may be totally unaware of their involvement in the value chain. The same

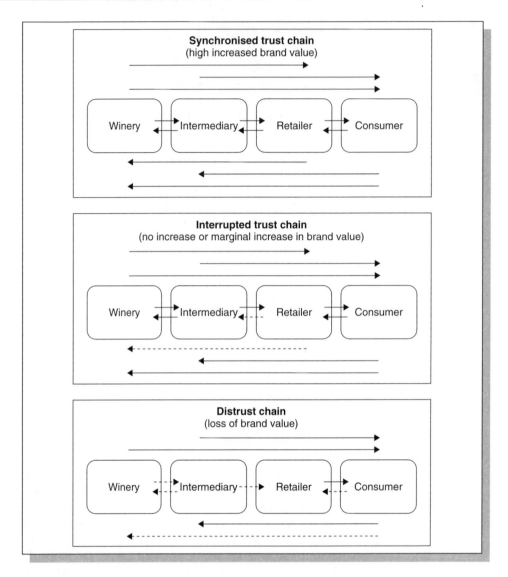

Figure 5.4
Synchronised, interrupted and distrust wine trust chains.

cannot be said of the winery and the consumer, as ultimately it is the winery's wine that is sold to the consumer.

The example presented in Figure 5.4 illustrates the importance the intermediary and the relationships that they hold with other actors in the value chain. Therefore it is useful to discuss relationship marketing as a means of managing the value chain (see Hall et al., 2003 for more discussion of issues of trust in relation to food supply chains).

Relationship marketing

According to Beaujanot and Lockshin (2003, n.p.) relationship marketing is particularly useful for the wine industry '… wineries have to do business with wholesalers, distributors or agents instead of final consumers, which is even more obvious in an export context'. In Chapter 4, we introduced the concept of relationship marketing as a tool for wineries to use at the cellar door when they are interacting directly with the consumer. Grönroos (1996, p. 8) suggests that this should be considered as a fundamental component of marketing as

…marketing includes all necessary efforts required to prepare the organization for, and implement activities needed to manage, the interfaces with its environment. Markets are, of course, of several kinds: customers, distributors, suppliers, networks of co-operating partners, etc.

Several authors have recognised the value of relationship marketing as a tool in the wine value chain (e.g. Lindgreen et al., 2000; Beverland and Lindgreen, 2001; Hingley and Lindgreen, 2002; Beaujanot and Lockshin, 2003) and almost all acknowledge that the wine industry could do a better job at implementing such a strategy. Beaujanot and Lockshin (2003, n.p.) also suggest that:

Wineries should be aware of the importance of having a relationship approach when doing business, and that this orientation needs a commitment in terms of time, effort and money. Otherwise the likelihood of obtaining the desirable results can be very low.

Trust is key to the development of effective inter-organisational relationships (Svensson, 2001), as are commitment and co-operation (Hingley and Lindgreen, 2002). Knight et al. (2003, p. 39) further suggest that this trust and commitment is usually developed between individuals within a company and they evidence this with the following quote from 'a highly experienced distributor in the UK wine sector':

If I'm going to sell wine it's on personality. You sell it because people like you or they respect what you do or… they like your brand as well, they've got to like the wine, they've got to like the presentation, but they've got to like you. If they don't like you, they won't deal with you.

Box 5.2 provides some possible questions that different actors in the wine value chain may wish to ask themselves in the development of such relationships. It is apparent from these questions that there is a complex set of interplays that need to occur in the development of these relationships and some of these are quite objective and based on sound business principles, while others are quite personal and intuitive.

Box 5.2 Key questions in the winery–intermediary–retailer relationship

What wineries should ask themselves when selecting an intermediary

1. Do I need a 'marketmaker' or a 'matchmaker'?
   - Do I want or need to sell my wine to an intermediary in the market I am going into?
   - Would I be best represented in my chosen market by an agent working on my behalf?
   - Are there brokers that I could use to sell my wine to retailers?
   - What is my business strategy?

2. Which company do I choose?
   - What experience do they have in the market that I am entering?
   - What expertise do they have?
   - Do they sell to retailers and other outlets that serve my intended target market?
   - What other brands do they represent/stock and are they compatible with my own brand values?
   - Can I trust them?
   - Do they supply retailers that I can trust?
   - Will they be committed to my brand?

3. How do I measure their on-going value to me?
   - On-going sales
   - Feedback from their clients
   - Market intelligence
   - Price
   - Strong relationships with retailers and other outlets

What intermediaries should ask themselves when selecting a winery

1. What winery do I want to supply me?
   - Do they have the volume I need to supply my client base?
   - Can they consistently supply at this level? (i.e. Are they supplying to me at full capacity and will a poor vintage mean they cannot supply at this level?)
   - Does the winery produce the varieties and styles that my clients are looking for?
   - Are my clients looking for boutique specialised wines or more generic volume wine?
   - Can the winery supply wine at the price point that my clients are looking for?
   - Do they know who their target market is?
   - Do I have clients that match this market?

- Can I trust them?
- Do I have clients that I can trust to market this wine in a way that the winery will perceive as beneficial?
- What is my business strategy?

2. How do I measure their on-going value to me?
   - Reliable supply
   - Quality of wine supplied (consistency of quality, not necessarily flavour profile)
   - Information on the wines and winemaking process
   - Price
   - Strong relationships with retailers and other outlets

What retailers should ask themselves when selecting intermediaries

1. What intermediary do I want to supply me?
   - What experience and expertise do they have?
   - Do they have the volume I need?
   - Do they have a wide array of wines?
   - Do they have wines at the right price point?
   - Do they understand the needs of the end consumer and, more specifically my target market?
   - Do they keep abreast of market trends?
   - Do they have wines of the variety and style to meet consumer demands, especially my target market?
   - Can I trust them?
   - Can I trust the wineries that are part of their portfolio?

2. How do I measure their on-going value to me?
   - Reliable supply
   - Timely supply
   - Quality of wine supplied (consistency of quality, not necessarily flavour profile)
   - Information on the wines and their producers
   - Market intelligence
   - Price
   - Strong relationships with the wineries

Chapter summary

This chapter has introduced the complex area of wine intermediaries. Despite the fact that intermediaries are powerful gatekeepers in the wine value chain, they are poorly understood. The terminology used to describe different players can be confusing and categories are not always mutually exclusive. The typology presented here expands on that presented by Baritaux et al. (2006) in the hope that this will bring some clarity in defining different categories of intermediaries and their various roles.

Svensson's (2001) 'trust chain' concept has also been applied to the wine value chain to highlight how intermediaries have a crucial role in the wine value chain for wineries and retailers alike. Trust is important in the development of relationships and therefore plays a pivotal role in the implementation of a relationship marketing strategy between a winery, an intermediary (or intermediaries) and a retailer. This means that, while objective measures play an important role in the selection of intermediaries by wineries (and vice versa), they are also based on a high degree of 'gut instinct' and personal feelings about individual actors in the relationship.

Practical wine marketing insights

- Intermediaries must be chosen carefully by wineries as they can make or break the value chain.
- The development of relationships between wineries and intermediaries, and retailers and other outlets and intermediaries, is critical to the success of the wine value chain, especially for smaller players at all levels of the industry.
- These relationships require a high degree of commitment in terms of time and effort, as well as a degree of intuition (and perhaps even good luck).

Further reading

Baritaux, V., Aubert, M., Montaigne, E. and Remaud, E. (2006). Matchmakers in wine marketing channels: the case of French Wine Brokers. *Agribusiness*, 22(3), 375–90.
Discussion of the role of French wine brokers and their unique role in the wine value chain.

Hall, C.M., Sharples, L., Mitchell, R., Cambourne, B. and Macionis, N. (eds.) (2003). *Food Tourism Around the World: Development, Management and Markets*, Butterworth Heinemann.
A discussion of trust in food and tourism supply chains more broadly, including some discussion of wine tourism.

Hingley, M and Lindgreen, A. (2002). Marketing of agricultural products: case findings. *British Food Journal*, 104(10), 806–27.

Findings in relation to relationship marketing between New Zealand wine producers and UK importers and distributors (also explores fresh food distribution in the UK).

Svensson, G. (2001). Extending trust and mutual trust in business relationships towards a synchronised trust chain in marketing channels. *Management Decision*, 39(6), 431–40.
For discussion of how trust chains can be managed to best effect.

Retailing

This chapter is divided into two main sections. The first section takes a macro-retailing perspective and discusses some of the global trends in retailing and their implications for wine. Most significant here is the international growth of transnational supermarket chains with their market dominance and global supply and sourcing systems. The second section looks at retailing in terms of the concept of servicescape and how this affects wine purchasing decisions.

Introduction

Retailing represents one of the most important ends of the wine supply/value chain or marketing channel. A marketing or distribution channel describes the movement of a product from the site of production to the place of consumption and can include transportation, handling and storage, ownership transfers, processing, and distribution. Retailing is a set of business activities that adds value to the products and services sold to consumers for their personal or family use (Levy and Weitz, 2004). Retailers provide important functions that increase the value of the products and services they sell to consumers and facilitate the distribution of those products and services for those who produce them. Each type of retail outlet, whether it is a supermarket, speciality store or direct channel, has its own functions in the marketing of the wine product, and targets particular markets.

Retailing can be defined as selling products and services to consumers for personal use. Many wineries are therefore a retail outlet in the sense that they sell wine direct to customers.

However, usually cellar door sales (see Chapter 4) are distinguished from non-winery retail in any discussion of wine businesses. Retailing in this sense is usually described in relation to wine sold to consumers at supermarkets, high street chains and independent and specialist wine stores as well as web-based retailers.

In Chapter 1 we discuss the complex nature of the wine supply/value chain which highlights the fact that retailers are integral to wine distribution. Figure 6.1 presents a simplified version of the supply/value chain presented in Chapter 1, demonstrating that, apart from direct sales from the winery or a winery outlet (see Chapter 4), the retailer is the only party that sells the product to the end user or consumer. Wholesalers and agents are two forms of intermediaries that aid the distribution from the producer to the retailer and these are discussed in detail in Chapter 5.

There are a variety of ways in which retailers can be grouped in the distribution channel, however they are often grouped by the depth and breadth of their product assortment and the service and specialisation level that each retail outlet provides for example, supermarket chains, high street chains and independent/specialist retailers. In the UK the Institute of Grocery Distribution (IGD) (2006) categorise grocery stores (retail stores focussing on food products including wine) into four categories:

- *Convenience stores*: stores with sales area of less than 3000 square feet, open for long hours and selling products from at least eight different grocery categories (e.g. SPAR, Co-operative Group, United Co-op, Londis, Bestway).
- *Traditional retail and developing convenience stores*: sales area of less than 3000 square feet such as newsagents, grocers, off-licences, and some forecourts (e.g. Shell, BP, Total).

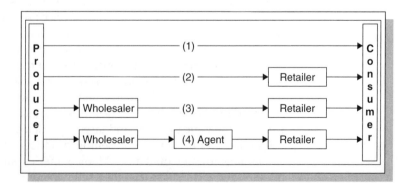

Figure 6.1
Distribution
channels

- *Supermarkets and superstores*: Supermarkets have a sales area of 3000–25,000 square feet selling a broad range of grocery items. Superstores' sales have a sales area above 25000 square feet, selling a broad range of mainly grocery items. In both categories non-food items are also sold (e.g. Tesco, Asda).
- *Alternative channels*: kiosks, markets, doorstep delivery, vending, home shopping.

The wine retailing implications of the various types of outlets are discussed in more detail below (see Plates 6.1–6.3).

The retail market power of supermarkets

Although many people have a romantic image of wine being sold from the cellar door the reality is that most wine is purchased from supermarkets. Euromonitor (2001) reported that grocery and discount store channels account for over 50% of wine sold in Italy, and over 70% of wine sold in the UK, the US, Germany and France. In Australia wine is not legally sold in supermarkets, but over 50% of the specialist retailers are owned by the major supermarket chains (Lockshin and Hall, 2003) and are often co-located, so much so that it is usually possible to walk directly from the supermarket into the liquor store.

The retailing of wine in supermarkets in New Zealand became lawful only in 1989 following legislative changes. By 1999 43% of wine purchases were from supermarkets (Advanced Business Research, 1999) and by 2005 65% of wine sales were through supermarkets, therefore these establishments are becoming an essential market for most wine producers as it reaches a larger audience than any other retail outlet (New Zealand Wine, 2006). The wine section is often extensive with the range of wines available catering well to various shoppers' needs, from cask wines to premium labels, and across a wide price point spread. Supermarkets have been responsible for the development of the wine industry in many countries. The environment provided by the supermarket gives a sense of security to inexperienced wine buyers and allows people to browse selections without interruption. The development of wine categories within these retail establishments has also further helped with the education of consumers (Jennings and Wood, 1994; Handley and Lockshin, 1997).

The significance of retailers in terms of sales in developed countries has meant that the international wine market and many domestic markets are becoming increasingly driven by the retailers because of their substantial market power. Global retail and trading companies are increasingly important in the international trading system, linking millions of producers to consumers worldwide. However, their role presents a double edge sword as it is simultaneously an opportunity and a threat in terms of market access. Therefore, large retailers and supermarkets are increasingly described as market gatekeepers (Lang, 2003). To the United Nations Development Programme (UNDP) (2005, p. 142): 'Supermarkets are now the main gatekeeper to developed country markets for agricultural produce. Their growth is transforming markets. To sell in world markets, especially markets for higher value-added crops, is increasingly to sell to a handful of large supermarket chains'. One of the most significant value-added agricultural crops of course being wine. Wine Australia similarly describe retailers as gatekeepers which:

have replaced the customer as king. Demands are now placed on wineries and winemakers to produce wine to specification at directed prices, with wineries that fall out of mainstream distribution networks facing difficult times. The ever-increasing presence of big retailers partnering with big brands backed by large companies is pointing to an increasing divide in retail, with smaller chains and independents forced to seek up and coming brands and points of difference.

(Wine Australia, 2007)

The market power of retailers is considerable. The top 30 supermarket chains and food companies account for about one-third of global grocery sales and this market share is increasing rapidly as a result of urbanisation and the rapid economic growth of two of the world's largest markets, China and India. Wal-Mart, the world's largest company, accounts for more than one-third of US food industry sales. In the UK the top five supermarkets account for 70% or more of grocery sales which is double the share that existed at the end of the 1980s, while throughout Europe there is increasing consolidation in the retail sector (Wrigley, 2002).

In 2007, the UK food market was estimated to be worth £72.8 billion, an increase of 18.5% since 2002, while the drinks market was estimated to be worth £30.5 billion, an increase of 20.7% since 2002. Alcoholic drinks account for the largest share of the UK's drinks retailing market, representing 51.4% of the market value share (British Retail Consortium, 2007). The UK retail market for still wine was estimated to have reached a value of £7.6 billion in current terms in 2004, up 5% on 2003 with a split between sales of red and white wine of around 50:50, though the value of the red segment remains larger because of the higher average price of red (Mintel, 2005). Significantly, an increase in wine sales within the supermarket sector in the UK has been identified as creating a downturn in off-license and speciality shops as supermarkets can offer discounts and a wide variety at a convenience and low price that attracts some consumers (Mintel, 2005).

The growth of supermarkets in the developed world is paralleled by growth in the developing world. For example, in the late 1980s supermarkets accounted for less than 20% of food sales in Latin America. That share has now climbed to 60% (Reardon and Berdegue, 2002; Reardon et al., 2003). 'In one decade Latin America experienced a scale of supermarket expansion that took five decades in Europe' (UNDP, 2005, p. 142). Supermarkets are also spreading in China faster than anywhere else in the world. Hu et al. (2004) report that supermarket sales are growing by 30–40% per year, two to three times faster than in other developing regions, as a result of rapid economic development and globalisation.

In the transition economies of Central and Eastern Europe the recently privatised retail sector has also experienced rapid supermarket growth. According to Dries et al. (2004) massive inflows of foreign direct investment and competitive domestic investments have driven a rapid take-off of large-format modern retail sector development from a tiny 'luxury' niche of around 5% of food retail in the mid-1990s to 40–50% by 2003 in 'first-wave' and 20–40% in 'second-wave' countries. In 'third-wave' countries such as Russia, and which is also a rapidly growing wine market, supermarkets are still only 10% of food retail but growing very fast. Dries et al. (2004, p. 525) conclude that 'in most countries there is rapid multi-nationalisation and consolidation of the supermarket sector, with profound changes in procurement systems affecting the conditions facing farmers, and creating important opportunities and challenges'.

Global sourcing and supply systems

Significantly for the wine market the concentration of market power has gone hand in hand with the development of global sourcing and supply systems (Figure 6.2). Indeed, such systems have also been a driver behind the increased internationalisation of the wine industry (see Chapter 2). Importantly, as well the traditional strength of large retail chains with respect to personal shopping has been enhanced by their development of on-line retailing. An example of the range available on Tesco.com is indicated in Table 6.1. Significantly, the Tesco range includes a number of wines from overseas that have been bottled under

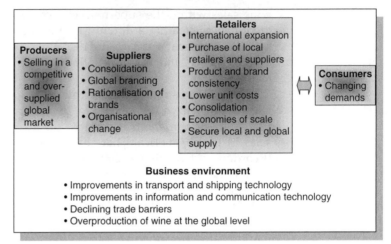

Figure 6.2
Drivers of global
retail sourcing and
supply systems

Tesco's own label which further reinforces the importance of a large retailer such as Tesco for wine exporters. For example, the UK is New Zealand's most important export market, although 60% of wine sales are through 'grocers' (supermarkets). In the late 1990s 94% of supermarket sales were below the critical price point in terms of profitable trade for New Zealand producers of £5.00, although the average selling price for New Zealand wines in that market was above that amount at £5.14 (Mikic, 1998 in Benson-Rea et al., 2003).

In the UK major retailers sell approximately 40% of their packaged grocery sales under their own brand. Research conducted by the IGD in 2003 indicated that a shop's own brand ranges were important for 19% of shoppers in their selection of supermarket, with own brand products being recognised for their lower price and being better value than the branded equivalent (IGD, 2004).

The gatekeeper role and the concentration of buying power in some of the most significant wine markets, including some of the fastest growing, means that large retailers have an enormous capacity to wield influence on the prices that producers receive (Wrigley et al., 2005). The over-production of low price bottled wine and bulk wine on a global scale and the success of varietal branding only serves to reinforce the strength of retailers as they have the capacity to substitute low cost yet reasonable quality varietals from one region for another. This has been facilitated by the development of global supply networks that gives supermarket chains the capacity to shift their demand between suppliers whether they be wineries or wholesalers

Table 6.1 Wine available at Tesco.com March 2007

Origin	Total number of brands available	Number of Tesco branded wines	Number of wines at under £6 per bottle	Number of wines at £5–7 per bottle	Number of wines at £7–10 per bottle	Number of wines at over £10 per bottle
Argentina	10	4	6	2	2	–
Australia	123	18	68	38	29	11
Austria	1	–	–	1	–	–
Bulgaria	4	2	4	–	–	–
Chile	32	12	23	9	4	–
Cyprus	1	–	1	–	–	–
England	1	–	1	–	–	–
France	157	44	71	27	18	55
Germany	19	2	16	2	1	–
Greece	2	–	2	–	–	–
Hungary	4	–	3	–	1	–
Italy	56	23	48	11	3	2
New Zealand	19	1	4	8	8	2
Portugal	25	7	8	4	7	8
South Africa	40	4	29	6	4	5
Spain	56	17	42	12	6	3
UK	5	3	5	–	–	–
USA	54	8	37	10	5	2
Wales	1	–	1	–	–	–

Notes: Analysis conducted 29 March 2007; brands defined as differently labelled wines; wines include sparkling and fortified wines.

(Gwynne, 2006). This has meant substantial discounting in many European markets. For example, in Germany around 60% of wine is sold under €2 per bottle due to the rise of discount retail stores, such as Aldi and Lidl. Most wine in the UK is still sold at between €3 and €5, but prices are under pressure due to the growing power of supermarkets like Tesco and Sainsbury's in the wine sector. These two chains plus Asda (Wal-Mart) account for half of UK wine sales (Beverage Daily, 2006). Nevertheless, such a situation poses substantial issues on the capacity of small wineries and even export wholesalers to compete when supply networks are being restructured via the centralisation of procurement, logistical upgrading, supply network shortening and new intermediaries, the imposition of quasi-formal contracts, and the development of private standards (Coe and Hess, 2005; Bernetti et al., 2006), all actions that favour large well-capitalised suppliers. Furthermore, Clarke (2000) has also argued that an increase in the retail power of major supermarket chains has served to redefine local consumer choice. This has meant that smaller retailers are particularly disadvantaged by the shift in retail power because it has directly affected the store and product choices of consumer groups, depending on their relative mobility.

Yet the growth of supermarkets as the dominant wine retailer should not be treated completely in a negative light, particularly by consumers seeking low-priced reasonable quality wine. For example, Anderson (2001) points out that one reason for the growth in export demand for Australian wine was the change in liquor licensing laws in the UK in the 1970s that allowed supermarkets to retail wine to the post-war baby boomers (by then adults). By the mid-1980s supermarkets, dominated by Sainsbury's, Marks and Spencer, Waitrose and Tesco, accounted for more than half of all retail wine sales in the UK (Unwin, 1991) a figure that has increased substantially since to over 70% (see above). Therefore, in an aggregate sense the growth of supermarkets as a retail force has tended to go hand in hand with the growth of many of the New World wines. Given that most wines are consumed within 24 hours of purchase and that much of the success of New World wines has been geared to that market, supermarkets offer a great opportunity for the promotion of fruity, easy to drink styles of wine. These can also be purchased by supermarket chains from larger suppliers and sold under either the wineries or the chain's own brand. Because of the ready availability of low-priced reasonable quality wine, supermarkets also have an important role in growing the wine market overall and potentially introducing consumers to wine as a product in a non-threatening environment (Box 6.1).

Small is beautiful?

In order to be able to survive in such a competitive market smaller retail stores, especially independent and specialist stores, will tend to focus on small and interesting winery brands and varietals that have not received significant coverage in the supermarkets by virtue of price, customer recognition, or even small amount that can be supplied. In addition, specialist retailers will often utilise expert wine knowledge as a means of maintaining and building customer relationships (Figure 6.3).

Box 6.1 UK wine retail discounting: The great wine rip-off?

The average discount on branded wine was estimated at around £1.50 in major supermarkets in the UK at the beginning of 2007 (Mercer, 2007). It is estimated that over two-thirds of the wine sold in the UK is done so on the basis of special promotions while Jon Moramarco of Constellation, the company behind wine brands such as Banrock Station and Hardy's, said in 2006 that for some of his company's brands more than 80% of sales were made at 'half-price' (in Moore, 2007) leading to a situation of lower earnings because cost increases were not passed on in the UK (Mercer, 2007). Such a situation raises substantial questions about the nature of supermarket discounting and artificially created promotions (i.e. when the initial price of a wine is set deliberately higher so that a discount can be applied later) and its flow on effects back along the supply chain. According to Allan Cheeseman who oversaw Sainsbury's wine department for over 20 years:

When it comes to wine offers, we're living in a fool's paradise ... I think perhaps some of this is my fault ... During the late 1990s and early 2000s at Sainsbury's we began promoting wine. The difference was that those were genuine promotions. We took a hell of a bat on the margin, but we set the whole thing in train and it's now got out of hand. Today many wine offers are created artificially. They aren't what you'd call genuine promotions at all. But unfortunately, there are an awful lot of special-offer junkies out there and it's slowly strangling the wine industry ... I'm very sceptical about many of the half-price offers ... They're often poor-quality, inferior wines that have been sold at a 'full', concocted price for the absolute minimum period.

(Moore, 2007)

Because of the market share of supermarket chains with respect to wine retail, Moore (2007) reported that, not only may some consumers be duped by pricing strategies, but 'Such is the tyranny of the big retailers that the wine companies are losing out too, particularly the smaller, more individual ones – big brands that produce in bulk and have deep resources can more easily negotiate the perils of the modern retailing jungle'. However, the situation is likely only to get worse as it estimated that Britons will only be drinking an extra 1.5 litres of wine each in 2010, compared to the 27 litre per person rate in 2005 which is a far cry from the 75% growth in wine consumption between 1990 and 2005 (Mercer, 2007). Such a situation means that the market power of supermarkets is likely to only increase.

According to Moore (2007) a wine company will likely have paid ten to twenty thousand pounds for promotional displays in the middle or end of an aisle in order to secure such a premium selling position as well as paying for mention of their wine in the in-store magazine or recommendation on a food and wine recipe card. For example, 'Waitrose charges suppliers a "nominal fee of £300" for a mention in its Wine List magazine, and Tesco too takes money "as part of the business plan we have with wineries" to appear in certain spots of the wine magazine that is sent out to customers' (Moore, 2007).

As she noted, such business methods work against smaller producers who do not have the marketing budgets of larger companies and therefore find it difficult to be mentioned in promotions. Nevertheless, discounting is now so established in the UK market that it may be difficult to change the purchasing behaviours of many consumers while it may also introduce new consumers to wine. As Dan Jago, Tesco's wine, beer and spirits category director, stated:

Asda experimented with not promoting as part of their everyday-low-prices strategy, but people didn't like it. We like to think our wines offer value at all prices but customers tell us they like promotions, because they allow them to try new things, plus there is so much choice and they like to be directed towards certain wines. Younger drinkers – 18 to 25 years – like to have as many clues as possible.

(Moore, 2007)

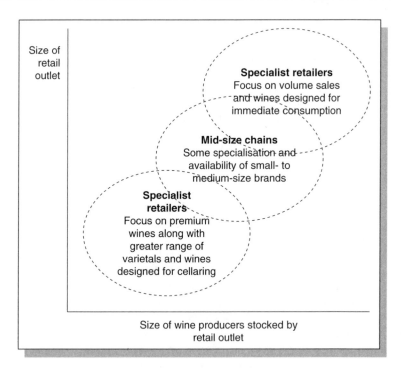

Figure 6.3
Relationship between retailers and wine brands

Table 6.2 outlines some of the characteristics and advantages and disadvantages of different retail outlets from the perspective of producers. High street and banner group chains have an important intermediate role between the high volume transnational supermarket chains and specialist retailers combining some of the characteristics of both. The term high street chain is used to distinguish between retailers with smaller outlets on high streets (main street if North America) than the larger

Table 6.2 Advantages and disadvantages of different retail outlets

Outlet	Characteristics	Advantages to producer	Disadvantages to producer
Supermarket/ hypermarket chains	High volume sales, low margins and low retail prices; usually low level of wine knowledge of staff	• Quantity purchases • High brand awareness • Can help create mass appeal	• Lack of freedom to recommend price points • Low level of interest in experimental styles and varieties • Convenience of location and opening hours to customers
High street/ banner group chain	Intermediate between supermarket (volume retailer) and independents; increased level of wine knowledge	• Convenience of location and opening hours to customers • Wide exposure • Service focus • Purchase in reasonable quantity through chains and sometimes low quantity by individual stores	• Low level of interest in experimental styles and varieties
Independent/ specialist	Tends to cater to wine consumers with a higher level of knowledge through a high level of service and wine knowledge; accesses boutique and small producers	• 'Hand selling' approach through knowledge of wines and matching to consumer needs • Very strong service focus and development of customer relationships • Will often be interested in experimental styles or uncommon varieties	• Each outlet must be serviced and supplied individually • Small volumes

(Continued)

Table 6.2 (*Continued*)

Outlet	Characteristics	Advantages to producer	Disadvantages to producer
State monopoly retailer	Overall aim is to promote healthy drinking; often a high level of wine knowledge; accesses a range of suppliers	• A range of volumes may be purchased • Having the wine stocked may give producers national or region wide access	• If the monopoly does not stock the wine then it is excluded the from region or country in retailing terms, which means that even if it can be purchased separately by restaurants developing brand profile is extremely difficult
Duty-free retailer	Usually low level of knowledge and often focus on well-known brand items and luxury items	• Provides access to a higher-income level market with increased propensity to spend • Liquid container restrictions on planes may reduce appeal of wine as a purchase item	• Usually purchase through large distributors

supermarkets operating in malls or hypermarkets. Banner groups are a wholesaler-driven buying group of independent shops operating under the same banner or brand. For example, in New Zealand the Foodstuffs organisation, the country's biggest grocery distributor and one of New Zealand's largest businesses, has the characteristics of a high street chain in international terms. The Foodstuffs organisation consists of three separate, regionally based, retailer-owned cooperative companies and a Federation body, Foodstuffs (NZ) Ltd, which is based in Wellington, and includes retail brands such as New World, Pak'nSave and Four Square. Each regional company is owned by its retail members and operates entirely autonomously with its own Board and management. Although Foodstuffs manages the supply chain for members, thereby providing for collective purchase of wine and the advantages that provides to both the chain and wine producers, individual members may also purchase directly. Therefore, many of the New World supermarkets, for example, will often have a separate section of the wine shelves, set apart for wines produced from the region in which the supermarket is based and which will often include wineries with very limited production runs.

Specialised retailers have an extremely significant role to play in wine marketing as although they may carry some of the large volume producers they will usually hold wines from smaller producers and of unusual varieties which would not be economic for the larger retailers to carry given their economic models. Specialised retailers are therefore vital to small wineries and often reflect strong business to business relationships with individual producers. Specialist retailers will usually also host wine clubs and tasting opportunities that provide producers with an opportunity to interpret their wine to an audience which will also likely have an above-average level of wine knowledge as well as providing an opportunity for producers to gain market information at a relatively low cost (see Chapter 9). Furthermore, there is often significant demand for such opportunities, for example, in the UK wine market Mintel (2005) reported that 37% of wine drinkers want more opportunities to taste before buying.

For specialist retailers the opportunity to host producers and/or their distributors for tastings and wine club meetings also allows them to reinforce the strong experiential and relationship marketing dimensions of their business (see Chapter 9). In many ways specialist retailers should also be regarded as wine knowledge brokers as their higher degree of knowledge of wines than other retailers allow them to introduce their customers to new and interesting wines that they may otherwise not have tried. Indeed, in the UK market Mintel (2005) reported that almost half (47%) of wine drinkers have an appetite for experimentation, with the most adventurous being males, 35–44 and 55–64-year old.

State alcohol monopolies

The retail structure for wines in any country is ultimately determined by regulatory and institutional arrangements which have been established. This means that in many jurisdictions there are state alcohol monopolies to varying degrees, as well as limits on electronic retailing of alcohol or purchase and shipment of wines between jurisdictions (see Chapters 1 and 2). For example, in the increasingly important markets of Finland, Sweden and Norway wine is retailed by a state monopoly as it is also in some of the provinces of Canada and states in the

USA. The reasons for this primarily relate to a desire to restrict alcohol consumption because of the perceived negative health and social impacts of alcohol. For example, the English version of the Systembolaget website, the Swedish Alcohol Retail Monopoly, states that the organisation 'exists for one reason only: To minimise alcohol-related problems by selling alcohol in a responsible way, without profit motive'.

However, state monopolies do not necessarily mean poor-quality wine or service. In fact overall trade liberalisation and, in the case of Europe, the openness of borders to bring in alcohol for private consumption means that state monopolies are often starting to act like specialist wine retail chains. In the case of Sweden, the mission of Systembolaget is 'to sell alcoholic beverages and to be at the forefront of developing a healthy drinking culture. We will exceed customer expectations by constantly developing our product range, knowledge, service and responsibilities' (Systembolaget, 2003, p. 2). Systembolaget argues that by being a monopoly they 'can maintain a more comprehensive product range, more rigorous quality control and better trained employees than anyone would be capable of in a market open to competition' (2003, pp. 4, 6). The Systembolaget product range is actually among the most extensive in the world, with a regular range of around 3000 brands of beer, wine and spirits from around 40 countries, and just as many products available to order. The number of Systembolaget stores has increased from 384 in 1995 to 411 in 2005 (Systembolaget, 2006). Significantly, even a small rural Systembolaget store has around 700 brands available with larger ones more than 1500. Around 900 new products are introduced each year with each one being tasted before hand. In 2005, Systembolaget received 17,773 tenders and sampled 11,859 products (Systembolaget, 2006). In addition, staff receive an extensive training programme.

Some aspects of the Systembolaget marketing system are exemplary and would be regarded as good practice for any large wine retailer. For example, a customer satisfaction index (CSI) has been developed and serves as one of Systembolaget's strategic key performance indicators at both an overall operational level and for every store. A total of over 60,000 people are questioned as part of the survey (150 per store) and the survey is carried out once a year. In 2005, the areas that customers regarded as being of most importance in terms of their satisfaction with Systembolaget were social responsibility and product range, but store personnel and the store itself was also regarded as important. Interestingly, support for the monopoly has also increased with just over half (52%) of respondents in 2005 indicating that they would be likely to vote to retain the monopoly.

The 2005 survey also indicated that Systembolaget's customers are more satisfied with their Systembolaget store than their food store. The difference being most pronounced when it comes to satisfaction with personnel which is one of the highest values in the survey. Customers also rate Systembolaget's product range and stores more highly, but, interestingly, rate value for money lower (Systembolaget, 2006).

The contemporary retailing model developed by Systembolaget is now being emulated by other monopolies and arguably for some of the same reasons. First, growing competition for the alcohol dollar as a result of increased, albeit restricted competition, from cross-border purchasing, partial deregulation of the alcohol market (usually beer), and increased capacity of restaurants to purchase direct. Second, so as to decrease the likelihood that monopoly retailers will be further deregulated or even abolished. For example, the Liquor Control Board of Ontario (LCBO) embarked on a modernisation plan in 1998 which sought to position the LCBO as Ontario's 'source for entertaining ideas' and which resulted in major changes to the store network:

- Improving stores street frontage and location.
- Improving look inside and out.
- Making the look consistent, including displays and signage.
- Improving accessibility and parking.
- Closing or consolidating stores that no longer met customer needs.
- Creating value adding for customers, for example, larger destination stores offering a full range of products including tutored tastings and advice on food matching.
- Improved consumer research.

This strategy was further enhanced by the five year strategic plan (2003–2008) which developed a new brand vision 'Discover the World' that 'calls on employees to engage customers in a journey of discovery, to take the mystery out of the bottle and the perceived risk out of the purchase' (LCBO, 2007).

Although the LCBO's mission is similar to that of other monopolies ('To be a socially responsible, performance-driven, innovative and profitable retailer, engaging our customers in a discovery of the world of beverage alcohol through enthusiastic, courteous and knowledgeable service' (LCBO, 2006, p. 8)), it should also be noted that the LCBO is an important driver for purchase of local Ontario wines. For example, one of the six corporate objectives of the LCBO is to promote the domestic wine industry and grow sales of Ontario wines. The Liquor Distribution Branch (LDB) in British Columbia, trading as BC Liquor Stores, has similarly been involved in the promotion of British Columbia wines. However, the long-term capacity of a retail monopoly to have that role may be endangered in the light of increased reduction of barriers on international trade in wine (Box 6.2).

Box 6.2 Market segmentation of retail customers in Ontario

In 1997, the customer segmentation of LCBO customers was based on consumer interest in learning more, social habits, shopping and product preferences. In 2006–2007, a new segmentation strategy was launched that was based more on behaviour than attitudes, particularly with respect to what is actually being purchased and the likelihood of spending more. According to the LCBO (2006, p. 9) 'this gives the LCBO more insight into their interests and helps us align our strategy better to cross-sell, up-sell and migrate customers to other product categories'. The new segmentation was based on a one-off study of more than 1000 interviews conducted Ontario wide, an annual Corporate Tracking Study, which included in-depth interviews with 2400 customers, and focus groups held in the major urban centres Toronto, Brampton, London, Ottawa and Sudbury to gain more insight into likes and dislikes and preferences. The six segments and their characteristics identified in 2006 (LCBO, 2006) were:

- *Experience seekers*: Mostly interested in red and imported wines. Usually browse the aisles and are interested in learning about new products. Buy on advice of employees, media and culinary magazines. Well educated, married, aged 40 to 59 years with high income.
- *Mixers and shakers*: Interested in coolers, spirits and beers. Like to browse, open to suggestions and willing to pay more for premium products. Influenced by recommendations from employees, media and incentive shopping schemes. Single and under 25 years.
- *Peers and cheers*: Interested in beer, spirits and occasionally Ontario white wine. Knowledgeable about beer but have little interest in learning about other products. Shop often but make quick in and out visits. Young married men.
- *Young Experimental Sociables*: Mostly interested in wines from all regions. Buying decisions influenced by product features, bonus airmiles and value adds. Food matching also an interest. Open to suggestions. Young and single.
- *Aspiring stay-at-homes*: Interested in wine, but sometimes beer, usually imported. Purchases based on brand, price and incentive schemes. Occasional shopper for beverage alcohol but open to learning more about all beverage alcohol. Married.
- *Comfy at homes*: Interested in Ontario white wine, but sometimes beer, usually domestic. Occasional shoppers, their purchasing decisions are based on price and incentive shopping. They have little interest in learning more. Older women with lower income.

Duty-free retail

Another specialist type of wine retailer is the duty-free store found in airports, ports and border crossings which enable purchasers to take designated quantities of wine across borders. In 2005, the world's total trade in duty-free and travel retail goods reached US$27 billion, corresponding to a growth of 8.0% on 2004. This percentage figure is about 3% points higher than the 5–6% growth rate recorded for the number of international tourist arrivals in 2005. Airport shops represent 52.2% of global duty-free and travel retail sales (Group Generation, 2006). According to Wine Industry Report (2006) wine represented 28% of global duty-free and travel retail sales in 2005, up from 12.5% in 1990. Harry Loebenstein, the General Manager of South African group Distell's global duty-free division, suggests that Singapore and Dubai are amongst the top five airports in terms of luxury spend by travellers. Stockholm airport is another high-value shopping destination, along with Frankfurt. 'Amongst travellers using duty-free retail at these airports, price is less of a factor than quality. Shoppers want uniqueness, style and exclusivity' (in Wine Industry Report, 2006). Nevertheless there are significant differences in regional markets with respect to duty-free purchase. For example, in the Indian travel market wine and spirits, cigarettes and confectionery are preferred purchases at duty-free shops. Shopping at duty-free shops for Indian travel consumers is more impulse driven than pre-planned (Tax Free World Association, 2006). However, for Asia Pacific travel consumers (Peoples Republic of China, Hong Kong, Japan, South Korea, Singapore, and Taiwan) airport shopping was primarily motivated by price and the purchasing tends to be pre-planned rather than impulsive (Tax Free World Association, 2005).

In the European market traditional duty-free items (cosmetics and fragrances, tobacco and liquor) are the most frequently purchased among products at airports and most of these purchases are pre-planned. According to a European traveller survey conducted by the Tax Free World Association (2002) liquor was purchased by 32% of respondents of which almost 85% was pre-planned.

A major challenge for the wine retail component of duty-free retail is the introduction of new security measures on liquids that was introduced initially on the trans-Atlantic route in 2006 and for most international carriers in major markets in 2007. In April 2007, the International Civil Aviation Organisation (ICAO) issues new guideline recommendations to its 189 member airports on tamper-free bags as well as security principles for retail liquids, most significant of which was that liquids should be carried in containers of no greater than 100 millilitres (Newhouse, 2007), thereby potentially significantly affecting outbound wine retail sales. For example, on the 30 March 2007 Australian Federal Minister for Small Business, Industry and Tourism Fran Bailey announced new procedures that permit full duty-free shopping to continue in Australia's downtown duty- and tax-free stores as well as at post security 'airside' stores. However, the decision only occurred after weeks of lobbying by the Australian Duty Free Association (ADFA) to ensure that duty-free and tax-free items purchased in off-airport locations could still be purchased by customers and exported.

Internet retail

The final category of retail is that of internet retail. However, arguably the internet is an extension of existing categories of retail undertaken via a different distribution channel as all categories of wine retail, as well as wineries themselves, can sell by the internet although a major difference is that for some retailers their shop front may now only be on the web rather than the high street. Such multi-channel wine distribution systems offer an array of retail experiences, and in the process, deliver not only more value, but also different kinds of value for customers.

The greatest difficulty for internet wine retailers are the legal and regulatory issues associate with selling alcohol although these primarily relate to restrictions on selling alcohol to under-age purchasers and sending wine into other jurisdictions, whether they be national or provincial/state boundaries. From the consumers perspective the greatest advantage of the internet is the capacity to gain access to a far greater range of wine. Producers can utilise the internet as a means of making their wines available to a far greater range of customers while retailers can similarly use the internet as an alternative sales outlet. For all retailers the internet is a good means of maintaining customer relationships when customers are otherwise unable or unwilling to visit the normal retail outlet. In the USA, wholesalers have been the most vocal opponents of direct shipping, because such a system bypasses them and undermines the foundation of the 'three-tier' alcohol distribution system that has mandated the wholesaler's role in the supply chain (Tedeschi, 2005). Under that system, which many states adopted after the repeal of Prohibition, alcohol producers must sell to wholesalers, who must sell to retailers, who then sell to the public. However, a 2005 US Supreme Court decision meant that states that allow in-state wineries or retailers to direct ship, using the internet for example, must allow out of state wineries or retailers to do the same thing. This does still mean that states have the power to bar all direct sales but it did at least allow the loosening up of regulatory constraints on the wine trade (see Chapter 1). Mathwick et al. (2001, p. 40) argue that:

On-line shoppers are veterans of the direct retail environment, accustomed to dictating the terms of exchange. Whether on- or off-line, these shoppers have come to expect retailers to know who they are, what they've ordered in the past, and how they like to be contacted. They expect to be able to interact through whatever means (mail, phone, web, faxes or in-store) they choose, demanding personalized service, 24/7 access and memorable shopping experiences.

Whether this perspective paints the complete picture of internet retail is still open to substantial debate, particularly as internet usage widens. Nevertheless, the absence of face-to-face contact in technology based retail service encounters means that in order for internet retailing to provide customer satisfaction it must (Zeithami et al., 2006):

- Solve an intensified need, that is a customer can get a desired bottle of wine via the internet that was unobtainable by other means.
- Be better than the alternative, by saving time and money, was easy to use (well designed) and was available when required.
- Ensure the technology works, that is by ensuring the system is online.
- Ensure the process works, if a product is ordered and paid for it must then be delivered on time and be the correct product.

The retail servicescape

The servicescape is the physical setting within which service occurs and which influences customers' perceptions of the servicescape (perceived quality) and the subsequent internal (i.e. degree of satisfaction) and external (i.e. behaviour with respect to patronage and purchase) response (Figure 6.4). The servicescape is regarded as important for consumer experiences because this environment gives customers and employees tangible and intangible signs and signals about potential service delivery (Bitner, 1992; Luomala, 2003) as well as the level of pleasure and arousal of the customer (Mattila and Wirtz, 2001). As Mudie and Pirrie (2006, p. 65) comment, 'The control by the designer of corporate elements that form interior spaces can impact on the success of that delivery in a variety of ways.

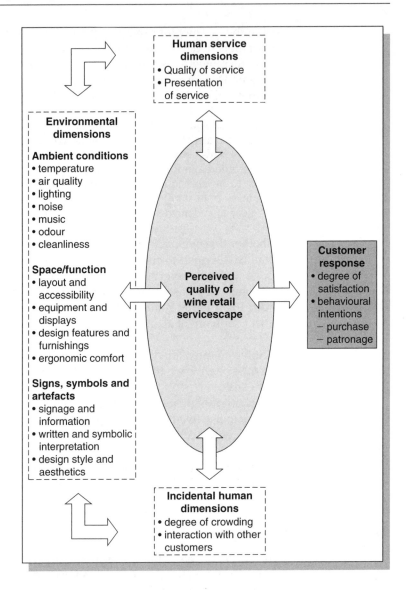

Figure 6.4
Wine retail
servicescape

It can influence the ... customer's perception of the particular service sector and can enhance the function, appropriateness and ambience of the activity'.

The environmental dimension of the servicescape refers to the physical components of the environment that can be controlled by the firm to enhance the customer's experience. These are the features that influence an individual's responses and behaviour in the servicescape and were originally categorised by Bitner (1992) as ambient conditions; spatial layout and functionality; and signs, symbols and artefacts (Figure 6.4).

Servicescapes occur over different scales and can range from individual rooms or areas within rooms through to the external built and cultural environment. For example, the servicescape of a winery will often range from the tasting room to the winescape of the surrounding vineyards and human settlements. The wine retail servicescape can usually be divided into two different settings. The overall servicescape of the retail outlet and the servicescape of the wine retail category. This is because with the exception of specialist retailers who deal only in wine, other retailers such as supermarkets and high street retailers also sell other products. Therefore, the category of wine products, often along with other alcoholic products, tends to have its own discrete retail pace and therefore environment. This has developed partly as a result of the retail approach of 'category management' by which products, such as different wines and alcoholic beverages, are grouped together in a manner that reflects customer needs based on how a product is consumed or purchased and, in some cases, regulatory requirements.

Donovan and Rossiter (1982) demonstrated that levels of pleasure (the degree to which a person feels happy, joyful, good or satisfied with the retail situation) and arousal (the degree to which a person feels alert, excited, stimulated or active in the retail situation) could predict customer behaviour in retail settings. The development of appropriate servicescape factors has been clearly identified as being positively related to the level of customer excitement and/or desire to stay longer in retail situations, such as a mall (Wakefield and Baker, 1998) or stores (Baker et al., 1992), thereby increasing the likelihood of increased purchasing (Donovan et al., 1994; Turley and Milliman, 2000).

Ambient conditions

Ambient conditions are the stimulus characteristics that affect perception, that is the sensory elements that consumers can sense in the environment. These include factors such as weather, temperature, light, air quality, noise, music, odour and colour. All these stimuli can effect how people think, feel and behave in a retail environment (Mattila and Wirtz, 2001). An example of stimuli affecting behaviour in an environment is that of odour. Scent has an effect on customer behaviour by acting as an olfactory cue to influence behaviour. Scent is used in a range of retail settings such as bakeries, coffee shops, and supermarkets in order not only to attract customers, but also to encourage spending more time within the environment. Scent can also improve store evaluations (Spangenberg et al., 1996). Many consumers implicitly associate cleanliness with the quality of the servicescape. For example, whether or not floors, shelving and display units are clean, whether restrooms are polished and disinfected, and whether garbage cans or waste bins are overflowing or not, will all affect the perceived quality of the retail outlet. Indeed, cleanliness has been found to exert a strong influence on consumers' perceptions of retail stores and services (Turley and Milliman, 2000). In general the longer the individual spends in the environment the greater the effect the ambient conditions will have.

Spatial layout and functionality

The spatial layout and functionality of a servicescape are particularly important for fulfilling the needs of a consumer within the servicescape. Spatial layout refers to how equipment is arranged within the servicescape and the relationship between different equipment. For example, the grid layout of most supermarket chains with long gondolas of merchandise and aisles in a repetitive pattern minimises the time spent shopping by customers and enhances the space productivity (Levy and Weitz, 2004). In the case of retail stores accessibility is an important aspect of spatial layout. Display space, particularly at the end of shopping aisles or in premium positions is regarded as a significant influence on purchasing, particularly when combined with appropriate signage and information (Varley, 2001). Furthermore, where a product is placed on shelves may also be significant with respect to likelihood of purchase as a result of visibility and accessibility. Such issues may become particularly pertinent with respect to elderly or disabled consumers who may find it difficult to reach high or low shelves (Leighton and Seaman, 1997). Functionality is the degree to which the equipment and layout facilitates the goals of the consumer. The experience a consumer has will likely be positive if the equipment facilitates the consumer intentions and the layout is aesthetically pleasing.

Signs, symbols and artefacts

Servicescapes provide explicit and implicit signals that communicate the features about a retail space to the individual. Examples of explicit communication would be signs or labels displaying the name of the company, types of wine, rules of behaviour with respect to legal age of purchase, as well as signs about entrances and exists. These signs may reduce stress that consumers may feel within the servicescape, which is likely to influence the consumer experience. In addition, specific interpretation or information may be made available on particular wines or varieties including wine and food matching or information with respect to history and culture.

Implicit communication may be done through symbols and artefacts; these give cues to the user on how to behave in the environment. These implicit cues are largely culturally based, for example a wine servicescape of a specialist retailer that uses high-quality construction materials with respect to wine shelves, such as quality wooden shelves, in contrast to metal and plastic shelving of supermarkets communicates symbolic meaning to the individual.

When consumers are unfamiliar with a servicescape they will look to environmental cues to help with their perceptual interpretation process, firstly categorising the servicescape and then forming inferences about it (Zeithami et al., 2006). Indeed, such features will act as a 'filter' with respect to consumer interest in particular retail environments and serve to match customer attributes with the perceived attributes of the retailer.

Influencing customer behaviour

The perception of retail store attributes along with shopping motives can have a significant influence on customer behaviour (Eroglu et al., 2003; Morschett et al., 2005). As with all areas of wine marketing it is important to recognise that there is no 'average shopper' in the real world and that research is required to determine the specific market attributes of each retail outlet and how they add value to the development of brand as well as to the consumer. A good retail example of the need to undertake research on consumer preferences is with respect to different cultural perception of consumer–consumer interactions, as perception of crowding can be important environmental factors affecting consumers' retail experience. For example, Pons et al. (2006) found that Middle Eastern consumers perceived both a lower level of density and appreciated crowded situations more than their North American counterparts.

However, in all cases it is important to recognise that no matter what the wine retail outlet the retail experience must deliver value if it is to turn a one-time visitor into a repeat customer. This perceived value is the essential outcome of marketing activity and a primary motivation for customers and providers to enter into marketing relationships (Holbrook, 1994; Peterson, 1995). Different retail environments and services will meet those values in different ways. For many high street and supermarket retailers this will generally be in terms of the extrinsic benefits it provides which will be quite utilitarian in terms of an exchange encounter. In contrast, for specialist wine retailers (as well as for many cellar door experiences, see Chapter 4) there will typically be much more intrinsic value derived from the 'appreciation of an experience for its own sake, apart from any other consequence that may result' (Holbrook, 1994, p. 40). Indeed, the specialist retail environment will often provide a context for active or participative value which implies greater collaboration and a stronger relationship between the customer and the retailer. Significantly, such a situation reflects the perspective of this book with respect to the importance of the co-creation of wine experiences. As Deighton and Grayson (1995) observed, consumer collaboration is a necessary prerequisite to creating a playful, game like exchange experience which takes the buyer across a threshold from distanced appreciation to active collaboration, and in the process, opens the door to a broad range of value sources for consumer, producer and, in the case of this chapter, the retailer. Chapter 4 presents several strategies for the cellar door that may also be useful in the development of relationships with consumers (Box 6.3).

Box 6.3 Good wine retailers

A good retail store specialising in wine should:

- Cater to their customers, not only via their selection of wine, but also through their willingness to provide help and provide friendly efficient service.
- Offer variety and selection.
- Provide a balance between value and quality for their customers.
- Know the value of visual presentation and merchandising. Shelf space should be fresh and filled and the store should be well maintained, clean and well lit.
- Have a clear return's policy.
- The retailer's knowledge of wine should be apparent when the customer seeks advice.
- When a wine retailer offers additional, upscale merchandise, consider it a bonus for the wine shopper.
- Derived in part from Merchant of Vino. http://www.thewineman.com/m_vino.htm

---

Conclusions

This chapter has analysed some of the macro- and micro-marketing dimensions of wine retailing. Internationally, retail market trends favour further rationalisation of retailing with growing market dominance of fewer chains. These chains utilise global supply and sourcing systems in order to keep prices low so as to maintain or grow market share. The implications of this structure for wine marketing is profound as in both developed and developing countries supermarket chains' share of retailing overall, and wine retailing in particular, is growing. This has meant that smaller wineries find it increasingly difficult to get their wines on to supermarket shelves and instead must focus on independent chains and specialist retailers for such opportunities. However, even large wine companies, even though they may be better able to enter mutually beneficial business to business relationships with supermarket chains, are under pressure particularly as many retailers are able to develop own brand labels in a market that is oversupplied with cheap yet reasonable-quality wine. Those companies that do enter relationships with supermarket retailers will also likely have to financially support in-store promotions of their wines in order to gain market profile unless they have been able to utilise other avenues to generate demand through either their own promotion and marketing activities in general or specialist media or have received publicity via wine write-ups or winning awards (see Chapter 9). Smaller wineries will need to enter into specific business to business relations with specialist retailers who have an interest in selling smaller brands and varieties to customers as well as exporting agents and distributors who, in turn, will have a network of retailers that support such labels.

Consideration of the retail servicescape will be significant no matter what type of retail outlet. Consideration of the wine retail servicescape applies at two different scales. The building or retail space as a whole and the specific wine retail space. In specialist retailers these two scales are combined. Importantly, consideration of the servicescape means paying attention to how design features and complementarity with a wine's branding and positioning as well as more mundane issues such as ease of accessibility. However, the goal of all servicescapes and retailer strategies should be to positively influence consumer behaviour so as to ensure purchase.

Practical wine marketing insights

- The internationalisation of wine retailing and the development of global source and supply systems reinforces the intensity of competition in the wine market.

- Supermarket chains are increasingly dominating retail wine sales.
- Supermarket chains tend to focus on high volume low price wines and enter B2B relations with larger distributors.
- In order to maximise retail opportunities in supermarket chains, wine companies will usually have to financially support in-store promotional activities in addition to any external promotion they will be doing.
- Independent and specialist retail stores offer the best possibilities for retailing the wines of small producers and non-mainstream wine varieties; although some national and provincial alcohol monopolies will also be promising.
- Specialist retail stores offer opportunities for direct customer contact through tastings and wine clubs as well as the development of personal relations with the owner/ manager of the outlet.
- Consideration of retail servicescapes is integral to successful wine retailing from both the retailers and the producers perspectives.
- Producers should consider how particular retail environments reinforce or diminish the brand values of particular labels and how it fits within the overall positioning of their products.

Further reading

Institute of Grocery Distribution (IGD): http://www.igd.com/
UK-based non-profit organisation that provides substantial resources on the UK, European and international food and grocery chain.

Bitner, M.J. (1992). Servicescapes: the impact of physical surroundings on customers and employees. *Journal of Marketing*, 56(2), 57–71.
A seminal article with respect to considering the physical evidence of service.

Lockshin, L.S., Spawton, A.L. and Macintosh, G. (1997). Using product, brand and purchasing involvement for retail segmentation. *Journal of Retailing and Consumer Services*, 4(3), 171–183.
Details ways in which different purchasing factors with respect to wine can be used as a basis for retail market segmentation.

Reibstein, D.J. (2002). What attracts customers to online stores, and what keeps them coming back? *Journal of the Academy of Marketing Science*, 30(4), 465–473.
Paper concludes that what attracts customers to a website are not the same dimensions critical in retaining customers on a longer-term basis.

Varley, R. (2001). *Retail Product Management: Buying and Merchandising*, Routledge.
A very good text on the retailing process and its management.

Licensed premises

Chapter objectives

After reading this chapter you will

- Appreciate the importance of food trends as a factor influencing consumption of wine in licensed premises, particularly licensed restaurants
- Understand the role of gatekeepers in supply and sourcing systems for licensed premises
- Understand the influence of different sourcing systems on wine lists
- Appreciate some of the different approaches to developing wine lists
- Understand some of the different pricing strategies for wine at restaurants
- Appreciate the importance of wait staff or menu recommendation as a determinant of wine purchase

In this book the term licensed premises denotes businesses or organisations that have legal permission to sell alcohol that is consumed on site. In the UK, this is also known as an on-licence (and the in the wine trade the on-trade), as opposed to an off-licence (off-trade) which requires the purchaser to consume the alcohol off-site. The category includes restaurants, hotels, and public houses (pubs and bars, including wine bars) and, in some jurisdictions cafes and institutions. Different national and regional jurisdictions have different licensing categories therefore making international comparisons difficult. This chapter will focus on restaurants and public houses as places within which wine is sold and served. The primary difference between the two being the supply of food, although increasingly categories are blurred as pubs and bars provide food and restaurants and bistros a range of alcoholic beverages. Indeed, this is in part a reflection of the notion that alcohol, and wine in particular, is something that accompanies food. As Walker and Lundberg (2001, p. 8) commented 'Restaurants are places where the public comes to be restored, nutritionally and psychologically'. Nevertheless, there are significant differences between restaurant marketing and the role of restaurants in wine marketing. The focus of the present chapter is on the latter.

The chapter is divided into two main sections. The first discusses trends with respect to eating and drinking out of the home environment. The second looks at various aspects of the micro-marketing environment of restaurants and pubs by which increased value can be provided to the customer and wine businesses.

Eating out

One of the paradoxes of modern society is that although food, including wine, has become more of a focus of fashion, consumption and identity than ever before, fewer and fewer people actually know how to cook. This therefore means that greater numbers of people in westernised consumer societies are either eating out or purchasing ready-made meals from supermarkets and retailers. In both cases there are marketing opportunities for wine. In the case of those that buy pre-packaged meals this will primarily be from retailers (see Chapter 6) although a number of restaurants also provide home-meal replacement services. However, for those eating out at restaurants this will most likely be from the restaurant itself. In some cases, where licensing laws allow, in the form of Bring Your Own (BYO) wine, wine may also be purchased from retailers and taken by the consumer to licensed premises (see Plate 7.1).

There are a number of trends affecting the propensity of people to dine out, many of which are the same trends affecting wine (see Chapter 2). Foremost, there is the cultural context of restaurants and dining out. In some western countries, such as Scandinavia, Australia, New Zealand, the UK and the USA, dining out has historically generally been seen as a luxury or something reserved for special occasions. However, major changes in lifestyle and consumption since the 1970s (including changes in leisure time, leisure and work patterns, increase in disposable income, the development of food media, growing multiculturalism and greater levels of travel) have lead to a radical change in eating behaviour within two generations (Kinsey and Senauer, 1996; Bianchi et al., 2000; Warde and Martens, 2000; Blisard et al., 2002). For example, Mintel (2004) reported that Britain now seems to have a pervasive 'food' culture, in part generated by the onslaught of television celebrity chefs (see also Chapter 9), as well as the ongoing product and service improvements made in the food and beverage industry. Furthermore, western lifestyles tend to result in an increased desire for speed and convenience and this is changing the way eating out establishments operate. For example, in the USA spending on away-from-home foods as a percentage of total food expenditure rose steadily by approximately 5–6% per decade between 1960 and 2000, reaching over 40% in 2000, a doubling from approximately 20% in 1960 (Kant and Graubard, 2004).

In contrast, eating outside of one's own home environment has been traditional in many Mediterranean cultures although even here there have been substantial shifts in eating behaviour. Some of the national differences in dining out, as well as a gradual increase in expenditure in relative terms, can be seen in Table 7.1 which details consumption expenditure on restaurants and hotels as a percentage of total household expenditure for key European markets and the USA.

Restaurants are a major and growing sector of the economy of developed countries. Since the 1950s the restaurant sector has usually been divided into three major segments: fast food, casual dining and fine dining. However, in recent years the sector has become increasingly diversified as new service opportunities arise, leading to new segments such as home-meal replacement and quick casual (also referred to as fast casual), which are restaurants that combine the food and atmosphere of full-service restaurants with the speed of fast-food restaurants. In the USA restaurant industry sales account for approximately 4% of gross domestic product (GDP) employing an estimated 12.8 million people, making it the largest employer outside of the public sector (National Restaurant Association (NRA), 2007). In the US commercial restaurant establishments are divided

Table 7.1 Restaurants and hotels as percentage of total household consumption expenditure (at current prices)

Jurisdiction	1995 (%)	2000 (%)	2005 (%)
EU (25 countries)	8.2	8.8	9.0
EU (15 countries)	8.3	8.9	9.2
Euro area	7.8	8.3	8.8
Austria	11.1	11.2	12.3
Finland	7.0	6.4	6.5
France	5.9	6.2	6.1
Germany	5.7	5.7	5.3
Ireland	14.5	14.4	13.8
Italy	8.6	9.5	9.8
Poland	3.2	3.1	2.9
Portugal	10.6	10.4	10.3
Spain	18.4	18.1	18.9
Sweden	4.5	5.0	5.1
UK	11.4	11.5	11.9
USA	6.5	6.4	

Source: derived from Eurostat, http://epp.eurostat.ec.europa.eu/

into: eating places; drinking places; managed services; lodging-place restaurants; and retail, vending, recreation and mobile restaurants. According to the NRA (2007):

- Average unit sales in 2004 were US$795,000 at full-service restaurants and US$671,000 at limited-service restaurants.
- More than 7 out of 10 eating-and-drinking places are single-unit (independent) operations.
- Nearly half of all adults have worked in the restaurant industry at some time during their lives and 32% of adults got their first job experience in a restaurant.

In terms of the market, the NRA (2007) report states:

- The average household expenditure for food away from home in 2005 was US$2634 or US$1054 per person.
- Four out of five – consumers agree that going out to a restaurant is a better way to use their leisure time than cooking and cleaning up.
- 38% of table service-restaurant operators anticipated that takeout would represent a larger proportion of their total sales in 2007.
- 43% of table service restaurant operators offering organic menu items anticipated that they would represent a larger proportion of their total sales in 2007.
- 37% of consumers have used curbside takeout at a table service restaurant.
- 59% of table service restaurant operators offer televisions for customer entertainment.

Significantly, the NRA (2006) also reported that wine is becoming increasingly popular at US restaurants. A survey of over 1000 chefs indicated that among fine-dining operators, 65% expected wine to represent a larger proportion of sales in 2007, while 50% of casual dining and 37% of family dining operators expected the same (see Plate 7.2).

Such figures are important as they reflect the diversity of the restaurant market and emphasise that not all restaurants are fine dining. Moreover, the US is often regarded as a trendsetter with respect to restaurant chains and the extent to which such models may be emulated in Europe and elsewhere. For example, Caterer and Housekeeper (2006) commented, 'The challenge for European foodservice is how to emulate the US dynamics where burgers gave way to pizzas, which in turn were overtaken by coffee chains, and now subs (the US term for long baguette-type sandwiches that are filled to order for takeaway) are leading the way'. Nevertheless, US chains have found it hard to establish themselves in Europe with only 12 US-foodservice chains that operate in Europe having more than five outlets. Between them they operate fewer than 14,000 stores (out of 1.5 million popular eating places) with McDonald's accounting for over half of those units.

Although chains do not appear to have been as successful in the European restaurant sector as in the US, in a number of European countries chains and transnational firms own a significant number of licensed premised, particularly in the hotel sector. For example, in the UK in November 2006 there were 58,197 pubs of which only 17,800 were independent. The rest were either brewer or pub company owned. In addition there were approximately 63,000 other outlets with an on-licence (hotels, wine bars, restaurants), 27,000 licensed and registered clubs and 53,000 off-licences (British Beer and Pub Association, 2006).

European and North American restaurant trends are increasingly being repeated elsewhere (e.g. Restaurant Association of New Zealand, 2006). Significantly, research demonstrates that as per capita income increases so per capita expenditure on dining out increases, and at a rate faster than per capita expenditure on food for at-home consumption (Blisard et al., 2002). This suggests that demand for eating out, and therefore restaurant experiences, will continue to increase in the developed world. This is also true in the rapidly industrialising economies of Asia where a considerable consumer class exists, even when other factors, such as an aging population, are taken into account. Of course such trends only provide a limited indication of the potential of restaurants and other licensed premises for wine consumption and sales. Other factors that are significant include:

- Regulations surrounding the consumption of alcohol.
- Food trends, particularly as the rapid growth of cuisines from non-wine regions of the world, such as South Asia, East Asia, and North Africa and the Middle East, in Europe and North America, provides a significant challenge for wine and food matching and wine promotion in relation to other traditional accompanying beverages. The westernisation of foodways in Asian markets, of course, creates new opportunities for wine.
- Perceptions of the health benefits of wine, which may be significant for promoting greater wine sales in restaurants.

In an examination of the economic impacts of the Californian wine industry using benchmarking analysis from the NRA plus information from restaurant, retail and distribution industry experts, MKF Research (2007) conservatively estimated that about 5% of the revenues of all US full-service restaurants may be attributed to sales of wine. However, such a figure will be extremely variable depending on the nature of the restaurant. For example, in 1989 Susan Koral of Spectrum Foods in San Francisco estimated that perhaps 60% of the premium table wine sold in the US was sold in restaurants (in Walker, 1989). Yet the reality is that then, as now, we do not really know, although there is no doubt that restaurant sales are a very important segment in the premium wine market. Nevertheless, the value of wine for restaurants is not just the direct revenue received from sales but also the contribution that the availability of wine makes to the attractiveness of the restaurant to consumers as well as the contribution that wine makes to the overall meal experience.

Licensed restaurants and premises are therefore a very important conduit for wine sales. However, in terms of wineries this should also be seen as only one of the benefits of restaurant sales. New brands can get quick recognition on a wine list because of the potential customer exposure while existing brands can add value by being available in certain restaurants that reinforce their positioning. The brand awareness provided by a restaurant listing is arguably extremely important for small wine producers who otherwise may be limited in their distribution. Indeed, distribution issues are as significant for licensed premises as they are for the retail sector.

Making wine available at restaurants and licensed premises

A key issue for the role of restaurants in wine marketing is how they source their wine. This means understanding distribution and supply systems in different national and regional jurisdictions as well as restaurant perception of customer preferences (see Chapter 5). Figure 7.1 indicates some of the factors that influence the selection of a wine list for restaurants. However, some generalisations can be made.

- *Chain restaurants or licensed premises* will usually be 'locked in' to a supply agreement with distributors or sometimes larger producers with a broad range of brands. This therefore offers very little opportunity to small wineries even if they are located close by to the restaurant, as supply contracts will usually be exclusive. Indeed, in some countries, the UK for example, many public houses are either owned or leased by breweries or pub companies, who will determine not only

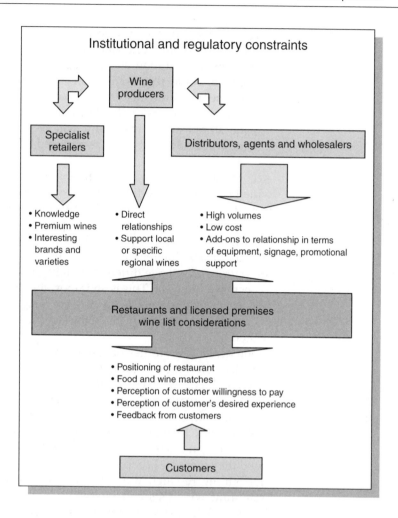

Figure 7.1
Factors
influencing the
development of
a restaurant and
licensed
premises wine
list

the beer sold but all other beverages. Such arrangements will obviously favour those wine brands that are already part of the distributor's range of brands and other large distributors.

- Some *smaller restaurants*, particularly bistros and themed restaurants, will often enter into an exclusive contract with alcohol distributors so as to take advantage of other aspects of the relationship such as supply of equipment (e.g. fridges), signage, free or subsidised restaurant promotional activities and underwriting the cost of producing the wine and beverage list. Again, this relationship favours wine brands already part of a distributor's stable of wines.
- *Independent full-service restaurants* will often enter into a range of supply relationships in order to build up a wine list appropriate to their food. In such situations key suppliers will usually be specialised wine retailers who offer an important

knowledge function in supplying smaller brands, interesting offerings and premium wines for a wine list, as well as reserve wine list preparation and management. In addition, where possible, some restaurants will also enter direct purchase agreements with wineries. However, unless a restaurant has a large storage area suitable for wine then the amount of wine stored at the restaurant will be relatively small and wine will be ordered on an as required basis.

According to Fattorini (1997) the main focus in developing a wine list should be to find a balance between what customers want to spend and can spend, and the absolute need to turn over the wine stock at a reasonable profit in a reasonable time. On the other hand, considerations must also be devoted to expectations of different markets, for example non-local restaurant patrons may have different 'taught preferences' of what to expect on a wine list. This is an important factor particularly in full-service restaurants as tourists are a significant proportion of customers, particularly given the significance of food tourism related motivations.

One of the few studies of restaurant policies with respect to wine list selection was undertaken by Thorsen and Hall (2001) who conducted a survey of New Zealand restaurants in 2001. Eighty-nine replies were received back from a mail survey of 254 restaurants. Of these 64 (25.2% of mail-out) were usable replies, with 18 replies being non-usable because they were either without a license or were BYO only. All respondents indicated they were on-licence holders or BYO and on-licence holders. Survey research was also complimented by analysis of restaurant wine lists and interviews with restaurant owners. Table 7.2 details some of responses of restaurants to a series of questions with respect to wine policies while an outline of results is provided below:

- *Origin of Wines*: Nearly all respondents carried non-New Zealand wines. Four respondents specified in writing that their policy was to list New Zealand and local wines only. The three most frequent overseas wines carried by respondents were Australia, France and Italy. Most respondents indicated Australian red wine in the wine list, while nearly half of the respondents indicated French Champagne. South African and Chilean wine was increasingly being adopted by restaurants, in part because of value perceptions. Fine-dining restaurants carried the most extensive stocks of international wines although they had a wider selection of wine varieties regardless of winery origin and region.

Table 7.2 Wine policy in restaurants

Statement	Strongly agree (%)	Agree (%)	Disagree (%)	Strongly disagree (%)	Mean score
It is important for a restaurant to put a strong emphasis on the wine list	31.3	59.4	9.4	–	1.78
Our business puts a strong emphasis on local wine products	26.6	59.4	14.1	–	1.88
The house wine is the flagship of the wines on the wine list	1.6	25.4	49.2	23.8	2.95
It is important to have a selection of vintage wines on the wine list	9.4	46.9	39.1	4.7	2.39
It is important to have a wide range of grape varieties in the wine list rather than origin of wines	14.1	65.6	20.3	–	2.06
It is important to arrange wine tasting courses for relevant staff in order to maintain a good wine knowledge among staff	37.5	54.7	7.8		1.70

$N = 64$.
Notes: Mean score on the basis of a 4-point scale (1 = strongly agree, 2 = agree, 3 = disagree, 4 = strongly disagree).
Source: After Thorsen and Hall (2001).

- *In charge of wine purchase and design of wine list*: Slightly over half the respondents indicated the owner as the person in charge of wine purchase and design of wine list. A general characteristic of this group showed that a significant share was small-scale operations in terms of size and wine turnover. About 25% indicated food and beverage manager or restaurant manager and the remaining the owner in cooperation with either the chef, restaurant manager or food and beverage manager. Only fine-dining restaurants with an extensive wine list selection employed a sommelier.

- *Method of wine purchase*: Most respondents only purchased their wines via a wine distributor, while 25% mooted alternative methods in addition to sourcing from a wine distributor, such as direct from wineries. Approximately 15% of respondents indicated direct purchase from specialised wine shops as a source of their wine stocks. Information from interviews suggested that in these cases the specialist advice available in such shops was the critical factor in purchasing from this source. Only one respondent indicated wine auctions as a source of wine.
- *Wine mark-up*: Over 60% of respondents indicated a mark-up between 50% and 100% of bottle cost, while 17% indicated 101–150% mark-up policy. Hotel operations had the highest mark-up of low-priced wines. A limited wine stock was the main characteristic of those with a low mark-up policy on low-priced wines. Fifty per cent of respondents indicated 51–100% mark-up for more expensive wines, while almost a third indicated 101–150% mark-up. The characteristics of the low and high mark-up operations were the same as in the variable for low-priced wines.
- *House wine*: Approximately 70% of respondents had a house wine on the wine list, with almost half of these operations indicated that their house wine was from a regional winery. Family style and hotel restaurants had the highest use of the house wine feature.

Issues associated with the difficulties that restaurants experience in establishing a wine list have also been examined by Davis and Charters (2006) who analysed some of the problems of wine list development within the context of consumer behaviour. The research findings indicated that how restaurateurs perceived their customers' desires influenced their wine list offering. However, the six interviews undertaken for the research also uncovered a greater struggle that the restaurateurs faced in creating a wine list, reflecting business and emotional needs, in the face of their perception of a customer's desire for safe but new experiences (Box 7.1). As Davis and Charters (2006, p. 12) concluded:

Restaurateurs wish to provide wines that create an experience and generate revenue. Customers want to select wines that they know or that they are comfortable trying. At times the inherent conflict becomes too much and the customers, if given the option, may simply make the decision outside the restaurant and bring their own wine. The process remains a challenge, as one restaurateur commented, 'on paper, wine lists are very easy to do'.

Box 7.1 Wine pricing at restaurants and licensed premises

One of the most vexed issues for customers at restaurants is the pricing of wine at higher than standard retail price. For restaurant managers and their wine suppliers it is also a significant issue as it affects rates of return, the experience and the brand. Here are some explanations for pricing at restaurants.

Pricing by the bottle

Most restaurants will have a mark-up on the price of a bottle of wine at a restaurant. There is enormous variability in the mark-up around the world and it is determined by a number of factors including the customer's willingness to pay and perception of the overall value of the wine. For example, Wansink et al. (2006) report 200% to 300% margins on restaurant wine sales which is far higher than Australian and New Zealand equivalents (Thorsen and Hall, 2001). Mark-ups tend to be lower in BYO restaurants in which you can also buy wine and higher in non-BYO fine-dining restaurants and hotels. Some businesses will do a simple percentage mark-up on the purchase price although when a simple percentage mark-up is applied some higher end wines may be too expensive. Some businesses will undertake a mark-up strategy based on the gross profit method of inventory estimation while others will establish a limited number of selling prices. Experience suggests that most restaurants will set their prices by the bottle based on their perception of customer choice, the quality and availability of the wine and consideration of costs incurred in providing the wine and there is no hard and fast rule that applies. Some also develop their wine list based on having a range of wine styles within several price points (e.g. a range of wines under $US10, a range at $10–25 and a range at more than $25) to allow for a range of consumer budgets and preferences.

Pricing by the glass

Given that purchasing wine by the glass is growing in popularity at many restaurants consideration also has to be given to pricing by the glass. Prices by the glass are usually determined after consideration of the bottle pricing strategy as it is easy to calculate how many glasses can be poured from each bottle. Some restaurants will divide the bottle price exactly and charge accordingly although some wine per glass prices are often lowered as an incentive for customers to purchase a specific wine and food matching. However, in the majority of cases the price by the glass will be slightly higher than a straight divide of the bottle price as account should be provided for spillage and wastage. The same price point strategy that may be employed for wine list development for bottles may also be applied to glasses.

Pricing for cellared wines

The above discussion of pricing by the bottle and by the glass assumes that the pricing is primarily undertaken by restaurants and licensed premises that have purchased wines ready to drink and do not have the associated costs of storage and inventory control. However, where establishments are purchasing wines that are likely to be cellared so that they can be drunk when aged and/or for their rarity value, additional considerations come into the pricing strategy including replacement and storage costs. One relatively common practice is to establish a procedure for mark-up over time for each vintage so that an extra percentage is added on for each vintage of a wine or year of production.

Corkage or service fees

Where it is legal for customers to bring a bottle of wine to a restaurant a corkage or service fee is usually applied. This is usually a flat fee per bottle, but may alternatively be charged per person. There are several reasons for charging this fee. First, you are still using the restaurants glassware which means that the costs of purchase, washing and breakage have to be allowed for, as well as wine service. Second, you are compensating the restaurant for a loss of purchase and therefore potential returns if you would have otherwise purchased from the restaurant. Third, ideally a restaurant or licensed premises has expended considerable thought as to what wines should be available, therefore if wine is not purchased there is still a cost to be incurred in terms of storage.

Restaurant wine marketing strategies

Once a wine is available at a restaurant it still has to be sold. This requires it being brought to the notice of the customer usually through a wine list. However, additional considerations include the extent to which servers are familiar with the wine and its food matching potential or its characteristics when consumed on its own. Even in casual dining establishments or bars the manager and/or the chef should have provided such information to waiting staff themselves. Unfortunately, this often is not the case and, where possible, wine businesses or their agents may offer to provide information and training to waiting staff themselves. Unfortunately, outside of a local region this is beyond the capacity of the majority of wineries although it is often undertaken by larger distributors with some direct winery to restaurant relationships being established in the case of the upper end of fine dining. Such connections are important as they may increase the likelihood of a wine being recommended by the waiting staff to customers.

Wine lists themselves can be a reason for a wine aficionado to visit a restaurant, although these restaurants (and customers) are few and far between, so for the vast majority of restaurants other considerations come into play in presenting the wine list. In some cases wines are recommended with the various dining options and the wine list is integrated into the menu. However, even in such cases there is often a separate wine list to enable customers to select. There are several ways of organising a wine list:

- by categories, that is sparkling wines, whites, reds, dessert wines, digestifs; which in turn are often sub-categorised into countries and regions;
- by price;
- by vintage;
- by variety;
- by style.

It is extremely important that the design of the wine list and the level of information provided be consistent with the positioning of the restaurant and the level of knowledge of the customer. Unfortunately, too many wine lists fail to connect with customers and the information they are seeking. One strategy may be to provide some tasting notes and/or some personal information on the winery/winemaker but again this needs to be done in a carefully considered fashion so as not to be intimidating and particularly reinforce stereotypes of 'wine wankers'.

Given public interest in not only drinking healthier but also trying different styles of wine many food and beverage establishments now provide wine by the glass. One of the best examples of this approach is Bacar (meaning wine goblet in Latin), a restaurant in San Francisco's SoMa (South of Market) district that offered contemporary northern Californian cuisine (see http://www.bacarsf.com/menus.html). At the time of writing Bacar had 1400 international and domestic wine selections available by the bottle (US$20 to US$700) with 65 choices served in two- and five-ounce pours, or in 250 or 500 millimetre decanters (US$1.50 to US$75), and in flights. When purchasing decanter portions, there is no upcharge from the bottle price. Three 250 millilitre decanters cost no more than one bottle. Information on wine availability by the glass and the bottle is available on their web site.

According to Bacar wine director and co-founder, Debbie Zachareas (who left the restaurant in February 2007). 'I think in order for a restaurant to stand out and to succeed, you need something special. That's what I'm trying to do with the wine program. I love it when I see a table with two or three or four decanters, all with different wines. That makes it worth the labor' (in Walker, 2001). When interviewed Zachareas stated that the restaurant was selling 85% of their wines by the glass or decanter with 40% to 45% of total sales coming from wine, probably double the normal for Californian licensed restaurants. Although many customers do not bring their own wine the restaurant charged US$25 for corkage, but waived that if a bottle was ordered off the list. With respect to Bacar's basic pricing policy about 70% of wines were 2.75 times of cost, but it could range from two to three times cost with Zachareas noting, 'I have found that people will pay $300 for a wine that cost $200, but they won't pay $600' (in Walker, 2001).

A 12 week study of wine restaurant promotions at two restaurants of the Texas chain, Rockfish Seafood Grill (Wansink et al., 2006), provided a number of insights into the potential success of restaurant wine marketing strategies. The study's conclusions included (Firstenfeld, 2006; Wansink et al., 2006):

- More recommendations equal more wine sales. Promoting five wines increased sales of the promoted wines by 39%, without 'cannibalising' other wine sales.
- A table-tent promotion of five wines increased wine sales of promoted wines more than promotions recommending a single wine or three, leading to a 39% increase for the five featured wines, a 12% increase in overall sales and a 4% increase in total restaurant sales.
- Suggested wine and food pairings are effective, but no more than three wine recommendations.
- Tasting portions sell: The single US$2 tasting promotion increased subsequent sales of full glasses by 18.2%, but when five tastes were offered (a $10 flight of five different wines), the total increase in sales for all five wines grew 47.3% week on week.
- Promotions can cannibalise: Between 69% and 87% in sales of promoted wines came from other wines that patrons would have ordered anyway. Instead it was recommend that higher-margin wines, mid-priced or above be promoted, and margin-cutting price promotions be avoided.
- Proper waiter education is necessary to prevent over pouring and thus control costs.

The Wansink et al. (2006) study provides a number of useful marketing insights that are congruent to other restaurant marketing experiences (Scanlon, 1999). Much of it is good common sense. However, it is important to remember that these were derived in a particular wine and restaurant context and that some promotional methods used in one context might not be as successful used in another (Box 7.2).

Box 7.2 Licensed restaurants' response to the screwcap wines initiative

In 2001, a screwcap initiative was launched in New Zealand to encourage the adoption of screwcaps on fine wines (see http://www.screwcap.co.nz/). This initiative has since gone global as the International Screwcap Initiative (ISI) (Hughes, 2006). In 2005, a survey was conducted of various stakeholders in the New Zealand wine industry in order to understand the innovation diffusion processes that were occurring and the level of understanding of screwcapped wines as a technical and marketing strategy.

In the case of licensed restaurants the purpose of the study was to identify and characterise the knowledge of and service with regard to Stelvin screwcapped wines. This was done in order to enable the identification of information needs in the sector and perceptions passed on to patrons, and therefore the role of these opinion leaders in informing the greater public. Forty-eight respondents in three urban centres participated in the study.

Just over 60% of respondents felt positively toward the initiatives as opposed to just over 10% opposed. The remainder saw both positive and negative aspects of the initiative. The more informed respondents understood the advantages of screwcap with regard to wine quality and the decrease of tainted wines, while still feeling that there was a loss in ceremony and professionalism with the use of a screwcap as opposed to a cork. Those with negative attitudes tended to be non-management staff members whom were either ill-informed or uninformed, one manager had even said that the screwcap was negative because it oxidised the wines. Interestingly, many of those feeling positively about screwcapped wines did in fact say that they would prefer a screwcapped wine when buying for personal use, with many still admitting that they would buy a white in screwcap and a red in cork, and often both in cork. Only a few people said that the wine alone would influence their decision.

There was an ongoing consistency to be found between the attitudes of management and the subsequent attitudes of wait staff. This indicates the importance of having fully informed managers to create a conducive atmosphere for the acceptance of screwcapped wines in licensed restaurants as it is these attitudes that are passed on to patrons and thus to the wider public.

The most common form of information on screwcaps was wine representatives (40%), followed by trade magazines (23%) and pamphlets (17%). Tastings were only used as a source by 10% of respondents. Magazines such as *Cuisine, Decanter*, and *Harpers*, were cited as important to understanding balanced arguments over the closures. Pamphlets also featured as an important source, however it is important that these pamphlets make it passed management and on to wait staff if they are to be effective. Ten per cent of respondents said that they would not want or need any more information on screwcapped wines, which is a concern with regard to the ongoing development of the marketplace.

A very important dimension to note in the information arena was the fact that the internet never featured as a best source of information and was used by only 4.2% of those surveyed, management and non-management alike. None had used the Screwcap Initiative website and none identified it as a site to gain continued information. As the most cost-effective source of information on the initiative it is interesting that so few 'professionals' were continuing to update their information about their industry in what is a highly competitive environment. For the Initiative it is important to acknowledge this and work to increase visits to the site by restaurant managers or to understand that this is not an effective means to communicate with this sector.

Only two restaurants of those surveyed actively promoted wines as being screwcapped although this was not done as a form of advertising for the screwcap but as a means to avoid being asked questions and 'wasting time' talking about them. No restaurants had ever had a wine returned because it was screwcapped, thus indicating that patrons did not feel strongly enough about the closure to reject them. This illustrates the unified feeling of respondents that New Zealanders are very accepting of the closures and that it is no longer an issue of major importance and argument in the general marketplace. All restaurants involved in the survey had seen a change in perception over the past couple of years towards this positive acceptance of the closure. Some of those interviewed said that there had been a lingering misperception about screwcapped wines as 'cheap' wines but that appears to be diminishing. However, unlike New Zealanders, Americans and those from the UK were viewed as commenting the most often about the screwcapped wines and also as being resistant to them even when they had been informed of the qualities of the screwcap. Asians and those from Singapore and Hong Kong in particular, showed initial resistance to the closures but were regarded as open to information and experience.

Tsasha Russek and Michael Hall

Conclusions

This chapter has analysed some of the macro- and micro-marketing dimensions of wine on licensed premises. At the macro-level some of the same considerations with respect to gatekeepers and sourcing and supply systems that occur in the retail sector (Chapter 6) are shown to operate in the licensed premises, particular pubs and restaurants. In addition, licensed premises are clearly subject to significant issues of regulation with respect to alcohol sales. This means that wineries will need to understand the particular sets of relationships that will lead to the adoption of their wines on restaurant and licensed premise's wine lists. Nevertheless, it is important to note that the value of such listing is more than just financial in terms of sales, but may also be important with respect to brand values, positioning and creating customer awareness of product.

At the micro-level consideration of the wine list is important however so too is the provision of information to the customer and the means by which wine is sold, that is by the glass, bottle and/or decanter. Personal recommendations by wait staff are regarded as particularly important as are other information sources that may be provided, but in both cases wineries, agents and/or distributors will often need to engage in educational exercises so as to maximise the likelihood of appropriate recommendations. However, regardless of why wine is purchased at a licensed premise it needs to be recognised that the purchasing event should not be seen as an isolated occurrence but as part of a larger chain of value that will potentially contribute to the ongoing purchase of that brand in the same way as a visit to the winery may also contribute to a long-term and loyal customer relationship.

Practical wine marketing insights

- Much of the access of wines to licensed premises is determined by distributor and agent relationships, particularly to chain restaurants
- Independent restaurants offer some of the best opportunities for access by smaller wineries, although this may be via specialist retailers or agents
- When selling and marketing wine to and through restaurants and other licensed premises issues of relationship to brand positioning are an important long-term consideration
- Wine lists can be provided to customers in a number of different formats although at all terms they should be developed with a consideration of the level of knowledge, interests and needs of the target market
- Wine by the glass is an important initiative in a market which is not only increasingly health conscious but also potentially interested in trying new wines.

Further reading

Wines and Vines: http://www.winesandvines.com/
The magazine and the website often has extremely useful information with respect to wine marketing in relation to restaurants.

Restaurant Wine: The Full Service Guide to On Sale Beverage Profits : http://www.restaurantwine.com/
This is an American bi-monthly wine industry journal published in the USA and primarily geared for the North American market.

National Restaurant Association: http://www.restaurant.org/research/
This US national association has a range of information available on their website and to their membership.

Caterer and Housekeeper: http://www.caterersearch.com/
Is a leading UK trade hospitality magazine and accompanying website.

Restaurant Startup and Growth Magazine: http://www.restaurantowner.com/
Official website of the magazine and a good source for understanding restaurant management and marketing in its own right.

British Beer and Pub Association: http://www.beerandpub. com/
Website of a key UK association with respect to public houses.

Australian Wine and Brandy Corporation (2007b). *Restaurant Wine Lists*, http://www.wineaustralia.com/Australia/ Default .aspx?tabid=850
Provides some interesting ideas with respect to wine lists and restaurant purchasing of wines.

Thorsen, E.O. and Hall, C.M. (2001). 'What's on the wine list? Wine policies in the New Zealand restaurant industry, *International Journal of Wine Marketing*, 13(3), 94–102.
Study of the policies by which restaurants select their wine list.

Fattorini, J.E. (1997). *Managing Wine and Wine Sales*, International Thomson Business Press, London.
A guide for restaurant and food and beverage managers in particular.

Wansink, B., Cordua, G., Blair, E., Payne, C. and Geiger, S. (2006). Wine promotions in restaurants: Do beverage sales contribute or cannibalize? *Cornell Hotel and Restaurant Administration Quarterly*, 47(4), 327–338.
Examination of the efficacy of different promotional strategies in a US restaurant chain.

Wall, E.A. and Berry, L.L. (2007). The combined effects of the physical environment and employee behavior on customer perception of restaurant service quality. *Cornell Hotel and Restaurant Administration Quarterly*, 48(1), 59–70.
Article provides into the environmental (servicescape) and human clues in restaurants that provide a message about the quality of service.

Wine events

Wine events, otherwise referred to as hallmark or special events are fairs, festivals, expositions, cultural and industry events which are held on either a regular or a one-off basis. Hallmark events have assumed a key role in international, national, regional and firm wine marketing and promotion strategies. Their primary marketing function being to provide the sponsors and host community with an opportunity to secure high prominence in the market place while also adding brand value and building customer and consumer relationships.

This chapter is divided into two main sections. The first discusses trends with respect to eating and drinking out of the home environment. The second looks at various aspects of the micro-marketing environment of restaurants and pubs through which increased value can be provided to the customer and wine businesses.

Wine events and festivals

Events have long been synonymous with wine and the wine industry from pre-Christian bacchanalia – mystical festivals dedicated to the Roman god of wine (in Greek mythology Bacchus was know as Dionysus or Eleutherios) that were originally held in mid-march but later extended to be held 5 times a year – through to festivals for Christian saints. Indeed, a significant connection exists between the two as some of the saints days that were celebrated as carnival were days in which moral behaviours could be inverted. Religious festivals and celebrations were also often entwined with the various stages of vine growth: budbreak, flowering, fruit set, veraison and harvest. However, in recent years events have become far more secular in nature although in a number of countries, such as Spain and Italy, wine festivals and religious thanksgiving still go hand in hand.

Community wine festivals and local wine celebrations can be described as wine events in relation to their regional, local and cultural significance. Festivals are a celebration of something the local community wishes to share and which involves the wider public as participants in the experience. Festivals are 'an event, a social phenomenon, encountered in virtually all human cultures' (Falassi, 1987, p. 1) and are likely to be one of the following five categories:

1. A sacred or profane time of celebration, marked by special observances.
2. The annual celebration of a notable person or event, or the harvest of an important product.
3. A cultural event consisting of a series of performances of works in the fine arts, often devoted to a single artist or genre.
4. A fair.
5. Generic gaiety, conviviality, cheerfulness.

Festivals are intimately related with the maintenance and celebration of community values. 'Both the social function and the symbolic meaning of the festival are closely related to a series of overt values that the community recognizes as essential to its ideology and worldview, to its social identity, its historical continuity and to its physical survival, which is ultimately what festival celebrates' (Falassi, 1987, p. 2). However, as a result of greater cultural and economic connectedness between places, community wine festivals have increasingly taken on a role as a commoditised product that is used externally promoted in order to attract visitors, promote the region or community, or promote consumption of specific wines – all usually with an economic motive. This is not to deny that such festivals may still have an important function for community celebration of wine but that such celebrations increasingly have an economic and commercial dimension to them. Wine events are therefore important not only because they constitute a reason to consume wine but because they have become significant for promoting wine, wine regions and wineries (see Plates 8.1 and 8.2).

As with wine itself, the number of wine events and related wine and food festivals appears to have grown substantially in recent years leading to an extremely congested market (Hall et al., 2003). Nevertheless, two major categories of wine event can be recognised. The first are industry wine events, such as conventions, expositions and symposia that are primarily internally focussed (also discussed in Chapter 9). The second, category of wine event is that which is externally focussed and is being specifically used as a marketing tool.

Industry wine events

Although industry or internally focussed wine events contribute to wine marketing, it is primarily with respect to business-to-business relationships and the media, as well as with promoting the development of economic relations and networks, as from this perspective events can be seen as a form of short-lived business cluster. Examples of industry wine events include wine shows and trade fairs and exhibitions. The size of such events varies substantially. For example, Vinitaly 2007 one of the world's largest wine trade events had more than 150,000 visitors from more than 100 countries of which 38,000 were international attendees. In addition, there were more than 2600 journalists from 52 countries. In terms of numbers of businesses the exhibition attracted 4300 companies from more than 30 countries (VeronaFiere Press Office, 2007). The International Wine Competition held as part of Vinitaly included almost 3500 wines from 31 different countries. The 2005 London International Wine and Spirits Fair (LIWSF) attracted 19,024 visitors in 2005 on which 25% were international visitors. John McLaren, UK Director of the Wine Institute of California, commented: 'As part of our international marketing strategy of building Brand California, the LIWSF is a vital element. We found it a very successful and effective event' (in ExCel London, 2007). Attendance at the trade days of the 2006 Vancouver Playhouse International Wine Festival (VPIWF, 2007) was 5845 people of which 52% were owners/managers, including managers, executive chefs, sommeliers and wine buyers. For many producers and other wine businesses which are part of the wine supply and customer chains such industry events are therefore an integral part of business and, at least, require attendance at such events if not registering as an exhibitor. Box 8.1 indicates some of the best ways that exhibitors can make such events work for their wine business and marketing.

Public wine events

Externally focussed wine events can be defined (after Ritchie, 1984; Hall, 1992) as a major one-time or recurring events of

Box 8.1 Making exhibition stand attendance work for your wine business

Do's

- Always greet the consumer with a smile. Introduce yourself to each visitor. Remember it is within the first four seconds that impressions are made, so be cheerful and welcoming – make the consumer feel important.
- Find out what visitors to your stand are interested in before launching in to sell and promote your product.
- Highlight the reason your business products are special. Focus on your 'unique selling points' as these will help you stand out from the crowd.
- Speak clearly and do not rush – not only is it advisable given the international nature of the wine industry and the number of people for whom English or French is a second language but it is also better for your business image and to get a few key points across to your audience than confuse them with too much information. If they are interested they will ring or e-mail you or check your brochure if they need to clarify anything.
- Ensure you have sufficient information packages on your business and/or products, even if this is just a business card and/or a brochure. However, given the cost of producing quality brochures it is advisable that brochures are saved for genuinely interested consumers rather than passed out to anyone who walks by. Brochures should also direct consumers to your website (and, yes, unless you are aiming to use exclusivity as a point of differentiation, you must have one!).
- Some exhibitors use a lead generation system to target distribution, that is, taking down e-mail addresses or phone numbers to provide information after the show. Some potential public consumers may feel uneasy about this approach for a consumer show because of privacy concerns, although this can be promoted in terms of 'being on the mail-order list'.
- Tailor your presentation to reflect the style and feel of your product and overall brand image.
- Network with other industry colleagues by attending exhibitor functions and other social activities.
- Spend some time looking around the show at competitors' products and looking for new products and innovations, such information may be extremely useful for identifying trends or shifts in the market. Importantly, also review what other businesses are doing to promote their products and the effectiveness of such strategies.
- Research the list of attendees to identify potential buyers and then research these buyers to identify which present the best opportunities for you. If you can, make appointments with those the strongest potential.

Do not's

- Sit down while on the stand as this gives the impression that you are lazy, do not care about the market or doing business or that you are 'closed for business'.
- Read while on the stand as this limits eye contact.
- Talk on your mobile phone or use your blackberry or laptop unless absolutely necessary – as this deters people from engaging with you on the stand.
- Barricade access to the stand with your presence.
- Ignore visitors to the stand. Acknowledge everyone who visits the stand regardless of whether you think they 'look like' potential purchasers of your product.
- Cluster with other representatives on the stand as this decreases your approachability.

Measuring your investment

Exhibitions are more than just social events. To enable wine businesses to better measure the return on investment from attending exhibition, trade and consumer events, it is important to have a tracking tool in place such as:

- Develop vouchers for redeemable discounts or value added products or services (for consumer shows).
- Cellar door survey (or other wine business survey such as restaurant, region or even specialist retailer) to ascertain where consumers heard about your product (for consumer shows).
- Take details of consumers or businesses you talk to who show interest and then e-mail or send them further product details. In this way you are able to develop a database of customers and interested consumers which can then be used to calculate actual short- and long-term sales arising from contact at the event (consumer and trade shows).

limited duration, developed primarily to enhance the awareness, appeal and profitability of a wine product in the short and/or long term. Such events rely for their success on uniqueness, status or timely significance to create interest and attract attention. A primary function of the wine event is to provide the sponsor and/or host community with an opportunity to secure a position of prominence in the market for a short, well defined, period of time. Significant, secondary functions include building and promoting brand values, maintaining relationships with customers, encouraging new wine consumers and promoting visitation. For example, with respect to the 2006 VPIWF primary reasons for attending were:

- 40.1% 'to discover new wines';
- 21.4% 'wine education';
- 11.8% 'for the fun of it';
- 8% 'learn more about food and wine pairing' (VPIWF, 2007).

In the case of tourism-related wine events such events are also often a strategic response to the problems that seasonal variations in demand. Wine events occur over a range of scales not only in terms of the numbers of people they attract but also the promotional base (i.e. brand, firm, multi-firm, community or region).

In the same way that there is no average winery visitor there is also no average set of visitors to a wine event. Event attendees do not constitute a single homogeneous market, instead different events attract different audiences (Nicholson and Pearce, 2000, 2001). For example, Box 8.2 provides a brief description of the visitor profiles to a number of wine events.

Box 8.2 Visitor profiles to wine events

Breedekloof Outdoor Festival, South Africa

Almost 36.7% of attendees were between 36 and 50 years, almost 32.2% were single, the majority were female (57.4%), and were mostly Afrikaans-speaking (78.1%). The results suggest that the overwhelming majority of the event attendees were domestic visitors primarily from the Cape Town conurbation. The travelling party to the event consisted mostly of two persons (25.9%) and the majority (68.7%) only visited the event for one day. Those that did not stay at home stayed with friends and relatives (VFR) (36.6%) or camped (22%) (Tasslopoulos and Haydam, 2006).

Winter Wine Fest, Australia

Fifty-two percent of visitors were female; 7% were aged between 18 and 24 years old, 42% between 25 and 44, 47% between 45 and 64 and only 4% were 65 years or over; 87% were working full or part time. In terms of social groups the largest proportion visited with friends (48%), followed by couples (33%), families (15%) and only 4% attended by themselves. Nearly all visitation was domestic primarily from the Melbourne conurbation (Weiler et al., 2004).

Rutherglen Winery Walkabout, Australia

A high number of young people (31.2% of respondents were aged 18–30 years) and a low number of older people (5% of respondents aged 61 years

---

and over attended the festival; 22.2% of respondents had family incomes lower than A$35,000) (Houghton, 2001).

Tastes of Rutherglen, Australia

In terms of age 31.6% of respondents were 31–40 and 29.8% 41–50. In comparison with the Rutherglen winery walkabout 14% of respondents to this event were aged 61years or over; 10.5% of respondents had family incomes lower than A$35,000 (Houghton, 2001).

Vancouver Playhouse International Wine Festival

19.3% of attendees were aged less than 30 and 4.3% were over 60. The average age of attendees was 39. Females made up 58% of the audience. The average monthly expenditure on wine was C$152 and 31.3% of attendees spend between C$51–100 on wine a month; 40.5% of attendees were single (VPIWF, 2007).

Critical factors that determine visitation to a wine event include, from the production perspective (Taylor and Shanka, 2002; Hall et al., 2003; Tasslopoulos and Haydam, 2006):

- location,
- timing,
- event facilities and activities,
- event programming,
- promotion and marketing.

From the consumers' perspective important considerations are (Hall et al., 2003; Brown and Getz, 2005; Yuan et al., 2005):

- travel time in relation to the overall availability of free time of the potential visitor,
- economic budget of visitor,
- accessibility,
- motivations, particularly social motivations,
- prior experience and positive recommendations via word of mouth,
- programming,
- perceptions.

In a study of a wine festival staged in the Swan Valley, Western Australia, Shanka and Taylor (2004) reported that the most common source of festival information was personal through word of mouth across all visitor groups. Other sources of information that also had some significance include newspapers and radio.

Event marketing management

Events are related to wine marketing in two major ways. First, as an extension of broader wine market strategies undertaken with respect to marketing of wine regions (including as tourism destinations), wineries, and wine labels or brands. Second, as a wine related product in their own right. The two roles are clearly interrelated although it is only in recent years that the potential synergies between events and broader promotion and branding strategies has been utilised.

Marketing is a critical element in the hosting and management of a successful event. To modify Kotler and Levy's (1969) definition of marketing in event terms: marketing is that function of event management that can keep in touch with the event's participants and visitors (consumers), read their needs and motivations, develop products that meet these needs, and build a communication programme which expresses the event's purpose and objectives. Certainly selling and influencing will be large components of event marketing; but, properly seen, selling follows rather than precedes the event management's desire to create experiences (products) which satisfy its consumers. Market research should also be an integral part of wine event management and planning (Box 8.3).

Box 8.3 Wine event market research

Even the smallest of wine events can benefit from a basic research survey programme with the value being:

- ensuring event objectives were met;
- assessing attendee satisfaction;
- identifying market profiles and segments;
- providing information that can be supplied to sponsors so that they can assess the benefits of sponsorship;
- monitoring the wine event over time.

Unless the event is small, it is extremely difficult and time-consuming to survey all attendees. In an industry context a survey can be placed in every attendee's conference, meeting or event package. However, for public events it is usually most efficient to undertake a convenience sample of respondents which can hopefully be estimated as a proportion of total attendees. Although the larger the sample the more accurate it will tend to be in statistical terms for volunteer run events the time costs of gaining a sample of over 300 people are likely to be prohibitive and, in statistical terms, are realistically unnecessary. Mail out surveys are costly and are likely to be wasteful and may not bring the desired returns. Depending on the human resource power available to event organisers we therefore recommend the conduct of either short face-to-face interviews at the event or an opportunity for respondents to drop surveys off as they leave the event. The former being the best option where resources allow but in both cases an inducement or prize should be provided for completion and return. Most importantly organisers should ensure that surveying is done systematically so that volunteers are not just approaching a certain type of attendee.

In considering the survey questions reflect on the type of information that will be required and wherever possible provide closed questions as this is easier and quicker to code for data entry and produce results. By all means have an open-ended question but it is best to leave it to last. Depending on the regulatory requirements on the country in which research is being conducted it may also be necessary to provide a guarantee of privacy of information to respondents.

Likely questions will include

- Age
- Gender
- Household income
- Place of permanent residence
- Occupation
- Highest level of education
- Marital/relationship status
- Number of companions accompanying to the event
- Primary reasons and motivations for attending event
- Event related purchases
- Where did people get information on the event from
- Is the event part of an overnight trip? If so what type of accommodation are they staying in and how long are they staying for
- Have they attended previous wine events, either this and/or others
- Most appealing/satisfying aspects of event (least appealing can also be asked)
- Overall spending habits with respect to wine
- Overall information sources with respect to wine
- Recognition of sponsors

In terms of results simple tabulations and descriptive statistics are usually more than suited for the needs of wine event marketers and planner and can provide the basis for effective planning in to the future.

A successful wine event marketing plan will focus on the development of a marketing process which revolves around activities and decisions in three main areas:

1. market segmentation and targeting;
2. market entry strategy, including time and location of event;
3. marketing mix variables.

Unfortunately, many wine events, particularly small ones, are conducted without the benefit of a marketing plan or strategy.

Market segmentation

Visitors to wine events are a diverse market. However, no event can be all things to all people. Therefore, it is essential that any business, community, destination or organisation that is planning an event should incorporate an understanding of the behaviour of event visitors into their marketing and promotional strategies. Event organisers should identify market segments which are in tune with the nature and character of an event and its objectives or, alternatively, and less in tune with the philosophy of this book with respect to adding value to wine over the supply/value chain, the event should be staged in such a way as to meet the needs of the market. In other words, wine events should ideally be held as part of a broader marketing strategy rather than being held for their own sake. Whichever way the market is segmented, it should be emphasised that an attractive market for a wine event will be one in which:

- the market segment is of sufficient size to make the event viable;
- the market segment has the potential for growth or, depending on the objectives, of keeping to a sustainable size (this is particularly important for events organised by volunteers so as to avoid the potential for volunteer burn-out);
- the market segment is not 'taken' or 'owned' by existing events;
- the market segment has a relatively unsatisfied interest or motivation that the event can satisfy.

Market entry strategy

Each new event needs to develop a market entry strategy. Although many wine events are constrained in terms of their location, especially community events that must, by definition, be based within the community, the timing of when an event is held will be crucial to its success in attracting visitors and attendees. The objectives which underlie an event are again crucial to decisions regarding the timing of holding an event. Where there is some flexibility in hosting an event, organisers should consider (a) what other events and attractions the wine event will be competing with and (b) given the seasonality of visitation to the destination and of the wine industry, can the event be utilised to boost visitor arrivals in shoulder-season and off-peak periods or 'down-times' in growing wine?

The marketing mix

The design of an appropriate marketing strategy for an event consists of analysing market opportunities, identifying and targeting market segments, and developing an appropriate market mix for each segment. Key factors are identified below:

- *Product/service characteristics*: Wine event management must understand the difference between the generic needs the event is serving and the specific products or services it is offering. In order to meet the demands of the marketplace, it is essential that event organisers focus the wine event product/s in light of the needs of specific market segments.
- *Promotional channels and messages*: Promotional programmes for even the most modest local wine event require exactly the same kind of organisation, planning, allocation of responsibilities and attention to detail that the larger events require. In promoting events to the market various promotional methods are used, including advertising, personal selling, sales promotion and publicity. Promotional methods should be selected on the basis of their capacity to achieve the objectives of the event with respect to target audience and their relative cost.
- *Price*: Although many wine events are 'free' in terms of entry costs too participants and visitors, particularly community events, the issue of price is significant at all levels of event management and marketing. Prices may cover costs, maximise profits, subsidise all participants or certain market segments, encourage competition, or result in unanticipated consumer reaction. Prices should be set according to a wide range of factors including past history, general economic conditions, ability to pay, revenue potential, costs, level of sponsorship and the competition. Pricing may even be used as a mechanism to appeal to particular markets. Rather than

set a standard price to all entrants to an event, organisers may also wish to lower price levels to certain demographic groups, such as students or under 25s, in order to broaden the market base and encourage new wine drinkers.

- *Place and methods of distribution*: Despite the 'fixed' nature of the majority of wine events, distribution issues are also of significance to organisers. As noted above, the time and place in which wine events are held will be a major factor in determining the event's success. Time and place are actually questions about the most appropriate manner in which to 'distribute' the event product to its current and potential audience. Furthermore, issues of distribution will be tied up in the promotion of events. For instance, given a limited budget how can event organisers best distribute promotional materials to the market that they have identified?

- *Packaging and programming*: Packaging is the combination of related and complimentary services in a single-price offering. For larger, wine events packages may consist of a selection of sub-events being sold together or the event plus transportation. Programming is the variation of service or product in order to increase customer spending and/or satisfaction, or to give extra appeal to an event or package. For example, many wine festivals, such as the VPIWF noted above, have a programme of different activities and tasting which are timed to follow and interrelate with each other over the various days on which the festival is held. The specific mix of activities which are developed with the overall wine event framework may have the capacity to extend the interest of certain markets and hence, potentially, increase their level of satisfaction. Programming should consider such factors as the event venue and location, inclement weather options if part of the event is to be staged outside, and the needs of different target markets, and their relative availability to attend (e.g. if an event is appealing to a domestic market and is held during the week some potential target markets may not be able to attend during the day because of work commitments), and balance within the choice of activities.

- *Partnership*: Collaboration is a very important part of wine event marketing management, particular with respect to bringing together the various sectors of the wine industry but also the needs of sponsors. Sponsorship may come in many forms: financial assistance, facilities, provision of event infrastructure, management skills, labour and, of course, donations of wine. Sponsors see events as a means of raising corporate profile, promoting particular products through enhanced profile and image, obtaining lowers costs per impression than those achieved by advertising, improve sales, and in being seen as good corporate citizens. Nevertheless, from the perspective of wine event organisation and the host community it is essential that the potential sponsor be appropriate to the objectives, needs and image of the event (Box 8.4).

Box 8.4 Wine Marlborough Festival 'New Zealand's Premier Wine and Food Experience' (festival tagline)

The Wine Marlborough Festival is New Zealand's longest running wine festival and is the largest and, arguably, the most famous wine event in the country. Formerly, known as the BMW Wine Marlborough Festival or the Air New Zealand Marlborough Wine and Food festival, depending on sponsorship arrangements, the event is held at the Brancott Estate, formerly owned by Montana wines, which is now part of the Pernod Ricard Group. Although interestingly no mention of hosting the event was made on the Brancott Vineyards website at the time of writing.

The festival is run by local volunteers through an incorporated society with some paid assistance for some of the event management functions such as marketing and promotion. The festival has long been a showpiece of the region's wines but, since the 1990s, the festival has also been regarded as a separate tourism event in its own right. For example, the incorporated society that owns and manages the event aims to 'attract attention to Marlborough and its produce, to assist the district's economy and ... as a consequence (to) provide increased opportunities for tourism, both domestic and international' (Festival News 1994 in Pratt, 1994, p. 32). Nevertheless, the growth of general tourist interest in the festival has generated its own problems related to the capacity of a volunteer organisation to manage a large event but also the expectations and images that the event creates, particularly when the event is meant as a showpiece for the regions wines rather than a concert type event. For example, in 1993 admission was limited to 12,000. Although this figure was relaxed in the late 1990s they were reimposed again in 2002 following concerns over the positioning of the festival in terms of how it related to the region's wines rather than just being seen as a source of entertainment (Hall and Mitchell, 2004, 2005).

This case presents information with respect to the 2003 festival and where possible compares it to previous festivals so as to illustrate that not only do different wine events have different market profiles but that the profile of the same festival may even change each year.

Visitor origins

54.7% of respondents came from outside the Marlborough region, including 10% from overseas; 45.2% of survey respondents were from the Marlborough region.

Demographics

In 2003 28.4% of respondents to the festival survey (*n* = 229) were aged 24 years or below. The 2003 survey indicated a significant increase in festival goers in the 20–24 age group over 2002, while the 25–34 age group had not changed significantly. The sample shows that there has been a significant decline in numbers in the 40–59 age group. This group has almost halved from 2002, down from 43.5% to 23.1%. The 60+'s have remained reasonable constant when compared to previous years. The shift to the 20–29 age group is consistent with results of surveys undertaken in 1999 and 2000. Arguably shifts in age group may be related not only to a growth in interest in wine in certain age groups, but, possibly more important, the range of musical entertainment that may be available.

Accommodation

In 2002, festival goers where as equally likely to stay with 'friends and family' as in a motel. Visitors to the 2003 festival, that indicated they had or were using accommodation, were more significantly likely to be staying with 'friends and family' (15.7%) than to stay in a motel (9.6%) or a hotel (7.9%).

Number of companions

In general respondents came to the festival with others (only three respondents indicated that they came alone); 30.6% came with three to four companions, groups of one to two (24.5%) and five to six (47%). These results indicate the importance of the social dimension of the wine event experience.

Attendance at previous Wine Marlborough Festivals and other events

More than half of the respondents in 2003 indicated they had previously attended the festival; 11% had been once, 5.2% had attended twice before and 4.8% three times before. The festival appears to continue being successful in securing repeat visitation with just over 20% of 2003s respondents indicating three or four previous visits to the festival. A further 12% indicate five or six prior visits. Respondents were also asked what other type of events they had attended during the year prior to the Wine Marlborough Festival. Of particular importance were major sports fixtures (18%), beer fests (15.4%), wild food events (12.7), followed by outdoor concerts (11.6%), and other New Zealand food and wine festivals (11.4%). The survey also indicated that there was a marked decrease in respondent attendance at events such as art festivals (7.1%) and agricultural/gardening shows (6.0%) over that indicated for 2002.

Appealing aspects of Wine Marlborough

The most appealing aspects of the event were atmosphere (74.7%) and social (58.7%) closely followed by variety of wines (56.4%), and the 'outdoors/sun'

(52.9%). The 2003 respondents rated the social aspect of the event two places higher than in 2002 relegating variety of wines and outdoors/sun in order of preference.

Wine Marlborough Festival: http://www.wine-marlborough-festival.co.nz/
Brancott Vineyards: http://www.brancottvineyards.com/

Both industry and public events can contribute to a region's tourism development by serving to attract visitors from outside of the destination. Industry events attract business visitors and contribute to the development of economic networks. Visitors to industry events and conferences also tend to have an extremely high per day spend. Yet despite this the tourism focus on wine events tends to be on public events, which are regarded as providing an opportunity for destinations to establish themselves as wine tourism destinations and contribute to regional economic development (Brown et al., 2002). For example, in reflecting on the experience of the Breedekloof Outdoor Festival in South Africa, Tasslopoulos and Haydam (2006, p. 69) commented that, 'Wine events provide wine regions with an opportunity to promote the wine and build market identity and, therefore, result in the transition of traditional rural areas into modern service economies.' Nevertheless, it is becoming increasingly recognised that wine events need to be seen not just as an opportunity to increase visitor numbers or sell wine but to seek to build wine brands at various scales (i.e. region, producer, label) (Mowle and Merrilees, 2005), often by using the event to increase brand loyalty, and by creating long-term relationships with consumers. However, it is also important for wine event organisers to consider the communities in which they are located and connected so as to ensure that an events potential contribution in terms of community cohesiveness, economic benefits and social incentives, are not outweighed by environmental and social costs (Gursoy et al., 2004).

Conclusions

This chapter has provided an overview of some of the marketing dimensions of wine events. Although wine events have been demonstrated to have a long history it is argued that there are now primarily two types of events – industry-oriented internally focussed events and public externally focussed tourism events. The marketing values of industry events are business to business and media focused while the public events tend to be more consumer oriented. Both contribute to brand and relationship building, as well as to sales, but in different ways. Consumer wine events, for example, can be an extremely useful way to attract new consumers to wine overall as well as to specific brands, because they are often seen as less intimidating than other customer contact opportunities such as wine clubs, specialist retailers or, in some cases, even the wineries themselves (Houghton, 2001; Hall and Mitchell, 2005).

With respect to wine marketing management the chapter has emphasised the need for wine events to have clear objectives that can then be utilised with respect to understanding market segmentation and targeting; market entry strategy, including time and location of event; and marketing mix variables. It is also recommended that appropriate research strategies are developed that reinforce the appropriateness of event objectives. Overall, the chapter reinforced the notion that although events and festivals can be a wonderful thing, from a wine marketing perspective, wine events need to be integrated into wine marketing strategies so that they add value to the overall wine product and experience rather than being organised in isolation.

Practical wine marketing insights

- Do's and do not's of exhibition stand attendance.
- Evaluate attendance at exhibition and events.
- Wine events should be organised with clear objectives in mind.
- From a wine marketing perspective, wine events needs to be integrated into wine marketing strategies so that they add value to the overall wine product and experience rather than being organised in isolation.
- A successful wine event marketing plan will focus on the development of a marketing process which revolves around activities and decisions in three main areas:
  - market segmentation and targeting;
  - market entry strategy, including time and location of event;
  - marketing mix variables.
- Undertake systematic research on attendees at wine events in order to:
  - ensure that objectives are being met;
  - profile and segment attendees;
  - assess attendee satisfaction;
  - meet sponsors' requirements.

Further reading

Local Wine Events: http://www.localwineevents.com/
Is a US-based Internet site that claims to be the world's largest food and drink calendar. It does have an extensive listing of wine events although its listings are primarily US based.

Wine Events Calendar: http://www.wineevents-calendar.com/
US Internet site that includes lists of public wine events in the USA as well as international wine trade events and meetings. The site also includes other useful market and wine information.

ViniItaly: http://www.vinitaly.it/
One of the world's largest wine trade events which also includes an International Wine Competition and an International Packaging Competition.

Monterey Wine Country Events page: http://www.winee vents.org/
Regional wine events site that otherwise gives a very good example of the marketing opportunities made possible by an events focus.

Vancouver Playhouse International Wine Festival: http://play-housewinefest.com/
One of North America's top wine festivals that also includes trade days.

Hall, C.M. and Mitchell, R. (2005). Wine Marlborough: a profile of visitors to New Zealand's oldest wine festival. *Journal of Hospitality and Tourism*, 3(1), 77–90.
Study of visitation to New Zealand's longest running wine festival.

Hall, C.M., Sharples, E., Mitchell, R., Cambourne, B. and Macionis, N. (eds.) (2003). *Food Tourism Around the World: Development, Management and Markets*, Butterworth-Heinemann.
The leading text on food tourism which profiles numerous wine and food events.

Houghton, M. (2001). The propensity of wine festivals to encourage subsequent winery visitation. *International Journal of Wine Marketing*, 13(2), 32–41.
A very useful paper indicating how festivals can contribute to consequent winery visitation.

Wine brand image agents: advertising, endorsements, reviews and media

Chapter objectives

After reading this chapter you will

- Understand some of the issues surrounding advertising for wine
- Understand the pivotal role that different forms of media play in the marketing of wine
- Understand the importance of critics, medals, awards and wine shows in the marketing of wine
- Understand that there are different strategies available to wineries with respect to wine shows
- Appreciate the increasing significance of new media to the marketing of wine
- Appreciate that different market segments react to the influence of media and critical acclaim in different ways

Introduction

Premium wine, as a complex, symbolic and highly technical product, relies on a complex interaction of information sources and impressions for the development of brand image. Image is an abstract concept that incorporates the influences of past promotion, reputation, and peer evaluation of the alternatives and connotes the expectation of the user (Gensch, 1978; Stern et al., 2001). This information can be from many sources, some of which can be controlled or influenced by the winery and some which are primarily controlled by third parties. This chapter explores these image agents by adapting a framework, used to understand how destination image is formed (Gartner, 1993) in the context of wine image formation agents (see Figure 9.1). Tourism destinations have a number of characteristics in common with wine:

- Both products are extremely complex
- Both products change over time
- Both have a range of individual products within the overall brand (e.g. different attractions at destinations or different varieties and styles of wine) and sometimes have sub-brands
- Perceptions of both are heavily influenced by images and representation of place
- Both are likely to rely on the reputation of other brands in close proximity
- Quality is heavily dependent on subjective qualitative assessments by consumers which may be influenced by situation or occasion

Agent Type	Wine Image Agents	Control
Overt Induced I	Advertising, PR and sales promotions	Winery
Overt Induced II	Information at retail or other outlets (e.g. labels, 'table talkers', POS promotions)	Winery
Covert Induced I	Paid endorsement by a celebrity, chef or wine critic, product placement or event sponsorship	Winery
Covert Induced II	Hosting of wine media, critics, chefs and other influencers at the winery	Winery
Autonomous I	Wine shows, medals, reviews in wine media	Third party
Autonomous II	Non-wine media (e.g. news, lifestyle movies)	Third party
Unsolicited Organic	Recommendation volunteered by friends or family	Third party
Solicited Organic	Recommendation sought from friends or family	Third party
Organic	Tasting and consuming wine	Consumer

Increasing credibility (left axis) — *Decreasing control* (right axis)

Figure 9.1
Wine image formation agents

- Both benefit from 'independent' endorsement (e.g. travel guides and quality/accreditation systems such as star ratings for individual businesses and wine reviews and wine judges or critics), especially for first time purchasers
- There are a huge number of brand choices available
- Both rely heavily on intermediaries to distribute the product
- Choices are dependent on situation and occasion
- Both purchases have perceived risk and therefore are high involvement purchases

Three basic types of image formation agent can be identified (Gunn, 1972; Gartner, 1993; see also McKay and Fesenmaier, 1997):

- *induced*, which are the result of a conscious effort of image formation by the wine producer (whether at a wine grower or regional scale);
- *autonomous*, where third parties provide information or impressions of the wine;
- *organic*, which are unbiased and trusted others such as friends or relatives that have knowledge of the wine.

These three categories are further subdivided into four induced, one autonomous and three organic categories, while we have added a second autonomous category that allows for the fact that wine has experts that judge and evaluate wine in shows and specialised media (see Figure 9.1).

Induced and autonomous categories will be discussed in this chapter as the winery has little control over organic agents. This is not to deny the importance of organic agents in the purchasing of wine, as there is considerable evidence to suggest that word of mouth recommendations are very important for wineries (Quinton and Harridge-March, 2003; Mitchell, 2004), as they are highly credible sources of endorsement. This chapter therefore explores:

- advertising and public relations (PR);
- the role of point of sale packaging (labels and in-store displays);
- the role of medals, shows and reviews in promotion and price;
- the role of non-wine media in influencing perceptions of wine.

Induced wine brand image agents

Induced image agents are an important part of any promotional strategy for a wine producer as these are the elements that they can most easily control. The amount of paid promotional activities will depend on the size of the producer, their target markets and the overall budget available for such activities. Many advertising channels exist and each has a varying degree of reach and ability to communicate to the consumer about different aspects of wine (Table 9.1). Many of these channels are discussed in detail below.

Advertising (overt induced I)

Print media are widely used by wine producers for advertising and sales promotions for two main reasons. The first relates to the fact that there is a long history of wine-specific print media, with consumer oriented wine writing developing as early as the beginning of the 19th century (Charters, 2006). This, Charters (2006) says, was a result of the consumer revolution of the time which resulted in purchasing of goods such as wine to set oneself apart from others. This required knowledge to assist in the collection and aesthetic appreciation of wine. Ultimately this then leads to the second reason for the use of print media for advertising: an ability to target wine consumers. Readers of wine-specific print media tend to be highly involved consumers

Table 9.1 Use and capacity of selected advertising communications channels in developed countries with respect to premium wine and food products

Communications Channel	Reach*	Ability to communicate**		
		Wine price	Wine quality	Wine product information
Television	High	Good	Moderate	Moderate
In-store advertising	High	Moderate	Moderate	Moderate
Radio	High	Poor	Poor	Poor
Newspaper	High	Moderate	Moderate	Moderate
Magazine	High	Moderate	Moderate	Moderate
Internet advertising	High	Moderate	Poor	Poor
Websites	High	Good	Moderate	Good
In-store retail/farmers market samples	Medium	Excellent	Excellent	Good
Coupons, price promotions	Medium	Moderate	Poor	Poor
Home mailings	Medium	Poor	Poor	Poor
Friends and family recommendations	Medium	Excellent	Excellent	Excellent
Magazine or newspaper inserts	Medium	Moderate	Poor	Poor
Cinema advertising	Medium	Poor	Poor	Poor
Toll free numbers	Medium	Poor	Poor	Poor
E-mails	Medium	Poor	Poor	Poor
Event sponsorship	Low	Poor	Moderate	Poor
Recommendations from experts	Low	Moderate	Excellent	Good
Restaurant table tent promotion	Low	Poor	Moderate	Moderate
Travel by public transport	Low	Poor	Poor	Poor
Travel by airplane	Low	Poor	Moderate	Poor

*Extent of use/exposure to communication channel categorised as: high (over two-thirds of adult population); moderate (between one-third and two-thirds of adult population) or low (less than one-third of adult population).
**Capacity to communicate rated as poor, moderate, good and excellent.
Source: Author's data.

and therefore are more likely to be high-end purchasers and consumers of wine. This ability to target highly involved consumers with print media is common where products and activities involve a high degree of technical expertise and knowledge (e.g. wine, crafts, antique collecting or adventure sports) or where purchases involve a degree of social risk and/or aesthetic appreciation (e.g. wine, fashion, design, antique collecting and art). This also reflects behaviour by those undertaking, what

Stebbins (1992, p. 3) describes as, 'serious leisure' where individuals 'find a career ... in the acquisition and expression of ... special skills and knowledge' in an amateur hobby. Those involved in serious leisure may also be a member of a club or group of individuals with similar interests and they may read similar technical or specialist literature. For example, in 2000 73% of members of the USA Wine Club read *Wine Spectator* on a regular basis. Christensen (2004) also found that 43% of attendees of a wine club in New Zealand read specialist wine magazines. This figure jumped to 52% for those that could be considered to be taking part in serious leisure and these 'specialist wine consumers' were highly involved in wine as well as purchasing on average 25% more wine (by volume, 40% by value) than the other club members.

Several key specialist wine magazines are present in the major Anglophone wine markets, including, but by no means limited to: *Decanter* (UK: www.decanter.com); *Wine Spectator* (USA: www.winespectator.com); *Winestate* (Australia: www.wine state.com.au); *Gourmet Traveller Wine* (Australia: http://gourmet.ninemsn.com.au/gourmettraveller/) and *Vines* (Canada: http://www.vinesmag.com/). These five magazines have a total readership in the order of around 3 million readers worldwide, but *Wine Spectator* has by far the greatest reach. *Wine Spectator's* total audience is more than 2.1 million readers, with around 80% having a wine cellar or private collection, purchasing wine by the case and/or reading every issue (Wine Spectator, 2007a). There are also more than 500,000 visits to their website each month and 200,000 subscribers to the online newsletter *Sip & Tips* (*Wine Spectator*, 2007b). Advertising in such wine publications, along with other such specialist wine and food magazines (e.g. *Gourmet* (US), *Bon Appetit* (US), *Cuisine* (*New Zealand*)) presents the most targeted opportunity for wine producers and is relatively cost effective when compared to other advertising channels such as television or print media with wider readership.

Television advertising by wine producers is relatively rare for a number of reasons. One reason is that alcohol advertising may be restricted or banned in certain media. Charters (2006, p. 281) also suggests that 'even where formal restrictions are not in place, informal controls and the power of lobby groups may impose practical limits, such as influencing the advertising of wine on commercial television stations'. However it is just as likely that only large producers can afford the high cost of production and transmission of television advertisements. Television also has a relatively broad market and it is therefore more difficult to target wine consumers, although particular shows would likely appeal to the wine market and these could be useful to be associated with. One such example is a long association that Montana Wines (New Zealand) (now a division of Pernod Ricard) had with a series of 'art house' movies and mini series called *Montana Sunday Theatre* shown at 8.30 pm on a Sunday. Montana saw an opportunity for such television programmes that would attract their target market and they developed the concept and approached Television New Zealand who ran the programme for several years following Montana's brief for the type of movie/series to be shown in the slot. Montana was, however, New Zealand's largest producer of wine and one of only a few that could have afforded such an association.

Radio has a more targeted audience as radio stations usually attract a very narrow demographic of listeners. For nationally syndicated radio programmes and primetime listening slots advertising airtime can be expensive, but most radio stations have cheaper off-peak slots and local stations can be a very cheap advertising channel. However, care must be taken to ensure that a radio station's listeners are a demographic that matches the brand's target market, as the narrow demographics may mean that the advertisement completely misses its target.

Billboards can be very effective at reaching a wide audience, but may not necessarily have a high degree of conversion to sales. Breweries around the world have been very effective at using billboards and often they involve innovative concepts and many use humour to great effect. Humour is one way that billboards can be particularly effective, but Solomon (1992) suggests that, while humourous advertisements do get attention, especially those relating to alcoholic beverages, care must be taken to ensure that humour is appropriate for the product. While wineries might find it useful to use billboards as an advertising channel, it may not be appropriate to follow the lead of breweries and it would be advisable to seriously consider whether humour would be appropriate for their brand image.

Bus shelter billboards have been used effectively in Australia by Beringer Blass to promote their Yellowglen range of 'value market' sparkling wines. 2007 was the eighth year of the 'Seriously Bubbly' advertising campaign, which Yellowglen says is 'synonymous with the excitement that accompanies drinking Yellowglen – it's feminine, fun, celebratory and seriously bubbly' (Beringer Blass Wine Estates Limited, 2007). The campaign used digitally enhanced images of female models wearing evening dresses made of sparkling wine bubbles and drinking a glass of the wine (see www.yellowglen.com.au). Along with print media campaigns, billboards were placed in tram and bus shelters in inner city areas and along routes to and from suburbs that matched their target demographics. The message was simple and clearly associated with the brand. According to Yellowglen, by 2007 the brand had become a leader in the Australian sparkling wine category, '… with a value market share twice it's nearest competitor' (Beringer Blass Wine Estates Limited, 2007). For some general tips on advertising see Box 9.1.

Box 9.1 General tips for wine advertising

You should always employ a professional to prepare advertising copy and images, but you should also have a knowledge of what to expect of them. The following are some of the key things to be aware of:

- Do market research first and test campaign ideas before implementing them.
- Ensure the chosen media matches your target market.
  - If they cannot tell you what their audience is, then don't use them!
- Keep the message simple and clear.
- Ensure that advertising sends the message that you want it to.
  - What is your desired brand image?
  - What is the take home message (i.e. what do you want the audience to know)?
  - What is the intention of the campaign (i.e. is it a teaser, a sales promotion or a general brand awareness campaign)?
  - What are the motivations, desires and lifestyles of the target audience?
- Give the audience a 'call to action' (e.g. website, free call phone number, stores where they can buy the wine, address of the cellar door).
- Set a realistic advertising budget. This should include money for the running of campaigns throughout the year as well as costs set aside to prepare the copy and imagery for the campaign at the beginning. Advertising budgets should not be set based on 'what's left when all the other bills have been paid', but rather as a necessary and legitimate business expense or investment.

Public relations (Overt Induced I)

In many instances PR can be more important for wine producers as it is less uni-directional (i.e. broadcast) than advertising and therefore can be useful in the development of relationships with consumers and other groups and individuals that are of interest to wineries (e.g. suppliers, shareholders, government officials, employees or the local community) (Summers et al., 2003). PR is also useful for wineries as it does not have to pay for the broadcasting of the stories, rather it develops PR campaigns and strategies in the hope that media will pick up on it and run with stories. It may also communicate directly with the target audience rather than broadcast the message.

Wine producers are likely to have many different PR strategies and there are many opportunities to have campaigns throughout the year. For example, the changing seasons on the vineyard allow for the development of campaigns that inform consumers and other stakeholders of what is happening: springtime release of the new vintage; summertime visits to the winery; fall/autumn harvest season and; winter festivals and events. There are also many channels that wineries can use for PR, especially as wine has strong lifestyle appeal and a 'feel good factor' in markets such as the USA, Australia, the UK and Canada that, providing press releases and events are well crafted and managed, are likely to be picked up in popular media.

New media such as the Internet also present wine producers with good opportunities to undertake PR activities and these can be fully managed by the wine producer. The advancement of technologies in the Web2.0 environment are adding sophistication to Internet based PR and publicity through: podcasts (audio and video); blogs (web logs or diaries); RSS feeds (which are a form of push/broadcast media on the Internet that reach a highly targeted audience) and wikis (which allow readers/viewers to contribute their own content) on a webpage (see Box 9.2 for examples).

Box 9.2 Virtual wine and connectivity

No, we do not think that virtual wine will replace real wine for a long time, we are still a long way away from Star Trek-like virtual worlds. However, for many people interested in wine the experiences provided by virtual communities and new media are providing a whole new dimension to their interests. The experiential marketing opportunities provided by the web can allow the wine industry to create a lot of new relationships with consumers, as well as maintain existing relationships; help reinforce brand loyalty; provide feedback not only on the wines that are produced but even comment on marketing strategies; and also serve to promote word of mouth. However, the connectivity and openness provided by the Internet is a two-way relationship as the more a firm allows its customers to develop brand ownership by becoming a part of the brand community the more it also becomes necessary for companies to work with its customers and meet their needs. Arguably this has become even more necessary in the so-called Web2.0 environment in which blogs, wikis, social networking and folksonomies, all of which emphasise collaboration and sharing, have become commonplace. In this environment co-creation becomes more than just a seemingly academic concept as it means that firms have to guide the strategic process in order to build brand communities. Indeed, the smartest companies are understanding that products are in many cases customer made.

Examples of some interesting web strategies include:

Stormhoek ('The best South African wine for the money, end of story' also 'The Unofficial Geek Wine of Silicon Valley'): http://www.stormhoek.com/. Producer that demonstrates a great combination of blogging, viral marketing, YouTube, cartoons and tie in with more conventional marketing, including a coupon for use at Threshers (largest independent specialist alcohol retailer in the UK). Designed to maximise Internet linkages so as to spread the word about the wines as fast as possible and at low cost.

Threshers: http://www2.threshergroup.com/. Noted above! Interesting because of its wine club (On Taste) and the development of a niche on Fairtrade wine.

Fat Bastard Wine: http://www.fatbastardwine.com/. A premium wine that deliberately plays on its humour and lack of pretension which is reinforced via its US website where drinkers have the opportunity to tell their own fat bastard stories, buy merchandise, read the story behind the name, listen to radio advertisements and, of course, find out where to purchase it. At the time of writing it was also possible to vote for the top 10 most pretentious figures as well.

Click Wine Group: http://www.clickwinegroup.com/. A website that is geared more to the interests of distributors, retailers and licensed premises though also has much of interest to the consumer. The Group is the importer of the Fat Bastard as well as a range of other wines from Australia, Chile, Germany, Italy and Spain. The website is interesting because of the selling materials and packaging and positioning information provided on the various wines which we note also includes some excellent small winegrowers and wines that elsewhere may be regarded as 'unfashionable'. Apart from the range of wines and their various branding strategies the website also provides excellent recommendations with respect to creating wine flights and tastings for restaurants.

Sales promotions (In-Store) (Overt Induced II)

Like advertising and PR, there are many options available for sales promotions. In most cases they will either involve printed material (as it is easily used in the retail environment and relatively inexpensive to produce) or personally delivered by sales staff or the owner or winemaker themselves (see Table 9.2).

Personally delivered sales promotions are likely to have a greater impact as they allow the consumer to have direct contact with the wine producing company and thus are much more conducive to relationship marketing (see Chapter 4). One way that wine producers can do this is by attending retailers' wine clubs to present their wines (see Box 9.3 for an example). Alternatively in-store tastings at retailer premises or supermarkets (where

Table 9.2 Examples of retail promotions

	Print	Personal
Information	• Neck tags • Shelf tags • Brochures • 'Table talkers' • Tasting notes	• In-store tasting • Tutored tasting • Seminars/workshops • Food matching
Experience (tasting)		• In-store tasting • Tutored tasting • Food matching
Image	• Neck tags • Brochures • 'Table talkers' • Tasting notes	• In-store tasting • Tutored tasting • Food matching
Offers	• Contests • Neck tags • Brochures • 'Table talkers' • Tasting notes	• In-store tasting • Tutored tasting

Box 9.3 Wine club members as high involvement consumers

Wine clubs

Although no uniform definition of a wine club exists, possibly due to their wide and varied existence, the primary function of such clubs could be surmised to be two things: a promoter and sales conduit, and a channel for fostering wine knowledge. Wine clubs therefore act as a sales vehicle for the retail outlets such as liquor stores, specialty wine stores, online wine stores and wineries themselves who offer club-type memberships.

Attendance at wine clubs is likely to be a reflection of a high involvement in wine, especially, as Lockshin and Spawton (2001) suggest, highly involved individuals are eager to continually learn about their area of interest and, Christensen (2004) says, take part in 'serious leisure'. Furthermore, they value the opportunity to discuss their interest with friends.

Involvement

Involvement is widely used as a measure of attachment to products and brands. It can be used both to show how highly involved a product/brand is and to segment markets (e.g. low versus high involvement consumers). Involvement has been described as 'the degree of personal relevance which a product holds for the consumer' (Schiffman and Kanuk, 1987, p. 255). Yet, while there is general agreement on the principles behind involvement, few agree on a universal definition. As a result there are several different measures of involvement, including: product, brand, purchasing, situational and enduring involvement.

These measures can be quite different. Product involvement, for example, explores attachment to a product category (e.g. wine), while situational involvement looks at how involved people are when purchasing and consuming in different circumstances (e.g. buying wine for a gift versus for everyday consumption).

Wine and involvement

Wine is widely acknowledged as a high involvement product as it has a relatively high degree of risk associated with its purchase, can be expensive, is part of most people's discretionary spending and is often used by individuals to say something about who they are (see Chapter 4). Other high involvement products include fashion, jewellery, houses and luxury goods.

It is not surprising then that there have been a number of studies of wine involvement. These have used various measures of involvement to explore the nature of the relationship between the wine and its consumer and include, amongst others studies of:

- retail wine shopper segments using product, brand and purchasing involvement (Lockshin et al., 1997);
- wine consumption situation using product involvement (Quester and Smart, 1998);
- regional wine branding and consumer choice using product involvement (Rasmussen and Lockshin, 1999);
- wine choice behaviour using product involvement (Lockshin and Hall, 2003);
- wine consumption behaviour given different situations using product and situational involvement (d'Hauteville, 2003);
- wine club, wine consumption and wine tourism behaviour using enduring involvement (Christensen, 2004).

It is the last of these studies that is discussed very briefly here: an investigation into members of a small New Zealand specialist wine retailer's wine club.

Decanter Club

The 'Decanter Club' is a wholly owned entity of Munslow's Fine Wines, a specialty wine store located on Dunedin's George Street. The 'Decanter Club' has been in existence since the mid-1990s, and enjoys a loyal following. In addition to acting as a channel through which fine wines are sold, the Decanter Club operates as an educator and promoter of wines. The Decanter Club holds meetings most weeks from February to November. Although overall attendance numbers are restricted, non-members are also welcome to participate in club activities when space permits. The Decanter Club hosts a range of events including tastings conducted by wineries, winery representa-tives and wholesalers, as well as other specialists aligned to the industry. The format for each tasting differs, as the running of the evening is facilitated by the respective visitor.

The Decanter Club has an e-mail membership of approximately 650 mem-bers, in addition to a smaller number of paper-based members. Each month a newsletter is e-mailed to the membership list, advising readers of recently tasted wines and upcoming events, as well as staff picks and in-house spe-cials. The Decanter Club owners' willingness to assist with this study, and their preference for e-mail communication appeared to provide an effective and valuable means of accessing potential respondents. On this basis the Decanter Club was chosen to be the pool from which potential respondents would be sought.

The value of Decanter Club

This serves as both sales promotion and PR for Munslow's wines and for wine producers and wholesalers who attend the meetings to present their wines. It is particularly useful for wine producers that attend, as its members are wine involved and are, in the main, high-end consumers of wine.

Decanter Club members were found to high levels of 'enduring involvement' (described by Higie and Feick (1989, p. 690) as 'a stable trait that represents an individual's degree of interest or arousal for a product on a day-to-day basis; that is, an ongoing, long-term interest') towards wine drinking, club par-ticipation and, to a lesser extent, winery visitation (Christensen, 2004). As highly involved consumers they also exhibit extremely positive purchasing behaviour, such as:

- They purchase an average of around 10 bottles a month, at an average of NZ$20 per bottle.
- Around one in three drink wine daily.
- More than two out of five have a wine cellar of more than 100 bottles.

However, it was amongst a core of club members that attended meetings more than 12 times a year (dubbed 'wine specialists' by Christensen, 2004), that involvement was highest and purchasing behaviour most lucrative:

- They purchase an average of around 12 bottles a month, at an average of $NZ22 per bottle.
- More than two out of five drink wine daily.
- Almost one in three have a wine cellar of more than 250 bottles (one in fact had more than 1800 bottles of wine in his cellar).
- More than half were also influenced to attend by the chance to meet rep-resentatives from the winery (almost double that of other club members).

David Christensen and Richard Mitchell

local laws permit it) can be a useful way to allow consumers to reduce perceived risk by trying before they buy.

Labels (Overt Induced II)

Labels are an important part of the promotional mix for wineries. They are critical at the point of sale as they attract the consumer to a particular brand. In some stores there could be several thousand different labels and consumers must make a choice based on what impression the label makes. There is a lot information that a label presents and Lockshin and Hall (2003, p. 13) describe this as the 'Brand Constellation' and it might include: 'the company name … [;] colour of the wine; country, region, sub-region and vineyard; price including discounts; varietal names or combinations; winemaker(s); and style (sweet, light, heavy, tannic, etc. – often on the back label)'. However, more importantly front labels in particular must also evoke more abstract concepts about the wine and its brand image (Rocchi and Stefano, 2006). Charters (2006, p. 199) suggests that wine label has therefore become a work of art and 'the artistic label acts as metaphor for the wine; the consumer may be unable to appreciate the aesthetic qualities of the drink, at least until the cork is pulled, but the label signifies what its aesthetic value will ultimately be'. The overall message about the wine is therefore developed through the choice of colours, materials and graphic elements and artistic design of the label (Rocchi and Stefani, 2006).

The design of the wine label is critical to the marketing strategy of the winery as it is ultimately what sets the brand image for the wine and the expectations of consumers. The image presented in the label should follow through into other design elements for the winery, including stationary, websites and advertising and promotional material. It is vital that professional designers are used and that an appropriate budget is set aside when developing the brand. Box 9.4 provides a hypothetical example of a wine label showing some of the key informational and aesthetic elements.

Box 9.4 Key design elements: Greenstone Wines

This is a fictitious wine label. Any references to actual past, present or future wines or wineries of similar name or brand concept are purely coincidental and this case study does not reflect the views of any such company.

The following is a brief discussion of some of the principles behind the different elements of the label and reasons for the information that is presented.

(Note: This is to be read with Plate 9.1). Readers will need to refer to national legislative requirements with respect to wine labelling in terms of both information as well as positioning, although this task has now been made easier thanks to new international agreements on labelling (see Chapter 2).

Brand Logo (A)

The Koru is an iconic symbol of New Zealand flora and this is intended to ensure strong recognition of the wine's New Zealand origins. The Koru is the Māori name given to the unfurling fern frond, depicting life, growth and movement. The Koru depicted here is also hand-crafted greenstone and this has been used to reinforce the image of a hand-crafted wine. Green is also important as it represents the environment, while Greenstone can be seen as coming from the earth, suggestive of a strong affiliation to terroir. The white background is also used to represent purity and the use of only three colours (white, black, and green) is suggestive of elegant simplicity.

Brand Name (B)

The name Greenstone, as suggested above, has many positive connotations for the brand and these are reinforced by further use of green in the font of the brand name. The use of green only for the brand name also differentiates it from other product information and provides a further association with the brand concept which may aid recall. The fonts used also represent the traditions of the old world wines and the contemporary New World wine producers.

Other front label information

Place of origin (C) is particularly important if the region is well known and should be relatively prominent on the front label. In this case, the association between Marlborough and Sauvignon Blanc (D, the grape variety) is particularly important. Percentage of alcohol by volume (E) and volume of wine in the bottle (G) are required by law, while the vintage (F) is important product information as there may be some vintages that are better than others and it is important in terms of cellaring of the wine. Country of origin and producer information (H) may be mandatory in some markets.

Back label

The summarised brand information (I) reinforces the information provided on the front label. It is also presented in a way that reinforces the brand image presented on the front label. The Koru motif also appears (subtly) under the wine description (J). The wine description is presented in simple language and also tells the consumer something of the company (family owned) and its philosophy (handcrafted), as well as information such as cellaring potential.

Further reinforcement of the message behind the Koru logo is presented on the back label (K) in a poetic, perhaps even enigmatic, reference to the philosophy behind the wine. Importer information (L) and further product information (M) are also presented on the back label in accordance with the legal requirements of the market that this wine is to be exported to.

Design concept and label by Clare Nicholls and
Hamish Nicholls

Celebrity endorsement (Covert Induced I)

The use of celebrities is widespread in many product categories and these are often used as reference groups (Schiffman and Kanuk, 1987). Reference groups can be used in a number of ways, but two are pertinent to wine. The first is the use of celebrity 'experts' to provide a form of validation of the quality of the wine. For example, Australia's oldest family owned winery, Yalumba (http://www.yalumba.com/) used celebrity chef Jamie Oliver in advertising campaigns to take advantage of his celebrity status and popularity, as well as his perceived expertise in all things food and wine as one of the world's best known chefs. Celebrity chefs have arisen because of what is known as the 'cult of celebrity', where celebrities have gained widespread public followings, with fandoms, social status and cultural cachet. Gillespie (1994) suggests that these chefs actively court the media, cultivating a highly marketable public persona and that '… they have been aided and abetted by a copy hungry media' (Gillespie, 1994, p. 22). This is useful for wine producers that are able to gain favour with these chefs, especially if they are convinced that the wine will assist them in their quest to increase their public profile. The chef's endorsement might be paid for by the producer or it may be cultivated by the development of a relationship with them. Endorsement may also be through advertising campaigns, which will almost always involve direct payment to the celebrity.

The second is the use of celebrities as a role model. In this case the consumer is considered to be an aspirant and, in choosing the wine, they are expressing a desire to be like the celebrity or to have the lifestyle of the celebrity. Sports stars, movie and television stars, also part of the 'cult of celebrity', may also be involved in wine endorsements. However, it would not necessarily seem obvious for a sports star to endorse a wine. However, there are examples of sports star endorsements for wine companies. One such example is Australian cricket star Shane Warne doing a paid endorsement for a range of Zilzie Wines (http://www.zilziewines.com/). The Shane Warne Collection, as the range was known, was a somewhat risky venture for Zilzie given Warne's image as a beer-drinker, smoker and all-round 'bad boy'. However, the publicity received was enormous. According to one reporter at the launch of the wine for example:

At most wine launches you get a few lifestyle journalists, a few free-lance photographers looking for a drink, and too many wine-writing egos. Not at this particular launch, though. There were mainstream media and sporting celebrities. It all rather deflated the egos of the wine writers, who stood up the back, not getting the sporting jokes and generally being ignored. If Warne's wines do no more than this, they are already to be praised.

(Anon, 2002)

One of the effects of this approach by Zilzie was to broaden the media appeal of their wines but it also had the effect of democratising wine more broadly in the Australian market, as Warne is an important cult hero for many Australian men – he may be a larrikin, but people trust him and many can relate to his antics in some way. As the journalist at the launch continued:

... from a cultural point of view (yes, I am talking about a cricketer and culture in the same sentence), Warne has the ability to bring wine to those millions of Australians who don't drink it, or at least don't drink much of it.

My favourite rant is the one about Australia's poor wine-drinking habit: 20 litres per capita, compared with Italy or France, at about 60 litres per head a year. We rely on export markets for our wine; wine is the new sheep's back. That's good while the export markets are buoyant, but what happens if ... We never wore enough of our own wool; will we make the same mistake with our wine? Perhaps not if Warney has more to do with it.

(Anon, 2002)

Whether celebrities are used because of their expertise or their role model status, they must have a degree of credibility with the target market and this relates to their trustworthiness (Schiffman and Kanuk, 1987). For example the association between Zilzie and Shane Warne was relatively short lived and this may reflect the fact that Warne was found guilty of taking banned drugs in the year after the launch of the range. This would potentially have had a negative impact for Zilzie in some markets, especially as Warne had become less trustworthy in the eyes of the public, regardless of whether his breach of anti-doping laws for cricket was intentional or an innocent mistake on his part.

Product placement and event sponsorship (Covert Induced I)

Product placement involves the appearance of a product at special events or in movies or television programmes (Summers et al., 2003). According to media research company, PQ Media, 'global paid product placement grew 37.2% to $[US]3.36 billion in 2006 and is forecast to grow 30.3% to $[US]4.38 billion in 2007' (PQ Media, 2007). They also suggest that non-paid placements are also commonplace including 'barter' and 'added-value' placements and Patrick Quinn, President/CEO of PQ Media says:

As a new media order has emerged in recent years, our research indicates that we are entering an era of alternative advertising and marketing strategies .... Brand marketers are seeking to better engage consumers with emotional connections and media companies are searching for new revenue streams as traditional advertising methods suffer from negative perceptions. As a result, product placement has emerged from a novel marketing tactic just a few years ago to a key marketing strategy worldwide.

(PQ Media, 2007)

The use of product placement by wineries is relatively common and there are many examples of where effective placements have been achieved, including the following high profile examples:

- Ruffino Chiati Classico which appeared in *The Soparanos* television show and the movie *The Devil Wears Prada* in 2006 (Greenfield, 2006).
- Clos Du Val being order by Tom Hanks' character in Steven Spielberg's *The Terminal* and *The OC* in 2004 (Styles, 2004b).
- An E&J Gallo wine, Rancho Zabaco, appearing on *Queer Eye for a Straight Guy* in 2004 (Styles, 2004b).

According to Styles (2004b) the practice of paying for product placements is not widely used by wine producers, but there are strategies for increasingly the likelihood of gaining exposure. For example E&J Gallo use the fact that they spend a considerable amount on advertising to influence television networks to include their wine in shows that they produce (Styles, 2004b). Meanwhile, Clos Du Val has a more proactive strategy, paying a marketing firm around US$5,000 a month to 'keep its wines in directors' minds' (Styles, 2004b). In 2004, this involved distributing around 240 cases (around US$36,000 worth) of their wine at premieres and other big show business events. Although they cannot quantify the impact that this has on the end consumer, they reported a 50% jump in the sales following the implementation of the strategy. They can however measure the exposure that they received, as their wines ended up appearing in around 100 films and television shows.

Product placement can also be useful at high profile events, as can sponsorship of such events. Champagne houses have long recognised the value of being involved in high profile sports events and used it as a deliberate strategy in the creation of a luxury brand image (Beverland, 2004). Champagne G.H. Mumm, for example, has been involved in international sailing events (e.g. Admirals Cup, the Vendée Globe, the Hermes G.H. Mumm Regatta and the Skandia Cowes Regatta) and has been the 'Official Champagne' for Formula One motor racing since 2001. This association between Champagne and sports events has been important in developing and maintaining the champagne's image as a drink of celebration as winners often pop the cork and spray the crowd at the end of the race, game or contest. As such there are both indirect (i.e. the image of Champagne as a product category) and direct (i.e. brand image and sales for the brand associated with the event) benefits to be gained. It may also be useful for wine producers to have an involvement with events with aesthetic appeal (e.g. fashion shows, arts festivals, classical music and opera events and theatre events) as this may have positive benefits for premium wine brands which, as Charters (2006) points out, also have strong aesthetic value. Box 9.5 expands on this notion of wine as aesthetic and explores the relationship between wine and fashion.

Naming rights sponsorship of events can be expensive, especially for those events with a wide audience, and is likely to be out of the reach of most wineries. However, smaller wineries may be able to develop strategies that will allow them to become involved in smaller local events in locations that have high concentrations of their target market. They may also be indirectly involved with major events by providing wines for private hospitality suites/corporate boxes, although these may not necessarily be accessible as often major stadia and events centres or events may require these facilities to only stock sponsors' products.

Sponsorship is a complex area that is likely to require an understanding of contractual arrangements, intellectual property issues, management of press and PR and how to maximise your exposure over what may be a very short period. If the investment in an event is significant, then it can be beneficial to employ professionals to assist in the management of the process.

Hosting media (Covert Induced II)

In Chapter 4 we highlighted the value of hosting media at the winery as a powerful tool for creating media interest in a wine brand and, as such the discussion on this topic is brief. However we do not wish this brevity to be seen as a sign that it is not a useful tool. On the contrary, it can be very effective, relatively inexpensive and can have long lasting effects, especially if the media representative is likely to be involved in reviewing your wines in the future. One of the reasons that hosting media can be important is that resulting stories are likely to be perceived by consumers as being autonomous (hence its categorisation as an induced covert agent). This has more credibility than overt (induced) advertising and promotion, as it is seen to be coming from an independent third party.

The most important thing to remember about media visits is that the experience must be well managed, but not scripted or contrived, as the journalist can just as easily write negative comments about the visit and this can be very damaging to brand image.

Autonomous wine brand image agents

As has already been suggested, autonomous image agents can have more credibility as they are provided by a third party that is perceived to be independent. Further, as discussed in Chapter 4, wine involves a high degree of social risk for most consumers and, if they are unable to taste the wine before purchase, then they are likely to seek external validations of quality that will reduce this risk. For example, Orth and Krška (2002) found that Czech wine consumers felt that wine exhibition awards provided '… quality assurance since they are recognized by the consumers for building confidence and for signaling value for money. Additionally, the respondents firmly belief [sic.] in the independence of awarding committees'. Independent (autonomous) wine quality endorsements can come in several forms – awards, medals, star ratings and reviews by critics – but all can play a crucial role in the marketing of wine. Like any aesthetic form (e.g. art, fashion, movies, music, theatre), critical acclaim can make or break a wine.

Wine shows, medals and awards (Autonomous I)

Wine shows and exhibitions are where wine producers can submit wines to be measured against other wines of a similar type/style (class) by independent wine judges. Wines are tasted 'blind' (i.e. the wine is only labelled with a number and therefore the judge gets little or no information about the wine) and they are judged by a panel of judges against a set of 'organoleptic' criteria (i.e. sensory criteria such as colour, clarity, aroma, taste, mouth feel, acid–sugar balance, structure as well as how 'typical' they are for the wine class for which they are entered). Wines are typically scored either out of 20 or 100, depending on the system employed by the show, with those achieving an appropriate score receiving a medal (bronze, gold or silver) or a trophy for the highest scoring wines in their class and or at the show. Charters (2006, p. 220) suggests that the Australian show system is 'possibly the best developed and most cohesive in the world', but that it is not without criticism. He highlights the fact that:

- a lack of hierarchy in shows means that wines can perform well at one show and not another;
- the predominant use of winemakers as judges means the wines are judged primarily on their technical proficiency and therefore atypical (interesting) wines usually perform less well;
- large classes (often with as many as 200 wines) means that for a wine to stand out it must be a 'blockbuster' and therefore high quality, yet subtle wines also tend to perform less well;
- the processes of a show wine tasting itself, especially the short time available, limits the ability of judges to make appropriate judgements;
- these professional judgments may have no connection with consumer likes and dislikes.

In New Zealand questions have also been raised over the wine show process with respect to the potential for wineries to submit batches of wine for tasting that were different from those available from retailers under the same label. As Walsh (2007, p. 46) notes, in 1997 Cooper's Creek winery 'was accused of selling two different chardonnays under the same label, one ranked five-star by *Cuisine*, another a three-star; in 1998 ... the same winery was accused of mislabelling; in 1998 the now defunct Martinborough Lintz Estate won a gold medal at the Air New Zealand Wine Awards for a shiraz that wasn't the shiraz on the market'. More recently, there has been substantial public controversy over a Wither Hills Sauvignon Blanc that was submitted into *Cuisine's* annual tasting and was awarded five stars and ranked in the top ten Sauvignon Blanc's but then shown to be a different production batch with different characteristics from that available from retailers (Walsh, 2007). The furore surrounding this issue called into question not only the manner in which wine awards are judged but also the extent to which audits of wine are independent or even used, and the close relationship that can exist between wine judging, wine making and wine media, where the same person can be involved in all three. Such issues are significant for winegrowers as wine awards are often used by new wine drinkers and those with a low level of wine knowledge to reduce the risk in wine purchasing.

Despite this wine shows continue to be popular and they do provide a useful baseline by which the industry can maintain and improve quality. However, they do appear to be more favoured by consumers in New World markets and emerging markets than Old World. As has already been suggested the medals that are awarded can also be one of the bases by which consumers make decisions about wines when they purchase them. The credence placed on medals will depend a lot on the consumer and purchase and consumption situation and therefore there are likely to be some segments for which medals are more important. For example Lockshin et al. (2006, p. 175) found that, while gold medals positively impact on wine choices for low involvement wine consumers, 'high involvement consumers discount the effect of a gold medal, especially with large well-known wine brands'. Other segmentation bases may also be useful in determining the relative importance of medals in decision making.

Wine shows also require different strategies by different wine producers. As Charters (2006, after Robinson, 1999) suggests '… the very best producers will rarely enter their wines in a competition; they have little to gain if they win, and much potential damage to their wine's reputation may occur if they lose'. In New Zealand, in 2006, 260 out of 540 wineries did not participate in the Air New Zealand Wine Awards (the country's top wine show in which 70% of gold medal wines were audited). As Walsh (2007, p. 52) observed, this was 'not necessarily because their wines are below par. They might be making great wines, but in a style that's out of favour. They might be making wines that go with pizza as opposed to the tannic fruit bombs that howl for attention in a crowded line-up'. Some wineries, however, have a deliberate strategy to enter as many high profile shows and competitions as possible. Villa Maria, New Zealand's second largest producer, is one such producer. Between 2000 and 2006, they report having entered 26 major domestic shows and seven international shows. In 2005, for example, they entered two major domestic shows and two international shows in Australia, where they won a total of: nine trophies (placing runner-up in five); 35 gold medals (or equivalent); 27 silver medals; 20 bronze medals (Villa Maria Wines, 2007). This strategy forms part of Villa Maria's marketing strategy, with medal stickers placed on winning wines to indicate their success to consumers and a print advertising campaign that serves to reinforce the award winning status. These stickers are often used by wineries to indicate show success as they are easily identifiable in retail outlets and this may act as a strong visual cue that can narrow some consumers' choice very quickly.

There are many different levels of wine show and each is of varying quality and value to a wine producer and consumer (Charters, 2006; Walsh, 2007). Shows can range from small regional shows, to state and national shows and ultimately to large international shows. They can also either be primarily producer focussed, trade focussed or have a commercial focus and which is open to the public. In reality most larger shows, at least at an international level and probably at a national level, will have a focus on producer, trade and end consumer (see also Chapter 8). Each of these shows will have a different level of influence on trade, consumers and media (see Table 9.3). Therefore wineries need to select the shows that present the best opportunities for them, especially if their intention is to use the awards as part of their marketing strategy. A small regional producer-focussed show may be useful in terms of gauging how their wines rate against other producers in the region, but it is likely to have only a minimal impact on sales.

Wine reviews and the role of wine critics (Autonomous I)

Charters (2006) says that wine shows and their judges perform a 'gatekeeping' role in the wine value chain; he also says that wine critics act as gatekeepers. Reviews of wines by wine critics are the mainstay of many wine-specific magazines (see above) and an important form of external independent information about wine. They differ from wine show judgements in that they are often the opinion of just one critic (although most magazines or wine annuals may also have blind tastings by tasting panels) and they will include descriptions of the wines, potential food

Table 9.3 Influence of wine shows/awards

	Producer show			Trade			Commercial		
	TI	MI	CI	TI	MI	CI	TI	MI	CI
Regional	Low	Low	Low	Low	Low	Low	Low	Med	Low
State/National	Med	Low	Low	Med	Med	Med	High	High	High
International	High	Med	Med	High	Med	Med	High	High	High

TI = Trade Influence; CI = Consumer Influence; MI = Media Impact (reach).

matches and cellaring potential. This not only gives consumers a measure of 'quality', it also gives them more of an appreciation of its aesthetic values, perhaps even including which occasions its style is best suited to. As such critics are telling consumers what is good and what is not (Charters, 2006), as well as what they should taste and even how they should consume it. In this fashion they are 'gatekeepers of taste' like the music press (Shuker, 1994) and art critics (Greenfeld, 1988).

While there are thousands of wine critics, their power as gatekeeper varies considerably and there are a relative few that have a high degree of influence in the main Anglophone markets. In the USA at least, Robert Parker is the most powerful of these critics and has been termed the 'Emperor of Wine' (McCoy, 2005). Charters (2006, p. 216) suggests that:

As Robert Parker's reputation increased so consumers tended to buy wine according to his recommendation ... This gave him great influence, but there are suggestions that there is a 'Parker-style' and fears that he spawns stylistic homogeneity and has become too powerful in influencing markets.

Similarly, Ellis (2005) in a review of McCoy's book on the influence of Robert Parker commented:

Although Parker always said his scores should be used in conjunction with his tasting notes, it wasn't long before wine merchants – and wineries – started trumpeting the Parker scores alone as a quick way to decipher a wine's worth. Soon, a high Parker score, especially a 90+, meant higher prices for producers and a lot more sales for retailers ... It also didn't take long for winemakers to note Parker's preference for big wines that are packed with oak and fruit and have lots of texture. Critics charge that wines that don't fit Parker's favored profile receive lower scores and, therefore, have poorer sales – pushing winemakers to adapt.

Beverland (2003, 2004) suggests that this has been particularly influential in Bordeaux, where a Parker rating of 90 out of 100 can have positive impacts on price, yet an 89 out of 100 can be 'disastrous'. Despite this Beverland (2004, p. 457) also found that endorsements by wine writers are important in the development of luxury wine brands as they gained credibility from '... an external system such as an independent wine writer, or in the case of Europe, an institutionalised quality classification system' (see Charters, 2006 for an extensive discussion of these classification systems). Moreover, Beverland (2004, p. 462) continues that 'younger firms, having little history to draw on, may place less weight on this component, and more weight on endorsements and product integrity, whilst more established firms may place greater emphasis on history and their endorsements'.

There is no denying that wine critics are influential as several authors have found a relationship between critics' evaluations and reviews of wine and price (Landon and Smith, 1997; Jones and Storchmann, 2001) and winery and individual wine reputation. Most wine reviews are undertaken following the submission of wines by wineries and therefore the winery does have some control over which critics taste and review their wines. Some critics will also seek out wines to review and in these instances wineries have little control. This lack of control, coupled with the influence and power of the critic, makes wine reviews somewhat problematic, yet necessary, in wine marketing.

Non-wine media (Autonomous II)

Increasingly lifestyle media are providing reviews of wines, wineries and wine regions as food, wine and travel become an important component of the burgeoning middle class lifestyle (see Hall et al., 2003). The rise in popularity of wine and food as lifestyle commodities can be found in the proliferation of food and wine sections in general lifestyle magazines (e.g. *House and Garden* or *Condé Naste Portfolio*) or specialised spin-offs of these magazines (e.g. *Gourmet Traveller Wine*) and the development of lifestyle and food and wine channels on television networks.

The value of this media as an image forming agent can be quite indeterminate. The difficulty with this media is that it is difficult to identify the level of trust which a consumer might place in the reviewer or critic and/or this source as a source of wine information. It could be that the total independence from wine-related media and the wine industry may be seen by some as beneficial (perhaps mostly amongst wine novices or those less involved in wine), but as either neutral or negative by others (most likely amongst those more involved in wine). The influence of wine articles in such media will also depend on the style of review or article and how this relates to the readership. For example, an article about life on the winery or the family that owns a winery may be more beneficial to brand image in these media than reviews of the wine, especially as it may assist in building relationships with (potential) consumers.

Fashion media – which is increasingly aligned with more general lifestyle – can also be influential as similar principles of aesthetic appeal may be at play and, it can be argued, wine can be perceived as haute couture. Box 9.5 discusses wine as fashion and how Louis Vuitton–Moët Hennessy (LVMH) has married these two worlds.

Box 9.5 Wine as fashion: Moët & Chandon and Dom Pérignon

There are many elements that relate the concept of fashion to wine. This box highlights some of these elements and discusses them in the context of two of the world's most famous champagne brands Moët & Chandon and Dom Pérignon, both of which are part of the Louis Vuitton–Moët Hennessy (LVMH) luxury (fashion) brand group of companies.

Wine as fashion

Clothing is the consumer product most frequently associated with fashion. However fashion may refer to the style of a consumer product, the symbolic meaning attached to a product, or the process by which a product is temporarily adopted by an individual or social group within a cultural context (Sproles and Burns, 1994). The fashion process is a dynamic mechanism of change, the origins of change being as diverse as the channels within a society that facilitate the change (Sproles and Burns, 1994).

Wine, as a product of aesthetic and symbolic value (Charters, 2006), has the potential to be conceptualised as a fashion item. For example, the release of a new vintage of wine is to the wine enthusiast (connoisseur) what the launch of a new season's clothing range is to the fashion leader: it is much anticipated; it is the focus of critics and journalists; it may be released to its public at a show; and as Bruwer et al., (2002) suggest, it is something with which the consumer can make a (fashion) statement about themselves. Wine, like clothing, also has fashion cycles. Different wine varieties go in and out of fashion like clothing. Pinot Gris may be perceived as being more fashionable than un-oaked Chardonnay or Pinot Noir more than Merlot and, like clothing, these cycles can be influenced by the media and the critical acclaim of experts.

If wine is synonymous with fashion, then Champagne could be viewed as the Haute Couture of the wine industry. Champagne embodies prestige and luxury and as such some brands have a close affiliation with the fashion industry. Champagne, like denim in clothing fashion, has become such an iconic product that it is difficult to imagine it ever being out of fashion. Both denim and Champagne have a heritage from their origins in France more than 250 years ago and they may be subject to various fashion fads or trends but the product continues to be timelessly fashionable.

Moët & Chandon and Dom Pérignon: timeless fashion labels

As part of the LVMH stable, Moët & Chandon and Dom Pérignon are part of a multinational company with a portfolio of approximately 60 of the world's most luxurious fashion brands. The mission of the LVMH group is to represent the most refined qualities of Western 'Art de Vivre' from around the world. LVMH products, and the cultural values they embody, blend tradition and innovation, elegance and creativity. LVMH aims to tightly control its brands in order to maintain and enhance the perception of luxury relating to their products, and to ultimately create 'star brands' (Wetlaufer, 2001). Bernard Arnault, chairman of LVMH, states that a star brand exists when the company manages to make products that paradoxically 'speak to the ages' but feel intensely modern (Wetlaufer, 2001). LVMH claim to have achieved star branding with Moët & Chandon and Dom Pérignon Champagne in that it is described as being timeless, modern, and highly successful (Wetlaufer, 2001).

Established in 1743, Moët & Chandon is today the largest producer of Champagne in the world. How does this brand that has such a long tradition continue to be perceived as modern, or fashionable? One way is LVMH's commitment to creativity and innovation. Another is that Moët & Chandon has set out to embrace the fashion world and one way that it has done so is to be the official Champagne sponsor of the New York and London Fashion Weeks (Nassauer, 2007).

Dom Pérignon too is an iconic Champagne brand with a long heritage. Dom Pérignon places emphasis on the reinvention of the Champagne each vintage by only producing a Vintage Champagne in exceptional years. The company refers to the paradoxical tension between the distinctive qualities of a year and the timeless spirit of Dom Pérignon. Through this 'continual reinvention of the exceptional', the Champagne house keeps the fashion process alive.

Rosé Moët: Wine style and the fashion process

In 1998, Moët & Chandon produced a non-vintage rosé in a process which can be compared to the first stage of the fashion process. A new fashion was created (rosé Champagne); a style that was different to current fashion (white Champagne). This is part of the process of new product design, which begins with radical innovation that allows the product to stand apart from others (Wetlaufer, 2001). New fashions are adopted by fashion leaders as they are highly visible and create attention and interest (Sproles and Burns, 1994).

Consumers perceived rosé as young and extroverted, in comparison with the traditional perception of Champagne as being elitist (Nassauer, 2007). A number of factors contributed to the success of rosé Champagne including the search by increasingly educated wine consumers for something new, and a general fashion trend toward 'all things pink' (Nassauer, 2007). It was no accident, then, that Moët & Chandon chose the London Fashion week for the UK launch of their non-vintage rosé in 1998 (Nassauer, 2007).

Once the decision to invest in non-vintage rosé production was made, Moët & Chandon increased its visibility through other marketing efforts. This started with rose petal coloured Valentine's Day advertisements in glossy magazines and special packaging in the late 1990s (Nassauer, 2007). As sales increased, and the fashion of rosé Champagne gained larger social acceptance, marketing was spread to all parts of the world year round (Nassauer, 2007).

Creating fashion through packaging

All fashions have life cycles, culminating in eventual obsolescence as fashion leaders look for something new (Sproles and Burns, 1994). Moët & Chandon (and LVMH, in general) look to constantly reinvent the brand, to stay modern (Wetlaufer, 2001). As an example, Moët & Chandon has produced a hand-made Moët Rosé picnic bag complete with magnums of Rosé Imperial. This was an exclusive and expensive accessory that the company used to create a further association with fashion.

A wine label can communicate a visual image, provide recognition, stimu-late interest and enhance thought (Thomas, 2000). Furthermore, the label, the wine and its overall packaging may go beyond the point of purchase to make a statement about its purchaser (Thomas, 2000). Brand image, and product presentation, namely bottle labelling and additional packaging, are important determinants of prestige and luxury perceptions of Champagne (Mortan et al., 2004). For example, in 2007 Dom Pérignon unveiled a limited edition packaging for Dom Pérignon Vintage 1998 in Sydney (Walsh, 2007). Designed by Marc Newson the neon green cooler in the shape of an over-sized Dom Pérignon bottle transformed the packaging into a work of art. 'Dom Pérignon by Marc Newson' was the first creation of the newly established Dom Pérignon Designers' Studio, and has been described as 'a true object of desire' (Vienna Art Week, 2007).

Advertising campaigns: the worlds of fashion and wine collide

In 2005, fashion guru and photographer, Karl Lagerfeld was commissioned by Dom Pérignon to prepare an advertising campaign for the release of its 1998 Vintage Champagne. The result was '7 Fantasmes of a Woman', in which Lagerfeld 'brings to life his vision of a woman's sensual fantasies' melding these with the '18th century origin of Dom Pérignon into a series of photographs filled with sensuality, mystery and sexual ambiguity' (Steidl, 2007) (see www.dom-perignon.com). This association with Lagerfeld has continued and in the second campaign called 'Room Service', this time for the 1998 Rosé Dom Pérignon. The campaign photos and subsequent book and short film (which includes an unusual version of 'Diamonds are a Girl's Best Friend') follow a plot where:

After an orgy of shopping, [supermodel] Eva Herzigova checks into a sumptuous hotel. She takes the biggest suite, where she tip-taps around in beautiful clothes, lolls about in bed, takes luxurious baths, sips pink champagne, loves her own company. Flowers arrive, but she sees nobody, wants nobody. She is lavishing all her attention inward. Her only distraction is the man on the other side of the connecting door. Finally, bored, she instructs a maid to let her into his room, whereupon she seduces him without hesitation.

(Spicer, 2006).

Spicer (2006) suggests that 'This is Karl Lagerfeld's idea of a woman's perfect fantasy ... It's a delicious tableau, composed by the grande dame of fashion'.

According to one review of the book and film, 'The storyline he created was an ultra-contemporary fairy tale that recounted an irresistible attraction between two solitary and seductive hedonists whose paths cross at one of Paris's finest hotels' (Amazon, 2007)

This collision between wine, fashion, art and film is further reinforced by the candid interviews with supermodel Helena Christensen that describe her role in the photo shoot (the only material available on the 1998 Vintage Dom Pérignon website). In somewhat of a post-modern moment, the boundary between documentary, fashion shoot, erotica and advertising campaign seems to disappear.

Moët & Chandon's 'Be Fabulous' advertising campaign also demonstrates a strong association with fashion. This is especially evident in the 'Be Fabulous: Turn an exit into an entrance' poster, which sees two models alighting from a black Maserati limousine on to a red carpet holding a magnum of Moët & Chandon as if entering the premier of a new movie or opening of a West End show. The website that accompanies the campaign presents a 'making of video', which gives a behind the scenes look at the photo shoot for this and the other posters with images reminiscent of catwalks and fashion photo shoots (see www.moet.com).

In these campaigns, played out in various forms of media, fashion and wine have become one!

For more details see:
www.lvmh.com
www.moet.com
www.domperignon.com

Clare Nicholls and Richard Mitchell

Movies and other fiction (Autonomous II)

We have already discussed the significance of product placement in movies and television, yet the role of movies and other forms of fiction can go well beyond simple product placement. Where a wine forms an integral part of the story (whether by product placement or not) the impact on the consumer can be quite profound. In these works of fiction the reader/viewer is immersed in diegetic (diagetic) reality where they may experience 'vicarious emotions'. As Lazarus (2006, p. 28) puts it:

The emotions we experience in the theater, movies, or when we read a book are usually attenuated compared with the real thing. Because we know we are reasonably safe in a theater or at home reading, these vicarious emotions are likely to be less intense than they would be in actual life. We understand that the events being portrayed are simulations of reality and the actors are merely playing parts. Yet, if the story is written and performed well, it has the power to move us.

These emotions may be expressed as laughter or crying or in sympathy or empathy for the characters and these are powerful markers for our memory. Emotions such as these are widely acknowledged to have an impact on our recall and attachment to a product or brand (Ambler and Burne, 1999). The level of impact of this image formation agent is therefore potentially huge. Nowhere is this more obvious than with the cult movie *Sideways* (see Box 9.6).

Box 9.6 The 'Sideways Effect'

Sideways

In 2004, the movie *Sideways* was released and soon met with popular and critical acclaim. It was ultimately nominated for five Academy Awards (including best picture) and won two Golden Globes including 'best picture: musical or comedy'. However, even with such adulation, few could imagine what a profound impact it would have on the world of wine. According to the website of the Sideways™ Wine Club (http://www.sidewayswineclub.com/) which is operated by Wine Marketing Enterprises of San Francisco, 'The movie Sideways did more for U.S. wine sales than any media event in 15 years. We continue in the spirit of Sideways, sharing our passion with new as well as experienced wine fans. We also feature an extensive collection of wine quotes and wine books to build your library – perfect gift ideas!'

One line in the movie is credited with changing the drinking habits of a nation: 'If anyone orders merlot, I'm leaving. I'm not drinking any F***ing merlot' (Miles, drunk, to Jack outside a restaurant before dinner with potential 'love interests', Maya and Stephanie). However, there are many scenes in this movie that changed attitudes and behaviours towards two grape varieties: Merlot and Pinot Noir.

Pinot Noir impact

In fact it could be argued that Pinot Noir had become the target of Miles' affection following his break up with his wife, as he waxes lyrical about its somewhat enigmatic beauty. For example, when Maya asks: 'Why are you so into Pinot?', Miles replies:

I don't know. I don't know. It's a hard grape to grow, as you know, right? It's thin-skinned, temperamental, ripens early. It's not a survivor like cabernet which can just grow anywhere and thrive even when it's neglected. No, Pinot needs constant care and attention. In fact, it can only grow in these really specific little tucked away corners

---

of the world. And only the most patient and nurturing of growers can do it, really. Only somebody who really takes the time to understand Pinot's potential can then coax it to its fullest expression. It's flavours, they're just the most haunting and brilliant and thrilling and subtle and ancient on the planet. Now, cabernet's can be powerful and exalting too but they seem prosaic to me for some reason by comparison. I don't know.

(Sideways, Directed by Alexander Payne, Twentieth Century Fox, 2004)

These romantic images of what Pinot Noir represents are mirrored by the clear sexual tension between Miles and Maya, which enhances the power of the dialogue to influence attitudes towards Pinot Noir. This is just one example of Mile's infatuation with Pinot Noir which is a central part of his character, with Pinot often, it seems, being used as metaphor for aspects of his life. Pinot Noir ultimately comes to stand for Miles and his plight and it is his fragile and desperate, yet lovable, character that the audience empathise with (a vicarious emotional response).

As a result of these powerful images and emotions, *Sideways* changed Pinot Noir consumption overnight. Dubbed the *Sideways Effect*, according to ACNielsen figures on US wine sales this saw Pinot sales jump 16% from the previous year in the 12 weeks that ended 15 January 2005, less than six months after the movie's release (Locke, 2005). A year after the film's release Bonné (2005) suggests that 'Twelve months ago, it was a grape appreciated by the more geeky among wine lovers (plus the French and a handful of Californians and Oregonians with a penchant for masochism)'. He continues that

Pinot noir sales have spiked by nearly 45 percent since July 2004, according to ACNielsen. That's just a drop in the overall wine bucket (a mere 1.6 percent of all table wine sold), but for a once obscure variety and the winemakers who devote themselves to the grape's finicky nature, it has been a rare moment in the limelight

(Bonné, 2005).

Merlot impact

Some have suggested that at the same time there was a slump in the sale of Merlot (Sauer, 2005) that is often accredited to Mile's disdain for merlot in the quote above, but this is overstated. ACNeilsen figures at the time actually revealed a rise of 3% for the 12 weeks to 15 January 2005 (Locke, 2005).

Brand impact

The impact was also felt by individual brands, including:

- Wild Horse winery from the region where the movie is set, reporting a 135% increase in sales of its Pinot Noir from supermarkets in the four weeks to 15 January (Locke, 2005).
- Hitching Post II, the restaurant where Maya worked and the focus of several scenes, sold 900 cases of a wine used in the movie (their 2004 Highliner Pinot Noir) within weeks of bottling (Bonné, 2005).

- Blackstone Pinot Noir sales increased by almost 150% in the six months following the film's release (Sauer, 2005).
- Sanford Pinot Noir, Miles' Pinot of choice, tripled in price soon after the film's release (from US$10 to US$30) and maintained the new price through to at least two years after the movie's release (Nothaft, 2007)

Wine tourism impact

Tourism to the Central California Coast region also increased, with the development of *Sideways* maps and cycle, van and coach tours that stopped at movie locations to dine and take part in wine tasting (Thies, 2005). Evidence of the impact includes:

- Hitching Post II's restaurant patronage rose 30 percent in the six months post-release (Sauer, 2005).
- Santa Barbara and Central Coast regions reported a 'huge tourism boom' in the 12 months after the release of the movie (Bonné, 2005, Locke, 2005).

Sideways effect

Just how significant *Sideways* was in the upswing in the popularity of Pinot Noir is hard to quantify but few can deny that it did have at least some impact. As Danny Brager, vice president of ACNielsen Beverage Alcohol Team, put it 'it looks like more than a coincidence that this varietal's sales have been stronger than ever since the movie's release' (cited in Locke, 2005). And, as Californian Pinot maker, Tony Soter, rejoiced, 'I've been making pinot since 1980, so I've been waiting for this train to come for some time' (cited in Bonné, 2005).

Official Sideways website: http://www.foxsearchlight.com/sideways/

The website includes pages on Wine Tasting 101, a Snob-Free Guide to Wine, links to Santa Barbara tourism website and the Sideways wine club (http://www.sidewayswineclub.com/) operated by Wine Marketing Enterprises of San Francisco.

Sideways is by no means the only fictional story where wine plays a pivotal role in defining the characters or is part of the plot and the publicity is not always as favourable. For example, the British television comedy *Absolutely Fabulous* (http://www.bbc.co.uk/comedy/abfab/) sees the two central characters, who are usually either drunk or stoned, regularly getting drunk on there favourite cocktails called a 'Bolli Stolli' (Champagne Bollinger and Stolichnaya vodka) and a 'Veuve and Bourb' (Champagne Veuve Clicquot and bourbon). Throughout the several years of the series glass door fridges are also visible in the main set that are filled either with Veuve Clicquot or Bollinger.

While the series has a cult following and the cocktails have become (in)famous, it could be suggested that the brand association with the drunken characters of Patsy and Eddy is far from flattering for either Champagne house.

A note on organic wine brand image agents

Organic agents are well outside the control of the winery, however, the credibility with which they are usually perceived means that they are important. In essence organic agents provide word of mouth endorsements for a wine and this is usually following their own first hand experience with the wine. This experience might have been under the control of the winery (e.g. at the cellar door or at a tasting at a retail outlet) and therefore it is important that all consumers of a wine are considered to be potential brand ambassadors. As has been noted in Chapter 4, a relationship marketing approach to direct contact with consumers will assist in reinforcing the brand values that the winery wishes to be passed on by word of mouth recommendations (see Chapter 4).

Chapter summary

Many external factors can influence the image of a wine and only some are under the full control of the wine's producer. Advertising is where the winery has the greatest control, but where the brand message has least credibility. At the other end of the scale, word of mouth recommendations (organic agents) are almost completely outside the control of the winery, yet are perhaps the most credible and powerful of brand image vectors.

The wine critic and wine show judges have also been shown to be particularly important image agents for wineries as the external validation of quality that they provide for consumers places them as powerful gatekeepers of taste. As autonomous agents of image they are seen as 'unbiased' and therefore they have a high degree of credibility, especially those that have gained a reputation for their expertise. Works of fiction where wine plays a central role can also be a powerful agent of image and there is no better example than the cult movie *Sideways*.

A range of induced agents are available to wineries for the development of their brand image and these can be largely controlled by the winery, yet may not have as great an impact as might be hoped. However, irrespective of which agent is used strategic and tactical planning is crucial to the maximisation of the impact that they can have.

Practical wine marketing insights

- Wine brand image formation agents can be a powerful tool and external force that impact on wine marketing.
- Induced agents such as advertising and PR, information at retail locations, celebrity endorsements and hosted media can all be used as brand communication tools for wineries.
- Autonomous agents (e.g. wine shows, awards and reviews, and wine critics) are independent and therefore are largely out of the control of the wine producer, however they are powerful gatekeepers of consumer choice and they must not be ignored in any marketing strategy. An effective strategy can be the difference between success and failure in the marketplace.
- Movies and other fictional works can also be very powerful advocates for a wine and if this is married with effective product placement (covert induced) then the impact can be massive. Once again effective strategy and investment in such a strategy are important to success.

Further reading

Charters, S. (2006). *Wine and Society: The social and cultural context of a drink*. Elsevier Butterworth Heinemann.
Chapter 10 includes a discussion of wine literature, wine critics and wine shows.

Lockshin, L., Jarvis, W., d'Hauteville, F. and Perrouty, J-P. (2006). Using simulations from discrete choice experiments to measure consumer sensitivity to brand, region, price, and awards in wine choice. *Food Quality and Preference*, 17(3/4), 166–178.
An empirical study of the relative importance of several factors that impact on wine choice, including wine medals.

Orth, U. R. and Krška, P. (2002). Quality signals in wine marketing: the role of exhibition awards. *International Food and Agribusiness Management Review*, 4(4), 385–397.
An empirical study of the impact of wine awards on price.

Stern, B.M., Zinkhan, G.M. and Jaju, A. (2001). Marketing images. *Marketing Theory*, 1(2), 201–224.
Provides a review of how the concept of image has been used in the marketing literature.

Marketing cooperation: regions, networks and clusters

Chapter objectives

After reading this chapter you will

● Appreciate the value of cooperative marketing for wineries, wine regions and countries
● Understand the value of cooperation with complementary industries such as tourism
● Appreciate the value of place in the branding of wine and how cooperation can develop and enhance a sense of place
● Identify that there are different forms of legal protection of the intellectual property of place that are best implemented cooperatively

---

Introduction

In Chapter 1 we highlighted the fact that in most wine regions around the world there is a dichotomy between a very small number of large wineries who control the vast majority of production and a relatively large number of small businesses who compete for a relatively small proportion of the market. For these smaller wineries, it is difficult to have a significant presence in the marketplace as they do not have the economies of scale to undertake large-scale marketing activities. As a result it is important for these smaller wineries to work together in order to have a greater impact in their chosen markets. In particular the development of formal networks and clusters has provided New World and, to a lesser extent, Old World wine industries with positive outcomes that have allowed these smaller wineries to 'punch well above their weight' in the international marketplace. As Aylward and Zanko (2006, p. 9) suggest:

Trends in a number of New World [wine] industries appear to point to the fact that wine firm clusters create a disproportionately positive influence. Infrastructure, knowledge flows, supply chains, research and education bodies, regulatory frameworks, advisory organizations and general firm interaction appear to be significantly more intense within these clusters than in non-cluster regions.

They also suggest that this has resulted, at least in part, from the 'emergence of regionalism/localization' in New World wine regions (Aylward and Zanko, 2006, p. 8). This form of cooperation is sometimes dubbed 'co-opetition' (Brandenburger and

Nalebuff, 1996) or 'co-ompetition' (McKibbin, 2000), which sees businesses cooperating to compete in the broader marketplace and is the focus of much of this chapter.

Wine is also one of the few products whose attributes are naturally conducive to cooperation at a regional level, as the wine region itself can be a source of differentiation, added value and reputation. Place-based marketing is critical to the success of individual brands, wine regions and the image of entire nation's wine production. This means that a discussion of the role of place is useful in relation to wine marketing and how this is played out in cooperation at a regional and national level. This chapter therefore discusses different forms of marketing cooperation including:

- regional marketing clusters and networks that cooperate within the wine industry;
- wine and food tourism networks that cooperate across a number of sectors at both a regional and national level;
- industry-wide marketing initiatives at a state and national level, by industry, quasi-governmental and governmental agencies;
- policy and regulatory cooperation at an international level that impacts on different marketing functions of individual companies, wine regions and countries.

Wine networks and clusters

There is a considerable body of literature on the value of networks and clusters for all industries and the wine industry is no exception. The benefits that accrue from cooperative behaviour, both formal and informal, are widely acknowledged to go beyond the firm level to include groups of businesses, regions and entire nations (Hall et al., 1998). The focus here, however, is on the benefits that accrue to individual businesses in terms of marketing. The marketing benefits might include, cooperative promotional and advertising activities, the exchange of marketing know-how and market intelligence, increased research capacity (especially in the development of new markets), joint training of employees and the sharing of marketing infrastructure (Hall et al., 2000).

From the outset it is important to develop an understanding of two important concepts – networks and clusters – that are used to describe different forms of cooperative behaviour. Networks are characteristic of '... a wide range of cooperative behaviour between otherwise competing organizations and between organizations linked through economic and social relationships and transactions' (Hall et al., 2000, p. 206, after Hall et al., 1998). These networks gain mutual benefit from sharing resources by working together towards a common goal in a way that is accommodating and complementary to other members of the network (Powell, 1990). Hall et al. (2000, p. 208) suggest that 'Networks are ... particularly important for the wine industry, e.g. wine cooperatives or regional wine associations which may pool expertise or equipment or may engage in joint promotional activities'.

The concepts of clusters and 'clustering' have also been closely associated with the wine industry. Indeed, Porter (1990, 1998, 2000), who coined the term cluster, used the California wine industry cluster as an example to illustrate some of the attributes of clusters. Clusters are also important in the context of this book as they form value chains (Porter, 1990) and the development of value chains, rather than supply chains, is one of the core premises on which this book is built (see Chapter 1). According to Porter (2000, p. 15):

Clusters are geographic concentrations of interconnected companies, specialized suppliers, service providers, firms in related industries, and associated institutions (e.g. universities, standards agencies, trade associations) in a particular field that compete but also cooperate. Clusters, or critical masses of unusual competitive success in particular business areas, are a striking feature of virtually every national, regional, state, and even metropolitan economy, especially in more advanced nations.

Blandy (2001, p. 80) suggested 'that there is no precise, "right" (one size fits all) formula for developing industry clusters'. However, Hall et al. (2003, p. 38–39) suggest that a number of factors may be important in the development of effective networks and clusters, including:

- the life cycle stage of innovative clusters;
- government financing and policies;
- the skills of the region's human resources;
- the technological capabilities of the region's R&D (Research and Development) activities;
- the quality of the region's physical, transport, information and communication infrastructure;
- the availability and expertise of capital financing in the region;
- the cost and quality of the region's tax and regulatory environment;
- the appeal of the region's lifestyle to people that can provide world-class resources and processes;

- spatial separation – the existence of substantial spatial separation of vineyards and wineries within a wine region due to physical resource factors;
- administrative separation – the existence of multiple public administrative agencies and units within a region;
- the existence of an entrepreneurial and innovative 'champion' to promote the development of a network;
- the hosting of meetings to develop relationships.

A number of analyses of New World wine industries have found examples of different levels of cluster, including:

- *California*: A wine cluster based in the Napa and Sonoma Valleys and beginning in the late 1970s/early 1980s (Porter, 1990, 1998, 2000).
- *South Australia*: Beginning in the 1980s (Blandy, 2001; Aylward, 2004; Aylward and Zanko, 2006).
- *Australia*: National wine industry as a 'meta-cluster' (Marsh and Shaw, 2000).
- *Chile*: An emerging national cluster (Visser, 2004).
- *Colchagua Valley (Chile)*: A knowledge-based cluster (Giuliani and Bell, 2005).
- *Hawkes Bay (New Zealand)*: A private sector initiated wine, food and tourism cluster (Hall, 2003, 2004).
- *Central Otago (New Zealand)*: A government funded marketing cluster (Mitchell and Schreiber, 2006).
- *Serra Gaúcha (Brazil)*: A cluster responsible for 80% of Brazil's wine production (Fensterseifer, 2006).

Ditter (2005) contrasts these New World 'Porterian' clusters with the French *'terroir/AOC'* approach, suggesting that the French approach is not conducive to cooperative behaviour. In particular he suggests that:

The fragmented supply [in the French wine industry] is ... both the cause and the consequence of a "non-competitive/non-cooperative" tradition among producers which is diametrically opposed to how Porterian clusters work; individual strategies of traditional producers aim to avoid all forms of comparison with neighbours and potential competitors.

(Ditter, 2005, p. 50)

So it seems that wine clusters and networks are largely the preserve of New World wine regions and that Old World wine regions, such as those in France, are hamstrung by archaic notions of the need to protect 'wine as a cultural expression' at the expense of business imperatives (rather than the culture of wine as a way to add value) and laws and regulations that reinforce the status quo and hinder innovation (Ditter, 2005). As a result Ditter (2005) asks whether the terroir model should be abandoned by French wine producers, and concludes:

Most certainly not, since the nature [and] structure of winemaking in France would not allow the industry to compete with the Californian or Australian one: French producers are unwilling and unable to produce standardised wine in large quantities backed up by heavy marketing investment and would certainly be wiped out of the world market in a few years if they tried to. The terroir/AOC strategy aiming at the production in small quantities of high quality 'typical' products remains the most relevant considering French wine making structures.

(Ditter, 2005, p. 50)

Despite this there is some evidence of wine regions in France that have a high degree of cooperative, perhaps even Porterian, behaviour (see Plate 10.1). For example, Ditter himself acknowledges that the *Comite interprofessionnel du Vin du Champagne* (CIVC) is one notable exception to the rule. The CIVC has been in existence since 1945 and cooperates to maintain the quality of champagne, protect the intellectual property of the name and promote the region and its wines around the world (see Box 10.2). Meanwhile *Inter-Rhône*, the recently refocused and rebranded regional body for the Rhône region in the south of France is also a good example of attempts towards more of a Porterian approach (see Box 10.1).

Box 10.1 Inter-Rhône

In 1999 the *Comité Interprofessionnel des Côtes du Rhône* (CIDR) renamed and repositioned itself as *Inter-Rhône* after initially being developed at the request of vignerons and negotiants in 1955 (http://www.vignovin.com/). According to Guibert (2006, p. 261):

The Rhône Valley [(RV)], comprising 77,000 ha of AOC wines, is the second largest French wine producing area behind Bordeaux (117,000 ha), and one of the world's largest high quality wine producing regions. It is also a first class tourist area, so RV AOC wines function as the flagship for leading wine producers. In 2001–2002, 480 million bottles of RV AOC were sold. RV production, valued at 1.3 billion €, also represents 16 per cent of total French AOC wine exports in volume and 20 per cent of official French quality-wine production. In 2002, 28 per cent of RV production, valued at 30 million euros, was dispatched to over 150 countries, mainly in Europe.

RV AOC wines are produced and marketed by 1,529 private producers, 113 cooperatives, 43 wine traders and six cooperative groups. Local wine merchants bottle 50 per cent of the volume produced (representing 233 million bottles in 2003) and wine merchants from outside the area bottle 24 per cent, direct sales by producers representing 24 per cent of the total volume.

Inter-Rhône comprises of a General Assembly made up of 42 members (21 producers and 21 merchants) plus several advisors from local administrations, professional organisations and consumer associations and an executive made up of 26 members (13 producers (nine Côtes du Rhône an one each from Côtes du Ventoux, Costières de Nîmes, Coteaux du Tricastin and Côtes du Luberon) and 13 wine trade) (Inter-Rhône, 2005). Its four main objectives are based on: (1) undertaking supply and demand research and hold these centrally so as to aid adaptation and regulation of the supply; (2) implementing marketing rules and 'conditions of payment'; (3) undertaking scientific research to aid quality improvement and (4) organising the domestic and international promotion of Rhone Valley AOC wines.

Strategy

Two hundred of the region's wine professionals and experts took part in a conference to set the strategic direction for the region through to 2010. Entitled, *Côtes du Rhône: the next generation – Côtes du Rhône in 2010*, the strategy has 10 strategic initiatives:

1. Improving quality, developing the traceability of products while taking into account the expectations of the consumers and respect for the environment.
2. Improving the coherence and effectiveness of the tools for checking wine quality.
3. Strengthening partnerships and improving management of the market.
4. Protecting and preserving winemaking heritage.
5. Significantly improving the qualifications of producers.
6. Improving the image of Rhône wines in France by developing communication, promotion and tourism in the winemaking trade.
7. Developing market share in France, segmenting supply and attracting new consumers.
8. Increasing export sales by significantly developing the means (collectively and at the firm level) to reach 40% of the sales.
9. To improve competition between winemaking firms and ensure their durability.
10. Implementing a real internal and external information policy.

Market research

In 2004, Inter-Rhône had a budget of €17.5 million, €12.5 million (72%) of which was devoted to promotional activities, with a further €222,000 used for market research and economic activities. Part of this market research was a qualitative study undertaken in over 100 counties that identified four segments for Rhône wines:

(1) The 'Food' segment should logically demand regularity, a safe buy, consistency, easy-to-handle packaging, wide distribution and reasonable prices.
(2) The 'Fun' segment should correspond to standard wines. It is the 'Soda' model of consumer habits. What is of value for the consumer is a universal, durable and recognizable taste, and the ability to find it easily in a crowded supply context.
(3) The 'Tasting' group covers people who look for something special, specific or a different taste – as characterized by 'terroir' and origins.
(4) The 'Art' segment looks for an exceptional or unique sensation.

(Guibert, 2006, p. 265)

Guibert (2006) suggests that this market research has been used by different players within the Rhône to develop new marketing strategies that allow them to target one or other of these segments.

For more information see:
http://www.inter-rhone.com/en/
http://www.vins-rhone.com/index.asp?lng=en&rub=7600

For a discussion of network activities in the Rhône region's marketing channels see:
Guibert, N. (2006). Network governance in marketing channels: an application to the French Rhône Valley AOC wines industry. *British Food Journal*, 108(4), 256–272.

It is perhaps important at this juncture to make a clear distinction between networks and clusters as, while these two terms are used by some interchangeably and they are not necessarily mutually exclusive, they are quite different phenomena. Braun and Lowe (2005) provide perhaps the most useful distinction between the two terms (see Table 10.1). They suggest that the two terms are 'different, yet interdependent' and that:

High levels of networking and trust create embeddedness, strong ties and dependable behaviour, enabling open exchange of knowledge and ideas across the cluster domain, which in turn fosters high levels of localised collective learning, competitive advantage and innovation.

Table 10.1 Clusters versus network characteristics

Networks	Clusters
Networks allow firms access to specialised services at lower costs	Clusters attract needed specialised services to a region
Networks have restricted membership	Clusters have open membership
Networks are based on contractual agreement	Clusters are based on social values that foster trust and encourage reciprocity
Networks make it easier for firms to make complex products	Clusters generate demand for other firms with a variety of similar and related capacities
Networks are based on cooperation	Clusters take both cooperation and competition
Networks have common business goals	Clusters have collective visions

Source: Braun and Lowe (2005, n.p., after Rosenfeld, 2001).

The success of regions is, however, conditional on regional network and governance conditions.

(Braun and Lowe, 2005, n.p.)

One of the key things for the wine industry, whether discussing networks or clusters, is the fact that the wine region is usually (but not always) the basic unit for marketing cooperation. This is largely because of the significance of place in the marketing of wine and therefore it is useful to discuss place-based wine marketing and the importance of place in marketing cooperation.

Place-based marketing and cooperation

Wine is inextricably linked to place. A wine's character and flavour relies on the interaction between winemaking and viticultural techniques, grape variety and the combination of physical environment of the region in which the grapes are grown. The impact of the combination of these regional attributes is greater than the sum of all of the individual components (i.e. climate, soil, vegetation, aspect, topography and micro-flora and fauna) and, as such, this complex milieu cannot be replicated (Vaudour, 2002; Trubek, 2005). Trubek (2005, p. 261) suggests that '*Terroir* and *goût du terroir* [literally "taste of the locality"] are categories for framing and explaining people's relationship to the land, be it sensual, practical, or habitual.'

Meanwhile Charters (2006, p. 106) observes that, 'it is not merely that the wine tastes different, but that it is –almost philosophically – a different object because it represents a specific plot of land. In this way the physical substance of the wine is subordinate to its role as a marker for where it came from.'

For the French *terroir* is something 'almost mystical' (Halliday, 1998) and it is imbued with multiple meanings. Vaudour (2002, p. 119), for example, suggests that 'Uniqueness, origin, persistence, specificity and personality are at the very heart of the notion of terroir, which comprises the varied facets of "nutriment", "space", "slogan" and "conscience" terroirs.' Of particular significance to any discussion on wine marketing is Vaudour's notion of *'slogan terroir'*, which pertains to the relatively recent phenomena of the use of *terroir* as a marketing and advertising tool which sees the term used as a metonym for 'rural/ecological and communal values' (Vaudour, 2002, after Letablier and Nicolas, 1994).

The French also talk of the *typicité* (literally its typicality) of wine, a term closely related to *goût du terroir*. According to Vaudour (2002, p. 121), *typicité*:

characterises a collective taste memory, which has matured over a long time, through several generations of people, and refers to geographically referenced products. It is the shared perception of how generations of people from a given place expect the wine should taste, when made from grapes grown in that place and when the wine has been made in that place.

As such when wine is marketed there is a significant impact on consumer perceptions of the wine. d'Hauteville et al. (2006) found that in a blind tasting non-expert wine tasters were not able to distinguish between five different wine brands, but when given the region, they made clear distinctions about the quality of the wines. Region, as an extrinsic driver of expectations of wine quality is very important and it is therefore important for wine regions to work together to develop, promote and protect a reputation for good quality wines. Box 10.2 demonstrates how the champagne wine region worked together to develop and protect perhaps the most enviable reputation of any wine region and perhaps any place-based brand for any product.

Legal protection of place brands

It is useful at this juncture to briefly introduce some of the international legal framework that sees wine regions and wine producing countries, rather than individual producers, work together to protect the intellectual property associated with

---

Box 10.2 Champagne: the world's foremost place brand

An inauspicious start

Champagne has not always been known for its wine and it is far from being a lucky region. Champagne lies strategically in the middle of Western Europe at the crossroads of ancient trade routes and has therefore been the site of conflict and deadly bloodshed for several millennia. From pre-Roman plundering by such tribes as the Vandals and the Goths to the Hundred Years' War, the Thirty Years' War, the Napoleonic Wars and some of the bloodiest battles of World War I (to name but a few), champagne has been one of the most contested regions on the planet (Kladstrup and Kladstrup, 2005).

From the 17th century, however, the Champenois began to cultivate a product that one day they could call their own – sparkling wine. Contrary to popular belief, champagne was not 'invented' and certainly not by Dom Pérignon (a Benedictine monk resident at the Hautvillers Abbey of Saint-Pierre from 1668 to 1715) (Kladstrup and Kladstrup, 2005). Champagne was originally a quirk of nature that saw the cold autumn and winter temperatures of this northerly region putting yeasts into hibernation and warm springtime temperatures restarting fermentation once the wine was sealed inside the bottle. In fact, this was generally seen as a fault in wines at the time and winemakers, perhaps none more so than Dom Pérignon, did what they could to avoid this.

The myth of Dom Pérignon

Despite many of the fallacies surrounding the legend of Dom Pérignon, perhaps even because of them, Dom Pérignon is an important figure in champagne's reputation. Over almost 50 years Dom Pérignon made several important innovations that improved viticulture and winemaking in champagne, many of which are still used today, but the systematic production of sparkling wine was most certainly not one of them (Kladstrup and Kladstrup, 2005). It was another monk from the Abbey of Saint-Pierre, Dom Grossard, who from 1821 campaigned to have almost all of the winemaking practices of champagne attributed to Dom Pérignon without any evidence to support this (Guy, 2003). According to Guy, by the 1860s Dom Pérignon was 'unquestioningly' attributed with the almost miraculous discovery of sparkling champagne. In 1889 this legend was picked up by the *Syndicat du commerce des vins de Champagne* (which was an organisation of négotiants and one of the first region-wide marketing organisations) and they distributed illustrated pamphlets telling the story of how he was the 'father' of champagne. They further reinforced this in 1896 when they released another pamphlet that stated 'unequivocally' that it was he who had ' "discovered" champagne by following "ancient tradiditions" ' (Guy, 2003, p. 28). Various other promotional efforts took place around commemorations of 'historic' significance in the life of Dom

Pérignon that further reinforced the myth of champagne, engendering it with a sense of place far beyond any reality. As Guy (2003, p. 29) suggests, the myth:

served the more secular purpose of seducing the champagne-drinking public. A wine originally associated with dissipation and hedonism was now believed to have been invented by a monk; the holy origins of champagne helped to legitimize a drink originally associated exclusively with aristocratic frivolity and decandence ...

Despite the almost industrial techniques used in sparkling wine production, the Dom Pérignon myth distanced champagne from any association with assembly lines, technology, and backbreaking labor. The monk's 'simple' invention was cultivated in public relations campaigns to create an image of champagne as being as effortless to create as it was to drink, a symbol of a balance between old-world traditions and the 'good life' of the modern period.

The development of this image would not have been possible without a cooperative effort and Guy suggests that the *Syndicat du commerce* was ahead of its time in terms of marketing. They were an organisation specifically set up to promote the region, not individual brands, and they used techniques that would not look out of place today, including a focus on packaging, public relations spectacles and print journalism.

Royal seal of approval

The region of champagne has also enjoyed an important association with French royalty, while the wine has been a favourite of royalty, nobility and powerful people throughout history. For example, the city of Reims, home to many champagne houses, was the site of French coronations from 898 to 1825 and Clovis (the first French King) was baptised there in 498 (www.champagne.fr). Louis XIV, the 'Sun King', was a contemporary of Dom Pérignon and loved the still wine that was to become the champagne we know today, rarely drinking anything other than wine from the region. He was introduced to it at his coronation in Reims at the age of 16 years and from then on Louis set the fashion for nobility throughout France who eat and drank what he did (Kladstrup and Kladstrup, 2005).

The Duc d'Orléans, Loius XIV's successor, also had a passion for champagne but he preferred it sparkling (despite continued suggestions that this was a fault) (Robinson, 2006). His patronage was hugely influential, so that 'By 1730, sparkling champagne had conquered the courts of Europe, with copious amounts being drunk in the palaces of London, Brussels, Vienna and Madrid' (Kladstrup and Kladstrup, 2005). But it was Russia where champagne had the greatest impact with Peter the Great taking four bottles to bed with him each night, his daughter (Czarina Elizabeth) designating it for official toasts and Catherine the Great famously using it to 'fortify' her young officers whom she would then seduce (Kladstrup and Kladstrup, 2005).

Meanwhile several brands of champagne have also enjoyed success with royalty and powerful people for around 200 years. For example, Tsar Nicholas I was a customer of Moët and Chandon in the early part of the 19th century, as was Napoleon Bonaparte (http://www.nextdaychampagne.co.uk/). In 1876, Champagne Roederer developed Cristal cuvée for Tsar Alexander II of Russia and in 1909 they were nominated by Tsar Nicolas II as the official supplier to the Imperial Court of Russia (www.champagne-roederer. com/). Sir Winston Churchill also had a strong association with Champagne Pol Roger, who produce a wine in his memory.

Such patronage is important to the image of champagne and this has greatly enhanced its image. Today this image of luxury lives on.

Internal conflicts

The story of the champagne wine region is far from one of 'wine and roses'. In fact, as well as being invaded and controlled by several external powers, conflict within the Champenois winemaking community was not uncommon right up to World War I (Guy, 2003; Kladstrup and Kladstrup, 2005). Ravished by phylloxera (a highly invasive and destructive root mite), poor harvests (especially 1907–1909), prohibition in many of its main markets and rural economic depression (albeit punctuated with short periods of high prosperity) (Charters, 2006), the region was under considerable stress at the beginning of the 20th century.

In December 1908 the Aube, a region which is considered by some to have been a core part of the region for centuries, was excluded from the wine region by officials in Paris attempting to delineate the region (Guy, 2003), the beginning of the French *Appellation d'Origine Contrôlée* (AOC) system (see below). The Aubois were furious at the government and the people of the Marne, which had been included in the government's drawing up of champagne, and they pitted themselves in a war of words against the Marne that would last three years.

Delimitation was designed, at least in part, to minimise the 'fraud' that was perpetrated by some champagne producers who imported grapes from outside the region to produce sparkling wine (Guy, 2003; Kladstrup and Kladstrup, 2005). This practice was an affront to the grapegrowers of the region and was beginning to cost some their livelihood and the exclusion of the Aube from the region also caused significant financial stress for the grapegrowers there. Over the three years following the 1908 delimitation tensions grew, so that by March 1911 125 Aubois town councils had quit in protest and on Palm Sunday more than 40,000 Aubois rallied in the town of Troyes (Kladstrup and Kladstrup, 2005). Two days later the Senate in Paris rescinded the 1908 law and the Marne exploded into frenzied riots. By the end of the unrest, a little under 24 hours later, more than 40,000 vines had been burned and trampled (Guy, 2003), at least 40 buildings and six champagne houses lay in ruin, nearly 6 million bottles of champagne had been destroyed, dozens were injured and two grapegrowers had committed suicide (Kladstrup and Kladstrup, 2005).

Ultimately this conflict led to the formation of the *Comité Interprofessionnel du vin de Champagne* (CIVC), which involves grapegrowers and champagne houses in the joint management of the region's wine. But, interrupted by the

Great War and the Depression of the 1930s, this was not to come to fruition until 1941. Jancis Robinson (2006) suggests that this pioneering organisation has been 'much copied elsewhere'.

Working together to protect the name

With such a strong brand, the champagne wine region is constantly on the look out for others attempting to pass-off wine and other products using this name. The first successful case against a company outside the region claiming to be champagne was in 1843 (Duval Smith, 2004) and there were two decades of court victories over producers from Saumur in the latter half of the 19th century. However, it was not until international treaties on intellectual property were put in place in 1893 that the Champenois were able to prosecute non-French producers, such as those in Germany and Russia who were prolific producers of sparkling wine and who were using the name champagne.

The CIVC is now responsible for seeking out and, if necessary, prosecuting hundreds of cases of fraud around the world each year, spending hundreds of thousands of euros each year in the process. Table 10.2 shows a number of prominent prosecutions that CIVC have successfully made since the 1960s.

Table 10.2 Examples of cases of intellectual property actions taken by the Champagne region

Year	Location	Product	Action
Direct competition			
1960	London	'Spanish Champagne'	Prosecution
1972	Japan	Wine	Bilateral agreement
1973	Spain	Wine	Bilateral agreement
1974	Québec	'Champagne canadien' (Canadian Champagne)	Prosecution
Indirect competition			
1987	Germany	*Perrier* water	Prosecution
1994	UK	'Elderflower Champagne'	Prosecution
Challenges to reputation			
1984	France	'Champagne Cigarettes'	Prosecution
1990	Switzerland	'Schaumpanger Paris – Night'	Prosecution
1993	France	'Champagne de Yves St Laurent' perfume	Prosecution
2002	Sweden	'Arla' yoghurt with 'the taste of Champagne'	Prosecution

Source: Mitchell (forthcoming, after CIVC, 2003, p. 36).

For more information on Champagne (wine and region) visit the following sites:

http://www.champagne.fr/en_indx.html# (CIVC)

http://www.maisons-champagne.com (*Union Des Maisons De Champagne*)

http://www.champagnesdevignerons.com/ (*Syndicat Général des Vignerons de la Champagne*)

The following books are two different social histories that provide an insight into how Champagne has become what it is today:

Guy, K.M. (2003). *When Champagne Became French: Wine and the Making of a National Identity*, Johns Hopkins University Press.

Kladstrup, D. and Kladstrup, P. (2005). *Champagne: How the World's Most Glamorous Wine Triumphed Over War and Hard Times*, William Morrow.

their region and/or country name. One of the key concepts is the notion of place names as 'geographical indications' which '… possess qualities or a reputation that are due to that place of origin' (WIPO, 2006). This reputation of the region adds value (i.e. place brand value) to products from the region and therefore they have intellectual property (cultural capital) that can be legally protected.

Tokaji (Hungary) in 1700, Chianti (Italy) in 1716 and the Duoro Valley (Portugal) in 1756 were the first wine regions to put in legal delimits to protect wine producers from passing-off (i.e. the use of the region's name by those from outside the region) (Charters, 2006). However, it was the French that pioneered the modern systems of 'geographical indications of source' for wine in the form of their *Appellation d'Origine Contrôlée* (AOC) system (Charters, 2006). According to one influential grape grower of the 1900s, this saw 'terroir made into a legally defined area' (Guy, 2003, p. 126). As a result of these laws, producers from outside of the premium wine regions of Champagne, Burgundy and Bordeaux (or any other AOC region) were no longer allowed to use these place names to market and sell their wine (Guy, 2003; Charters, 2006). Charters (2006) also suggests that one function of the AOC system was marketing and that this 'is perhaps most apparent in Burgundy, where, for the very best wines (the *grands crus* and *premiers crus*), the [AOC] is coterminous with the vineyard boundary; the vineyard, in turn may be owned by just a few owners, or even a single person.' While the benefits may accrue to individual producers the development and maintenance of such a system requires collective action at a regional level. AOC wines form just part of the wine classification system different levels of the French (AOC) regional classification system works (Box 10.3).

Box 10.3   The French regional classification system

The French wine industry classifies four levels of wine: *Appelation d'Origine Controlee* (AOC), *Vin Délimité de Qualité Supériere* (VDQS), *Vin de pays* and *Vin de table*.

Appelation d'Origine Controlee

This is the top tier of wine and accounts for around for 52% of French wine production. Wines are labelled by the AOC that they come from and not by the grape variety or varieties used. It not only defines the boundaries of wine regions, it also legally prescribes a range of elements of viticultural and wine-making practice, including grape varieties, ripeness and alcohol, yields, viticulture, and winemaking and distillation.

Appellation can also apply to a range of different geographical scales and generally speaking smaller scale AOCs are better quality than the larger regional appellations. The scales are as follows:

- A large region (e.g. Bourgogne)
- A district (e.g. Côte de Beaune)
- A village (e.g. Nuits Saint Georges)
- A single vineyard (e.g. Château Latour)

There are also several regional 'quality' classifications within most AOC regions. These are all different and are based on different criteria, however several talk about *grand cru* (literally 'great growth') wines which are generally of a higher quality and are of higher value than other wines. Some regions have other names for these premium wines. In some regions *grand cru* wines are not automatically designated every vintage as some years may be below the accepted standard. A second tier classification may also exist *premier cru* or *premier cru classé* (literally 'first growth') in some regions, while there are other variations such as *premier grand cru* and *premier cru supérieur* (St-Émillion and Chateau d'Yquem in Bordeaux) which are in fact higher quality than *grand cru*.

Vin Délimité de Qualité Supériere

This is the second tier of French wine and is similar to AOC but the yields permitted are generally higher. VDQS accounts for less than 1% of French wine production and it is generally accepted that wines in this classification are moving towards becoming an AOC wine.

Vin de pays

These wines are still regulated by regional tasting panels and must conform to geographical restrictions. These are largely new vineyards and many are labelling their wines by grape variety rather than (or as well as the region).

This category of wines accounts for 33% of all production. *Vin de pays* also has three levels of geographical classification:

1. 4 large regions,
2. 39 départments,
3. almost 100 small zones.

Vin de table

This is not a delimited classification and, as such, grapes can be planted anywhere. This accounts for around 15% of French wine production and is dominated by wines from the Languedoc and Roussillon regions in the warm climes of the south, but there is some *vin de table* grown in most parts of France. There are also no limits on yields and wines are often lighter reds. It is sometimes also known as *vin ordinaire* ('everyday wine'), which is a slightly derogatory term.

Other European classifications

Several European countries also have classifications that are similar to the AOC classification. Table 10.3 provides examples from Italy, Spain and Portugal.

Table 10.3 Italian, Spanish and Portuguese equivalents to the French AOC system

France	AOC	VDQS	Vin de pays	Vin de table
Italy	Denominazione di Origine Controllata e Garantita	Denominazione di Origine Controllata	Indicazione Geografica	Vino da tavola
Spain	Denominación de Origen Calificada and Denominación de Origen	Vino de Calidad Producido en Región Determinada	Vino de la tierra	Vino de mesa
Portugal	Denominação de Origem Controlada	Indicacao de Proveniencia Regulamentada	Vinho regional	Vinho de mesa

A number of international treaties are now in place to protect intellectual property rights including geographical indications and these are administered by World Intellectual Property Organisation (WIPO) and the World Trade Organisation (WTO).

Table 10.4 lists the most relevant treaties for protecting geographical indications, the three most important of which are:

1. The *Paris Convention for the Protection of Industrial Property* (1883).
2. The *Lisbon Agreement for the Protection of Appellations of Origin and Their International Registration* (1958).
3. Articles 22–24 of the *Agreement on Trade-Related Aspects of Intellectual Property Rights (TRIPS)*.

Importantly for this discussion, these treaties are primarily used to protect the regions rather than individual companies and they are most often used to prosecute individual companies. In the case of the Paris Convention, wine is also afforded a greater degree of protection than other agricultural and food products. As such they reinforce the power of place branding for wine and the value of collaboration at a regional level.

Regional collaboration

The French AOC system is based on the idea of protecting terroir and is deeply rooted in a sense of place. However, regional cooperation is also widespread in New World wine regions, especially those that are newly emerging. In these regions the purposes of cooperation might be quite different from those in France and other Old World regions, as they tend to have a focus on innovation and marketing rather than tradition and production. These differences are made very clear in the findings of a study by Jordan et al. (2006), who examined differences in the business strategies of Australian and French wineries. They not only found that Australians were more likely to collaborate and with more partners, but they also found clear differences in the reasons for collaboration. In France the three main reasons were: logistics support, like lending of machines (65%); promotion, like the same wine tasting stand in a trade fair (60%) and production (50%). In Australia, on the other hand, the three main reasons were: promotion (76%); exchange of information about the market or about the competitors (60%) and logistic support (55%).

Jordan et al. (2006, p. 16) conclude on the basis of these and other findings that:

... Australian wine companies benefit from a much more favourable environment insofar as it encourages firms to be market/marketing oriented, to be proactive in their strategic orientation, to be entrepreneurial and innovative, and to work together in order to be more efficient.

Table 10.4 Key international agreements involving intellectual property rights

Treaty/agreement	Year first signed	Number of signatories*	Revisions	Description

Paris Convention for the Protection of Industrial Property	1883	171	• Brussels (1900)
			• Washington (1911)
			• The Hague (1925)
			• London (1934)
			• Lisbon (1958)
			• Stockholm (1967)
			• Amended 1979
				• Applies to industrial property in the widest sense, including:
				  • patents, marks, industrial designs, utility models
				  • trade names
				  • geographical indications
				  • the repression of unfair competition
				• Must treat one's own nationals and foreigners equally
				• Protection in own country is effectively concurrent in all contracting states
				• Indications of source: each contracting state must act against direct or indirect use of a false indication of the source of the goods or the identity of the producer, manufacturer or trader

Madrid Agreement concerning the International Registration of Marks and *Madrid Protocol*	1891 1989	56 69 (total = 79)	• Brussels (1900) • Washington (1911) • The Hague (1925) • London (1934) • Nice (1957) • Stockholm (1967) • Amended 1979	• Protection of a mark in a large number of countries • International registration effective in contracting states • Open to any state which is party to the Paris Convention • Parallel and independent from Paris • States may adhere to either or both
Madrid Agreement for the Repression of False or Deceptive	1891	34	• Washington (1911) • The Hague (1925) • London (1934) • Lisbon (1958)	• Goods bearing a false or deceptive indication of source must be seized on importation, or importation prohibited, or other actions and sanctions applied

(Continued)

Table 10.4 (Continued)

Treaty/agreement	Year first signed	Number of signatories*	Revisions	Description
Indications of *Source on Goods*			• Stockholm (1967)	• Prohibits the use of all indications capable of deceiving the public as to the source of the goods
Lisbon Agreement for the Protection of Appellations of Origin and Their International Registration	1958	26	• Stockholm (1967) • Amended 1979	• Protection of appellations of origin • Names registered by the WIPO • WIPO communicates registration to other contracting states • A contracting state may declare, within one year, that it cannot ensure the protection of a registered appellation
Agreement on *Trade-Related Aspects of Intellectual Property Rights (TRIPS)*	1994	149 (32 observers)		• Introduced intellectual property rules into the multilateral trading system • Must treat one's own nationals and foreigners equally • Equal treatment for nationals of all trading partners in WTO • Protection should contribute to technical innovation and the transfer of technology to mutual benefit of producers and users
Doha Development Agreement (DDA)	2001	149 (32 observers)	• Cancún (2003) • Geneva (2004) • Hong Kong (2005)	• Platform for negations on 21 multilateral issues • Includes intellectual property rights dealt with in TRIPS • All geographical indications to be given a 'higher level of protection' • 'Traditional Knowledge' also introduced as a place-based concept

*Numbers as of October 2006, except TRIPS and Doha (December 2005).
Source: Mitchell (forthcoming).

In emerging wine regions, such collaborative behaviour is as much the result of necessity as it is the result of a supportive environment. In these regions it is generally small producers who begin to establish viticulture and as individual companies they have fewer resources to allow them to compete in the marketplace. Working together allows them to gain the economies of scale to promote themselves to a wider audience and to develop export markets. Collaborative behaviour such as this is also important in a highly competitive marketplace as this allows for consistent messages, a greater degree of selling power through collective bargaining and increased efficiencies in distribution and sales (Box 10.4).

Box 10.4   Central Otago Pinot Noir Limited, New Zealand

Central Otago Pinot Noir Limited (COPNL) has been highly successful at marketing the Central Otago region on the international stage. This commercial cluster was formed as an independent company by the Central Otago Winegrowers Association (COWA) in 2003 to '… market Central Otago wine (primarily to export markets) and promoting the Central Otago wine brand' (www.centralotagopinot.co.nz). COPNL's stated objectives are to:

- Meet the global marketing challenge through cooperative marketing. Grouping resources for marketing and promotion make this type of marketing more effective but also an economically viable option.
- Work hard through promotion, coordination of events and working with media to ensure a consistent positive image for Central Otago wine.
- Position Central Otago Pinot Noir at the very top of the market through regional cooperation and activities.
- Make use of available Government funds through the 'cluster approach'.
- Encourage premium quality and protect and support the quality brand.

(www.centralotagopinot.co.nz)

The group formed a commercial company for a number of reasons, but one of the main reasons was that, under New Zealand Trade and Enterprise (NZTE) criteria the Central Otago Winegrowers Association (a not-for-profit organisation) was not eligible for government funding for cluster/network development. The New Zealand government (through the Ministry of Economic Development and NZTE) is highly supportive of such clusters and provided more than NZ$65,000 as seed funding for the first three years of the cluster under its Cluster Development Programme.

Membership of COPNL is only open to members of COWA, but '… it is only those actively producing wine … that have chosen to participate' (Mitchell and Schreiber, 2006, p. 93). In 2007 around 50 members each paid an annual fee of between NZ$2925 and NZ$5175 depending on the volume of production (non-producers/new entrants paying NZ$562.50), which pays for the basic administration of the cluster. Members may also choose to participate in optional marketing and promotional activities which incurs additional costs for the participating members. These activities have included:

- media and trade promotions in partnership with NZTE's 'marketnew-zealand.com';
- trade and consumer events in New Zealand and in main export markets (e.g. San Francisco, New York, London, Sydney and Melbourne);
- hosting wine writers, buyers, chefs and other opinion leaders (e.g. Masters of Wine);
- 'sneak preview' tastings with writers and buyers;
- the annual 'Central Otago Pinot Noir Celebration' event which hosts around 200 influential media, buyers, opinion leaders and consumers.

Mitchell and Schreiber (2006, p. 94) observe that COPNL serves an important function for Central Otago wineries as the '... markets for wine at the relatively high price level sought by the wineries in Central Otago are very small, and by using the organisation's marketing network, marketing costs are reduced.'

For more information see:
http://www.centralotagopinot.co.nz/

Cooperation with other sectors: wine tourism

Thus far in this chapter we have discussed the importance of relationships between wineries. However, it is also important to recognise the value of collaborating with other complementary sectors. According to Porter (1990), for example, a broad range of wine-specific businesses and organisations are part of the Californian wine cluster (e.g. public relations companies, universities, bottle suppliers, etc.), but also with related clusters. These include an agriculture cluster, a food cluster and a tourism cluster (see Plate 10.2 for French example). This is often discussed in terms of 'horizontal' integration (i.e. within the wine industry) and 'vertical' integration (i.e. between the wine and another industry) (Telfer, 2001a). Michael (2007, p. 26) also suggests that 'diagonal' clustering is important for optimal cluster development. He suggests that:

Here, each firm adds value to the activities of others, even though their products may be quite distinct and clearly belong to other industry classifications. Diagonal clustering occurs where firms working together create a bundle of separate products and services that the consumer effectively purchases as a single item. The situation is common in many tourism destinations, where separate firms with separate production processes supply activities, transport, hospitality, accommodation, etc. The co-location of complementary providers adds value to the tourism experience; while, conversely, the absence of key services will probably limit the growth of existing firms.

(Michael, 2007, p. 26)

The importance of the relationship between wine and tourism has already been established in Chapter 4 and many authors have discussed the value of networks that involve both wine and tourism businesses (e.g. Hall and Mitchell, 2000; Hall et al., 2000; Telfer, 2001a, b; Bruwer, 2003; Hall, 2003, 2004; McRae-Williams, 2004). According to Hall et al. (2000, p. 208), '… in the context of wine tourism such networks are critical as there is a need to create linkages between businesses which have previously identified themselves as being in separate industries with separate business foci.' Box 10.5 provides an example from Vancouver Island, Canada.

Box 10.5 The Wine Islands Project: A successful cooperative (tourism) marketing venture

---

The project

The *Wine Islands Region* is situated on Vancouver Island and the outer Gulf Islands, British Columbia (BC) and is home to 32 wineries, cideries and meaderies (Smith, 2006). The *Wine Islands* is the newest wine region in BC and the fastest growing in Canada (British Columbia Wine Institute, 2006; Wine Islands Vintners' Association, 2006) and it has been energised by increasing wine tourism (Schreiner, 2005).

Recognising the need to capitalise on this emerging and evolving tourism market, a small group of wine interested locals began the search for an innovative plan to bring diverse sectors of the local agritourism economy together. From the outset the group faced the challenges that are faced by many networks of small to medium tourism enterprises (SMTEs): limited resources and disparate approaches to marketing.

Initiated in early 2006, the Wine Islands Project, a cooperative marketing initiative was designed to promote the Wine Islands Region and funnel potential visitors and media to market-ready wine and culinary businesses (Smith, 2006). Bringing together 80 partner businesses from several tourism sectors, this project acted as a networking and marketing hub for industry (Smith, 2006).

Guided by a common goal of creating a sustainable agritourism industry and supporting and nurturing regional businesses, several major public and private sector funding partners were also instrumental in the project's development. This includes the *British Columbia AgriTourism Alliance* (BCATA), *Investment Agriculture Foundation, Canadian Tourism Commission* (CTC) and the *Cowichan Region Economic Office*, while the *Wine Islands Vintners Association* (WIVA) has acted as the lead coordinating body for the project.

Development of marketing collateral

Partner organisations pooled their resources to create 10 regional wine touring routes that marked the location of tourism sector partners: accommodation, food and beverage, transportation, attractions as well as wineries, meaderies and cideries. These touring maps were incorporated into two major project deliverables. Firstly, a comprehensive project website (www.wineislands.ca) was designed to attract a world-wide audience featuring regional images, downloadable maps and partner listings and advertising. Secondly, the Wine Islands Guide, a 24 page rackable brochure contained consumer travel information on the region, partner advertising, a list of farmers' markets and an hours of operation grid. This second piece of marketing collateral was designed for those visitors already in the region and in particular the short haul, 'rubber tyre traffic' market (Smith, 2006). As such its brochure distribution included regional locations on Vancouver Island, mainland BC, Alberta and Washington State.

Indicators of early success

Called a *Wow Story* by the CTC (F. Verschuren, personal communication, March 1, 2007), and picked up by local print and television media, this innovative project has been particularly successful at meeting the needs of network partners in areas of media coverage while enhancing regional profile and building the Wine Islands brand. Partner businesses have commented that the project has been tremendously successful in this regard: 'We are overjoyed at the depth and scope of awareness it has brought forward to the local and international communities about Island wines' (B. Storen, personal communication, March 16, 2007).

On an individual level, several of the partners have experienced substantial revenue and visitor increases. Wineries in particular have realised an increased flow of visitors, with many arriving maps in hand at their cellar door. Not only has the Wine Islands Project been successful at directing visitors to partners' doorsteps, relationships between businesses have been built that have created a mutual benefits in terms of leverage on other wine tourism experiences.

For more information see:
www.wineislands.ca
Case prepared by: Carleigh Randall

Hall et al. (2000) suggest that in its most basic form wine tourism collaboration is evident in the development of wine routes (see Figure 10.1). As cooperation becomes more sophisticated, then more formal joint marketing may occur and ultimately a full range of network behaviours may emerge. In the case of the Niagara Wine Route Telfer (2001a) suggests that this has gone further as he found evidence of interactions with other clusters (including agricultural clusters and food clusters – like Porter found in California), organisations such as wine councils and marketing committees and the visitor bureau and governmental and research bodies. Using Telfer's case study Lynch and Morrison (2007) highlight the fact that businesses in this network work together to improve the quality and diversity of the regional wine tourism product, as well as undertaking joint marketing of the region. This, they say, is undertaken at a local and provincial level through:

Learning and exchange: through peer learning contributing to knowledge transfer, tourism education processes, communication, acceleration of the speed of implementation of support agency initiatives, and the facilitation of small business development;

Business activity: stimulated by co-operative activities that foster innovation, new product development and the extraction of marketing

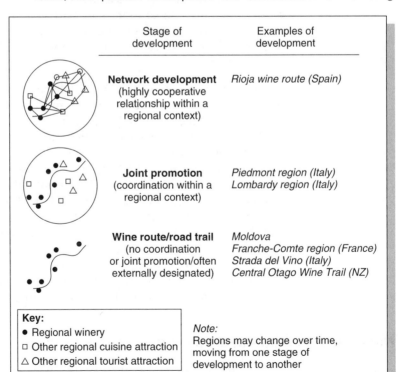

	Stage of development	Examples of development
	Network development (highly cooperative relationship within a regional context)	*Rioja wine route (Spain)*
	Joint promotion (coordination within a regional context)	*Piedmont region (Italy)* *Lombardy region (Italy)*
	Wine route/road trail (no coordination or joint promotion/often externally designated)	*Moldova* *Franche-Comte region (France)* *Strada del Vino (Italy)* *Central Otago Wine Trail (NZ)*

Key:
● Regional winery
□ Other regional cuisine attraction
△ Other regional tourist attraction

Note:
Regions may change over time, moving from one stage of development to another

Figure 10.1 Stages of wine tourism network development *Source*: Hall et al. (2000, p. 207).

synergies, which in combination serve to enhance the reputation of the region for wine tourism, increasing visitor numbers, extending the visitor season, and increasing the level of entrepreneurial activity; and

Community values: fostered through the network's common purpose and focus, engaging support for small enterprises in the destination's development, and the retention of more of the income earned by these developments within the destination.

(Lynch and Morrison, 2007, p. 54)

Despite the fact that there are many benefits of cooperation between wine and tourism there are a number of barriers to the development of clusters and networks. According to Hall (2003) barriers might include:

- Poor perceptions amongst wineries of the benefits of tourism for the wine industry.
- A dominant product focus on the part of many wine producers.
- A lack of experience in and understanding of tourism within the wine industry.
- A lack of entrepreneurial skills and abilities with respect to marketing and tourism product development.
- Spatial separation – distance between vineyards and physical and perceived barriers to access.
- Administrative separation – in particular multiple public administrative agencies within a region.
- The lack of 'champions' to promote formal cooperative behaviours.

If the full benefits of inter-industry collaboration are to accrue these barriers need to be overcome and in many cases it is the presence of individuals that are willing to champion collaboration that leads to the most sophisticated collaborative activities. In Central Otago, for example, many of these barriers were evident in a study by Schreiber (2004) (see also Mitchell and Schreiber, 2006, 2007), but two years after the conclusion of this study one local cellar door manager, with the support of her directors, began to develop an informal, but strong network of cellar door operators, wine tour operators and some tourism businesses. In the early phases of its development, the Central Otago Cellar Door Network, has held workshops to discuss collaboration on promotion and wine tourism product development and facilitated training for cellar door managers and staff.

National- and state-level marketing collaboration

Most countries and states that produce wine have at least one peak body that coordinates a range of functions for the wine industry. These may be fully administered and funded by the industry itself or have differing levels of governmental support, including legislation to enforce statutory levies on winemakers and grapegrowers. Marsh and Shaw (2000) report that Australia has perhaps the highest degree of collaboration of any wine producing country, with nine national bodies with various functions, sources of funding and resources available for the industry (see Table 10.5).

While Table 10.5 demonstrates that Australia has specialist organisations to undertake a wide range of activities, most other countries and states do not have the luxury of so many wine peak bodies. Despite this most will undertake a series of marketing functions.

Market research

One of the key functions of national and state wine organisations is the commissioning of market research and disseminating the results to wine industry members and stakeholders. For example, in 2005 the Australian Wine and Brandy Corporation (AWBC) commissioned Hudson Howells to undertake research into infrequent wine consumers in 25–30 age group in Australia with the intention to '… support the development of a domestic promotion strategy' and 'identify tactics and tools that could be used to stimulate increased wine consumption in this segment' (Hudson Howells, 2005). The report was made available to the industry in a document published on the AWBC website and it made recommendations on a range of poster, print and in-store promotional activities designed to attract these consumers to wine (http://www.wineaustralia.com/Australia/Default.aspx?tabid = 208). AWBC also produce an extensive set of export market reports that are regularly updated and available to subscribers on their website.

The California Wine Institute also provides its members with extensive export market reports in a members-only section of their website, as well as a less extensive section that is freely available (see e.g.: http://www.calwinexport.com/pages/Market Info.htm). This is a membership-based organisation that represents wineries and a wide range of providers of services and goods to the wine industry.

Marketing strategy

At a national- and state-level strategy is critical as peak wine bodies have to satisfy the needs of a wide range of stakeholders

Table 10.5 Principal Australian wine industry associations in 2000

	WFA	WGCA	AWBC	GWRDC	ASWE	AWRI	CRC	WISA	WIETG	WA
Mission	Represent producers	Represent growers	Statutory authority Quality regulation/ export promotion	Statutory authority Determine R&D strategy; fund R&D	Facilitate domestic wine education/ promotion	R&D	R&D	Represents suppliers promotion	Coordination between industry and educational institutions	Stage exposition every 2 years
Base	South Australia (also a Canberra Office)	South Australia	South Australia (representative offices in Canada, the Netherlands (continental Europe), Ireland, Japan, UK, USA)	South Australia	South Australia	South Australia	South Australia	South Australia	South Australia	
Funding sources	Member subscriptions Special levies (graduated scale)	Member subscription	Statutory levy	Statutory levy	Subscriptions and levies ($50,000 WFA)	GWRDC Contract research	GWRDC Contract research	Member subscription sponsorship		Exhibitor contributions

Governance	Elected board (11 members)	Elected board (9 members) Federal organisation (3 state councils)	Mixed nominee/ elected board	9 members appointed by minister	Subsidiary of WFA	Nominated board	Nominated board	Elected board (8 members)	Industry representatives nominated by associations	6 member board (WFA sponsored)
Staff	5	1	26	2.5	1	45 (15 PhD)	45		1 P/T provided by SA Wine Corp.	37
Outreach	Annual report newsletter	Periodic	Annual report Newsletters	Annual report		Annual report Newsletter Technical bulletin	Conferences/ training Newsletter Annual report	Annual report Newsletters Conference		

ASWE: Australian Society for Wine Education; AWBC: Australian Wine and Brandy Corporation (now branded under Wine Australia); AWRI: Australian Wine Research Institute; CRC: Cooperative Research Centre for Viticulture; GWRDC: Grape and Wine Research and Development Corporation; WA: Wine Australia; WFA: Wine Makers Federation of Australia; WGCA: Wine Grapegrowers Council of Australia (dissolved in 2004; new group Wine Grape Growers Australia); WIETG: Wine Industry Education and Training Group; WISA: Wine Industry Suppliers Australia.
Source: After Marsh and Shaw (2000).

(including wine producers, exporters, distributors, retailers and federal, state and local governments) by promoting the image of a nation and its wine to a diverse range of domestic and international markets. This is complicated by the fact that the 'product' that they are attempting to promote is very complex, consisting not just of wine, but potentially thousands of individual brands, images of the country or state as a whole and the values that these images engender in the consumer.

Promotion

Promoting national and regional brands in export and domestic markets is probably seen as one of the primary outcomes for individual wineries. Promotional activities might include generic country or state promotional campaigns; national or state wine promotional websites for trade and consumers; events for media, trade and consumers (see also Chapter 8); seminars and educational programmes; and domestic promotions. This is core business in most New World wine producing countries (see Box 10.6) and is becoming increasingly important for Old World regions. Hungary, for example, is re-emerging as a wine exporting nation, after lying dormant between 1930 and the late 1980s under state communist rule (Robinson, 2006), and there have been calls from a wide range of industry pundits for cooperative marketing and an improvement in the country's image (Bànfalvi, 2005). In Australia the AWBC has also begun to use new technologies to promote 'wine brand Australia' by using podcasts by well-known wine critic and journalist Max Allen that introduce a number of iconic Australian wine regions (see http://www.wineaustralia.com/Australia/Default.aspx? tabid = 1940).

Box 10.6   New Zealand wine promotion: 'the riches of a clean green land'

Under the tagline 'the riches of a clean green land', New Zealand spent NZ$4.5 million on generic marketing and promotional events in the 2005/2006 financial year (an increase of 30% on the previous year's budget) events in the 2005/2006 financial year and more than 190 wineries took part in New Zealand Winegrowers organised events. These events included a wide variety of activities that are outlined below.

Tastings

New release media and trade tastings were designed to '... provide media and key influencers an early and exclusive opportunity to sample wines not previously shown in the market. The key aims are to encourage positive press and broadcast coverage and to raise interest and generate listings amongst buyers' (New Zealand Winegrowers 2006, p. 22). Tastings were held in the key markets of Melbourne, Sydney, London, New York and San Francisco and were attended by more than 800 influential trade and media representatives.

Exhibitions

New Zealand Winegrowers also delivered wine fairs and general trade/consumer exhibitions in the UK, USA, Australia, Canada and Japan, which were a core element of the generic marketing programme. This included hosting a generic New Zealand stand at several exhibitions with a wider consumer and trade appeal. For example, 'the New Zealand stand at London International Wine and Spirits Trade Fair (May 2006) featured over 130 wines from 39 wineries and was attended by 13,569 trade visitors' (New Zealand Winegrowers, 2006, p. 22). In total these events saw New Zealand wines presented at events attended by more than 19,200 trade and media and well in excess of 110,000 consumers. This included the *Good Food and Wine Shows* in Sydney (30,000 attendees) and Melbourne (26,000 attendees), where 31 wineries exhibited at a Tourism New Zealand stand promoting food and wine tourism in New Zealand.

Seminars

The 2005/2006 promotional campaign also included a series of 30 educational seminars in New Zealand's main markets targeted at highly specialised audiences to increase awareness levels of knowledge of New Zealand wine. Six different themes were developed with the following titles: *A Regional Tour of New Zealand Pinot Noir, Awesome Aromatics; Sub-Regional Nuances of Sauvignon Blanc; Hot Reds from Hawkes Bay; The New World Fruit and Old World Structure of Syrah* and a general overview presentation entitled *Experience the Wines of New Zealand*.

Media and trade visits

New Zealand Winegrowers also hosted 24 media and wine buyers from nine countries on visits to New Zealand wine regions. This included supermarket representatives, specialist wine buyers, specialist wine media, fashion and lifestyle media and sommeliers. The aim of the visits were 'to create long-term supporters who will continue to generate positive media coverage/place listings of New Zealand wine in the years subsequent to their memorable experience in the country' (New Zealand Winegrowers, 2006, p. 23). One writer that attended subsequently wrote: 'New Zealand has positioned itself quite uniquely on the UK shelves, keeping volumes low, but prices high, with a reputation for producing classy wines for the discerning drinker that is the envy of most other nations' (Tom Cannavan, *Fine Expressions*, March 2006, in New Zealand Winegrowers, 2006, p. 23).

Generic promotion

Generic promotional campaigns were also conducted in New Zealand's main markets. In the UK a major promotion included, amongst others, working with the Waitrose supermarket chain to install in-store promotions in 173 stores nationwide as well as a *Waitrose Wine Direct* newsletter featuring New Zealand wine sent to over 100,000 people. In the USA a major promotion was piloted in 30 Safeway Supermarket stores and there was also a campaign to improve awareness of New Zealand wine in a number of New York restaurants.

Domestic public relations

Recognising that the domestic market is the number one market for New Zealand wines, a domestic public relations campaign was developed to target key opinion leaders. To this end 'New Release Tastings' were held for key trade and media in Auckland, Wellington and Christchurch. Over 200 wines were showcased from 49 wineries. Wine New Zealand 2005, a major trade and consumer show, also attracted 2445 visitors.

Source: New Zealand Winegrowers (2006).

Export facilitation

One important role of national- and state-level collectives is the development and maintenance of smooth export channels. This can be facilitated by working with governmental trade agencies from the exporting country to maximise the efficient importation of wine into a market. In New Zealand, for example, New Zealand Winegrowers work closely with New Zealand Trade and Enterprise (NZTE) to provide exporters with information and logistical assistance in many export markets. In Australia, AusTrade provides a similar service. This might not seem like a marketing function, but it ultimately leads to easier sales and distribution of wine.

Greater export facilitation is also occurring at an international or inter-agency level. As noted in Chapter 2 Argentina, Australia, Canada, Mexico, New Zealand, South Africa and the USA formed the World Wine Trading Group (WWTG) in order to compete more effectively with EU wine producing nations as well as facilitating improved trading conditions around the world. An example of an international wine trade initiative is the Agreement on the Requirements for Wine Labelling that was reached in January 2007 which enables wine exporters to sell wine into WWTG markets without having to redesign their labels for each individual market.

Table 10.6 Selected national and state/provincial offices in export markets

	National offices			State/provincial offices		
	Australia	New Zealand	South Africa	Bordeaux	California	Champagne
Australia		*			✓	✓✓
Belgium						✓
Canada	✓	*			✓	
China			✓		✓	✓
Denmark			✓	✓	✓	
Europe/The Haag	✓		✓		✓	
Germany				✓✓	✓	✓
Hong Kong					✓	
Ireland	✓✓					
Japan						✓✓
Korea						
Mexico					✓	
The Netherlands					✓✓	✓✓
Russia			✓			
Singapore					✓	
Spain						
Switzerland						
Thailand			✓		✓✓	
Sweden			✓		✓	
Taiwan			✓	✓✓	✓	✓✓
UK	✓✓	✓				
USA	✓✓	*				

*Contracted partner marketing services, not a full office.

For heavier exporting countries, states and provinces this function (as well as other export and marketing functions) may be facilitated by offices in major export markets. Table 10.6 shows that, for example, California has 13 offices around the world and that the UK, as a major importer of wine, plays host to many national and state wine offices.

Lobbying

National bodies also have the political status and power to also act as a lobby to influence government policy and law. Like export facilitation this may not seem to be a marketing function. However, there are many laws and regulations that can influence the marketing of wine (e.g. licensing, advertising and labelling laws) (see also Chapter 2). Effective lobbying of government agencies can also help to optimise sales conditions in domestic markets. For example, the Free the Grapes organisation is partly funded by the California Wine Institute and they are actively lobbying against state laws that restrict the movement of wine across state borders (see also Chapters 1 and 2). The Conseil Interprofessionnel du Vin de Bordeaux (CIVB) have also attempted to lobby, with limited success, against France's prohibitive wine advertising laws, known as the Evin law.

There are also examples of organisations that represent all parts of the wine supply/value chain being involved in lobbying to influence the sales and marketing of wine. For example, the Wine and Spirit Trade Association (WSTA) are an important lobby group for the wine industry in the UK. WSTA was established in 1824 and currently has over 300 members representing wine producers, suppliers (e.g. consultants, warehouses and freight forwarders), importers, distributors and retailers. They advocate for their membership on a range of issues, including tax, licensing, EU wine and alcohol policy, packaging and social responsibility (see http://www.wsta.co.uk/).

Conclusions

Collaborative marketing is very powerful for the wine industry and is being applied at a number of different geographical scales. The key concepts of networking and clustering are important here and the wine industry has been put forward as a prime example of these concepts in action. The New World is perhaps more advanced than its Old World counterparts as they are less constrained by legislation that seeks to preserve tradition. Australia and New Zealand, in particular, provide many examples of best practice in collaborative wine marketing and, as such, several have been discussed here.

The link between place and wine means that the regional collaboration is both important and, in the absence of any regulatory obstructions, is relatively easy to achieve. Marketing based on wine region is commonplace around the world and this is steeped in history in the Old World of wine, perhaps nowhere more so than in France where it is enshrined in AOC law. These laws cause somewhat of a conundrum for French wine producers, as they clearly add value for some producers, but they also restrict their ability to be innovative and they can work against effective collaboration.

At a regional-level collaboration between the wine and tourism sectors is also beneficial as wine tourism can reinforce and enhance regional brand image (see also Chapter 4). Once again the New World dominates in such collaboration, but Old World wine regions are fast seeing the potential that wine tourism networks can have.

Collaboration at a national level (or state or provincial level in some cases) is critical if wine producing countries are to survive in an increasingly competitive global marketplace. This allows countries to position themselves effectively and to put in place the mechanisms necessary for wine producers to effectively market and sell their wine in export markets.

Practical wine marketing insights

- Collaboration is critical for survival in the domestic and export marketplace and in many countries governments actively support such collaboration.
- Place-based marketing is a useful tool for marketing wine and this is likely to be most effective where wineries work together to develop the region's brand image and reputation.
- In most wine regions organisations have been established that facilitate such collaboration, some have voluntary membership while others have compulsory membership with government enforced levies. National bodies have also been set up that operate in a similar manner for entire countries.
- Collaboration with tourism businesses can be an effective positioning tool for wineries, but this requires wineries to recognise that they will be part of the tourism industry and a commitment to and understanding of the tourism industry.

Further reading

Hall, C.M. (2004). Small firms and wine and food tourism in New Zealand: issues of collaboration, clusters and lifestyles. In Thomas, R. (ed.), *Small Firms in Tourism: International Perspectives*, pp. 167–81, Elsevier.
For a discussion of the wider benefits of wine tourism networks and clusters.

Hall, C.M., Johnson, G.R. and Mitchell, R.D. (2000). Wine tourism and regional development. In Hall, C.M., Sharples, E., Cambourne, B. and Macionis, N. (eds.), *Wine Tourism Around the World: Development, Management and Market, pp. 196–225, Butterworth Heinemann.*

Marsh, I. and Shaw, B. (2000). *Australia's Wine Industry: Collaboration and Learning as Causes of Competitive Success.* Australian Business Foundation, Sydney. Available at: http://www. abfoundation.com.au/ext/ABFound.nsf/0/1cf34f0d97d7cca94a2569380 009079f/$FILE/wine%20study.PDF
For an extensive report on collaboration in the Australian wine industry.

Mitchell, R.D. and Schreiber, C. (2007). Wine tourism networks and clusters: operation and barriers in New Zealand. In Michael, E. (ed.), *Micro-Clusters and Networks: The Growth of Tourism*, pp. 79–106, Elsevier.
For a case study of the New Zealand and, more particularly, Central Otago wine region and wine tourism collaboration.

Porter, M.E. (2000). Location, competition, and economic development: local clusters in a global economy. *Economic Development Quarterly*, 14(1), 15–34.
Provides a useful background to the value of clustering as a marketing management strategy and provides an overview of Porter's more recent thinking on the subject.

CHAPTER 11

Conclusions:
To market to market

Chapter objectives

After reading this chapter you will

- Reaffirm the importance of a humanistic experiential marketing approach with respect to the intangible dimensions of wine production for consumers and marketing
- Appreciate some of the key international trends associated with wine consumption and consumer behaviour
- Appreciate some of the key international trends associated with wine production and production behaviour
- Reaffirm that value is added to wine brands at all stages of wine production, distribution and consumption where the consumer makes contact

This final chapter seeks to outline some of the key findings, issues and trends that will be faced in wine marketing in the immediate future. This chapter is divided into sections that address consumption and production factors with respect to wine and their marketing implications.

Introduction

One of the great myths of the wine industry is that 'a great wine will sell itself'. Unfortunately, while this is a wonderful sound bite that is often heard at tastings, wine clubs, the cellar door and industry meetings, it just is not true. In order to be sold the wine and the consumer have to be brought together. This means at the very least there has to be a distribution channel. But more than that the consumer has to know about the wine and then decide to purchase it, often in the face of competition from many other options, many of which will not even be wine. Furthermore, the decision to purchase is also situational in terms of motivations, needs, atmosphere, social situation, budget, convenience, fashion, peer pressure and many other factors. Indeed, a key realisation in understanding wine purchasing patterns is that the vast majority of wine is consumed within 24 hours of purchase, something which is not akin to the image of buying a bottle 'to put it down' often, perhaps unwittingly still conveyed in the popular wine media. In fact, one of the things that we would like to 'put down' is the archaic production focus that still exists with many in the industry.

The above comments should not be construed to mean that we do not believe that efforts should not be directed into making technically excellent wine, we do. However, in the same way that a great wine shows great balance so it is that balance needs to be achieved in the understanding of how wine businesses, and wine growers in particular, can increase their return on investment. First and foremost this requires the realisation that the value of wine, and what the wine product actually is, is co-created between the producer and the consumer. You cannot have one without the other. This therefore means that wine is not just a physical product but is in fact the entire bundle of meanings, experiences, values and desires associated with 'what's in the bottle' and how it got there. If this is appreciated then we are more than halfway to understanding the essential nature of wine marketing because the mechanics of marketing, in terms of segmentation, selection of communication channels and marketing management, can then be most efficiently and effectively applied (see Plate 11.1).

Trends in wine consumption and production behaviour

The future, by its nature, is unknown. 'Wildcards' – high impact, low probability events – such as unpredictable economic events, for example, the Great Depression of 1929 or the Asian economic crisis of 1997, or natural disasters, for example, the spread of phylloxera in the 19th century, can have substantial mid- to long-term affects depending on the scale of their impact. Nevertheless, in seeking to understand the short- to medium-term prospects for wine and wine marketing it is useful to identify factors that will affect the business environment. Box 11.1 identifies major trends and issues in wine consumption and consumer behaviour.

Box 11.1   Trends and issues in consumption and consumer behaviour to 2015

- On the basis of world consumption trends since 1995 (OIV, 2006), world wine consumption will continue to increase. However, this increase will not keep up with the rate of estimated population growth and therefore world wine consumption per capita will continue to fall.
- National markets showing continued economic growth and rising incomes per capita demonstrate some of the best growth potential for increasing wine consumption. However, the potential of such markets needs to be understood

in relation to such factors as religious and cultural attitudes to alcohol and wine in particular; adoption by existing and emerging middle class of western-oriented consumerism in which wine has a role as a status good; and increased competition from other beverages, alcohol and otherwise. On the basis of such analysis in terms of non-traditional wine growing areas India and China will be primary markets for growth in wine consumption, and Korea, Japan, the Nordic countries and Singapore significant secondary markets. In terms of areas in which wine growing is established then the USA and Russia appear to be primary growth markets, and South Africa and some of the transition economies of Eastern Europe significant secondary markets.

- Existing wine-growing countries will continue to be the most significant markets for premium wines, with the possible exception being Singapore. India and China will be important but primarily by virtue of the sheer size of their markets rather than the overall pattern of consumer behaviour and consumption.
- The health benefits of moderate wine consumption will continue to grow as an important selling feature especially as population ages in developed countries.
- Women will continue to become even more significant as the drivers behind wine brand choice and as consumers of wine.
- The take home wine market will continue to grow with this primarily being purchased from supermarkets. Continued drink driving campaigns in a number of developed countries will serve to reinforce this trend.

At a global scale it is likely that wine consumption will continue to slowly increase although on a per capita basis it will decrease. As a result of the slow rate of global consumption volume oriented producers will continue to pay substantial attention to the emerging markets of Asia. By virtue of their sheer size and the growing middle class China and India will attract marketing attention from premium producers but their primary focus will be with the mature markets of Europe and the still growing premium markets of the USA, UK and the Nordic countries.

The lifestyle and fashion dimensions of wine which have developed substantially in recent years will have particular influence on the increasingly gendered nature of wine brand choice in which women are becoming more important as household drivers of brand choice, particularly in a retail environment. This may well have substantial implications for wine marketing strategies including channel choice for medium to larger wine companies while also having implications for some of the specialised marketing strategies of small wineries. The health dimensions of wine are also increasingly likely to become a focal point of wine promotion, where alcohol advertising regulation makes this possible, as a result of the aging populations of many western societies. In the various countries in which alcohol advertising law prevents such statements from being made it is likely that companies will become more inventive with respect to circumventing regulations, that is, through encouraging appropriate stories in the media, as well as direct lobbying on lawmakers to change alcohol advertising law.

With respect to wine production the industry will continue to face increasingly competitive conditions as a result of global overproduction in relation to levels of consumption (Box 11.2). Although non-premium (bulk) producers are the most affected by overproduction, such is the scale of production that premium producers are also increasingly being affected. The financial and business pressures that are being brought to bear on many small and boutique premium producers will therefore continue well into the foreseeable future. This does not mean that there are no opportunities for flexible and innovative producers, there clearly well be, instead it will reflect a reality that for many microproducers the wine industry will represent in great part a lifestyle choice rather than a strategy for short-term profit maximisation, that is, it is likely that in the majority of many winegrowing business start-ups greater returns would be possible from alternative investment strategies. Indeed, the competitive nature of the industry will require greater consideration of allocation of scarce resources than ever before as well as carefully considered marketing strategies. Examples of greater flexibility of winegrowing operations from integrated business models (in which grape production, wine production and wine promotion and distribution are all owned within the same business structure) include:

- bypassing of traditional retail channels to focus on new forms of online retailing and presence;
- greater flexibility in grape and/or grape juice purchase from a greater range of providers and utilising international supply chains;
- greater flexibility in use of contracted winemakers, viticulturalists, managers and marketers (i.e. human resources), and becoming even more of an international labour market;
- greater flexibility with respect to use of plant, that is, crushing, fermentation tanks, bottling plants, being utilised on a short-term contract or lease basis, again potentially;
- greater flexibility with respect to relations between winegrowers, intermediaries and retailers as capacities for substitution of suppliers remains high in a buyers market.

Box 11.2 Trends and issues in production and production behaviour to 2015

- Competition between wine producers and wine regions will continue to increase.
- There will be ongoing turbulence in the production of wine as a result of overproduction relative to consumption. EU and other national support schemes for the wine industry, including vine pull schemes, will only have marginal impacts on world wine production overall although they will have significant regional impact.
- The industrial structure of wine production, particularly in New World wine countries, will continue to emphasise a small number of very large companies and a large number of very small companies. Such structures will increasingly give rise to policy tensions as grapegrowers and small wineries come under increasing financial pressures.
- Winegrowers will face increased competition for access to increasingly scarce water supplies in a number of regions including Southern Europe, USA, British Columbia, South Africa and Australia.
- As a result of increased mobility of people, freight and agricultural commodities the rate of transmission of pests and diseases will increase.
- The role of transnational supermarket and other retail chains will continue to grow in importance in terms of volume of wine sold.
- Wine growth internationally will continue to come from high value rather than high-volume markets.
- Wine tourism and wine events will be increasingly adopted by wine regions and some winegrowers as a business and market strategy.
- Web2.0 will provide wineries with new networking opportunities but will require new business strategy approaches in order to be able to manage the co-creation possibilities.

While there are limits to the extent of flexible production the case described in Chapter 5 of 'virtual winemakers' who own no grapes or winemaking capacity and simply buy all of the services necessary to make wine that they bottle and label under their own brand indicates the development of a new modern form of négociant. In fact, the freeing up of the global wine market with respect to trade barriers will only serve to reinforce the potential for growth in this dimension of the wine business.

Ironically, at the same time as international trade negotiations within Organisation Internationale de la Vigne et du Vin (OIV) and the World Wine Trade Group are opening up new possibilities for the further internationalisation of the wine industry and therefore the development of new markets for many wine-growers, there are increasing concerns about market constraints. One of the key themes to emerge from the various chapters of the book, and one that we did not really expect to emerge so strongly when we started researching its content, is the extent to which gatekeepers affect successive stages of the wine value chain. The term 'gatekeeper' is a long-used concept that refers to the capacity of an individual or company to act as points that function as gates blocking the flow of some material while allowing other material to pass through (White, 1950). Importantly, material does not just refer to physical products such as wine but also, and perhaps even more significantly in the longer term, information.

In this book we can distinguish between gatekeepers of distribution and supply and gatekeepers of knowledge, taste and experiences although their roles will often overlap. With respect to gatekeepers of distribution and supply the increasing concentration of larger and larger firms with respect to distribution and retailing clearly creates potential difficulties for smaller winegrowers particularly in light of the fact that more and more wine is being purchased from supermarket retailers (Burt and Sparks, 2003; Hollingsworth, 2004). According to Wine Australia (2007):

The current market has seen retailers take a far greater role in directing consumer tastes, such is the overwhelming choice offered to a wine buyer. Retailers are taking a gatekeeper role, and it could be argued they have replaced the customer as king. Demands are now placed on wineries and winemakers to produce wine to specification at directed prices, with wineries that fall out of mainstream distribution networks facing difficult times.

As Montgomery (1975) recognised over three decades ago with respect to the influence of supermarket buyer decisions, 'The ability to obtain distribution is clearly a key factor in the success of a new consumer product. If a product is not available, the sales results are obvious' (1975, p. 225). In short, if you can't get it to customers then you can't sell it. The international concentration of the retail grocery market, particularly in an environment of over-production even with respect to premium wines, means that it is harder and harder to bring sufficient returns on investment if wines are easily substitutable. Therefore, in addition to managing how supply and production best fits together, and in some cases developing 'alternative' distribution chains, where possible, via the internet, farmers markets and cellar door, winegrowers have also been seeking to identify points of difference with respect to their wine and their marketing that may help in distinguishing themselves in an otherwise congested market. Points of difference will often relate to brand development and usually include factors such as place, variety and nature of winemaking and wine-growing (particularly the environment). As Penn (2006) observed with respect to how global sourcing of wine will affect the future of the California wine industry:

Global competition has made it imperative that vintners and growers find a way to make their regions stand out. Associations will take the lead in explaining to consumers how the products from their region are different than the grapes and wines available from other regions. Associations are coordinating the marketing efforts of vintners and growers in each region to deliver a unified message (Penn, 2006).

Where place or variety is not used as a major source of differentiation then other specific marketing characteristics that relate to experiential dimensions, such as fun, for example, Fat Bastard wines, or status and fashion, as in some champagne houses (see Chapter 9), can be used.

As Weingarten and Adler (2005) commented: 'To a connoisseur, the last thing a wine should be is 'fun.' But times change, and even as the overall quality of the wine produced worldwide continues to improve, the imperatives of marketing are being felt from Napa (home of Marilyn Merlot) to Australia (Crocodile Chase) and South Africa (Goats Do Roam and Bored Doe)'. Or, as Domaine Paul Mas from the Languedoc region did, produce a red wine called Arrogant Frog for the Australian market (Smith, 2006). According to Jean-Claude Mas the wine was designed as a way of penetrating the Australian wine glut and overcoming the even worse situation in France:

The phrase 'made in France' is no longer sexy ... That is a major problem for the whole country. Made in France is no longer appealing, and we are not appealing on price, because our costs are too high, or because people do the job better than we do. We have to compete on innovation now, and new ideas. We think we do it right, but we have to present it differently, for example, Arrogant Frog (in Smith, 2006, p. 7).

Nevertheless, such wines still have to be drinkable! 'The days of hiding inferior quality wine behind good packaging or strong distribution and promotion are numbered. The consumer is not as concerned about where it comes from as how good it tastes and costs; and the chain buyers and the retailers know it' (Penn, 2006). As Peter Click, whose company the Click Wine Group (see Chapter 9) imports Fat Bastard wines from France, where they are not sold, stated, 'But if the wine isn't good, it doesn't matter how clever the name is' (in Weingarten and Adler, 2005).

Fat Bastard has actually been one of the bright spots for French wine in the North American market, primarily because they have thought of their customer and have sought to make wine accessible. Such strategies will not be for everyone, but it does show the desirability of focussing on the customer, a concept that is not implemented anywhere near as often by companies as it is said. Importantly, such brands also play a very significant part in getting curious consumers purchasing wine in the first place so that, over time, those who become substantially wine interested then migrate to more premium varietals and brands that are often perceived as being more authentic (Penn, 2007b).

One of the great difficulties with differentiation strategies is being able to sustain the advantage over time as many elements can be copied or even become standard over time. For example, if all wineries were to adopt sustainable winegrowing practices it may cease to be an advantage for an individual winegrower although the region and wine as a beverage over all would likely benefit. Therefore, it means that firms and regions need to not only be consciously developing their brand but also seeking to protect them.

Consumer preference is obviously going to be a major determinant of what winegrowers produce. However, consumer preference cannot be seen in isolation from some of the factors that influence fashion and taste overall (see Chapter 2). Gatekeepers of taste refer to how the flow of information affects wine purchasing both within the distribution channel as well as by the end consumer. Although there is overlap here with retailers in terms of in-store promotions as well as in the proclivities of retail buyers the most significant gatekeepers of taste lie in the media and the recommendations made by reviewers and cooking personalities and in the awards at wine shows (see Chapter 9). That stated, recommendations by friends and family in whom a consumer has trust are also extremely important in influencing taste. Such recommendations can be influenced by winegrowers and other wine businesses which deal direct with consumers (see Chapter 4). Word of mouth is the most powerful promotional channel of them all and therefore attention to providing positive service experiences whether at the winery, wine club or the restaurant are important as they all affect the overall perceived value and quality of the wine product.

Gatekeepers of experience arise in the settings in which wine is consumed. This includes the cellar door (see Chapter 4) where recommendations are made over what wine to try but, more significantly, it applies to sommeliers and waiting staff who make recommendations over what wine to match with a meal or to try (see Chapter 7). Winegrowers can influence gatekeepers of experience, particularly by seeking to run education and training programmes at the restaurant or, if possible, at the winery. Obviously at an international level such programmes are best undertaken in conjunction with cooperative promotions by all except the larger firms. Yet, even the smallest of winegrowers and producers can engage in such programmes at a local level. This is perhaps the most basic – and some of the most effective – marketing of all, but we are consistently amazed about how staff of restaurants and licensed premises in a winery's locale as well as accommodation and hospitality providers and tourism staff have never been to the winery or sampled the wine. In this case good marketing is a phone call or visit away.

The growth in advertising and sales channels and opportunities will also provide new challenges to winegrowers to be able to harness the communicative power of new communication channels such as blogs, wikis and networks. In order to maximise the effectiveness of the Web2.0 environment, wine businesses must realise more than ever that communication is a two-way process. Just as significantly, the development of brand communities by the use of new information and communications technology means that wine brand committed customers feel like they have an investment or degree of ownership in the brand. These people, who are likely to be long-standing members of the newsletter list or a member of the wine club, visit the winery regularly or even the website on a regular basis, are the best ambassadors for the brand. In the design field it is increasingly common for products to be customer-made, creating brand communities does this for wine as well. The notion of 'customer-made' is a logical extension of the idea of co-creation with which we started this book (see Chapter 1). This refers to the process of wine businesses creating their products, particularly the experiences that surround them, in close cooperation with experienced and creative consumers, thereby drawing on their intellectual capital, and getting them involved in the brand production process. For some readers this may be taking things a little too far, but if you are serious about the business of producing something that consumers want then it makes huge sense to get them actively involved in the value-adding process.

In addition to the economic factors affecting winegrowing in the short to mid-term it is likely that environmental concerns, particularly with respect to water security, will become increasingly significant as climate change factors start to have an affect in many wine-growing areas. In some cases it is likely that growers will be able adapt by planting new varieties and/or developing new locations. These developments will, however, pose new marketing challenges as well as winegrowing challenges. For example, even though some excellent English premium wine is now being produced, English wine has long suffered an image problem which will take substantial time to address. Similarly the emerging northern wines of Denmark and Sweden will also require skilful marketing to move beyond being more than just novelty value (and, yes, there are vineyards in both countries!). Arguably, the Canadian experience, particularly the Niagara Peninsula region in Ontario and the Okanagan Valley and Vancouver Island in British Columbia, demonstrates that new premium wine regions cannot only be regarded as significant to a local market but also develop a significant international profile as well with a combination of good winegrowing and good marketing.

The wine industry is one that is constantly changing with the pace of change arguably hastening since the early 1980s as a result of international trade reforms, rural restructuring, adoption of new technologies and practices and increasing internationalisation. Nevertheless, there are also a number of cyclical adjustments that also affect wine markets including the affects of business cycles as well as normal climatic variation. Yet even considering the potential affects of cyclical adjustments on our understanding of the global wine industry it is apparent that further significant change is afoot. The further intervention of the European Commission (2006a; see Chapter 2) in European winegrowing, even despite the undoubted resistance from various stakeholders and regions, will also lead to substantial structural change. As Labys and Cohen (2004, p. 13) observed, the declines in wine exporting shares by France and Portugal:

… deserve serious attention by their respective domestic wine industries … However, for the new producers, the increase in market shares and exports symbolizes the impact of the important underlying factors that have transformed their wine industries. Given the changing nature of wine consumption habits and the mediocrity of the wines sold in many cases, one wonders whether or not old world producers are capable of reversing [their relative decline in wine export share].

Conclusions: Practical wine marketing

There's a lot of potential out there, but there are so many brands and so many new brands out there that it's tough to find shelf space and even to find distributors … The distributor network is to the point where they are throwing up their hands and saying, 'we don't want to see any new brands, we're so overloaded' – Ironstone Vineyards president Steven Kautz (see http://www.ironstonevineyards.com/).

(Penn, 2007b)

As an individual winery, the challenge is making sure you're differenti-
ated with a clear and direct story because there's so much clutter out
there ... I'm reminded every time I go to Safeway. It's overwhelming,
especially with all the competition from overseas. Have a clear message and stick to it – Hess Collection President Tom Selfridge (see
http://www.hesscollection.com/).

(Penn, 2007b)

Marketing is the late arrival to the wine industry, to some it is
probably even the bastard child, but marketing is now integral
to the business of wine. Historically, the focus of winegrowers
has tended to be on what happens in the vineyard and in the
winery. Since the 1960s attention also turned to issues of supply
and distribution chains. Since the late 1980s there has also been
a growing realisation that marketing is also important. There is
perhaps one exception to this – Champagne – and the benefits
of their focus on marketing and promotion from as early as the
late 18th century are clear. They are head and shoulders above
all others in terms product awareness, image and positioning.
Nevertheless, by far the greatest investment of winegrowers
(even in Champagne), whether it be time, money, research or
education is on the production of wine. In this age of environmental concern many winegrowers are, quite rightly, paying
increased attention to sustainable winegrowing (see Chapter 3).
However, what is often missing is the recognition that good
business practice, and particularly the consumer orientation
of the marketing dimension, is as much a part of sustainable
commercial winegrowing as anything that goes on in the
vineyard.

This book has therefore adopted a very contemporary approach
to understanding wine marketing. As well as discussing some
of the relevant 'Ps' of marketing (particularly for those who did
Marketing 101!) – including some of the practical insights of
wine marketing – it has a structure that emphasises that value
can be added to wine through all stages of the supply and distribution chains so that they become value chains for both consumer and producer. This approach also emphasises that, in the
long run, there is also a mutual dependency between the various businesses that lie within the value chain. However, as
emphasised in a number of chapters as well as in this one, the
role of gatekeepers is emerging as a crucial issue in the capacity
of some wine growers to get their wine to consumers, particularly in the increasingly important retail sector. Perhaps more
philosophically we have emphasised that ultimately wine is an
experience that includes everything from the intangible elements of wine and its brand image (e.g. symbolism, emotional
value, aesthetic and meaning) to the more tangible service

elements of economic exchange surrounding wine (e.g. the services provided by intermediaries, winery staff and retailers). In other words, we have expressed in marketing terms what most readers already know, that wine is much more than a 'drink'.

We termed the more humanistic marketing approach adopted by this book as an experiential (experience-driven) approach in order to emphasise how wineries and all the actors in the wine production and supply chains need to focus on the values that consumers derive from wine and other competing products as a whole and from the wines that they are providing in particular. This means that we have paid specific attention to the needs and experiences of consumers and customers and how wine businesses create and add value for customers in all elements of the chain as well as the issues in the business environment that affect the capacity of firms to act. To do this we have utilised a range of examples, cases and frameworks as well as reference to various methods and strategies. However, most fundamentally we advocate that it is the approach that should be the basis for wine marketing. This means that in practical marketing terms:

(a) As many people as possible in the wine business need to have adopted such a customer experience orientation, from the cellar door through to the vineyard.
(b) That as many firms and people as possible within the web of economic relationships and networks of the winegrower also need to have such an orientation. This is not just hyperbole, winegrowers must try and influence behaviours and attitudes throughout the value chain.
(c) That customer experience orientation needs to be built into realistic wine business decision-making and strategy and it is this that should then drive market research, marketing strategy and marketing management decision-making. This is extremely important for smaller winegrowers as well as other wine businesses, such as licensed premises and specialist wine retailers given the scarce marketing dollar and the need to use the most appropriate communications channel.

Unfortunately, a lot of marketing, including some wine marketing advice, is generated more by the needs of the marketing division, creatives, advertising firms and consultants than by the real needs of wine businesses. We hope that this book has in some small way helped you reflect on the business and marketing of wine and consider the means by which your business goals may be achieved. May your wine experiences be positive ones!

Recommended reading

Winecast – a wineblog and podcast: http://winecast.net/category/wine-marketing/
Produced by Tim Elliott, these provide comments on wine regions, varieties, tasting notes and a range of other wine-related topics. From a marketing perspective the site is interesting not just for the commentary but also for the links and marketing dimensions that are demonstrated. One of our favourite comments is with respect to the announcement of a Wine MBA in France, Elliott writes, 'The French have a lot better things to do than understand what an MBA is; they, like a lot of producers worldwide, need to understand their customers and make wine they like. That's it, no MBA required ...' (17 September 2006). We could not agree more – and we both work in Business Schools!

Click Wine Group: http://www.clickwinegroup.com/
The Group is discussed in Chapter 10 but we have included it here as the Group has the philosophy of 'bringing quality international wines within reach' by featuring 'easy-to-remember names and distinctive packaging, to take the intimidation out of wine'. Again, we couldn't agree more.

Wine Australia (2007). *Future Trends*, Australian Wine and Brandy Corporation, http://www.wineaustralia.com/Australia/Default.aspx?tabid = 826
An interesting account from an Australian perspective on the potential futures of the wine industry.

Wine Business Monthly: http://www.winebusiness.com/
The news section arguably provides some of the best discussions on business trends, albeit with more of a North American focus (see also a number of the other websites recommended in Chapter 2).

Bisson, L.F., Waterhouse, A.L., Ebeler, S.E., Walker, M.A. and Lapsley, J.T. (2002). The present and future of the international wine industry. *Nature*, 414, 696–699.

Organisation Internationale de la Vigne et du Vin (OIV). *State of Vitiviniculture World Report March*, OIV, Paris.
Readers should regularly assess the annual state of vitiviniculture world report released by the OIV which details global trends with respect to wine consumption and production.

References

Advanced Business Research (1999). *New Zealand Wine Market Research: Results of a Survey of New Zealand and International Visitor Wine Drinkers*, Ministry of Tourism, Wellington.

Ahmed, Z. (2004). Indians embrace wine-drinking. *BBCNews*, 4 February 2004, Available: http://news.bbc.co.uk/2/hi/business/3454429.stm

Ailawadi, K.L., Borin, N. and Farris, P.W. (1995). Market power and performance: a cross-industry analysis of manufacturers and retailers. *Journal of Retailing*, 71(3), 211–248.

Akerman, P. (2007). Wine trade sinking in red ink. *Daily Telegraph*, 19 March 2007, Available: http://www.news.com.au/dailytelegraph/story/0,22049,21403523-5001024,00.html

Allan, G. (1999). *Restoring the Native Vegetation Balance: Principles and Practices*. Sustainability of Viticulture in Central West NSWOrange Agricultural College – Friday 3 December 1999, Sustainable Viticulture, Greening Australia.

Amazon (2007). *Review of Room Service' by Karl Lagerfeld*. Available: http://www.amazon.com/Karl-Lagerfeld-Service-Devendra-Banhart/dp/386521326X/ref = pd_bxgy_b_img_b/002-8639616-6191230.

Ambler, T. and Burne, T. (1999). The impact of affect on memory of advertising. *Journal of Advertising Research*, 39(2), 25–34.

Anderson, K. (2000). The anatomy of Australia's wine boom: lessons for other industries. *Australasian Agribusiness Review*, 8. Available: http://www.agrifood.info/review/2000/Anderson Wine.html

Anderson, K. (2001). *Where in the World is the Wine Industry Going?* Discussion paper No.0101, Centre for International Economic Studies, Adelaide University, Adelaide.

Anderson, K. and Norman, D. (2003). *Global Wine Production, Consumption and Trade, 1961 to 2001*, Centre for International Economic Studies, Adelaide University, Adelaide.

Anon (2002). Warne, women and song. *Sydney Morning Herald* (Online Edition), 24 December 2002. Available: http://www.smh.com.au/articles/2002/12/23/1040511009509.html

Ardente, F., Beccali, G., Cellura, M. and Marvuglia, A. (2006). POEMS: A case study of an Italian wine-producing firm. *Environmental Management*, 38(3), 350–364.

Australian Associated Press (2004). *Southcorp restructure may close winery*. Available: http://www.vanguard.com.au/.

Australian Wine and Brandy Corporation (AWBC) (2007a) *Wine Australia*. Available: http://www.wineaustralia.com/australia/Default.aspx?tabid = 217.

Australian Wine and Brandy Corporation (AWBC) (2007b) *Restaurant wine lists*. Available: http://www.wineaustralia.com/Australia/Default.aspx?tabid=850

Australian Wine and Brandy Corporation (AWBC) (2006). New industry strategy 'a roadmap for wine sector sustainability', Media Release, 8 February 2006, Australian Wine and Brandy Corporation, Adelaide.

Aylward, D. (2004). Innovation-export linkages within different cluster models: A case study from the Australian wine industry. *Prometheus*, 22(4), 423–435.

Aylward, D.K. and Zanko M. (2006). *Emerging interorganizational structures in the Australian wine industry: implications for SMEs*. Faculty of Commerce Paper, University of Wollongong. Available: http://ro.uow.edu.au/commpapers/61

Azimov, E. (2006). In Champagne, the roots of pleasure are rare and pure. *New York Times*, 14 June 2006.

Baker, J., Levy, M. and Grewal, D. (1992). An experimental approach to making retail store environmental decisions. *Journal of Retailing*, 68(4), 445–460.

Bánfalvi, C. (2005). Image is everything for Hungarian wines. *Diplomacy and Trade: Hungary's International Monthly*, February 2005, Available: http://www.dteurope.com/2005_februar/09_business.html

Banrock Station (2005). *Banrock Station Leads the World With New Conservation Donations Milestone*, Banrock Station Media Release, Thursday, 8 December 2005.

Barclay, V. (2001). Is your winery production or marketing Driven? *Wine Business Monthly*, 8(9), Available: http://www.winebusiness.com/html/MonthlyArticle.cfm?dataId=11390

Barham, E. (2003). Translating terroir: the global challenge of French AOC labelling. *Journal of Rural Studies*, 19, 127–138.

Baritaux, V., Aubert, M., Montaigne, E. and Remaud, E. (2006). Matchmakers in wine marketing channels: the case of French wine brokers. *Agribusiness*, 22(3), 375–390.

Barrett, S. (1989). An assessment of the Vine Pull Scheme: A case study of the Southern Vales of South Australia. *Australian Geographer*, 20(2), 185–190.

Barthes, R. (1957/2000). *Mythologies* (A. Lavers, Trans.). Vintage.

BBC (2006). WTO 'to referee' alcohol duty row. *BBC News*, 20 November 2006, Available: http://news.bbc.co.uk/2/hi/business/6165660.stm

Beatty, S.E., Mayer, M., Coleman, J.E., Reynolds, K.E. and Lee, J. (1996). Customer-sales associate retail relationships. *Journal of Retailing*, 72(3), 223–247.

Beaujanot, A. and Lockshin, L. (2003). The importance of market orientation in developing buyer seller relationships in the export market: the link towards relationship marketing. In *Proceedings of the International Colloquium in Wine Marketing*. Adelaide, Australia, Wine Marketing Group, University of South Australia. Available: http://www.unisa.edu.au/wine-marketing/conferences/proceedings.asp.

Benson-Rea, M., Brodie, R.J. and Cartwright, W. (2003). Strategic issues facing the New Zealand wine industry in a global environment. In *Proceedings of the International Colloquium in Wine Marketing*, Wine Marketing Group, University of South Australia, Adelaide.

Bentley, S. and Barker, R. (2005). *Fighting Global Warming at the Farmers' Market: The Role of Local Food Systems in Reducing Greenhouse Gas Emissions*, Foodshare.

Beringer Blass Wine Estates Limited (2007). Advertising. Available: http://www.yellowglen.com.au/brands/yellow-glen/index.asp

Bernetti, I., Casini, L. and Marinelli, N. (2006). Wine and globalisation: changes in the international market structure and the position of Italy. *British Food Journal*, 108(4), 306–315.

Berry Brothers. and Rudd (n.d.) *Frequently asked question – wine investing*. Available: http://www.bbr.com/wine-knowledge/faq-investment.lml.

Beverage Daily (2006). Tough UK wine sector spoils the constellation party. *Beverage Daily*, 9 October 2006, Available: http://www.beveragedaily.com/news/ng.asp?id=71129-constellation-wine-uk-wine

Beverland M. and Lindgreen, A. (2001). Relationships or transactions? Marketing practice in the wine trade. In O'Cass, A. (ed.), *Proceedings of Australian and New Zealand Marketing Academy Conference (ANZMAC)*, Albany, Auckland, New Zealand, 1–5 December 2001.

Beverland, M. (2003). Building icon wine brands: exploring the systemic nature of luxury wines. In *Proceedings of 3rd*

Annual Wine Marketing Colloquium, University of South Australia.

Beverland, M. (2004). Uncovering 'theories-in-use': building luxury wine brands. *European Journal of Marketing*, 38(3/4), 446–466.

Bianchi, S.M., Milkie, M.A., Sayer, L.C. and Robinson, J.P. (2000). Is anyone doing the housework? Trends in the gender division of household labor. *Social Forces*, 79(1), 191–228.

Billingsley, K.L. (2004). Wine Wars: Defending E-commerce and Direct Shipment in the National Wine Market. *Pacific Research Institute*, San Francisco.

Biodiversity and Wine Initiative (2004). The biodiversity and wine initiative: why a biodiversity and wine initiative, *Wynboer A Technical Guide for Wine Producers*, December, Available: http://www.wynboer.co.za/recentarticles/0412bio.php3

Biodiversity and Wine Initiative (BWI) (2007). Current BWI members and champions. *Biodiversity and Wine Buzz: Newsletter of the Biodiversity and Wine Initiative*, 2(1), 4.

Bisson, L.F., Waterhouse, A.L., Ebeler, S.E., Walker, M.A. and Lapsley, J.T. (2002). The present and future of the international wine industry. *Nature*, 414, 696–699.

Bitner, M.J. (1992). Servicescapes: the impact of physical surroundings on customers and employees. *Journal of Marketing*, 56(2), 57–71.

Blandy, R. (2001). South Australian Business Vision 2010, Industry Clusters Program: A Review. University of South Australia. Available: http://business.unisa.edu.au/cid/publications/blandy/BV2010_clusters_report.pdf

Blisard, N., Lin, B., Cromartie, J. and Ballenger, N. (2002). America's changing appetite: food consumption and spending to 2020. *Food Review*, 25(1), 5–9.

Bonné, J. (2005). A year since 'Sideways,' the state of pinot envy. *MSNBC Interactive*, 16 August 2005. Available: http://www.msnbc.msn.com/id/8976742/.

Boothman, P. (2006). Marlborough man. *Decanter*, October, 282–284.

Boyle, D. (2003). *Authenticity: Brands, Fakes, Spin and the Lust for Real Life*, Flamingo/HarperCollins.

Brandenburger, A. and Nalebuff, B. (1996). *Co-Opetition*. Doubleday.

Braun, P. and Lowe, J. (2005). Trust in Rural Areas. In *Proceedings of 2nd Future of Australia's Country Towns Conference*, Bendigo, 11–13 July 2005, Centre for Sustainable Regional Communities, La Trobe University. Available: www.latrobe.edu.au/csrc/2ndconference/refereed n.p.

British Beer and Pub Association (2006). *Statistical Handbook 2006*, 33rd edn., British Beer and Pub Association, London.

British Columbia Wine Institute (2006). *Media resources: Quick facts about the BC Wine Industry*. Available: http://www.winebc. com/media.php

British Retail Consortium (2007). *Retail stats and info: Sector facts and stats*. Available: http://www.brc.org.uk/

Brooks, S. (1993). *Public Policy in Canada*, McClelland and Stewart.

Brook, S. (ed.) (2000a). *A Century of Wine: The Story of a Wine Revolution*, Mitchell Beazley.

Brook, S. (2000b). Wine, food, style and pleasure', In Brook, S. (ed.), *A Century of Wine: The Story of a Wine Revolution*, pp. 10–23, Mitchell Beazley.

Brown, G. and Getz, D. (2005). Linking wine preferences to the choice of wine tourism destinations. *Journal of Travel Research*, 43(3), 266–276.

Brown, M.D., Var, T. and Lee, S. (2002). Messina Hof Wine and Jazz Festival: An economic impact analysis. *Tourism Economics*, 8(3), 273–279.

Bruwer, J. (2003). South African wine routes: some perspectives on the wine tourism industry's structural dimensions and wine tourism product. *Tourism Management*, 24(4), 423–435.

Bruwer, J., Li, E. and Reid, M. (2002). Segmentation of the Australian wine market using a wine-related lifestyle approach. *Journal of Wine Research*, 13(3), 217–242.

Burt, S.L. and Sparks, L. (2003). Power and competition in the UK Retail grocery market. *British Journal of Management*, 14(3), 237–254.

Calder L. (1999). We Don't Need No Education......Or Do We?, *Wine Business Monthly* September, Available: http://Wine business.com/archives/monthly/1999/0999/bmi9924.htm.

Cambourne, B., Hall, C.M., Johnson, G.R., Macionis, N., Mitchell, R.D. and Sharples, E. (2000). The maturing wine tourism product: an international overview. In Hall, C.M., Sharples, E., Cambourne, B. and Macionis, N. (eds.), *Wine Tourism Around the World: Development, Management and Markets*, pp. 24–66, Butterworth-Heinemann.

Caputo, T. (2007). Wine X Officially ceases publication: Publisher cites lack of understanding, industry support. *Wines and Vines*, 20 February 2007, Available: http://www.wine sandvines.com/head_feb07_x.html

Carlsen, J. and Ali-Knight, J. (2004). Managing wine tourism through demarketing: the case of Napa Valley, California. In Carlsen, J. and Charters, S. (eds.), *International Wine Tourism Research*, CD-ROM.

Carpinter, B. (2004). Wine companies may have to blend. *The Dominion Post* (16 August 2004). Available: http://stuff.co. nz/stuff/0,2106,3003737a7775,00.html.

Castaldi, R.M., Cholette, S. and Hussain, M. (2006). A country-level analysis of competitive advantage in the wine industry. In *Proceedings of 3rd International Wine Business Research Conference, Montpellier, 6–8 July 2006*. CD-ROM.

Caterer and Housekeeper (2006). Marketing snapshot: US restaurant trends. *Caterer and Housekeepe*, 5 July 2006, Available: http://www.caterersearch.com/Articles/2006/07/05/307490/market-snapshot-us-restaurant-trends.htm

Charters, S. and Pettigrew, S. (2005). Is wine consumption an aesthetic experience? *Journal of Wine Research*, 16(2), 121–136.

Charters, S. (2006). *Wine and Society: The Social and Cultural Context of a Drink*. Elsevier Butterworth-Heinemann.

Charters, S. and Ali-Knight, J. (2002). Who is the wine tourist? *Tourism Management*, 23(3), 311–319.

Christensen, D. (2004). *Wine club members' enduring involvement toward winery visitation, wine drinking and wine club participation*. Unpublished Masters Thesis, University of Otago.

Christensen, D., Hall, C.M. and Mitchell, R. (2004). The 2003 New Zealand Wineries Survey. In Cooper, C., Arcodia, C., Soinet, D. and Whitford M. (eds.), *Creating Tourism Knowledge, 14th International Research Conference of the Council for Australian University Tourism and Hospitality Education, Book of Abstracts, 10–13 February 2003*, School of Tourism and Leisure Management, pp.144–149, University of Queensland.

Cirami, R.M., McCarthy, M.G. and Glenn, T. (1984). Comparison of the effects of rootstock on crop, juice and wine composition in a replanted nematode-infested Barossa Valley vineyard. *Australian Journal of Experimental Agriculture and Animal Husbandry*, 24(125), 283–289.

Clarke, I. (2000). Retail power, competition and local consumer choice in the UK grocery sector. *European Journal of Marketing*, 34(8), 975–1002.

Coe, N.M. and Hess, M. (2005). The internationalisation of retailing: implications for supply network restructuring in East Asia and Eastern Europe. *Journal of Economic Geography*, 5(4), 449–473.

Collins, D. (2005). *Tourism Research Australia Niche Market Report Number 5, A Profile of Wine Visitors in Australia 2003*. Tourism Research Australia.

Constellation Wines (2006). Australia's Banrock Station Wines announces $1.25 million milestone sponsorship to return Native Atlantic Salmon to Lake Ontario, *Just-drinks*, 28 April 2006.

Corbans Viticulture (2007). Corbans Viticulture News Update February 2007. Available: http://www.corbansviticulture.co.nz/cv/fms/Specialist%20Services/Market%20Trends%20Update.pdf.

Crescimanno, M., Ficani, G.B. and Guccione, G. (2002). The production and marketing of organic wine in Sicily. *British Food Journal*, 104, 274–286.

Croser, B. (1997). The Australian wine industry Perspective, *Agribusiness Review*, 5, Available: http://www.agrifood.info/review/1997/Croser.html.

d'Hauteville, F. (2003). *The Mediating Role of Involvement and Values on Wine Consumption Frequency in France.* In *International Colloquium in Wine Marketing*, University of South Australia.

d'Hauteville, F., Fornerino, M. and Perrouty, J.P. (2006). Disconfirmation of taste as a measure of country of origin strength. An experimental approach on French wines. In *Proceedings of the Third International Wine Business and Marketing Research Conference Montpellier, 6—8 July 2006.* CD-ROM.

Davis, N. and Charters, S. (2006). Building restaurant wine lists: A study in conflict. Paper presented at the *3rd International Wine Business Research Conference*, Montpelier, 6–8 July 2006.

Deighton, J. and Grayson. K. (1995). Marketing and seduction: building exchange relationships by managing social consensus. *Journal of Consumer Research*, 21, 660–676.

Demhardt, I.J. (2003). Wine and tourism at the Fairest Cape: Post-apartheid trends in the Western Cape Provinace and Stellenbosch (South Africa) In Hall, C.M. (ed.), *Wine, Food, and Tourism Marketing*, pp. 113–130, Howarth Press.

Department of Environment, Food and Rural Affairs (DEFRA) (2005). *Food Miles*, DEFRA.

Department of Industry, Tourism Resources (2005). Nice Markets Overview. http://isr.gov.au/content/itrinternet/cmscontent.cfm?objectID-F294F506-96C7-EC89-7E8ED5CAD0751824

Ditter, J.-G. (2005). Reforming the French wine industry: could clusters work? *Cahiers du CEREN*, 13, 39–54.

Dlott, J., Ohmart, C.P., Garn, J., Birdseye, K. and Ross, K. (eds.) (2002). *The Code of Sustainable Winegrowing Practices Workbook*, Wine Institute and California, Association of Winegrape Growers.

Donaldson, A (2004). Research your wine tourists – why are they coming to you? *The Australian and New Zealand Grapegrower and Winemaker* http://www.grapeandwine.com.au.

Donovan, R. and Rossiter, J. (1982). Store atmosphere: an environmental psychology approach. *Journal of Retailing*, 5, 34–57.

Donovan, R., Rossiter, J., Marcoolynn, G. and Nesdale, A. (1994). Store atmosphere and purchasing behavior. *Journal of Retailing*, 70(3), 283–294.

Dries, L., Reardon, T. and Swinnen, J.F.M. (2004). The rapid rise of supermarkets in Central and Eastern Europe: implications for the agrifood sector and rural development. *Development Policy Review*, 22(5), 525–556.

Duval Smith, A. (2004). Champagne battle set to bubble over. *The Observer*, 26 September 2004. Available: http://www. guardian.co.uk/france/story/0,,1312898,00.html.

Edwards, F. (1989). The marketing of wine from small wineries: managing the intangibles. *International Journal of Wine Marketing*, 1(1), 14–17.

Ellis, J.E. (2005). The power of palate. *Business Week*, 25 July 2005, Available: http://www.businessweek.com/magazine/content/05_30/b3944122.htm

Eroglu, S.A., Machleit, K.A. and Davis, L.M. (2003). Empirical testing of a model of online store atmospherics and shopper responses. *Psychology and Marketing*, 20(2), 139–150.

Euromonitor (2001). *Wine – Global Wine Trends*, Euromonitor, February.

European Commission (2006a). *Working Paper Wine Economy of the Sector*, European Commission, Directorate-General for Agriculture and Rural Development, Brussels.

European Commission (2006b). *Wine: Profound reform will balance market, increase competitiveness, preserve rural areas and simplify rules for producers and consumers*, European Commission, IP/06/824, 22 June 2006.

European Commission (2006c). *Towards A Sustainable European Wine Sector*, European Commission, Brussels.

ExCel London (2007). *Trade Show Case Studies: London International Wine and Spirits Fair*, ExCel London The International Exhibition and Conference Centre, London, Available: http://www.excel-london.co.uk/en/press_office/trade_show.html#

Fain, T. (2007). Sunday alcohol sales measure dead. *The Macon Telegraph*, 26 March 2007.

Falassi, A. (ed.) (1987). *Time Out of Time: Essays on the Festival*, University of New Mexico Press.

Fattorini, J.E. (1997). *Managing Wine and Wine Sales*, International Thomson Business Press, London.

Fensterseifer, J.E. (2006). The emerging Brazilian wine industry: Challenges and prospects for the Serra Gaúcha wine cluster. In *Proceedings of 3rd International Wine Business Research Conference, Montpellier, 6–8 July 2006*. CD-ROM.

Firstenfeld, J. (2006). Which restaurant wine promotions really work? Table-tent recommendations for high-margin wines can promote overall sales. *Wines and Vines* 14 December 2006, Available: http://www.winesandvines.com/headline_12_14_06_rest.html

Fischer Boel, M. (2007). *European Agricultural Policy Facing Up to New Scenarios*. Speech to Confederazione Generale dell' Agricoltura Italiana, Taormina, Italy, 23 March 2007. Member of the European Commission responsible for Agriculture and Rural Development, Speech/07/182, European Commission, Brussels.

Fluet, C. and Garella, P. (2002). Advertising and prices as signals of quality in a regime of price rivalry. *International Journal of Industrial Organization*, 20, 907–930.

Foo, L.M. (1999). A profile of international visitors to Australian wineries. *Tourism Research Report*, 1(1), 41–44.

Ford, G.A. (2003). *The Science of Healthy Drinking*, Wine Appreciation Guild, South San Francisco.

Fraser, R.A. and Alonso, A. (2003). Wine Tourism – A marginal economic activity; the vintners perspectives. In *Taking Tourism to the Limits: An Interdisciplinary Conference in the Waikato, Hamilton, New Zealand*, 8–11 December 2003, pp. 184–201, The University of Waikato, Department of Tourism Management, Hamilton.

Free the Grapes (2007). *Issues Summary*. Available: http://www.freethegrapes.com/research

Gartner, W. (1993). Image Formation Process. *Journal of Travel and Tourism Marketing*, 2(2/3), 191–216.

Gebauer, J. and Ginsburg, M. (2003). The US wine industry and the Internet: An analysis of success factors for online business models. *Electronic Markets*, 13(1), 59–66.

Geene, A., Heijbroek, A., Lagerwerf, A. and Wazir, R. (1999). *The World Wine Business*. Utrecht; Rabobank International.

Gensch, D.H. (1978). Image-measurement segmentation. *Journal of Marketing Research*, 15(3): 384–394.

Geraci, V.W. (2004). Fermenting a twenty-first century California wine industry. *Agricultural History*, 78(4), 438–465.

Gettler, L. (2004). Grape surplus to squeeze wine groups. *The Age* (online edition), 9 February 2004. Available: http://www.theage.com.au/.

Gillespie, C.H. (1994). Gastrosophy and *nouvelle cuisine*: entrepreneurial fashion and fiction. *British Food Journal*, 96(10), 19–23.

Giuliani, E. and Bell, M. (2005). The micro-determinants of meso-level learning and innovation: evidence from a Chilean wine cluster. *Research Policy*, 34(1), 47–68.

Gössling, S. and Hall. C.M. (eds.) (2006). *Tourism and Global Environmental Change*, Routledge.

Greenfeld, L. (1988). Professional ideologies and patterns of 'gatekeeping': evaluation and judgment within two art worlds. *Social Forces*, 66(4), 903–925.

Greenfield, J. (2006). Best Product Placement of the Week – Ruffino Wine. *Product Placement News*, 16 July 2006. Available: http://www.productplacement.biz/branded-entertainment/200607161802/best-product-placement-of-the-week-ruffino-wine

Greening Waipara (2006). *Greening Waipara*, Issue 1 (September).

Gregan, P. (2004). New Zealand Wine – Our Brand. In *Proceedings of the New Zealand Wine Exporters Forum: Succeeding in International Wine Business, 27–28 January 2004*. n.p.

Grönroos, C. (1996), Relationship marketing: strategic and tactical implications. *Management Decision*, 34(3), 5–14.

Grönroos, C. (2000). *Service Management and Marketing. A Customer Relationship Approach*, Wiley.

Group Generation (2006). *The Year in Review 2005*, Generation Research. 17 October 2006, http://www.generation.se.

Guibert, N. (2006). Network governance in marketing channels: an application to the French Rhône Valley AOC wines industry. *British Food Journal*, 108(4), 256–272.

Gunn, C.A. (1972). *Vacationscape: Designing Tourist Regions*, Bureau of Business Research, University of Texas.

Gursoy, D., Kim, K.M. and Uysal, M. (2004). Perceived impacts of festivals and special events by organizers: an extension and validation. *Tourism Management*, 25(2), 171–181.

Guy, K.M. (2003). *When Champagne Became French: Wine and the Making of a National Identity*, Johns Hopkins University Press.

Gwynne, R.N. (2006). Governance and the wine commodity chain: upstream and downstream strategies in New Zealand and Chilean wine firms. *Asia Pacific Viewpoint*, 47(3), in press.

Hall, C.M. (1992). *Hallmark Tourist Events*, Belhaven Press.

Hall, C.M. (1996). Wine Tourism in New Zealand. In Higham, J. (ed.) *Proceedings of Tourism Down Under II: A Research Conference*, p. 109–119, University of Otago.

Hall, C.M. (2003a). Biosecurity and wine tourism: Is a vineyard a farm? *Journal of Wine Research*, 14(2–3), 121–6.

Hall, C.M. (2003b). Wine and food tourism networks: a comparative study. In Pavlovich, K. and Akorrie, M. (eds.), *Strategic Alliances and Collaborative Partnerships – A Case Book*, pp. 258–268, Dunmore Press.

Hall, C.M. (2004). Small firms and wine and food tourism in New Zealand: issues of collaboration, clusters and lifestyles. In Thomas, R. (eds.), *Small Firms in Tourism: International Perspectives*, pp. 167–181, Elsevier.

Hall, C.M. (2005). Demography. In D. Buhalis and C. Costa (eds.), *Tourism Dynamics: Trends, Management and Tools*, pp. 9–18, Butterworth-Heinemann.

Hall, C.M. (2007). The fakery of 'the authentic tourist'. *Tourism Management* in press.

Hall, C.M. (2008). *Tourism Planning*, Prentice-Hall.

Hall, C.M. and Mitchell, R.D. (2000). Wine tourism and rural restructuring and reimaging. *Mediterranean Thunderbird International Business Review Special Issue: 'Mediterranean Tourism in the Global Economy: Transition and Restructuring*, 42(4), 443–463.

Hall, C.M. and Mitchell, R. (2004). BMW Wine Marlborough 2003: A profile of visitors to New Zealand's oldest wine festival, In Cooper, C., Arcodia, C., Soinet, D. and Whitford, M. (eds.), *Creating Tourism Knowledge, 14th International Research Conference of the Council for Australian University Tourism and Hospitality Education*, 10–13 February 2004, School of Tourism and Leisure Management, University of Queensland.

Hall, C.M. and Mitchell, R. (2005). Wine Marlborough: a profile of visitors to New Zealand's oldest wine festival, *Journal of Hospitality and Tourism*, 3(1), 77–90.

Hall, C.M., Cambourne, B., Macionis, N. and Johnson, G. (1998), Wine tourism and network development in Australia and New Zealand: Review, establishment and prospects. *International Journal of Wine Marketing* (special Australasian edition), 9(2/3), 5–31.

Hall, C.M., Johnson, G.R., Cambourne, B., Macionis, N., Mitchell, R.D. and Sharples, E. (2000a). Wine tourism: an introduction. In Hall, C.M., Sharples, E., Cambourne, B. and Macionis, N. (eds.), *Wine Tourism Around the World: Development, Management and Market*, pp. 1–23, Butterworth-Heinemann.

Hall, C.M., Johnson, G.R. and Mitchell, R.D. (2000b). Wine tourism and regional development. In Hall, C.M., Sharples, E., Cambourne, B. and Macionis, N. (eds.), *Wine Tourism Around the World: Development, Management and Markets*, pp. 196–225, Butterworth-Heinemann.

Hall, C.M., Mitchell, R.D. and Sharples, L. (2003a). Consuming places: the role of food, wine and tourism in regional development. In Hall, C.M., Sharples, L., Mitchell, R., Macionis, N. and Cambourne, B. (eds.), *Food Tourism Around the World: Development, Management and Markets*, pp. 25–59, Butterworth-Heinemann.

Hall, C.M., Sharples, E., Mitchell, R., Cambourne, B. and Macionis, N. (eds.) (2003b). *Food Tourism Around the World: Development, Management and Markets*, Butterworth-Heinemann.

Halliday, J. (1998). *Wine Atlas of Australia and New Zealand*, Harper Collin Publishers.

Handley, I. and Lockshin, L. (1997). Wine purchasing in Singapore: a supermarket observation approach. *International Journal of Wine Marketing*, 9, 70–83.

Hanson, D. (2007). National Prohibition of Alcohol in the US Sociology Department, State University of New York, Potsdam. Available: http://www2.potsdam.edu/hansondj/Controversies/1091124904.html.

Haxton, N. (2006). Grape glut: call for subsidised vine pull. Transcript from *PM, ABC National Radio*, Monday, 5 June 2006, 18:38:28, Available: http://www.abc.net.au/pm/content/2006/s1655724.htm

Hedberg, P.R., McLeod, R., Cullis, B. and Freeman, B.M. (1986a). Comparison of the effects of rootstock on grape, juice and wine composition in a replanted nematode-infested Barossa Valley vineyard. *Australian Journal of Experimental Agriculture*, 24(124), 283–289.

Hedberg, P.R., McLeod, R., Cullis, B. and Freeman, B.M. (1986b). Effect of rootstock on the production, grape and wine quality of Shiraz vines in the Murrimbidgee irrigation area. *Australian Journal of Experimental Agriculture*, 26(4), 511–516.

Heeger, J. (2007). Doctor says government tried to block info on wine, heart health connection. *Napa Valley Register*, 1 March 2007.

Hemingway, E. (1932). *Death in the Afternoon*, Scribner Book Company.

Higie, R.A. and Feick, L.F. (1989). Enduring involvement: conceptual and measurement issues. *Advances in Consumer Research*, 16, 690–696.

Hingley, M. and Lindgreen, A. (2002). Marketing of agricultural products: case findings. *Birtish Food Journal*, 104(10), 806–827.

Hoj, R.B. and Pretorius, I.S. (2005). Grape and wine biotechnology: challenges, opportunities and potential benefits. *Australian Journal of Grape and Wine Research*, 11(2), 83–108.

Holbrook M.B. and Hirschman, E.C. (1982). The experiential aspects of consumption: consumer fantasies, feelings, and fun. *Journal of Consumer Research*, 9, 132–140.

Holbrook, M.B. (1994). The nature of customer value: an axiology of services in the consumption experience. In R.T. Rust and R.L. Oliver (eds.), *Service Quality: New Directions in Theory and Practice*, pp. 21–71, Sage, Newbury Park.

Hollingsworth, A. (2004). Increasing retail concentration: evidence from the UK food retail sector. *British Food Journal*, 106(8), 629–638.

Houghton, M. (2001). The propensity of wine festivals to encourage subsequent winery visitation. *International Journal of Wine Marketing*, 13(2), 32–41.

Houghton, M. (2002). *Wine festivals: their effectiveness as a promotional strategy for wineries: A Case Study of the Rutherglen Region*. Masters Thesis, La trobe University, Bundoora.

Hu, D., Reardon, T., Rozelle, S., Timmer, P. and Wang, H. (2004). The emergence of supermarkets with Chinese characteristics: challenges and opportunities for China's agricultural development. *Development Policy Review*, 22(5), 557–586.

Hudson H. (2005). *Australian Wine and Brandy Corporation Domestic Promotion Strategy: Qualitative Research Final Report*. Available: http://www.wineaustralia.com/Australia/Default.aspx?tabid=208

Hughes, N. (2006). International Screwcap initiative founded. *Decanter.com*, 6 January 2006, Available: http://www.decanter.com/news/72875.html

Hughey, K.F.D., Tait, S.V. and O'Connell, M.J. (2005). Qualitative evaluation of three 'environmental managemnt systems' in the New Zealand wine industry. *Journal of Cleaner Production*, 13(12), 1175–1187.

Institute of Grocery Distribution (IGD) (2004). *Retailer Own Label, Factsheet*, IGD, Watford.

Institute of Grocery Distribution (IGD) (2006). *UK Grocery Retailing, Factsheet*, IGD, Watford.

Inter-Rhône (2005). Professional Organisation. Available: http://www.inter-rhone.com/en/fonctionnement.php.

Jennings, D. and Wood, C. (1994). Wine: achieving competitive advantage through design. *International Journal of Wine Marketing*, 6(1), 49–61.

Johnson, G.R. (1998). *Wine Tourism in New Zealand: A National Survey of Wineries 1997*. Unpublished Diploma in Tourism Dissertation, University of Otago, Dunedin.

Jones, G.V. and Storchmann, K.H. (2001). Wine market prices and investment under uncertainty: an econometric model for Bordeaux crus classes. *Agricultural Economics*, 26(2), 115–133.

Jordan, R., Zidda, P. and Lockshin, L. (2006). Behind the Australian wine industry success: Does environment matter? In *Proceedings of 3rd International Wine Business Research Conference, Montpellier, 6–8 July 2006*, CD-ROM.

Joseph, R. (2005). Wine Crisis. *Wine International*, 16 May 2005, Available: http://www.wineint.com/story.asp?storyCode=1805.

Judica, F. and Perkins, W.S. (1992). A means-end approach to the market for sparkling wines. *International Journal of Wine Marketing*, 4(1), 10–18.

Kakaviatos, P. (2006a). Aussie wine lake to drain into China. *Decanter.com*, 14 June 2006, Available: http://www.decanter.com/news/86654.html.

Kakaviatos, P. (2006b). Climate change forcing migration north. *Decanter.com*, 1 June 2006, Available: http://www.decanter.com/news/85946.html.

Kant, A.K. and Graubard, B.I. (2004). Eating out in America, 1987–2000: Trends and nutritional correlates. *Preventive Medicine*, 38, 243–249.

Kilikanoon Wines News (2004). *Wine Industry Needs WET Exemption Policy to Underpin Regional Growth*. Available: http://www.kilikanoon.com.au/kili/news/news.asp?article_id=160

King, C. and Morris, R. (n.d.). *The Flow On Effects Of Winery Cellar Door Visits* Unpublished Report, Edith Cowan University, Bunbury Campus, WA.

King, C. and Morris, R. (1999). Wine tourism: costs and returns. In Dowling R. and Carlsen, J. (eds.), *Wine Tourism: Perfect Partners. Proceedings of the First Australian Wine Tourism Conference, Margaret River, Western Australia, May 1998*, pp. 233–245, Bureau of Tourism Research.

Kinsey, J. and Senauer, B. (1996). Consumer trends and changing food retailing formats. *American Journal of Agricultural Economics*, 78(5): 1187–1191.

Kladstrup, D. and Kladstrup, P. (2005). *Champagne: How the World's Most Glamorous Wine Triumphed Over War and Hard Times*, William Morrow.

Knight, J., Holdsworth, D. and Mather, D. (2003). *Trust and Country Image: Perceptions of European Food Distributors Regarding Factors That Could Enhance or Damage New Zealand's Image – Including GMOs*, Marketing Department, University of Otago, Dunedin.

Koerber, K. (2000). Demographic and macroeconomic factors fuelling increased wine consumption. *Wine Business Monthly*, 7(5), Available: http://www.winebusiness.com/html/MonthlyArticle.cfm?dataId=4731

Kotler, P. (1984). Rethink the marketing concept – there are 6 Ps not 4. *Marketing News*, 18(19), 3.

Kotler, P. and Levy, S.J. (1969). Broadening the concept of marketing. *Journal of Marketing*, 33, 10–15.

Kromhout, D. (1999). On the waves of the seven countries study: a public health perspective on cholesterol. *European Heart Journal*, 20, 796–802.

Labys, W.C. and Cohen, B.C. (2004). Trends or cycles in global wine export shares, Paper prepared for the *OENOMETRICS XI* conference of the VDQS-AEA, Dijon France, 20–22 May 2004, *Division of Resource Management Working Paper RESMWP-04-03*, West Virginia University, Morgantown.

Lagendijk, A. (2004). Global 'lifeworlds' versus local 'system-worlds': How flying winemakers produce global wines in interconnected locales. *Tijdschrift voor Economische en Sociale Geografie*, 95(5), 511–526.

Landon, S. and Smith, C.E. (1997). The use of quality and reputation indicators by consumers: The case of Bordeaux wine. *Journal of Consumer Policy*, 20(3), 289–323.

Lang, T. (2003). Food industrialization and food power: implications for food governance. *Development Policy Review*, 21(5–6), 555–568.

Lazarus, R.S. (2006).Emotions and interpersonal relationships: toward a person-centered conceptualization of emotions and coping. *Journal of Personality*, 74(1), 9–46.

Lechmere, A. (2007a). Wine industry to blame for Wine X demise: Darryl Roberts. *Decanter.com*, 19 February 2007, Available: http://www.decanter.com/news/110238.html

Lechmere, A. (2007b). Budget: tax on sparkling angers wine lobby. *Decanter*, 21 March 2007.

Lecocq, S. and Visser, M. (2006). What determines wine prices: objective vs. sensory characteristics. *Journal of Wine Economics*, 1(1), 42–56.

Lee, K., Zhao, J. and Ko, J. (2005). Exploring the Korean wine market. *Journal of Hospitality and Tourism Research*, 29(1), 20–41.

Leighton, C. and Seaman, C. (1997). The elderly food consumer: disadvantaged? *Journal of Consumer Studies and Home Economics*, 21(4), 363–370.

Levitan, L. (2001). Not by wine alone: environmental impacts, risks and consequences of viticulture. *11th Australian Wine Industry Technical Conference*, October, Adelaide, South Australia.

Levy, M. and Weitz, B.A. (2004). *Retailing Management*. McGraw-Hill Irwin.

Lewis, D. and Bridger, D. (2000). *The Soul of the New Consumer: Authenticity – What We Buy and Why in the New Economy*, Nicholas Brealey Publishing.

Lindgreen, A., Brodie, R. and Brookes, R. (2000). An empirical investigation of contemporary marketing practices in the New Zealand wine sector: A study of contemporary marketing practices in an international importer-exporter context. In O'Cass, A. (ed.), *Proceedings of Australian and New Zealand Marketing Academy Conference (ANZMAC), Gold Coast, 28 November – 1 December 2000*, pp. 689–696.

Liquor Control Board of Ontario (LCBO) (2007). *Today's LCBO*. Available: http://www.lcbo.com/aboutlcbo/todayslcbo.shtml

Liquor Control Board of Ontario (LCBO) (2006). *LCBO Annual Report 2005–2006*, LCBO, Toronto.

Liv-ex (2006). *December 2006 Market Report*, London International Vintners Exchange, London.

Lixin, W. (2006). Imported wines widen appeal: Interview with ASC Fine Wines Managing Partner Don St. Pierre, Jr, *China International Business*, May.

Locke, M. (2005). 'Hooray for Hollywood,' say pinot noir producers. *Associated Press*, 21 February 2005. Available: http://www.usatoday.com/money/industries/food/2005-02-21-pinot-noir-sideways_x.htm

Lockshin, L. (2003). *Consumer Purchasing Behaviour for Wine: What We Know and Where We Are Going*. Research Paper (Cahier de Recherche), Marchés et Marketing du Vin, Centre de recherche de Bordeaux Ecole de Management, Bordeaux, n° 57-03 August 2003.

Lockshin, L. and Hall, J. (2003). *Consumer purchasing behaviour for wine: What we know and where we are going*. In *Proceedings of the International Colloquium in Wine Marketing*, Wine Marketing Group, University of South Australia, Adelaide.

Lockshin, L. and Spawton, T. (2001). Using involvement and brand equity to develop a wine tourism strategy. *International Journal of Wine Marketing*, 13(1), pp. 72–78.

Lockshin, L., Jarvis, W., d'Hauteville, F. and Perrouty, J.P. (2006). Using simulations from discrete choice experiments to measure consumer sensitivity to brand, region, price, and awards in wine choice. *Food Quality and Preference*, 17(3/4), 166–178.

Lockshin, L., Spawton, T. and Macintosh, G. (1997). Using product, brand and purchasing involvement for retail segmentation. *Journal of Retailing and Consumer Services*, 4(3), 171–183.

Lodi-Woodbridge Winegrape Commission (2005). *2003 and 1998 IPM Program Grower Questionnaires: 2003 and 1998 Report of Results*, Lodi-Woodbridge Winegrape Commission, Lodi.

Lodi-Woodbridge Winegrape Commission (LWWC) (2006). Lodi Wins Governor's Environmental Award, Press Release, 5 December 2006, Lodi-Woodbridge Winegrape Commission, Lodi.

Lofman, B. (1991). Elements of experiential consumption: an exploratory study. *Advances in Consumer Research*, 18, 729–734.

Loureiro, M.L. (2003). Rethinking new wines: implications of local and environmentally friendly labels. *Food Policy*, 28(5/6), 547–560.

Luomala, H.T. (2003). Understanding how retail environments are perceived: a conceptualisation and a pilot study. *The International Review of Retail, Distribution and Consumer Research*, 13(3), 279–300.

Lynch, P. and Morrison, A. (2007). The role of networks. In Michael, E. (ed.) *Micro-Clusters and Networks: The Growth of Tourism*, pp. 43–62, Elsevier.

MacCannell, D. (1973). Staged Authenticity: arrangements of Social Space in Tourist Settings. *The American Journal of Sociology*, 79(3), 589–603.

Macionis, N. (1994). Marketing the Canberra District wineries, *Unpublished Report. University of Canberra.*

Macionis, N. (1996). Wine tourism in Australia. In Higham, J. (ed.), *Proceedings of Tourism Down Under II - a Tourism Research Conference.* Dunedin, 1996, p. 264–286, University of Otago.

Macionis, N. and Cambourne, B. (2000). Towards a national wine tourism plan: wine tourism organisations and development in Australia. In Hall, C. M., Sharples, E., Cambourne, B. and Macionis, N. (eds.), *Wine Tourism Around the World: Development, Management and Markets*, pp. 226–252, Butterworth-Heinemann.

MacKay, K.J. and Fesenmaier, D.R. (1997). Pictorial element of destination in image formation. *Annals of Tourism Research*, 24(3), 537–565.

Maddern C. and Golledge, S. (1996). *Victorian Wineries Tourism Council Cellar Door Survey, Final Report May 1996*, Victorian Wineries Tourism Council, Melbourne.

Magrath, A.J. (1986.) When marketing services, 4 Ps are not enough. *Business Horizons*, 29(3), pp. 44–50.

Maher, M. (2001). On vino veritas? Clarifying the use of geographical references on American wine labels. *California Wine Review*, 89, 881–925.

Marette, S. and Zago, A. (2003). Advertising, collective action and labelling in the European wine markets. *Journal of Food Distribution Research*, 34, 117–126.

Marsh, I. and Shaw, B. (2000). *Australia's Wine Industry: Collaboration and Learning as Causes of Competitive Success.* Australian Business Foundation, Sydney. Available: http://www.abfoundation.com.au/ext/ABFound.nsf/0/1cf34f0d97d7cca94a2569380009079f/$FILE/wine%20study.PDF.

Marshall, R.S., Cardano, M. and Silverman, M. (2005). Exploring individual and institutional drivers of proactive environmentalism in the US Wine industry. *Business Strategy and the Environment*, 14(2), 92–109.

Mathwick, C., Malhotra, N. and Rigdon, E. (2001). Experiential value: conceptualization, measurement and application in the catalog and Internet shopping environment. *Journal of Retailing*, 77, 39–56.

Mattila, A.S. and Wirtz, J. (2001). Congruency of scent and music as a driver of in-store evaluations and behavior. *Journal of Retailing*, 77, 273–289.

Maxwell, K. (2005). Give us a B! 3 August 2005, *Wines of South Africa News*. Available: http://www.wosa.co.za/news.aspx?NEWSID=7226.

McCaffrey, S. (2007). Ga. Senate committee deals Sunday sales a setback. *The Macon Telegraph*, 28 February 2007.

McCarthy, J.E. (1960). *Basic Marketing: A Managerial Approach*. Richard D. Irwin, Homewood.

McCoy, E. (2005). *The Emperor of Wine: The Rise of Robert M. Parker, Jr, and the Reign of American Taste*, HarperCollins.

McCoy, E. (2007). Winemakers jump on 'biodynamics' bandwagon, with great results. *Bloomberg.com*, 5 March 2007.

McKay, D.H. (1985). *Report of the Inquiry into the Grape and Wine Industries*, Australian Government Publishing Service, Canberra.

McKibbin, S. (2000). *Network Building and the Institutional Environment: A Case Study of Innovation Strategies of the European Commission*. Institute of Social Studies Working Paper Number 314. Available: http://adlib.iss.nl/adlib/uploads/wp/wp314.pdf.

McKinna, D. (1987). *Developing Marketing Strategies for Wines*. David McKinna et al. Pty Ltd.

McRae-Williams, P. (2004). Wine and tourism: cluster complementarity and regional development. In Smith, K.A. and Schott, C. (eds.), *Proceedings of the New Zealand Tourism and Hospitality Research Conference 2004*, 8–10 December 2004. Victoria University, Wellington, 237–245.

Mercer, C. (2007). UK wine boom turns sour. *Food and Drink Europe*, 15 January 2007, Available: http://www.foodanddrinkeurope.com/news/ng.asp?n=73351-wine-uk-wine-report.

Meropa Communications (2006). Bio-wine reaches critical mass in Cape winelands. 8 August 2006, *Wines of South Africa News*. Available: http://www.wosa.co.za/news.aspx?NEWSID=8829

Michael, E. (2007). Development and Cluster Theory. In Michael, E. (ed.), *Micro-Clusters and Networks: The Growth of Tourism*, pp. 21–32, Elsevier.

Mikic, M. (1998). *The Impact of Liberalisation: Communicating with APEC Communities – Wine Industry in New Zealand*, Australian APEC Study Centre, Monash University, Melbourne.

Miles, M.P. and Munilla, L.S. (2004). The potential impact of social accountability certification on marketing: A short note. *Journal of Business Ethics*, 50(1), 1–11.

Mintel (2004). *Restaurants UK*, Mintel International, London.

Mintel (2005). *Wine Retailing – UK*, Mintel International, London.

Mitchell, R.D. (2004). *Scenery and Chardonnay: An exploration of the New Zealand winery visitor experience*. Unpublished Doctoral Thesis, University of Otago, New Zealand.

Mitchell, R.D. (2006). Influences on post-visit wine purchase (and non-purchase) by New Zealand winery visitors. In Carlsen, J. and Charters, S. (eds.), *Global Wine Tourism: Research, Management and Marketing*, pp. 95–109, CABI.

Mitchell, R.D. and Hall C.M. (2001). Wine at home: self-ascribed wine knowledge and the wine behaviour of New Zealand winery visitors. *Australian and New Zealand Wine Industry Journal*, 16(6), 115–122.

Mitchell, R.D. and Schreiber, C. (2006). Barriers to vertical integration between the wine and tourism industries: The case of Central Otago, New Zealand. In *Proceedings of the Third International Wine Business Research Conference*, Montpellier, 6–8 July 2006 (CD-ROM).

Mitchell, R.D. and Schreiber, C. (2007). Wine tourism networks and clusters: operation and barriers in New Zealand. In Michael, E. (ed.), *Micro-Clusters and Networks: The Growth of Tourism*, pp. 79–106, Elsevier.

Mitchell R.D., Hall, C.M. and McIntosh, A.J. (2000). Wine tourism and consumer behaviour. In *Wine Tourism Around the World: Development, Management and Markets*, pp. 115—135, Butterworth-Heinemann.

Mitchell, V.-W. and Greatorex, M. (1989). Risk reduction strategies used in the purchase of wine in the UK. *European Journal of Marketing*, 23(9), 31–46.

Mitchell, V.-W. (1999). Consumer perceived risk: conceptualisations and models. *European Journal of Marketing*, 33(12), 163–195.

MKF Research (2007). *The Impact of Wine, Grapes and Grape Products on the American Economy 2007: Family Businesses Building Value*, MKF Research, St. Helens.

Montgomery, D.B. (1975). New product distribution: an analysis of supermarket buyer decisions. *Journal of Marketing Research*, 12(3), 255–264.

Moore, V. (2007). The great wine rip-off. *The Guardian*, 5 April 2007, Available: http://lifeandhealth.guardian.co.uk/drink/story/0,2050524,00.html

Morschett, D., Swoboda, B. and Foscht, T. (2005). Perception of store attributes and overall attitude towards grocery retailers: the role of shopping motives. *The International Review of Retail, Distribution and Consumer Research*, 15(4), 423–447.

Morton, A-L., Healy, M. and Rivers, C. (2004). Beyond the Bubbles: identifying other purchase decision variables beyond country of origin effect that make Australians buy Champagne. In *Proceedings Australia-New Zealand International business Association Conference: Dynamism and Challengers in Internationalisation*, Canberra.

Mowle, J. and Merrilees, B. (2005). A functional and symbolic perspective to branding Australian SME wineries. *Journal of Product and Brand Management*, 14(4), 220–227.

Mudie, P. and Pirrie, A. (2006). *Services Marketing Management*, 3rd edn., Butterworth-Heinemann.

Nassauer, S. (2007). How Moët and Chandon Made Rose Champagne Fashionable. *Wall Street Journal*. (Easter Edition), 15 February 2007, B1.

National Restaurant Association (NRA) (2006). *New Report Says Americans Focused on Adventure, Health and Wellness When Dining Out While Still Valuing Convenience and Control, News Release*, National Restaurant Association, Washington, DC.

National Restaurant Association (NRA) (2007). *Restaurant industry facts*. Available: http://www.restaurant.org/research/ind_glance.cfm

National Wine and Spirits (2004). *Annual Report Pursuant to Section 13 or 15(d) of the Securities Exchange Act of 1934 (year ended 31 March 2004)*. Available: http://www.nwscorp.com/financials/10K032004.PDF.

New Zealand Wine (2006). *New Zealand's wine market*. Available: http://www.nzwine.com/education/.

New Zealand Wine Grower (1999). Winegrowers foresight: New Zealand to lead world of wine by year 2010. *New Zealand Wine Grower*, 2(3), 7–9.

New Zealand Winegrowers (2003). *2003/04 Half Year Statistical Update 6 months to 31 December 2003*. Unpublished Report, New Zealand Winegrowers, Auckland.

New Zealand Winegrowers (2004). *Statistics*. Available: http: www.nzwine.com/statistics.

New Zealand Winegrowers (2006). *New Zealand Winegrowers Annual Report Year End June 2006*. Available: http://nzwine.com/Annual_Report_06.

New Zealand Winegrowers (2007). *Statistics*. Available: http: www.nzwine.com/statistics.

Newhouse, D. (2007). ICAO's new retail security guidelines in full. *TREND: Travel Retail Executive News Digest*, 3 April 2007, Available: http://www.trend-news.com/default.asp?new sid=2701.

Nicholson, R. and Pearce, D.G. (2000). Who goes to events: A comparative analysis of the profile characteristics of visitors to four South Island events in New Zealand. *Journal of Vacation Marketing*, 6(3), 236–253.

Nicholson, R. and Pearce, D.G. (2001). Why do people attend events: A comparative analysis of visitor motivations at four South Island events. *Journal of Travel Research*, 39(4), 449–460.

Nothaft, M. (2007). Pinot noir still popular 2 years after 'Sideways'. *East Valley Tribune* (Online Edition), 24 January 2007. Available: http://www.eastvalleytribune.com/story/82875

O'Mahony, B., Hall, J. Lockshin, L. Jago, L. and Brown, G. (2006). Understanding the impact of wine tourism on post-tour purchasing. In Carlsen, J. and Charters, S (eds.), *Global Wine Tourism: Research, Management and Marketing*, pp. 123–138, CABI.

O'Neill, M. and Charters, S. (2000). Delighting the customer – how good is the cellar door experience? *International Wine Marketing Supplement*, 1(1), 11–16.

O'Neill, M. and Charters, S. (2001). Service quality at the cellar door: implications for Western Australia's developing wine industry. *Managing Service Quality*, 10(2), 112–122.

Ohmart, C. (2002). Vineyard Views, Lodi-Woodbridge Winegrape Commission. Available: http://www.lodiwine.com/whatis sustainableviticulture.pdf

Ohmart, C.P. and Matthiasson, S.K. (2000). *The Lodi Winegrower's Workbook: A Self-Assessment of Integrated Farming Practices*, Lodi-Woodbridge Winegrape Commission, Lodi.

Ordish, G. (1987). *The Great Wine Blight*, 2nd edn., Sedgwick and Jackson.

Organisation Internationale de la Vigne et du Vin (OIV) (2006). *State of Vitiviniculture World Report March*, OIV. Paris.

Orth, U.R. and Krška, P. (2002). Quality signals in wine marketing: the role of exhibition awards. *International Food and Agribusiness Management Review*, 4(4), 385–397.

Orth, U.R., McGarry Wolf, M. and Dodd, T. (2005). Dimensions of wine region equity and their impact on consumer preferences. *Journal of Product and Brand Management*, 14(2), 88–97.

Patterson, E. (2000). *Tourism Tasmania: Wine Survey 2000* Unpublished Report. Tourism Tasmania, Hobart.

Penn, C. (2006). Trends: how will global sourcing affect the future of the wine industry. *Wine Business Monthly*, 15 December 2006.

Penn, C. (2007a). Sipping news: wine, food and an intelligent sense of vice. *San Francisco Chronicle*, 23 February 2007.

Penn, C. (2007b). The top 30 US wine companies of 2006. *Wine Business Monthly*, 15 February 2007.

Peterson, R.A. (1995). Relationship marketing and the consumer. *Journal of the Academy of Marketing Science*, 23(4), 278–281.

Pirog. R., van Pelt, T., Enshayan, K. and Cook, E. (2001). *Food, Fuel and Freeways: An Iowa Perspective on How Far Food Travels, Fuel Usage, and Greenhouse Gas Emissions*, Leopold Center for Sustainable Agriculture, Iowa.

Pitcher, L. (2002). Interpretation of Wine: A cellar door perspective. In Croy, G (ed.), *New Zealand Tourism and Hospitality Research Conference Proceedings*, pp. 336, School of Tourism and Hospitality, Waiariki Institute of Technology, Rotorua, New Zealand.

Poincelot, R.P. (1990). Agriculture in transition. *Journal of Sustainable Agriculture*, 1, 9–40.

Pons, F., Laroche, M. and Mourali, M. (2006). Consumer reactions to crowded retail settings: cross-cultural differences between North America and the Middle East. *Psychology and Marketing*, 23(7), 555–572.

Population Reference Bureau (2004). *2004 World Population Data Sheet*, Population Reference Bureau, Washington, DC.

Port, J. (2007). Red, white and green. *The Age*, 27 February 2007.

Porter, M.E. (1980). *Competitive Strategy: Techniques for Analyzing Industries and Competitors*, Free Press.

Porter, M.E. (1990). *On Competition*, Harvard Business School Press, Massachusetts.

Porter, M.E. (1998). *The Competitive Advantage of Nations*, Macmillan Press Ltd., London.

Porter, M.E. (2000). Location, Competition, and Economic Development: Local Clusters in a Global Economy. *Economic Development Quarterly*, 14(1), 15–34.

Powell, W. (1990). Neither market nor hierarchy: network forms of organization, Straw, B. and Cummings, L. (eds.). *Research in Organizational Behaviour*, 12, 74–79.

PQ Media (2007). *PQ Media Market Analysis Finds Global Product Placement Spending Grew 37% in 2006; Forecast to Grow 30% in 2007, Driven by Relaxed European Rules, Emerging Asian Markets; Double-Digit Growth in US Decelerates*. Press release, 14 March 2007. Available: http://www.pqmedia.com/about-press-20070314-gppf.html.

Pratt, S.J. (1994). *Special Event Tourism: An analysis of food and wine festivals in New Zealand*, Unpublished Diploma in Tourism Dissertation, University of Otago, Dunedin.

Pugh, M. and Fletcher, R. (2002). Green international wine marketing. *Australasian Marketing Journal*, 10(3), 76–85.

Quester, P. and Smart, J.G. (1998). The influence of consumption situation and product involvement over consumers' use of product attributes. *Journal of Consumer Marketing*, 15(3), 220–238.

Quinton, S. and Harridge-March, S. (2003). Strategic interactive marketing of wine – a case of evolution. *Market Intelligence and Planning*, 21(6), 357–362.

Rasmussen, M. and Lockshin, L. (1999). Wine choice behaviour: the effect of regional branding. *International Journal of Wine Marketing*, 11(1), 36–46.

Reardon, T. and Berdegue, J.A. (2002). The rapid rise of super-markets in Latin America: challenges and opportunities for development. *Development Policy Review*, 20(4), 371–388.

Reardon, T., Timmer, C.P., Barrett, C.B. and Berdegué, J. (2003). The rise of supermarkets in Africa, Asia and Latin America. *American Journal of Agricultural Economics*, 85(5), 1140–1146.

Renaud, S. and de Lorgeril, M. (1992). Wine, alcohol, platelets, and the French paradox for coronary heart disease. *Lancet*, 339, 1523–1526.

Restaurant Association of New Zealand (2006). *2006 Restaurant Industry Forecast, Executive Summary*, Restaurant Association of New Zealand, Mount Eden.

Reuters (2007). *EU Opens Tender to Distil Wine Lakes Into Biofuel*, Reuters News Service, 21 March 2007.

Riekhof, G.M. and Sykuta, M.E. (2005). Politics, economics and the regulation of direct interstate shipping in the wine industry. *American Journal of Agricultural Economics*, 87(3), 439–452.

Ritchie, J.R.B. (1984). Assessing the impact of hallmark events: conceptual and research issues. *Journal of Travel Research*, 23(1), 2–11.

Robinson, J. (1999). Vine pull schemes. In Robinson, J. (ed.), *The Oxford Companion to Wine*, 2nd edn., pp. 751–752, Oxford University Press.

Robinson, J. (ed.) (2006). *The Oxford Companion to Wine*, 3rd edn., Oxford University Press.

Rocchi, B. and Stefani, G. (2006). Consumers' perception of wine packaging: A case study. *International Journal of Wine Marketing*, 18(1), 33–44.

Royce, J.E. (1981). *Alcohol Problems and Alcoholism: A Comprehensive Survey*, Free Press.

Rozelle, S. and Sumner, D. (2006). *Wine in China: Final Report to the California Association of Wine Growers*. University of California Agricultural Issues Center and UC Davis: California. Available: http://aic.ucdavis.edu/research1/Wine_in_China.pdf.

Rozelle, S., Sumner, D. and Huang, J. (2006). *Wine in China: Final Report to the California Association of Wine Growers*, Agricultural Issues Center, University of California, Davis.

SAFE Alliance (1994). *The Food Miles Report: The Dangers of Long Distance Food Transport*, SAFE Alliance, London.

Saffer, H. (1989). Alcohol consumption and tax differentials between beer, wine and spirits. *NBER Working Paper No. W3200*, National Bureau of Economic research, New York.

Sanjuán, A.I. and Albisu, L.M. (2004). Factors affecting the positioning of wineries based on the value added by the DO certification. *Acta Agriculturae Scandinavica, Section C – Economy*, 1(3), 163–175.

Sauer, A. (2005). Brandchannel's 2004 product placement awards. Available: http://www.brandchannel.com/features_effect.asp?pf_id=251.

Scanlon, N.L. (1999). *Marketing by Menu*, 3rd edn., John Wiley and Sons, New York.

Schiffman L.G. and Kanuk, L.L. (1987). *Consumer Behavior*, 3edn., Prentice-Hall.

Schmitt, B.H. and Simonson, A. (1997). *Marketing Aesthetics: The Strategic Management of Brands, Identity and Image*, The Free Press.

Schreiber, C. (2004). *The Development of Wine Tourism Networks: An exploratory case study into established networks and issues in Central Otago*, Unpublished Diploma in Tourism Dissertation, Department of Tourism, University of Otago, Dunedin.

Schreiner, J. (2005). *The Wines of Canada*, Mitchell Beazley.

Scott, D.G. (2006). *Socialising the Stranger: hospitality as a relational reality*. Unpublished Masters Thesis, University of Otago, Dunedin, New Zealand.

Shanka, T. and Taylor, R. (2004). A correspondence analysis of sources of information used by festival visitors. *Tourism Analysis*, 9(1–2), 55–62.

Sheppard, A. (2007). Eco-worrier: don't cling the clingfilm. *The Times*, 20 January 2007, http://www.timesonline.co.uk/tol/life_and_style/health/complementary_medicine/article1294332.ece.

Shuker, R. (1994). *Understanding Popular Music*, Routledge.

Simic, P. (1999). Editorial. *Winestate Magazine (Online edition) 1999 Annual Edition*. Available: http://www.winestate.com.au.

Sin, C.Y. (2006). 10Ps of the marketing mix. *The Star Online* (Malaysia), 5 February 2006, n.p. Available: http://biz.thestar.com.my/news/story.asp?file=/2006/2/5/business/13308101&sec=business

Singh, R., Dubnov, G., Niaz, M., Ghosh, S., Singh, R., Rastogi, S., Manor, O., Pella, D. and Berry, E. (2002). Effect of an Indo-Mediterranean diet on progression of coronary artery disease in high risk patients (Indo-Mediterranean Diet Heart Study): A randomised single-blind trial. *The Lancet*, 360(9344), 1455–1461.

Skinner, A.M. (2000). Napa Valley, California: a model of wine region development. In In Hall, C.M., Sharples, E., Cambourne, B. and Macionis, N. (eds.) *Wine Tourism Around the World: Development, Management and Markets*, pp. 283–296, Butterworth-Heinemann.

Smith, B. (2006). A frog in your throat and it's an Arrogant little drop. *The Age*, 10 April 2006, 7.

Smith, T. (2006). *The Wine Islands Project Final Report*, Unpublished Report.

Solomon, M.E. (1992). *Consumer Behavior*, Allyn and Bacon.

Spangenberg, E.R., Crowley, A.E. and Henderson, P.W. (1996). Improving the store environment: Do olifactory cues affect evaluations and behaviours? *Journal of Marketing*, 60(2), 67–80.

Spawton, T. (1986). Understanding wine purchasing: knowing how the wine buyer behaves can increase your sales. *Australian and New Zealand Wine Industry Journal*, 1(2), 54–57.

Spawton, T.J. (1991). Of wine and live asses: an introduction to the wine economy and state of marketing. *European Journal of Wine Marketing*, 25(3), 1–48.

Spicer, K. (2006). The ultimate fantasy. *The Sunday Times*. 23 July 2006. Available: http://www.timesonline.co.uk/tol/news-papers/sunday_times/style/article688061.ece

Sproles, G.P. and Burns, L.D. (1994). *Changing Appearances: Understanding Dress in Contemporary Society*, Fairchild.

Stebbins, R.A. (1992). *Amateurs, Professionals, and Serious Leisure*, McGill-Queen's University Press.

Steidl (2007). *7 Fantasmes of a Woman by Karl Lagerfeld*. Available: http://www.steidlville.com/books/346-7-Fantasmes-of-a-Woman.html.

Stern, B.M., Zinkhan, G.M. and Jaju, A. (2001). Marketing images. *Marketing Theory*, 1(2), 201–224.

Stimpfig, J. (2007). Decanter's wine investment guide in association with Berry Bros. and Rudd, *Decanter.com*. Available: http://www.decanter.com/specials/104729.html

Styles, O. (2004a). French wine exports continue to fall. *Decanter* (Online edition), 25 August 2004, Available: http://www.decanter.com/news/57701.html.

Styles, O. (2004b). Clos du Val wins product placement game. *Decanter.com*, 10 June 2004. Available: http://www.decanter.com/news/55839.html

Summers, J., Gardiner, M., Lamb, C.W., Hair, J.F. and McDaniel, C. (2003). *Essentials of Marketing*, Nelson Australia Pty Limited (Thomson).

Sutherland, K. (2002). China's wine frontier, *Shanghai Star*, 16 May 2002.

Svensson, G. (2001). Extending trust and mutual trust in business relationships towards a synchronised trust chain in marketing channels. *Management Decision*, 39(6), 431–440.

Systembolaget (2003). *About Systembolaget: A Presentation of Systembolaget*, Our History and Our Aims, Systembolaget, Stockholm.

Systembolaget (2006). *Annual Report 2005*, Systembolaget, Stockholm.

Systembolaget (2007). *Launch Plan 2/2007: Plan for Launches Autumn/Winter 2007/2008*, Systembolaget, Stockholm.

Tait, S.V., Hughey, K.F.D. and O'Connell, M.J. (2003). A comparison of the advantages and disadvantages of three voluntary environmental management systems used in the NZ wine industry, *The Australian and New Zealand Grapegrower and Winemaker* March, 70–72.

Tasslopoulos, D. and Haydam, N. (2006). A study of adventure tourism attendees at a wine tourism event: A qualitative and quantitative study of the Breedekloof Outdoor Festival, South Africa. In Carlsen, J. (ed.), *World Wine and Travel Summit and Exhibition Academic Stream Proceedings*, 13–17 November 2006, pp. 53–71.

Tax Free World Association (2002). *European Consumers as Travel Retail Customers*, Tax Free World Association, Paris.

Tax Free World Association (2005). *2004/5 Asia Pacific Consumers as Travel Retail Customers*, Tax Free World Association, Paris.

Tax Free World Association (2006). *The Indian Outbound Traveller Study – 2006*, Tax Free World Association, Paris.

Taylor, R. and Shanka, T. (2002). Attributes for staging successful wine festivals. *Event Management*, 7(3), 165–175.

Taylor, R.G., Woodall, S., Wandschneider, P. and Foltz, J. (2004). 'The demand for wine tourism in Canyon county, Idaho.' *International Food and Agribusiness Management Review*, 7(4), 58–75.

Tedeschi, B. (2005). Opening New York to Internet wine sales, *New York Times*, E-Commerce 25 July 2005.

Telfer, D.J. (2001a). From a wine tourism village to a regional wine route: An investigation of the competitive advantage of embedded clusters in Niagara, Canada. *Tourism Recreation Research*, 26(2), 23–33.

Telfer, D.J. (2001b). Strategic alliances along the Niagara wine route. *Tourism Management*, 22(1), 21–30.

Thies, W. (2005). 'Sideways' Effects 1 year later. KSBY 6 Action News. 16 August 2005, Available: http://www.ksby.com/home/headlines/1814977.

Thomas, A. (2000). Elements influencing wine purchasing: A New Zealand view. *International Journal of Wine Marketing*, 12(2), 47–62.

Thorsen, E.O. and Hall, C.M. (2001). 'What's on the wine list? Wine policies in the New Zealand restaurant industry. *International Journal of Wine Marketing*, 13(3), 94–102.

Tilden, F. (1957). *Interpreting Our Heritage*, University of North Carolina Press, North Carolina.

Tourism Victoria (2003). *Wine Tourism Activity 2002*, Tourism Victoria, Melbourne, Australia.

Trade Law Centre for Southern Africa (TRALAC) (2006). *South Africa v New Zealand in the International Wine Market*, TRALAC, Stellenbosch.

Treloar, P. (2004). *The youth market, wine and wine tourism: A behavioural context for wine tourism potential.* Unpublished Masters Thesis. University of Otago.

Trubek, A.B. (2005). Tasting Place. In Korsmeyer, C. (ed.), *The Taste Culture Reader: Experiencing Food and Drink*, pp. 260–271, Berg.

Turley, L.W. and Milliman, R.E. (2000). Atmospheric effects on shopping behavior: A review of the experimental evidence. *Journal of Business Research*, 49, 193–211.

Turrentine, B. (2001). Freud on Wine. *Wine Business Monthly*, 8(5). Available: http://www.winebusiness.com/html/MonthlyArticle.cfm?dataId=8186.

United Nations Development Programme (UNDP) (2005). *Human Development Report 2005: International Cooperation at a Crossroads: Aid, Trade and Security in an Unequal World*, UNDP, New York.

United States Constitution Amendment 18 (1919). *Prohibition of Liquor*. Available: http://www.usconstitution.net/xconst_Am18.html.

United States Constitution Amendment 21 (1933). *18th Amendment Repealed*. Available: http://www.usconstitution.net/xconst_Am21.html

Unwin, T. (1991). *Wine and the Vine: An Historical Geography of Viticulture and the Wine Trade*, Routledge.

Unwin, T. (1996). *Wine and the Vine: An Historical Geography of Viticulture and the Wine Trade*, Routledge.

USA Wine Club (2000). *USA: The Wine Club's '2000 Survey' Spotlights Buying Habits of California's Top Wine Consumers*, Gomberg, Fredrikson and Associates.

van Schoor, L. and Visser, D. (2000). ISO 14001 Environmental management systems: Background, elements and benefits. Wynboer: A technical guide for wine producers, *Wineland*, September.

Vancouver Playhouse International Wine Festival (VPIWF) (2007). *Demographics*, Vancouver Playhouse International Wine Festival, Vancouver.

Vargo, S.L. and Lusch, R.F. (2004a). The four service marketing myths: Remnants of a goods-based, manufacturing model. *Journal of Service Research*, 6(4), 324–335.

Vargo, S.L. and Lusch, R.F. (2004b). Evolving to a new dominant logic for marketing. *Journal of Marketing*, 68, 1–17.

Varley, R. (2001). *Retail Product Management: Buying and Merchandising*, Routledge.

Vaudour, E. (2002). The Quality of Grapes and Wine in Relation to Geography: Notions of Terroir at Various Scales. *Journal of Wine Research*, 13(2), 117–141.

VeronaFiere Press Office (2007). *Wine Exhibition Closes Today. Viniltaly 2007: Business is Here. International Operators up by 15%*, VeronaFiere Press Office, Verona.

Vienna Art Week (2007). *Vienna art week sponsors*. Available: http://www.viennaartweek.at/2007/sponsor-detail.php?page_id=31).

Villa Maria Wines (2007). *Wine awards*. Available: http://www.villamaria.co.nz/wine_awards.php?sid=14.

Vinewise (2006a). *About vinewise*. Washington Association of Wine Grape Growers, Cashmere, Available: http://www.vinewise.org/209.html

Vinewise (2006b). *Sustainability Survey*. Washington Association of Wine Grape Growers, Cashmere, Available: http://www.vinewise.org/212.html

Virginia Wine Wholesalers Association (2005). *Wine: The Courts and Virginia*. Available: http://www.vwwa.org/PDF/Wine%20%26%20The%20Courts%20Color%20Flyer.pdf.

Visser, E. (2004). *A Chilean Wine Cluster? Governance and Upgrading in the Phase of Internationalization*, United Nations, Santiago, Chile.

Wakefield, K. and Baker, J. (1998). Excitement at the Mall: Determinants and effects on shopping response. *Journal of Retailing*, 74(4), 515–539.

Walker, J.R. and Lundberg, D.E. (2001). *The Restaurant: From Concept to Operation*, Wiley, New York.

Walker, L. (1989). Let the restaurant do the selling; wine marketers should be looking at restaurants to boost flat wine sales, *Wines and Vines*, September.

Walker, L. (2001). Wine by the glass: A key marketing tool, *Wines and Vines*, March.

Walla Walla Valley Vinea Winegrowers' Sustainable Trust (2004). *Welcome*. Available:http://www.vineatrust.com/

Walsdorff, A., van Kraayenburg, M. and Barnardt, C.A. (2005). A multi-site approach towards integrating environmental management in the wine production industry. *Water SA*, 30(5), 82–87.

Walsh, K. (2007). RSVP. Dom Pérignon. *Vogue Australia*, 52(3), 209.

Wansink, B., Cordua, G., Blair, E., Payne, C. and Geiger, S. (2006). Wine promotions in restaurants: Do beverage sales contribute or cannibalize? *Cornell Hotel and Restaurant.*

Warde, A. and Martens, L. (2000). *Eating Out: Social Differentiation, Consumption and Pleasure,* Cambridge University Press, Cambridge.

Wehring, O. (2005). Supreme Court decides on interstate wine sales. *Just-Drinks News*, 17 May 2005. Available: www.just-drinks.com/article.aspx?ID=81881andlk=np.

Weiler, B., Truong, M. and Griffiths, M. (2004). *Visitor Profiles and Motivations for Visiting an Australian Wine Festival*, Department of Management Working Paper Series 19/04, Department of Management, Monash University, Melbourne.

Weingarten, T. and Adler, J. (2005). Drink me, I'm 'fun': With whacky labels, high-end wineries aim to please. *Newsweek* 17 October 2005.

Wetlaufer, S. (2001). The Perfect Paradox of Star Brands. *Harvard Business Review*, 79(9), 116–123.

White, D. (1950). The 'Gate Keeper': A case study in the selection of news. *Journalism Quarterly*, 27, 383–390.

White, M.A., Diffenbaugh, N.S., Jones, G.V., Pal, J.S. and Giorgi, F. (2006). Extreme heat reduced and shifts United States premium wine production in the 21st century. *PNAS Proceedings of the National Academy of Sciences of the United States of America*, 103, 11217–11222.

Wine Australia (2007). *Future Trends*, Australian Wine and Brandy Corporation, Available: http://www.wineaustralia.com/Australia/Default.aspx?tabid=826.

Wine Business Monthly (2004). Australian Exports: US Now Number One Destination by Value. *Wine Business Monthly* August. Available: http://www.winebusiness.com.

Wine Industry Report (2006). Distell sales push in airport duty free. *Wine Industry Report*, 17 October 2006, Available: http://wineindustryreport.finewinepress.com/2006/10/17/distell-sales-push-in-airport-duty-free/.

Wine Institute (2004). *U.S. wine exports up three percent in volume, strong dollar contributes to one percent decrease in revenues (News release 6 May 2002).* Available: http://www.wineinstitute.org/communications/statistics/Exports_01.htm.

Wine Institute (2007). U.S. Wine Exports. 95 Percent from California, Jump 30 Percent to $876 Million in 2006. Wine

Institute, 14 March 2007, Available: http://www.wineinstitute.org/industry/exports/2007/us_wine_exports.php.

Wine Islands Vintners' Association (2006). *Welcome to the Wine Islands*. Retrieved 8 January 2007, Available: http://wineislands.ca/index.php.

Wine Market Council (2006). *Consumer Research Summary*, Wine Market Council, Available: http://www.winemarketcouncil.com/research_summary.asp.

Wine Spectator (2007a). *Classified Rate Card*. Available: http://www.winespectator.com/Wine/Images/Graphics/ads/2007CLASSIFIEDRATECARD.pdf.

Wine Spectator (2007b). *Winespectator Online*. Available: http://www.winespectator.com/Wine/Images/Graphics/ads/ws-mediakit-06.pdf

Winemakers Federation of Australia (1996). Strategy 2025. *Australian and New Zealand Wine Industry Journal*, 11(3), 196.

Winetitles (2006). Australian Wine Industry Statistics. *Winebiz*. Available: http://www.winebiz.com.au/statistics/wineries.asp

Wiseman, A.E. and Ellig, J. (2004). Market and nonmarket barriers to internet wine sales: The case of Virginia. *Business and Politics*, 6(2), Article 4. Available: http://www.bepress.com/bap/vol6/iss2/art4

Wittwer, G. and Anderson, K. (2002). Impact of the GST and wine tax reform on Australia's wine industry. *Australian Economic Papers*, 41(1), 69–81.

World Intellectual Property Organisation (WIPO) (2006). *About geographical indications*. Available: http://www.wipo.int/about-ip/en/about_geographical_ind.html#P16_1100.

World Trade Organisation (WTO) (1994). *Agreement on Trade-Related Aspects of Intellectual Property Rights* (TRIPS), The TRIPS Agreement is Annex 1C of the *Marrakesh Agreement Establishing the World Trade Organization*, signed in Marrakesh, Morocco on 15 April 1994, Available: http://www.wto.org/english/docs_e/legal_e/27-trips_01_e.htm.

World Wildlife Fund South Africa (2004). *Why a biodiversity and wine initiative?*. Available: http://www.panda.org.za/article.php?id=404.

Wrigley, N. (2002). The landscape of pan-European food retail consolidation. *International Journal of Retail and Distribution Management*, 30, 81–91.

Wrigley, N., Coe, N.M. and Currah, A. (2005). Globalizing retail: conceptualising the distribution-based transnational corporation (TNC). *Progress in Human Geography*, 29(4), 437–457.

Wyatt, C. (2006). Draining France's 'wine lake'. *BBC News*, Available: http://news.bbc.co.uk/2/hi/europe/5253006.stm

Xuereb, M. (2005). *Food Miles: Environmental Implications of Food Imports to Waterloo Region*, Region of Waterloo Public Health, Waterloo.

Yuan, L.A.C., Cai, L A., Morrison, A.M. and Linton, S. (2005). An analysis of wine festival attendees' motivations: A synergy of wine, travel and special events? *Journal of Vacation Marketing*, 11, 41–58.

Zago, A. and Pick, D. (2004). Labelling policies in food markets: private incentives, public intervention and welfare. *Journal of Agricultural and Resource Economics*, 29(1), 150–169.

Zeithami, V.A., Bitner, M.J. and Gremier, D.D. (2006). *Services Marketing: Integrating Customer Focus Across the Firm*, 4th edn., McGraw-Hill International.

Index